Reading Literature

Purple Level
Yellow Level
Blue Level
Orange Level
Green Level
RED LEVEL

Reading Literature

Red Level

The McDougal, Littell English Program

Jacqueline L. Chaparro

Curriculum Coordinator, English Language Arts
San Diego County Office of Education,
San Diego, California

Mary Ann Trost

Specialist in Educational Materials
for the Middle Grades, Cleveland Heights, Ohio

McDougal, Littell & Company
Evanston, Illinois
New York   Dallas   Sacramento   Raleigh

Consultants

Terri Billmeier, Teacher, Apollo Junior High School, Richardson, Texas

Frances Brooks, Teacher, Carson Junior High School, Carson City, Nevada

Terry Cranford, Teacher, Ramsey Junior High School, Fort Smith, Arkansas

James Dedes, Teacher, Holmes Junior High School, Mount Prospect, Illinois

Joe Elkins, Teacher, Warrensville Heights Junior High School, Cleveland, Ohio

Richard H. Gray, Chairman, English Department, Enfield High School, Enfield, Connecticut

Mindy Moffatt, Teacher, Walker Junior High School, La Palma, California

Sandra J. Nash, Teacher, Salt Rock Junior High School, Huntington, West Virginia

Virginia Vargas, Teacher, Berta Cabaza Junior High School, San Benito, Texas

Frontispiece: *Endangered Species: Siberian Tiger,* 1983, ANDY WARHOL.
Photograph by D. James Dee, Courtesy of Ronald Feldman Fine Arts, New York City.

Acknowledgments

Abingdon Press: For "Florence Nightingale," "George Washington Carver," and "Jane Addams," from *Armed With Courage* by May McNeer and Lynd Ward; copyright © 1957 by Abingdon Press. Samuel W. Allen: For "To Satch" by Samuel Allen, from *Soon, One Morning*. Atheneum Publishers, Inc.: For "Earth" by Oliver Herford, *(continued on page 521)*

ISBN: 0-86609-227-7

Contents

Great Modern Stories   181

CHAPTER 6 *Nonfiction*   295

Dear Student,

You are about to embark on an adventure—the adventure of reading fine literature. You will travel through time and space, visiting cities of the past and worlds of the future. You will meet fascinating characters who face exciting challenges. This book and your imagination will guide you.

Reading Literature will introduce you to a wide variety of literature. You will read stories, poems, plays, and works of non-fiction. These works have been written by world-famous authors such as Leo Tolstoy, Rudyard Kipling, Edith Wharton, Emily Dickinson, Henry Wadsworth Longfellow, Isaac Asimov, and Anne Morrow Lindbergh. Some of the works may make you laugh and others may make you cry. All of them should make you think.

Literature is your inheritance. Great writers of the past and present have left you a wealth of ideas, experiences, and feelings. Through reading, you can share and enjoy these riches.

Reading Literature can stretch your mind, sharpen your senses, and enrich your life. You will improve your reading, thinking, and vocabulary skills. You will discover how professional writers write, and you will learn to use a similar process for your own writing. Most of all, you will have the thrill of losing yourself in literature and finding there the wondrous challenge that is life.

Sincerely,
The Authors and Editors

CHAPTER 1

Peaceable Kingdom (detail), about 1834, EDWARD HICKS.
National Gallery of Art, Washington, D.C.
Gift of Edgar Williams and Bernice Chrysler Garbisch 1980.

Reading Literature: Fables

What Is a Fable?

In this chapter you will read one of the earliest stories. This type of story is called a **fable**. It is a short story that teaches a lesson about human nature. The lesson is called a **moral**.

Here is an example of a fable, ending in a moral.

THE CAT AND THE MICE

The mice were constantly bothered by a cat. They held a meeting to decide what to do. One young mouse said, "There should be a bell on the cat's collar. Then we could hear her coming, and we could run away in time."

All the other mice agreed this was a fine idea, but there was one problem. Who would put the bell on the cat?

It is easier to think up a plan than to carry it out.

The History of the Fable

More than 2500 years ago, in Greece, there lived a slave named Aesop. According to legend, he had wonderful skill as a storyteller. The animals in his stories, or fables, were much like people. They faced the same sorts of problems that people face. In showing how the animals acted, the fables pointed out how clever, stupid, kind, and cruel we humans can be.

Aesop was not the only storyteller to make up fables. People of every country enjoyed these stories. Fables have been told in lands as far apart as Africa and China.

Fables have remained popular. In the 1600's, a French writer, Jean de La Fontaine, rewrote the Aesop fables as poems. Later, Leo Tolstoy, a Russian, wrote new fables. In our own century, James Thurber, an American, brought familiar fables up-to-date.

The Elements of a Fable

Moral. A **moral** is the lesson a fable teaches. Sometimes the moral gives you good advice such as "Be happy with what you have." Sometimes the moral states a fact, such as "It is hard to believe a liar even when he tells the truth."

The moral usually comes at the end of the fable. Occasionally, the writer doesn't write the moral. He or she wants you to think about the events that happened in the fable and to figure out your own moral. Different people may even see different morals.

Characters. The **characters** in fables are usually animals. However, these animals act just like human beings. When writers make animals or objects act like human beings, they are using **personification**. You have probably seen personification in cartoons and TV commercials.

In a fable, each animal may stand for one quality of humans. For example, the young mouse could stand for cleverness. You may read about animals, but soon you start to understand people.

How To Read a Fable

The way you read depends a lot on what you are reading. Reading a dictionary differs from reading a comic book. Reading a telephone directory differs from reading a story. Good readers know what to expect when they start to read. Knowing what they might find helps them understand what they read.

When you read a fable, keep these ideas in mind:

1. Notice that you never learn much about the characters in a fable. You learn only what you need to understand the story.
2. Remember that, in most fables, each character stands for a quality of humans.
3. You may wish to read each fable twice. The first time, read the story as a story. Enjoy it. It's fun. The second time, be more thorough. Look at what happens. Study the characters. Find the lesson.

Comprehension Skills: Time Order

Understanding Time Order

Have you ever told a joke? If you have, you know how important it is to tell what is done or said in the right order. One event or sentence out of order can spoil the joke.

Order is just as important in the material you read. As you read, you should place the events in the correct **time order**. What happened first? next? last?

In most stories, each event logically follows the event that came before. The second event could never happen before the first. Most times, you can see how one event causes the next.

Read this fable. See how each thing that happens is caused by what comes before it.

THE LION'S SHARE

One day a lion, a tiger, a leopard, and a jackal went hunting together. They caught a plump deer and divided it into four equal parts. Since the lion was king, the others asked him to give out the portions.

"The first piece," said the lion, "is for me because I am the lion. The second piece is for the bravest, and that's me again. The third piece is for the strongest, and I am stronger than any of you. As for the fourth piece—I dare any one of you to touch it!"

Some people believe that might makes right.

Every event that happens depends upon what comes before it. Here is the order of events in this fable:

1. The lion, tiger, leopard, and jackal hunted and killed a deer.
2. The animals divided the deer into four parts.
3. They asked the lion to give out the parts.
4. The lion took all four parts as his share.

Exercises: **Understanding Time Order**

A. Read this fable by Aesop. Then answer the four questions below.

THE FOX AND THE LION

The first time the fox saw the lion, he was terribly frightened. He quickly ran away into the woods. The next time he saw the lion, he stopped at a distance and watched him carefully. The third time that they came near one another, the fox went straight up to the lion and talked to him as if he were an old friend. Then, he walked away.

Familiarity breeds contempt.

1. What happened the first time the fox saw the lion?
2. What happened the second time?
3. What happened the third time he saw the lion?
4. List all the events in this story in time order.

B. Read this fable. Complete the sentences with **before** or **after**.

THE BALD MAN AND THE FLY

There was once a bald man who sat down after work on a hot summer's day. A fly came up and kept buzzing around his bald head, stinging him. The man slapped at his little enemy, but—whack—his palm hit his head instead. Again the fly buzzed around him, but this time the man was wiser and said: "You will only hurt yourself if you take notice of your enemies."

1. _____ the bald man sat down, a fly buzzed around him.
2. The man slapped his head _____ the fly stung him.
3. _____ the man learned his lesson, he slapped at the fly.

C. Read these sentences from a fable about a race between a tortoise and a hare. Arrange them in the correct order.

1. Tortoise keeps plodding on, passing the sleeping hare.
2. Hare boasts about how fast he can run.
3. Tortoise crosses finish line first.
4. Hare takes a nap just before crossing finish line.

Vocabulary Skills: Word Parts

Using Word Parts

Sometimes you come across a word you do not know. What do you do? You can take the word apart to find its meaning.

New words are frequently formed by adding a beginning or an ending to a word, called the **base word**. In the word *untie, tie* is the base word. The beginning word part *un–* is a prefix. A **prefix** is a word part added to the beginning of a base word.

Prefix + **Base Word** = **New Word**
un   +   tie   =   untie

The new word has a different meaning from the base word.
This chart shows several prefixes and their meanings.

---

dis– and **un–** mean "the opposite of" or "not." *Dislike* means "the opposite of like." *Untie* means "the opposite of tie." *Uncommon* means "not common."

non– and **in–** mean "not." *In–* is also spelled *im–, ir–,* or *il–*. Examples include *nonpoisonous, inactive, impossible, irresponsible,* and *illogical.*

mis– means "wrong" or "wrongly." To *misspell* a word is to spell it wrongly.

re– means "again." To *reuse* is to use again.

Look at the word *helpful.* The base word is *help.* The ending word part *–ful* is a suffix. A **suffix** is a word part added to the end of a word. It changes the meaning of the base word.

Base Word + **Suffix** = **New Word**
help   +   ful   =   helpful

Here are some common suffixes and their meanings.

> **–er** or **–or** means "a person or thing who does some-thing." A *teacher* is a person who teaches. A *conductor* of electricity conducts, or carries, electricity.
>
> **–less** means "without." *Homeless* is "without a home."
>
> **–able** or **–ible** means "can be" or "having the quality." *Comfortable* means "having the quality of comfort." A dessert that is *resistible* can be resisted.
>
> **–ful** and **–ous** mean "full of" or "having." Examples are *graceful* and *hazardous*.

Look for prefixes, suffixes, and base words when you meet a new word. You may know the meaning of each part. Then you can combine the parts to find the meaning of the new word.

Exercises: Using Word Parts

A. Match each prefix and suffix with its meaning.

Prefixes		Suffixes	
1. *in–*	a. not	5. *–ful*	e. having the quality
2. *re–*	b. opposite of, not	6. *–less*	f. a person who does something
3. *dis–*	c. again	7. *–er, –or*	g. without
4. *mis–*	d. wrong	8. *–able*	h. full of, having

B. For each underlined word below, identify the base word and the prefix or suffix. Then give the meaning of the word.

1. Cold weather killed the <u>unfortunate</u> bird.
2. The woman asked a <u>traveler</u> passing by to give her advice.
3. Because his food was in a jar, the fox was <u>helpless</u>.
4. The cruel wolf wanted a <u>believable</u> excuse for killing the lamb.
5. The hungry fox pretended to be <u>unconcerned</u> about the food.

The Goose That Laid the Golden Eggs

AESOP

Have you ever wondered what it would be like to become rich? Imagine that you are to receive $100 every day of your life. Would you be forever happy? Think about this question as you read the fable below.

A man and his wife had the good fortune to possess a goose that laid a golden egg every day. Lucky though they were, they soon began to think they were not getting rich fast enough. Imagining that the bird must be made of gold inside, they decided to kill it. Then, they thought, they could obtain the whole store of precious metal at once. But when they cut the goose open, they found it was just like any other goose.

Those who want too much lose everything.

Developing Comprehension Skills

1. What did the man and his wife imagine about their goose?

2. How did the man and his wife come to the decision to cut open the goose?

3. What was wrong with the couple's thinking when they made their decision to kill the goose?

4. Would this story make sense if the events happened in a different order? Why or why not?

5. Tell the moral of this fable in your own words. Then give a brief example from real life that shows either that the moral is true or that it isn't true.

Reading Literature: Fables

1. **Understanding a Character.** In most fables, animals stand for human qualities. In this fable, however, the goose is not personified. Instead, the people themselves represent human qualities. Which of these qualities do you think the owners of the goose represent?

   pride   determination   foolishness
   greed   laziness   inability to plan ahead

2. **Understanding the Moral.** The moral of this fable could have read: "If you cut your goose open to get more gold, you may end up empty-handed." However, that moral would describe this story only. What purpose does the author have in making a more general statement? Why is the moral of a fable usually stated in a general way?

Developing Vocabulary Skills

Recognizing Added Endings. You know that new words can be formed when endings are added to base words. In addition to the suffixes you learned on page 7, there are many other endings that make slighter changes in the meaning of a word. Some of these endings are the following:

$-s$	$-ed$	$-er$	$-y$
$-es$	$-ing$	$-est$	$-en$

Several words in "The Goose That Laid the Golden Eggs" end in letter combinations listed above. Find five words in the fable that combine base words and any one of the endings listed above. Be sure that you can identify each base word. Keep in mind that not all words that end in these letter combinations are built on base words. For example, the "en" cannot be taken from "then."

Developing Writing Skills

1. **Rewording a Story.** There are many different ways to tell the same story. For example, you could change the beginning sentence of "The Goose That Laid the Golden Eggs" to the following:

   Once there was a very lucky couple. They owned a goose that laid golden eggs, one each day.

   Rewrite the entire fable in your own words.

2. **Writing About Art.** In some pictures an artist tells a story. In other pictures the artist allows the viewer to decide for himself or herself what the picture is about. Study "Peaceable Kingdom" by Edward Hicks, at the beginning of this chapter. Choose one or two of the animals pictured in the painting. Describe what human quality the animal or animals you picked seem to have. Then write a fable about the animal or animals you have picked.

Developing Skills in Study and Research

Recognizing Important Ideas in Reading. Even in a story as short as "The Goose That Laid the Golden Eggs," some ideas are more important than others. Writers and editors often provide clues to help you spot the important ideas. In this textbook, for example, the short introduction alerts you to look for certain information as you read. The study questions usually concentrate on major ideas.

The way the page looks gives clues, too. Often the pictures show important happenings in a story. Type printed in different faces—such as italic, or slanted, letters—can point out something special in the reading material. Type in different sizes, different thicknesses, or in different colors can also stress important ideas or ways of thinking about the selection.

Examine pages 8, 9, and 10. Identify at least three clues that point out important ideas in the fable.

The Shepherd's Boy and the Wolf

AESOP

Here a shepherd's boy has some fun fooling people. Read to find out if anyone is laughing when the fable ends.

A shepherd's boy was tending his flock near a village. He thought it would be great fun to fool the villagers by pretending that a wolf was attacking the sheep. So he shouted out, "Wolf! Wolf!" When the people came running up, he laughed at them. He played this trick more than once. Each time that he yelled "Wolf," the villagers found they had been deceived, for there was no wolf at all.

At last a wolf really did come, and the boy cried, "Wolf! Wolf!", as loud as he could. But the people were so used to hearing him call that they took no notice of his cries. So the wolf killed off sheep after sheep at his leisure.

It is hard to believe a liar even when he tells the truth.

Shepherd and Shepherdess with Flock (detail), about 1770, ANN GARDNER. The Metropolitan Museum of Art. Collection of Mrs. Lathrop Colgate Harper, Bequest of Mabel Herbert Harper, 1957.

Developing Comprehension Skills

1. Why did the boy shout "Wolf" the first time?

2. Why didn't the villagers answer the boy's cries when a wolf really did attack?

3. List the events of this fable in the order that they happened.

    The villagers run to help.
    The sheep are killed.
    The shepherd boy tells a lie.
    The shepherd boy tells the truth.
    The wolf attacks the sheep.
    The villagers ignore the boy's cries.

4. You have probably heard the expression "He cried wolf." Think of the story you have just read. Then explain the meaning of the expression "He cried wolf."

5. After this experience, how do you suppose the boy and the villagers will behave in the future? Give reasons for your answer.

Reading Literature: Fables

1. **Understanding Personification.** Is the wolf in this story an example of personification? Explain your answer.

2. **Interpreting a Character.** What human quality might the boy in the fable represent?

3. **Applying a Moral.** The moral of this fable is easy to understand. Give some examples from your own experience that prove this moral is true.

Developing Vocabulary Skills

Making Spelling Changes When Adding Endings. Before a suffix or another ending may be added to some base words, one of the following spelling changes may be necessary:

1. Change *y* to an *i*   (*heavy* + *er* = *heavier*)

2. Double the final consonant   (*bat* + *er* = *batter*)

3. Drop the silent *e*   (*village* + *er* = *villager*)

In this selection find an example of each of these three spelling changes. Then find six other words in this selection that are built by adding some common suffixes or other endings to base words.

Developing Writing Skills

1. **Recognizing a Story as a Fable.** Review elements of a fable from the introduction on page 3. Then prove, in a paragraph, that "The Fox and the Lion" is a fable. Use specific examples from the story.

2. **Understanding Point of View.** Most fables are written about the characters involved. Some stories, however, are written as if a person in the story is telling the story. Such a story is written from the **point of view** of that person. Rewrite the fable "The Shepherd's Boy and the Wolf" from the boy's point of view. Imagine that the boy is speaking.

A Boy and False Alarums, 1931, ALEXANDER CALDER.
John M. Wing Collection, The Newberry Library, Chicago.

The Man and the Lion

AESOP

Not everyone thinks alike. Sometimes it is very hard to explain your point of view to someone. Read the next two fables to see how the lion and the stork make their opinions clear.

A man and a lion went on a journey together. As they talked, they began to boast about their abilities. Each claimed to be superior to the other in strength and courage. They were still arguing with some heat when they came to a place where there was a statue of a man strangling a lion.

"There!" said the man triumphantly, "Look at that! Doesn't that prove to you that we are stronger than you?"

"Not so fast, my friend," said the lion. "That is only your view of the case. If we lions could make statues, you may be sure that in most of them you would see the man underneath."

There are two sides to every question.

The Fox and the Stork

AESOP

A fox invited a stork to dinner, but all he provided was a large flat dish of soup. The fox lapped it up with great relish, but the stork with her long bill tried without success to share in the meal. Her obvious distress caused the sly fox much amusement.

Not long after, the stork invited the fox in turn. She set before him a pitcher with a long narrow neck, into which she could get her bill with ease. Thus, while the stork enjoyed dinner, the fox sat by, hungry and helpless, for it was impossible for him to reach the tempting contents of the vessel.

Two can play the same game.

Developing Comprehension Skills

1. In "The Man and the Lion," the man thought that the statue proved something. What did he think it proved?

2. The lion thought that the statue expressed only an opinion. Whose opinion did he think it expressed?

3. Why couldn't the stork eat the soup that the fox served?

4. Would you want the fox for your friend? Why or why not?

5. In "The Man and the Lion," the lion teaches the man a lesson. In "The Fox and the Stork," the stork teaches the fox a similar lesson. However, she does it in a different way. What is the difference between the two ways of teaching?

6. Can you think of a single sentence of advice for both the man and the fox? The sentence should tell them to do something or to avoid doing something.

Reading Literature: Fables

1. **Drawing a Time Line.** A time line is a way of picturing the order in which things happen. To make a time line, first draw a straight line from left to right. Draw a dot on the line for each event that happens. Next to the dot, write a few words to explain which event the dot stands for. The sample time line below shows the events in "The Mice and the Cat."

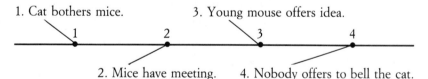

Draw a time line of the events in each of the two fables you just read.

2. **Understanding Character.** To understand a story you must understand why the characters in the story do the things they do. Why do you think the fox asked the stork to dinner? Why did the stork ask the fox to dinner? Were their reasons similar or different? Tell your opinion and give reasons for it.

Developing Vocabulary Skills

Using the Suffixes *–ful* **and** *–ly.* You have learned that the suffix *–ful* means "full of" or "having." Truthful words, for example, are full of truth. Another suffix is *–ly.* It means "in a _____ manner." For example, *sadly* means "in a sad manner."

1. The four words below are used in the two fables you have just read. Write the meaning of each. You may use clues that you find in the words and sentences around these words, or you may look up the words in the dictionary.

   a. boast   c. obvious
   b. distress   d. triumphant

2. Now make a new word from each of the four base words. Add the suffix *–ly* or *–ful.* Write the meaning of each new word.

Developing Writing Skills

1. **Writing an Original Fable.** Make up another fable that has the same moral as these two fables.

2. **Writing About a Personal Experience.** In "The Fox and the Stork," the fox learned his lesson the hard way. Write about a time when you learned a lesson the hard way.

Developing Skills in Critical Thinking

Making Comparisons. Sometimes what you read or hear seems confusing. At first, it seems different from anything you have read or heard before. However, as you think about the new information, you may see some likenesses with other things you know about. These likenesses help you understand the new information.

As you read stories, look for likenesses among characters. You can find likenesses among events or relationships or other elements.

Review the three fables you have read: "The Shepherd's Boy and the Wolf," "The Man and the Lion," and "The Fox and the Stork." Think about their characters. Are any of the six characters alike? How are they alike?

Then, think about the events in the three stories. Are any events similar? How are they similar?

List at least three similarities you find among the three fables.

The Milkmaid and Her Pail

AESOP

At some time almost everybody dreams of doing great deeds or obtaining fine things. Both the milkmaid and the wolf have dreams. See what the dreams lead to!

A farmer's daughter had been out to milk the cows and was returning to the dairy carrying her pail of milk upon her head. As she walked along, she began to daydream. "The milk in this pail will provide me with cream, which I will make into butter and take to market to sell. With the money, I will buy a number of eggs, and these, when hatched, will produce chickens. By and by I shall have quite a large poultry yard. Then I shall sell some of my chickens, and, with the money that they will bring in, I will buy myself a new gown, which I shall wear when I go to the fair. All the young fellows will admire it and try to flirt with me, but I shall toss my head and have nothing to say to them." Forgetting about the pail, she tossed her head. Down went the pail, all the milk was spilled, and her fine castles in the air vanished in a moment!

Don't count your chickens before they are hatched.

The Wolf in Sheep's Clothing

AESOP

A wolf decided to disguise himself so he could attack a flock of sheep without being detected. So he clothed himself in a sheepskin and slipped among the sheep when they were out at pasture. He completely deceived the shepherd, and, when the flock was penned for the night, he was shut in with the rest. But that very night the shepherd needed a supply of mutton for the table. He laid hands on the wolf, thinking he was a sheep, and killed him with a knife on the spot.

When you pretend to be what you are not, you must take the consequences.

Developing Comprehension Skills

1. Several events happened in "The Milkmaid and Her Pail." In addition, the milkmaid imagined other events. In the list below, identify the events that happened. Then identify those that the milkmaid imagined.

   The milkmaid carried a pail of milk on her head.
   She sold the milk.
   She bought chickens.
   She sold some chickens and made money.
   Young fellows flirted with the milkmaid.
   She tossed her head and spilled the milk.

2. Compare the milkmaid's feelings while she is daydreaming with her feelings after she spills the milk.

3. Do you think that the events in the milkmaid's daydream could really happen? Why or why not?

4. List these events in "The Wolf in Sheep's Clothing" in the proper order:

   The shepherd puts the flock and the wolf in the pen.
   The shepherd kills the wolf by mistake.
   The wolf puts on a sheepskin.
   The shepherd needs mutton to eat.

5. The wolf was talented at deceiving others. Was this talent worthwhile? Did it help the wolf? Explain your answer.

Reading Literature: Fables

1. **Understanding Proverbs.** Reread the moral at the end of "The Milkmaid and Her Pail." You may have heard this saying quoted by itself. It is a **proverb**, a popular saying that expresses a truth. Why would people use a proverb by itself? Why would they use it after a fable?

2. **Interpreting a Character.** The milkmaid's actions stand for, or represent, a common human habit. What is this habit? What could be the problem with thinking and acting the way the milkmaid did?

3. **Relating Literature and Life.** The wolf appears as a character in many fables. He is often given undesirable qualities. Can you think of any reasons for a bad opinion of wolves being this common?

4. **Understanding Expressions.** The phrase "wolf in sheep's clothing" is often used outside of this fable. What does it mean?

Developing Vocabulary Skills

Recognizing Base Words and Endings. Not every word that ends in −s, −er, −y, −ly, or −ing is built on a base word. Each of the words below appears in one of the fables you have just read. Find the words that are built on base words. For each, write the base word. Then write the ending. Follow the example. (If the word is not built on a base word, do nothing with it.)

Example: building = build + ing

1. dairy
2. order
3. farmer
4. very
5. castles
6. number
7. completely
8. supply
9. daughter
10. butter
11. his
12. poultry
13. nothing
14. thinking
15. fellows

Developing Writing Skills

1. **Writing an Explanation.** In "The Milkmaid and Her Pail," daydreaming hurt the milkmaid. However, daydreaming can also help people. Write at least one paragraph explaining how daydreaming might be helpful to a person.

2. **Rewriting a Fable.** Update either "The Milkmaid and Her Pail" or "The Wolf in Sheep's Clothing." Place the fable in a more modern setting. However, keep the moral the same.

Developing Skills in Speaking and Listening

Telling a Fable. From the fables you have read so far, choose your favorite. Reread it several times. Write out the events of the fable in the order in which they occur. You may wish to list the events on small note cards. It is easy to hold and refer to note cards when you speak. Practice telling the fable in your own words. Then, tell the fable to a group, using your notes on the time order of the events as a reminder.

The Spendthrift and the Swallow

AESOP

These two fables seem very different from each other. They have different morals. As you read them, see if you can find what makes them alike.

A spendthrift who had wasted his fortune had nothing left but the clothes in which he stood. One fine day in early spring, he saw a swallow. Thinking that summer had come, and that he could now do without his coat, he sold it. A change, however, took place in the weather. There came a sharp frost, which killed the unfortunate swallow. When the spendthrift saw its dead body, he cried, "Miserable bird! Thanks to you I am perishing of cold myself."

One swallow does not make a summer.

The Fox and the Crow

AESOP

A crow was sitting on a branch of a tree with a piece of cheese in her beak when a fox noticed her. He set his wits to work in order to discover some way of getting the cheese. Standing under the tree, he looked up and said, "What a noble bird I see above me! Her beauty is without equal, the color of her feathers exquisite. If only her voice is as sweet as her looks are fair, she ought without doubt to be Queen of the Birds."

The crow was hugely flattered by this, and, just to show the fox that she could sing beautifully, she gave a loud caw. Down came the cheese, of course, and the fox, snatching it up, said, "You have a voice, madam, indeed. What you need are wits."

Flattery is the best persuasion.

Developing Comprehension Skills

1. Tell the main events of each fable in order.

2. Explain the moral "One swallow does not make a summer" in your own words.

3. In "The Fox and the Crow," the fox said to the crow, "You have a voice, madam. What you need are wits." What did the fox mean? Why did he say this?

4. How else could the fox have gotten the cheese from the crow? Can you think of another solution?

5. The man in "The Spendthrift and the Swallow" and the crow in "The Fox and the Crow" each made a similar mistake. What was it?

Reading Literature: Fables

1. **Interpreting Character.** When the spendthrift saw the dead swallow, he became angry. He blamed the swallow for his being cold. What does this tell you about the spendthrift?

2. **Understanding Personification.** What human quality, or characteristic, does each animal in "The Fox and the Crow" stand for? Give reasons for your answers.

3. **Appreciating the Fable.** People who tell fables often use animals as their main characters rather than people. Why is it easier to accept the moral of a fable when the characters are animals?

Developing Vocabulary Skills

Understanding Expressions. Following are some words and expressions that make use of the word *crow*. Match the appropriate meaning in column B with the word or expression in column A. Use your dictionary if you need help.

A	B
1. crow's nest	a. a lookout
2. crowbar	b. the lines around a person's eyes
3. to crow about something	c. to boast, brag
4. crow's-feet	d. in a straight line
5. as the crow flies	e. a tool used for prying

Developing Writing Skills

1. **Presenting an Opinion.** The proverb "Flattery is the best persuasion" appears as the moral of "The Fox and the Crow." However, there is another proverb about flattery: "Flattery will get you nowhere." Which proverb do you believe is true? Can both proverbs be true? Write one or more paragraphs explaining and defending your opinion.

2. **Understanding Purpose.** The fable of "The Spendthrift and the Swallow" has the purpose of teaching a lesson. Rewrite the fable with a different purpose in mind. Choose one of these purposes or think of another. Change the moral to fit your new purpose.

   a. To sell Northerners airplane tickets to the warm South
   b. To encourage people to open savings accounts
   c. To encourage people to feed birds
   d. To pass a law against spendthrifts

Fox Hunt, 1893, WINSLOW HOMER. Pennsylvania Academy of the Fine Arts, Philadelphia.

The Wolf and the Lamb

AESOP

The next two fables are about hungry animals. However, the wolf and the fox have more than hunger in common. Read carefully to find something they both do.

A wolf came upon a lamb straying from the flock but felt guilty about taking the life of so helpless a creature without some believable excuse. So he cast about for a grievance and said at last, "Last year, sir, you greatly insulted me."

"That is impossible, sir," bleated the lamb, "for I wasn't born then."

"Well," said the wolf, "you feed in my pastures."

"That cannot be," replied the lamb, "for I have never yet tasted grass."

"You drink from my spring, then," continued the wolf.

"Indeed, sir," said the poor lamb, "I have never yet drunk anything but my mother's milk."

"Well, anyhow," said the wolf, "I'm not going without my dinner." And he sprang upon the lamb and devoured it without more ado.

The Fox and the Grapes

AESOP

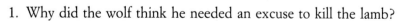

A hungry fox saw some fine bunches of grapes hanging from a vine that covered a high trellis. He did his best to reach them by jumping as high as he could into the air. But it was all in vain, for they were just out of reach. So he gave up trying. Walking away with an air of dignity and unconcern, he remarked, "I thought those grapes were ripe, but I see now they are quite sour."

Developing Comprehension Skills

1. Why did the wolf think he needed an excuse to kill the lamb?
2. What explanations or excuses did the wolf give before he ate the lamb?
3. Imagine that the lamb ate grass from the pasture and drank water from the spring. Would the wolf have a good reason for eating him? Explain your answer.
4. Why couldn't the fox eat the grapes?

5. What is wrong with the fox's reason for not wanting the grapes?

6. Think of something in your life that you want badly. How would you get it if you were the wolf? How might you handle this problem if you were the fox?

Reading Literature: Fables

1. **Understanding Personification.** In "The Wolf and the Lamb," what is the wolf doing that many people do?

2. **Interpreting Character.** The fox in literature is often sly and crafty. In "The Fox and the Grapes," how does the slyness of the fox help him to walk away with dignity?

3. **Understanding the Moral.** In your own words, write a moral for each fable.

Developing Vocabulary Skills

Using Word Parts To Find Meaning. The five words listed below are from "The Wolf and the Lamb" and "The Fox and the Grapes."

1. helpless   3. believable   5. unconcern

2. impossible   4. greatly

Copy each word. Write its base word and the prefix or suffix that has been added. Then write the meaning of the complete word.

Next, find each word in the fables. Copy the sentence in which each word appears. Rewrite the sentence, using the meaning of the word instead of the word itself.

Developing Writing Skills

1. **Rewriting a Fable.** Choose one of these two fables. Rewrite it so that the ending is the opposite of the original ending. Include a new moral.

2. **Writing an Original Story.** Some people are like the fox. When they can't have what they want, they claim "sour grapes." Write a brief story in which a person acts like the fox in the fable. The story may be about a real or a made-up event.

The Fox and the Grapes

JEAN de LA FONTAINE

Pretend you are a poet.
need an idea for a poem.
about using a fable? When Je
de La Fontaine did this, he
made some small changes. Try
to find the ways he changed the
fable on page 27.

A fox, almost with hunger dying,
Some grapes, upon a trellis spying,
To all appearance ripe, clad in
    Their tempting russet skin,
Most gladly would have eat them;
But since he could not get them,
    So far above his reach the vine—
'They're sour,' he said; 'such grapes as these,
The dogs may eat them if they please!'

    Did he not better than to whine?

Developing Comprehension Skills

1. List the main events of this fable in the order they happened.
2. Retell the last sentence of the poem in your own words.
3. Does the fox like dogs? Give a reason for your answer.
4. Do you think that the moral is as clear in this poem as it was in Aesop's story? Why or why not?

1. **Interpreting Character.** Compare the attitude of Aesop's fox and this fox. Which fox seems angry? Does the difference in the fox's attitude change your feelings about the fox? Explain your answer.

2. **Appreciating the Fable.** In some fables, the moral is stated. That is, the writer tells you the moral. In others, the moral is not stated. Can you think of any reasons for this difference? Explain your reasons.

Developing Vocabulary Skills

Understanding Prefixes and Suffixes. Each word below is built upon a base word used in "The Fox and the Grapes." Read the words. For each, find the base word and the prefix or suffix. Tell the meaning of the complete word. Then use the word in a sentence.

1. reappear 3. unripe 5. unreachable
2. disappear 4. reachable

Developing Writing Skills

Writing a Fable as a Poem. Notice how La Fontaine added details to the story of "The Fox and the Grapes." Instead of saying that the fox *saw* the grapes, he used the more specific word *spying*. He appealed to the reader's senses by describing the grapes: "ripe, clad in their tempting russet skin."

La Fontaine also used rhymes in his fable (*dying, spying*; *in, skin*; *vine, whine*; *these, please*).

Rewrite one of the other Aesop fables in this chapter in a poetic form. That is, write the story in lines instead of sentences. Imitate some or all three of the methods La Fontaine used:

1. Use specific words.

2. Appeal to the reader's senses; draw pictures with words.

3. Include some rhymes.

Two Ways To Count to Ten

LIBERIAN FABLE
Retold by Frances Carpenter

In this fable, as in the others you have read, animals do the talking. Which animals appear here that are not in the other fables? Why are these animals used?

In the long, long ago, animals were not so different, one from the other. Oh, they had different shapes, just as they do today. But they lived together in friendship and peace. Like people, those of one animal tribe sometimes took their wives from those of a different tribe. Like you and me, in those times beasts could talk. And, like people, they had a king to rule over them.

In the place of this story, the leopard was king. Rich he was, beyond telling. Mighty was he in his power over the other beasts. All the animals obeyed him.

"Whom shall I name to rule after me when I shall die?" King Leopard said one day to his pretty daughter. "I must find one who is wise enough so that he can rule well. Yes, my dear daughter, I must seek out the cleverest beast in our jungle land. I shall make him a prince. He shall have you for his bride. And to me he shall be a son."

King Leopard was pleased with his idea, and he planned a great feast. His royal drums carried word of it far and wide through the jungle, and all the animals came.

There were good things to eat. There was plenty to drink. The drums beat, and the guests at King Leopard's feast danced for three days.

At last the king called them to make a huge circle. Stepping into its center, he called his pretty daughter to come to his side. Then he spoke in a loud voice.

"Listen to my words, friends!" he cried. "Someday I must die. Someday another king must rule in my place. I will choose him now from among you, so that he will be ready."

There was a murmur of wonder all through the crowd. The king had to order them to be quiet.

"I shall seek the cleverest among you, for your king must be wise. I shall name him Prince. He shall be to me a son and to

Benin Leopard, 17th–18th Century, Nigeria, Africa.
The Metropolitan Museum of Art, the Michael C. Rockefeller Memorial Collection, gift of Nelson A. Rockefeller, 1972.

my dear daughter a husband. He shall share all my riches. And when I die he shall be your king."

Shouts came from the eager guests at the king's feast. No doubt each animal hoped that the good fortune would be his.

Then King Leopard held up his hunting spear. "Look at this, my people! Watch!" He flung the spear far up into the air.

"With this spear will I test you," he went on. "He who would be our prince must throw the spear toward the sky. He must send it so high that he can count to ten before it drops down to earth again."

There was a buzz of talk among all the animals then. This would not be so hard to do, they thought.

One after another, they came forward to try their skill. Each jungle beast danced before King Leopard and his pretty daughter. Each one sang a song that told how well he would rule, if he were chosen.

First to try his luck was the elephant. He was so big that he could push all the other beasts out of his way.

"I must be first," he said to himself. "This task is too easy. Almost any one of us can do it."

The elephant danced clumsily. He was very big and his body was heavy. Then, with his trunk in the air, he trumpeted all the fine deeds he would perform if he were prince.

The great beast threw King Leopard's spear up into the air.

"One! Two! Three!" he began counting. But he spoke slowly, as he did everything else. An elephant cannot easily hurry, you know.

Before the elephant had said, "Four!" the king's spear had dropped to earth. The proud beast hung his head so low that the tip of his trunk dragged on the ground. He knew he had failed.

Next came the bush ox. His wide gray horns swept the other beasts to the side.

"I'll throw the spear up to the sun," the huge animal sang while he danced. "I'll be a strong husband for King Leopard's daughter."

The bush ox picked the spear up in his mouth. With a mighty toss of his great head, he flung it far, far above his spreading horns.

"One! Two! Three! Four!" the bush ox counted more quickly than the elephant. But he, too, was slow. Before he could say "Five," the spear was down on the ground. He went off, ashamed, into the deep jungle.

The chimpanzee was third. He jumped up and down in a merry dance, and King Leopard's daughter laughed at his antics. He beat his hairy chest with his two fists, and he sang of how much he would like to be king in the leopard's place.

The young ape rose up straight on his hind legs. He held the spear in one hand, just like a man. With a twist of his long arm, he threw it up toward the sky.

"One-two-three-four-five-six-seven!" He chattered as fast as he could. The watching animals held their breaths. Surely, with such a quick tongue, the chimpanzee would make the count.

But he did not! He had not even said, "Eight!" before he had caught the spear once more in his hand.

One by one, other animals tried to count to ten while the spear was still up in the air. One by one, they all failed.

"It seems I must look somewhere else for a prince to rule when I am gone," King Leopard spoke sadly.

Then out from the crowd stepped an antelope.

Beside the elephant, the bush ox, and even the chimpanzee, the young deerlike antelope seemed puny and weak. His legs were long, yet so slender that it was almost a wonder that they would hold up his body. But the antelope spoke bravely.

"Let me try to throw your spear, O King," he cried. "I would like well to marry your pretty daughter."

"Ho! Ho!" The other animals burst into laughter. How could such a weak creature fling the king's spear high enough to say more than two or three words? However could he hope to count up to ten?

The antelope was not discouraged.

"I wish to try," he insisted. And King Leopard nodded his head. He had promised a fair trial for all who wished to take part in this contest.

"Who can say what any creature can do until he has tried?" The king spoke to the crowd. "The antelope may throw the spear." The other beasts were moved back to give him room.

When the antelope, on his slender legs, danced before the king, the leopard's daughter cried out with pleasure. No one could deny that his steps were more graceful than those of the elephant, or of the bush ox, or of the chimpanzee.

Then the antelope threw the spear. With a toss of his head, he flung it far up into the air. Before it could fall to earth, the clever beast called out two words. "Five! Ten!" he cried. "I have counted to ten. King Leopard did not say how the count should be made."

The leopard laughed then. He nodded his royal head.

"No, I did not say how the count was to be made," he agreed. "And as everyone knows, one can count by fives as well as by ones. The antelope has won the contest. He has proved he is the cleverest of you all. He shall wed my dear daughter. He shall be king when I am gone."

The other animals stared stupidly at the winner. They did not understand yet what had happened. But they could see that the antelope had outwitted them.

At the wedding feast that King Leopard gave for his daughter, they all cheered for the antelope, their new prince.

It is not always the biggest nor the strongest, but sometimes the cleverest who wins the prize.

Developing Comprehension Skills

1. What would the winning animal gain from the contest?

2. How did the elephant get to be the first contestant?

3. Why do you think the antelope was brought into the story last?

4. Do you think the daughter was happy with the outcome of the contest? Give a reason for your answer.

5. What quality was the king looking for? Why was the spear-throwing contest a good way to find that quality?

Reading Literature: Fables

1. **Reading Quotation Marks.** Frequently, there is conversation in a fable. The words that a character says are set off by **quotation marks** (" "). One set of marks is placed before the character's words. The other set is placed after the character's words. Read the fable once more and notice how much conversation there is in it. Be sure you know which character is talking each time you see quotation marks. Why do you think this story uses conversation?

2. **Interpreting Character.** A character can show strength in two ways. He or she can show physical strength. The elephant and bush ox had

that kind of strength. The other strength is inside the character. It is the second kind of strength that keeps a person going in spite of difficulties.

Do you think the antelope showed more of the second kind of strength than the other animals? What happens in the story to make you think so?

3. **Understanding Personification.** What human qualities did each of these animals show?

   a. the elephant   c. the chimpanzee
   b. the bush ox   d. the antelope

Developing Vocabulary Skills

Using Suffixes To Build Words. Review the meanings of these suffixes on page 7: *−er*, *−less*, *−able*, and *−ful*. Then read the sentences below. In each sentence, there is an underlined word taken from the African fable. Copy the sentence, adding the correct suffix to the underlined word. Remember that sometimes you will need to change the spelling of the base word before adding the suffix.

1. The leopard was a power___ king.
2. The drinking water was plenty___.
3. The storytelling time was an enjoy___ event.
4. The king wanted to appoint a new rule___.
5. Each animal tried to be the most skill___.
6. The antelope was more grace___ than the bush ox.
7. The elephant felt power___ when he knew that he had failed.
8. The win___ felt happy and proud.

Developing Writing Skills

1. **Writing an Original Fable.** Write a modern fable showing that "it is not always the biggest nor the strongest, but sometimes the cleverest who wins the prize." If you like, the fable may be based on a real experience you have had.

2. **Developing a Character.** Choose a different animal to win the spear-throwing contest. Tell what qualities he had that helped him win.

The Thief and the Bell

As you know, most fables are short. This fable from China may be one of the shortest. How does its shortness help to make the fable enjoyable?

CHINESE FABLE
Retold by Robert Wyndham

A man tried to steal a large bronze bell. It was too heavy to carry, so he tried to break up the valuable bronze with a hammer. But this made such a din that the thief feared he would be heard and discovered by the authorities. So he hastily stuffed his ears with cotton.

Only a fool would fool himself.

Bronze Bell, Courtesy of the Cultural Relics Bureau, Beijing, and The Metropolitan Museum of Art, New York.

Developing Comprehension Skills

1. List the events of the fable according to correct time order.

   The thief feared he would be discovered.
   The thief tried to steal the bell.
   The thief stuffed his ears with cotton.
   The thief tried to break the bell with a hammer.
   The bell was too heavy to carry.
   The bell made such a din.

2. Why did the thief stuff his ears with c⸱

3. "The Thief and the Bell" was written m
   country far away from us. Yet, we can ⸱
   you think of any reasons for the wide
   What are these reasons?

Reading Literature: Fables

1. **Understanding Personification.** D
   Explain your answer.

2. **Interpreting Character.** How would you describe the main charac⸱⸱
   in this story? Choose the qualities listed below that fit him.

generous	lazy	logical
dishonest	strong	unthinking
happy	admirable	
ridiculous	intelligent	

Developing Vocabulary Skills

Using Prefixes To Build Words. The prefixes *in–*, *non–*, and *un–* all mean "not." The prefix *mis–* means "wrongly." On a separate paper, write each of the following words, adding one of these four prefixes. Use a dictionary, if necessary, to choose the best prefix. Then use at least five of the new words in sentences about the Chinese fable.

1. __curable   4. __lucky   7. __understand   9. __finished

2. __human   5. __broken   8. __sense   10. __ability

3. __counted   6. __ashamed

Developing Writing Skills

1. **Writing a Comparison.** Does this fable remind you of TV or movie comedians? Write a paragraph showing how the character in this story is like one of the Three Stooges or another comedian.

2. **Revising a Fable.** Write a new ending to this story, showing a different moral.

King and the Shirt

LEO TOLSTOY

The next two tales were written about a hundred years ago. They are by Leo Tolstoy, an important Russian writer. As you read these newer tales, see if anything about them is different from the old fables.

A king once fell ill. "I will give half my kingdom to the man who can cure me," he said.

All his wise men gathered together to decide how the king could be cured, but no one knew. Only one of the wise men said what he thought would cure the king.

"If you can find a happy man, take his shirt, put it on the king—and the king will be cured."

The king sent his messengers to search for a happy man. They traveled far and wide throughout his whole kingdom, but they could not find a happy man. There was no one who was completely satisfied. If a man was rich, he was ailing. If he was healthy, he was poor. If he was rich and healthy, he had a cross wife. If he had children, they were bad. Everyone had something to complain of.

Finally, late one night, the king's son was passing by a poor little hut, and he heard someone say, "Now, God be praised, I have finished my work, I have eaten my fill, and I can lie down and sleep! What more could I want?"

The king's son rejoiced and gave orders that the man's shirt be taken and carried to the king, and that the man be given as much money as he wanted.

The messengers went in to take off the man's shirt, but the happy man was so poor that he had no shirt.

The Learned Son

LEO TOLSTOY

A son once returned from the city to his father, who lived in the country.

"We're mowing today," said the father. "Take a rake and help me."

The son did not want to work, so he said, "I am a scholar and have forgotten all those peasant words. What is a rake?"

As he walked across the yard, he stepped on a rake that was lying in his way, and it struck him on the forehead. He suddenly seemed to recall what a rake was. Clutching his head he cried, "What fool left a rake lying here?"

Haystack in Winter, 1891, CLAUDE MONET (Fr. 1840–1926).
Oil on canvas, 25¾ × 36⅜", 1970.253, Gift of the Misses Aimée and Rosamond Lamb in memory of Mr. and Mrs. Horatio A. Lamb, 1970. Courtesy, Museum of Fine Arts, Boston.

Developing Comprehension Skills

1. The following sentences tell about "The King and the Shirt." Fill in the blanks with "before," "after," or "then."

   _____ the king got sick, the wise men met to figure out a cure. _____ the king sent messengers to look for a happy man. _____ they found a happy man, the messengers traveled far and wide. _____ they found the happy man, they discovered he was too poor to have a shirt.

2. What made the poor man the happiest person in the kingdom?

3. In "The Learned Son," the son says, "I am a scholar and have forgotten all those peasant words." In your own words, explain what he means.

4. How do you think the father felt when his son said, "I have forgotten all those peasant words?"

5. Rich or educated people are often considered "better" than poor people. However, in both of these fables the poor peasants seem to be wiser than the richer or more educated characters.

   a. Tell how each fable makes this point.
   b. What does this fact tell you about Leo Tolstoy's attitude toward poor people?

Reading Literature: Fables

1. **Understanding the Moral.** In your own words, write a moral for each fable.

2. **Interpreting Character.** A scholar is someone who has studied many things and is very wise. In "The Learned Son," the son called himself a scholar. Do you think he was wise? Why or why not? Can you suggest any other words to describe him?

Developing Vocabulary Skills

Using Prefixes or Suffixes To Change Word Meanings. Some of the words on the following list are from fables in this chapter. The rest of the words were formed by adding prefixes or suffixes to words from the fables. Make sure you know the meaning of each word on the list.

Then review the prefixes and suffixes on the lists on pages 6 and 7. Choose a prefix or suffix that would change each word below to mean its opposite. You may change the prefix or suffix that is given as part of a word, or you may add a new prefix or suffix. Write the new words you form.

1. believable
2. prove
3. matched
4. helpless
5. curable
6. doubtless
7. hopeful
8. completely
9. known
10. fortunately
11. continued
12. unused
13. guilty
14. appearance
15. healthy

Developing Writing Skills

1. **Rewriting a Fable.** Both of these fables were written in times when life was quite different from the way it is today. Kings and queens ruled the land, and fields were tended by hand without the help of modern machinery. Write a modern-day version of either "The King and the Shirt" or "The Learned Son."

2. **Changing the Form of a Work.** Rewrite either of the two fables as a cartoon strip.

3. **Writing an Original Story.** In "The Learned Son," the son doesn't want to work. That's why he tells his father that he doesn't know what a rake is. Write about a time when you or a friend of yours got out of work with an excuse like that. Your story may be true or you can make it up.

Developing Skills in Critical Thinking

Recognizing Likenesses Among Characters. The thief in the fable "The Thief and the Bell" tried to fool others, but only fooled himself. What other characters in the fables you have read were this foolish?

Equal Inheritance

LEO TOLSTOY

In both of the following fables, the characters have learned lessons. One character has learned something very important, but the other character is a little confused. Which is which?

A certain merchant had two sons. The elder son was his favorite, and he intended to leave all his wealth to this son when he died. The mother felt sorry for her younger son, and she asked her husband not to tell the boys of his intention. She hoped to find some way of making her sons equal. The merchant heeded her wish and did not make known his decision.

One day the mother was sitting at the window weeping. A traveler approached the window and asked her why she was weeping.

"How can I help weeping?" she said. "There is no difference between my two sons, but their father wishes to leave everything to one and nothing to the other. I have asked him not to tell them of his decision until I have thought of some way of helping the younger. But I have no money of my own, and I do not know what to do in my misery."

Then the traveler said to her, "There is help for your trouble. Tell your sons that the elder will receive the entire inheritance, and that the younger will receive nothing. Then they will be equal."

The younger son, on learning that he would inherit nothing, went to another land, where he served his apprenticeship and learned a trade. The elder son lived at home and learned nothing, knowing that someday he would be rich.

When the father died, the elder son did not know how to do anything and spent all his inheritance. However, the younger son, who had learned how to make money in a foreign country, became rich.

Three Rolls and a Pretzel

LEO TOLSTOY

Feeling very hungry one day, a peasant bought himself a large roll and ate it. But he was still hungry, so he bought another roll and ate it. Still hungry, he bought a third roll and ate it. When the three rolls failed to satisfy his hunger, he bought some pretzels. After eating one pretzel, he no longer felt hungry.

Suddenly he clapped his hand to his head and cried, "What a fool I am! Why did I waste all those rolls? I ought to have eaten a pretzel in the first place!"

Developing Comprehension Skills

1. Draw a time line for each story. You may want to review Reading Literature: Fables, 1, page 16. Include the main events of the story.

2. In "Equal Inheritance," how did the father's decision affect the elder son's life? How did it affect the younger son's life?

3. Which son was wiser? Why do you think so?

4. In most stories, the order in which things happen is important. If the peasant in "Three Rolls and a Pretzel" had eaten the pretzel first, what difference would that have made?

Reading Literature: Fables

1. **Relating Literature and Life.** Fables are popular because they often use experiences that are familiar to many people. What familiar experience is in "Equal Inheritance"?

2. **Understanding the Moral.** What would be an appropriate moral for the first fable? Do you agree with this moral? Why or why not?

3. **Recognizing Humor.** Some fables teach their lessons through humor. "Three Rolls and a Pretzel" uses this method. What is funny about the story? How does the humor help you understand the point of the fable?

Developing Vocabulary Skills

Using Prefixes and Suffixes. Each of these base words was found in the fables in this chapter. Make new words by selecting a prefix, a suffix, or both from the lists on pages 6 and 7 and adding them to each base word. Make any spelling changes that are necessary. Be able to explain how each word changes in meaning. Then choose six of your new words, and write a sentence using each.

1. certain
2. hope
3. equal
4. thought
5. obtain
6. hand
7. satisfy
8. receive
9. home
10. place

Developing Writing Skills

1. **Developing a Point of View.** The first fable does not tell how each of the sons felt about the inheritance. Choose one of the sons. Write a paragraph from the son's point of view. Have the son tell his feelings about what happened.

2. **Writing About a Personal Experience.** When we expect nothing, often something special happens to us. Then we are pleasantly surprised. Describe a situation from your own life that illustrates this.

The Fox and the Crow

JAMES THURBER

"The Fox and the Crow" by James Thurber is a modern version of the Aesop fable on page 23. But this is a fable with a difference or two. Look for the differences as you read.

A crow, perched in a tree with a piece of cheese in his beak, attracted the eye and nose of a fox. "If you can sing as prettily as you sit," said the fox, "then you are the prettiest singer within my scent and sight." The fox had read somewhere, and somewhere, and somewhere else, that praising the voice of a crow with a cheese in his beak would make him drop the cheese and sing. But this is not what happened to this particular crow in this particular case.

"They say you are sly and they say you are crazy," said the crow, having carefully removed the cheese from his beak with the claws of one foot, "but you must be nearsighted as well. Warblers wear brilliant hats and colored jackets and bright vests, and they are a dollar a hundred. I wear black and I am unique." He began nibbling the cheese, dropping not a single crumb.

"I am sure you are," said the fox, who was neither crazy nor nearsighted, but sly. "I recognize you, now that I look more closely, as the most famed and talented of all birds, and I fain would hear you tell about yourself, but I am hungry and must go."

"Tarry awhile," said the crow quickly, "and share my lunch with me." Where-

upon he tossed the cunning fox the lion's share of the cheese and began to tell about himself. "A ship that sails without a crow's nest sails to doom," he said. "Bars may come and bars may go, but crow bars last forever. I am the pioneer of flight; I am the map maker. Last, but never least, my flight is known to scientists and engineers, geometrists and scholars, as the shortest distance between two points. Any two points," he concluded arrogantly.

"Oh, every two points, I am sure," said the fox. "And thank you for the lion's share of what I know you could not spare." And with this he trotted away into the woods, his appetite appeased, leaving the hungry crow perched forlornly in the tree.

MORAL: *'Twas true in Aesop's time, and La Fontaine's, and now, no one else can praise thee quite so well as thou.*

Developing Comprehension Skills

1. List the order of events in Thurber's "The Fox and the Crow." Then list the order of events of the original fable on page 23. Compare the two lists.

2. How did Thurber's fox trick the crow into giving him the cheese?

3. The word "crow" is used in many English phrases. Some of these phrases do not really refer to crows at all. Still, the crow in this fable referred to three of these phrases to show the importance of crows. What are the three phrases? What do they really mean?

4. A **parody** is a funny imitation of something that someone else wrote. Do you think that Thurber's version of the fable is a parody of Aesop's? Give a reason for your answer.

5. Does Thurber make the same point that Aesop made in this fable? Explain your answer.

Reading Literature: Fables

1. **Understanding the Moral.** Restate Thurber's moral in your own words.

2. **Understanding Personification.** In Aesop's fable, the fox represented the human characteristic of slyness, and the crow represented

vanity. In Thurber's fable, both the fox and the crow act a little differently. The fox still represents slyness. Do you think the crow still represents vanity? Is there any difference between Aesop's crow and Thurber's crow? Give a reason for your answer.

3. **Recognizing an Allusion.** Often a work of literature refers, or alludes, to another work of literature. This is called an **allusion**. Thurber's fable alludes to two fables that you have studied. Name the fables.

Developing Vocabulary Skills

Using Prefixes and Suffixes To Build Words. The sentences below tell about events that occur in the fables in this chapter. The words in parentheses, also, are taken from the fables. To make sense in its sentence, each word needs a prefix or a suffix from the lists on pages 6 and 7. Add the correct prefix or suffix to the word so that the new word will complete the sentence. Write the completed sentence on a separate sheet of paper. Remember to make any necessary spelling changes.

1. The boy was being _____ when he cried "Wolf!"   (deceit)
2. The lion argued that he was stronger and more _____ than the man. (courage)
3. The daughter of the _____ had been out to milk the cows. (farm)
4. The wolf disguised himself so he would go _____ in the flock of sheep.   (detected)
5. The grapes hanging from the vine were not _____.   (reach)
6. La Fontaine _____ the fable of the "Fox and the Grapes."   (told)
7. The thief was _____ that he would be heard and discovered by the authorities.   (fear)
8. The crow _____ the slyness of the fox.   (judged)

Developing Writing Skills

Writing a Parody of a Fable. Write a parody of another fable that you have read in this chapter. (See Developing Comprehension Skills, 4, page 46.) Remember that the moral does not have to be the same as the original.

Using Your Skills in Reading Fables

Read the following fable. Tell what human quality the crow stands for. Then write a moral for the fable. Remember to make the moral a general statement.

THE CROW AND THE PITCHER

A thirsty crow found a pitcher with some water in it, but there was very little of it. Try as she might, the crow could not reach the water with her beak. It seemed as though she would die of thirst within sight of water. At last she hit upon a clever plan. She began dropping pebbles into the pitcher. With each pebble the water rose a little higher. Finally the water reached the brim, and the clever bird was able to satisfy her thirst.

Using Your Comprehension Skills

The following paragraphs are taken from a tall tale you will read in Chapter 2 of this book. The tale tells how the cowboy hero, Pecos Bill, rode a powerful storm called a cyclone. Read this part of the tale. Then list the important events in the order in which they occur.

What Bill planned to do was leap from his horse and grab the cyclone by the neck. But as he came near and saw how high the top of the whirling tower was, he knew he would have to do something better than that. Just as he and his horse came close enough to the cyclone to feel its hot breath, a knife of lightning streaked down into the ground. It stuck there, quivering, just long enough for Bill to reach out and grab it. As the lightning bolt whipped back up into the sky, Bill held on. When he was as high as the top of the cyclone, he jumped and landed on its black, spinning shoulders.

By then, everyone in Texas, New Mexico, Arizona, and Oklahoma was watching. They saw Bill grab hold of that cyclone's shoulders and haul them back. They saw him wrap his legs around the cyclone's belly and squeeze so hard the cyclone started to pant. Then Bill got out his lasso and slung it around the cyclone's neck. He pulled it tighter and tighter until the cyclone started to choke, spitting out rocks and dust. All the rain that was mixed up in it started to fall.

Using Your Vocabulary Skills

The following sentences are from or about the selections you will read in Chapter 2. Read each numbered sentence or group of sentences.

In each item there is at least one word built from a base word and a prefix or suffix listed on pages 6 and 7. Find each of these words and write it on your paper. Think about what you know about the meanings of prefixes and suffixes. Also, look for clues within the sentence that lead you to an understanding of what the word means. (Do not use a dictionary.) Then write the meaning of each word that you wrote.

1. A man from Missouri is so successful as a fisherman that he can tie a hook and line to each foot and dive into the river and bring up a fish on each foot.

2. Paul hitched Babe the Blue Ox to the giant griddle and away they went. A few miles from the Big Onion lumber camp, Paul unhitched Babe and let the griddle roll on by itself.

3. Paul was naturally the best hunter, walker, runner, yeller, or mountain climber there was.

4. The horse was so thankful for being pulled from the trap that he swung his head around and gave Pecos Bill a smacking kiss.

5. Two of the tall tales have been retold by Adrien Stoutenburg.

Using Your Writing Skills

Choose one of the writing assignments below. Follow directions.

1. Compare Aesop's version of "The Fox and the Crow" with Thurber's version. You could discuss the characters, the personification, the moral, or the use of detail or conversation.

2. Write a new fable that uses one of these proverbs as its moral.

   a. Haste makes waste.   c. Birds of a feather flock together.
   b. A watched pot never boils.

American Folklore

A Double Crosser, 1946, WILLIAM R. LEIGH.
Joslyn Art Museum, Omaha, Nebraska.

Reading Literature: American Folklore

What Is American Folklore?

How are ghost stories and jump rope rhymes alike? One way they are alike is that we usually learn them from the people around us. As children, we heard older children or adults tell stories and recite rhymes. Later, we told the same stories and recited the rhymes. They are part of our folklore. **Folklore** includes the stories, customs, and beliefs of a whole group of people.

This chapter concentrates on one kind of folklore. You will read stories created by large groups of American people. The stories tell about American heroes, mostly imaginary. Each hero was special to the group that made up the stories. Now the stories have become part of the folklore of all the American people.

As these stories show, we Americans love tall tales. **Tall tales** are funny, exaggerated stories about real or invented characters.

The History of American Folklore

Early American settlers faced tremendous odds. How could they tame such a huge and wild land? Sometimes problems are so big that you have only two choices—you give up, or you make a joke, laugh, and keep trying. These Americans didn't give up.

When settlers got together, they told stories of mighty heroes who were bigger and stronger than any problem. Paul Bunyan, they said, carried trees in bundles and sneezed birds out of the air. John Henry worked faster and harder than a steam engine. Even ordinary people in tall tales did extraordinary things.

We don't know exactly where the idea for Paul—or John, or many of the other heroes—came from. It is possible that only one person invented each hero, but many other people added new parts to each story. Today there are many versions of each tale.

The Elements of American Folklore

Setting. The **setting** of a story is the time and place of its events. Usually the setting of a fable is not important. The setting of a tall tale, however, is important. Paul Bunyan, for example, was a giant lumberjack. He could be a hero only in the huge forests of a new land. John Henry was a heroic railroad worker. His story would have to take place after the invention of railroads.

Hyperbole. American folklore uses a special kind of exaggeration, **hyperbole** (hī pur′ bə lē). Hyperbole is wild exaggeration that puts an instant picture in the reader's mind. That picture is usually ridiculous, impossible, and funny. Here is an example:

One time snowflakes fell so large in Oregon that the ladies put handles on them and used them for umbrellas.

Narrator. The **narrator** is the person who tells the story. The narrator may be someone outside the story who knows everything that happens. The narrator may also be a character in the story. In this case, the writer uses *I* or *we*.

Often a writer tries to make the words of a tall tale sound as if a storyteller is saying them. The writer may use some old-fashioned words or words used in a particular part of the country. Sometimes the writer also makes up entirely new words.

How To Read American Folklore

When you read American tall tales, keep this in mind:

1. Let the narrator come to life in your mind. Imagine that the funniest, friendliest person you know is telling the story.
2. Imagine the setting. You can make more sense of the story if you create clear pictures of where it takes place.
3. As you read each hyperbole, picture the silly description.
4. When you come to a new word, try to guess its meaning. What is the narrator trying to tell you? If the meaning does not become clearer as you read further, use a dictionary.

Comprehension Skills: Cause and Effect

Understanding Cause and Effect

A good story makes sense. Its events are connected with each other in some way. We say the events are related to each other.

One way that events can be related is by time order. One event happens first. Another event happens second, and so on. For example, in the fable "Two Ways To Count to Ten," first the elephant threw the spear. Next the bush ox, the chimpanzee, and the other animals had a turn. The last animal to appear was the antelope.

Another way that events are related is by **cause and effect**. That is, the first event is the **cause** of the second, and the second event is the **effect** of the first.

For example, in "The Milkmaid and Her Pail," the milkmaid starts to daydream. This causes her to toss her head. Tossing her head is the effect of her daydreaming.

When the milkmaid tosses her head, she spills the milk she was carrying on her head. Now, tossing her head is the cause, and the spill is the effect.

As you read, notice how events are connected. You know that words like *first* and *last* warn about time order. There are also clue words that warn about cause-and-effect. Here are some:

because	so—that	if—then
since	in order that	

Read this example from the story of Pecos Bill. Which event is the cause? Which event is the effect? Can you identify the clue word that shows the connection?

> By the time Bill was ten years old, he could out-run and out-howl any coyote in the Southwest. Since he had not seen any other human being in all that time, he thought he was a coyote.

The cause was the fact that Bill hadn't seen any other humans. The effect was that he thought he was an animal. The clue word was "since."

Watching for clue words will often help you put the parts of a story together correctly. However, writers do not always warn readers of cause-and-effect relationships. Here is an example of cause and effect that does not use clue words:

A new family settled about fifty miles from the place where Bill's folks had built their homestead.

"The country's getting too crowded," said Bill's father. "We've got to move farther west."

Exercise: Understanding Cause and Effect

Answer the question that follows each sentence. Be able to identify the clue word that signals cause and effect.

1. The mustang was so thankful for being pulled from the trap that he swung his head around and gave Pecos Bill a smacking kiss.

   Why did the mustang give Pecos Bill a kiss?
   a. He swung his head around.
   b. He was thankful for being pulled from the trap.
   c. He was an old friend.

2. Davy braced himself against a log, so his own grin wouldn't knock him over backward, and went to work.

   Why did Davy brace himself against a log?
   a. He didn't want to be knocked over backward.
   b. He felt dizzy.
   c. He wanted to hold the log up.

3. These lumberjacks liked working for Paul Bunyan because he was always good to them, and he made sure that they had plenty of food.

   Why did the lumberjacks like working for Paul Bunyan?
   a. They were good to him.
   b. They didn't want to fight with anyone as big as he was.
   c. He made sure they ate well.

Vocabulary Skills: The Dictionary

Using Reference Sources

Often in your reading, you will find words you have never seen before. You may not be sure what they mean or how to say them. To find out more about these words, you can look them up in a dictionary. A **dictionary** is an alphabetical listing of words and their meanings. It gives other useful information, too. It can help you often in reading, and in speaking and writing as well.

Many books, such as this one, include a short dictionary at the back. This short dictionary lists only the difficult words in the book. It is called a **glossary**.

Using a Dictionary

Entry word. Each word listed in a dictionary is called an **entry word**. All the entry words are listed in alphabetical order.

Spelling. The correct spelling of each entry word is shown in boldface, or heavy type. The word is broken into syllables.

Pronunciation. The correct way to pronounce the entry word is shown in the **respelling**, usually inside parentheses. In the respelling, the word is again broken into syllables. Each sound in the word is shown by a letter or other symbol. The dictionary includes a **pronunciation key** to help you pronounce each symbol.

The respelling also includes accent marks ('). **Accent marks** tell you which syllables to stress when you say the word. Notice that for *coyote*, two pronuncia-

coy·o·te (kī ōt′ē *or* kī′ōt) *n.* **1.** a small wolf of North America. **2.** *Amer. Ind. Legend*, the culture hero and trickster of the American Indians of the West.
coy·o·til·lo (koi′ə tēl′yō) *n.* a thorny shrub of the buckthorn family found in Mexico and SW U.S.A.; its poisonous berries produce paralysis.

cow·pox (kou'päks) *n.* a disease of cows. People were once vaccinated with a mild virus of cow-pox to keep them from getting smallpox.

cow·punch·er (kou'pun'chər) *n. same as cow-boy: used only in everyday talk.*

cow·slip (kou'slip) *n.* a wildflower with yellow blossoms.

coy (koi) *adj.* shy or bashful, or pretending to be so, often in a flirting way. —coy'ly *adv.*

coy·o·te (kī ōt'ē *or* kī'ōt), *n.* **1.** a small wolf of North America. **2.** *Amer. Ind. Legend,* the culture hero and trickster of the American Indians of the West.

tions are correct. For each pronunciation, the accent mark is placed on a different syllable.

Part of Speech. The entry next lists the **part of speech** of the word. The following abbreviations are usually used.

n.	noun	*conj.*	conjunction
v.	verb	*prep.*	preposition
adj.	adjective	*pro.*	pronoun
adv.	adverb	*interj.*	interjection

Definition. The **definition**, or meaning, of the word follows the part of speech. Sometimes the word has more than one meaning. You should read all the possible meanings to find the exact one that you are looking for. Test each meaning in the sentence where you found the new word.

Exercises: Using Reference Sources

A. At the top of each page, dictionaries show the first and last entry words given on that page. Below are the first and last words on four dictionary pages. On which page would you find each of the following words?

1. thatch   2. disgust   3. griddle   4. straddle

Page 208 dip, distant   Page 734 storage, straight
Page 321 grease, grip   Page 770 that, there

B. Find the following words in a dictionary. On your paper, write the entry word, its respelling, and its definition.

1. sequoia   3. basin   5. ignoramus   7. disposition
2. nuisance   4. cactus   6. mutineer   8. mustang

C. Use the glossary of this book. Write the respelling, the part of speech, and the definition of each of the following words.

1. acquaint   2. drought   3. greedy   4. prairie   5. sagebrush

Paul Bunyan and Babe, the Blue Ox

TRADITIONAL AMERICAN
FOLK TALE
Retold by Adrien Stoutenburg

In a tall tale, a hero can solve normal problems in unusual ways. As you read about Paul Bunyan, watch for the problems he tackles. Can you suggest any other solutions that he could have tried?

Some people say Paul Bunyan wasn't much taller than an ordinary house. Others say he must have been a lot taller to do all the things he did, like sticking trees into his pockets and blowing birds out of the air when he sneezed. Even when he was a baby, up in Maine, he was so big he knocked down a mile of trees just by rolling over in his sleep.

Everyone was nervous about what might happen when Baby Paul grew older and started crawling. Maine wouldn't have any forests left.

Paul's father, and his mother, too, couldn't help feeling a bit proud of how strong Paul was. They knew, though, that the smartest thing to do was to move away. No one seems to know exactly where they went. Wherever it was, Paul didn't cause too much trouble for the rest of the time he was growing up. His father taught him certain things that helped.

"Don't lean too hard against smallish trees or buildings, Son," his father told him. "And if there are towns or farmers' fields in your way, step around them."

And Paul's mother told him, "Never pick on anybody who isn't your own size, Son."

Since there wasn't anyone his size around, Paul never got into fights. Being taller than other boys, by about fifty feet or so, he was naturally the best hunter, fisherman, walker, runner, yeller, or mountain climber there was. And he was best of all at cutting down trees and turning them into lumber. In those days, when America was new, people had to cut down a lot of trees. They needed the lumber for houses, churches, town halls, ships, bridges, ballrooms, stores, pencils, wagons, and flag poles. Luckily, the trees were there, stretching in tall, wind-shining rows across America. The trees marched up mountains and down again. They followed river and creeks. They massed up together in purple canyons and shoved each other out of the way on the shores of lakes. They pushed their dark roots down into rock and their glossy branches into the clouds.

Paul liked to flash a sky-bright axe over his head. He loved the smell of wood when it was cut and the look of its sap gleaming like honey. He didn't chop trees down in any ordinary way. With four strokes he would lop all the limbs and bark off a tree, making it a tall, square post. After he had squared up miles of forest in a half-hour, he would take an axe head and tie a long rope to it. Then he would stand straddle-legged and swing the axe in a wide circle, yelling, "T-I-M-B-E-R-R-R! Look out!" With every swing and every yell, a hundred trees would come whooshing down.

The fallen trees had to be hauled down to a river so that they could be floated to a sawmill. Paul grew a bit tired of lugging bundles of trees under his arms, and he wished he had a strong friend to help him. Also, at times he felt lonely, not having anyone his size around.

Babe, the Blue Ox

About the time he was feeling loneliest, there came the Winter of the Blue Snow. Paul, who was full-grown by then, had never seen anything like the blue flakes falling from the sky. Nobody else had

either, and perhaps no one ever will, unless it happens again. The blue snow fell softly at first, like bits of sky drifting down. The wind rose and the flakes grew thicker. The blue snow kept falling, day after day. It covered branches and roof tops, hill and valley, with blue, and Paul thought it was about as beautiful a sight as anyone could want.

One day when Paul was out walking in the blue snow, he stumbled over something the size of a mountain. The mountain made a faint mooing sound and shuddered.

"Excuse me," said Paul and looked closer.

Two huge, hairy ears stuck up above the snowdrift. The ears were as blue as the snow.

"Who are you?" Paul asked. There was no answer. Paul grabbed both of the ears and pulled.

Out of the snow came a shivering, clumsy, completely blue baby ox. Even its round, blinking eyes and its tail were blue. Only its shiny nose was black. The calf was the largest Paul had ever seen. Strong as he was, he felt his muscles shake under the creature's weight.

"Ah! Beautiful blue baby!" Paul said. He cradled the half-frozen calf in his great arms and carried it home. There he wrapped the baby ox in warm blankets and sat up all night taking care of it. The calf did not show much sign of life until morning. Then, as the dawn light came through the window, the ox calf stood up. The calf stretched its neck out and sloshed its wet tongue lovingly against Paul's neck.

Paul gave a roar of laughter, for his one ticklish spot was his neck.

Paul patted the baby ox and scratched his silky, blue ears. "We will be wonderful friends, eh Babe? You will be a giant of an ox and carry forests for me on your back."

That is how it happened that Babe the Blue Ox went with Paul Bunyan when Paul started out into the world to do his mighty logging work. By that time, Babe had his full growth. People never could figure out how long Babe was. They had to use field glasses even to see from one end of Babe to the other. And there were no scales large enough to weigh Babe. Paul did measure the distance between Babe's eyes, and that was exactly forty-two axe handle lengths and one plug of tobacco. Every time Babe needed new iron shoes for his hoofs, a fresh iron mine had to be opened. The shoes were so heavy that a man couldn't carry one without sinking up to his knees in solid rock.

Pancakes

Paul and the Blue Ox logged all over the northern timber country, from Maine to Michigan, Wisconsin, and Minnesota. Paul hired many men to help him. These lumberjacks liked working for Paul Bunyan, because he was always good to them and made sure that they had plenty of food.

The lumber crews liked pancakes best, but they would gobble up and slurp down the pancakes so fast that the camp cooks couldn't keep up with them, even when the cooks got up twenty-six hours before daylight. The main problem was that the griddles the cooks used for frying the pancakes were too small.

The winter that Paul was logging on the Big Onion River in Michigan, he decided that he had to do something about making a big enough griddle. He went down to the plow works at Moline, Illinois, and said, "I want you fellows here to make me a griddle so big I won't be able to see across it on a foggy day."

The men set to work. When they were finished, they had built a griddle so huge there was no train or wagon large enough to carry it.

"Let me think what to do," said Paul. "We'll have to turn the griddle up on end, like a silver dollar, and roll it up to Michigan." He hitched the Blue Ox to the upturned griddle, and away they went. It wasn't any job at all for Babe and Paul, though they had to hike a couple of hundred miles. A few miles from the Big Onion lumber camp, Paul unhitched Babe and let the griddle roll on by itself. When it stopped rolling, it started to spin as a penny does when it's ready to fall. It spun around and around and dug a deep hole in the ground before it flopped down like a cover over the hole.

The lumberjacks cheered and rushed off to haul a few acres of trees into the hole for a fire. The cook and a hundred and one helpers mixed tons of batter. When everything was ready, with the flames under the griddle blazing like a forest fire, Paul picked out a crew of men who could stand the heat better than others. He had them strap fat, juicy slabs of bacon on their feet.

"You men skate around on that griddle and that'll keep it well greased," he said.

The men skated until the griddle shone with bacon fat. White batter came pouring out onto the griddle and soon the smell of crisp, brown, steaming pancakes was drifting across the whole state. There were tons of pancakes—with plenty left over for Babe, who could eat a carload in one gulp.

Road Building

There wasn't much Paul couldn't do, especially with Babe's help. But there was one job that seemed almost too hard even for him. That was in Wisconsin, on the St. Croix River. The logging road there was so crooked, it couldn't find its own way through the timber. It would start out in one direction, then turn around and go every which way until it grew so snarled up it didn't know its beginning from its end. The teamsters hauling logs over it would start home for camp and meet themselves coming back.

Maybe even Babe couldn't pull the kinks and curves out of a road as crooked as that one, Paul thought, but there was nothing to do but try.

He gave Babe several extra pats as he put the Blue Ox's pulling harness on. Then he hitched Babe to the end of the road and stood back.

Babe lowered his head and pushed his hoofs into the earth. His muscles stood out like rows of blue hills. He strained forward, pulling at the road. He stretched so hard that his hind legs spraddled out until his belly nearly scraped the ground. The road just lay there, stubborn as could be.

"You can do it, my big beautiful Babe!" Paul said.

Babe tried again. He strained so hard that his eyes nearly turned pink. He sweated so that water poured from the tips of his horns. He grunted and pulled, and his legs sank into the ground like mighty blue posts.

There was a snap, and then a loud C-R-A-C-K! Paul saw the first kink come out of the road, and he cheered. The road kept fighting back, flopping around and trying to hold on to its crooked twists and turns, but it was no match for Babe. At last, the road gave a kind of shiver and then lay still. Babe pulled it straighter than a railroad tie.

Paul Bunyan's chest swelled up so with pride that it broke one of his suspenders. The broken suspender whizzed up into the sky like a long rubber band. Just then, thousands of wild ducks were flying overhead. The suspender wrapped itself around the ducks and strangled the whole flock. Paul felt sorry for the ducks, but there was nothing to do but gather them up and hand them over to the cooks.

That night after a wonderful duck dinner, Paul's bookkeeper, John Inkslinger, started writing down all that had happened. He was busily scratching away with his pen when he saw that he had only two barrels of ink left. He asked Paul what to do.

"That's easy," said Paul. "Don't bother to dot your *i*'s or cross your *t*'s. You'll save enough ink that way to get by until we can haul in another load of ink in the spring. Then you can fix up the *i*'s and the *t*'s."

Winters could be very cold there in Wisconsin and Minnesota. One year, Lake Superior froze solid from top to bottom. In the spring, Paul had to haul all the ice out of the lake and stack it up on shore to thaw.

That same winter, men's words froze in front of their mouths and hung stiff in the air. Brimstone Bill, who was a great talker, was frozen in by a solid wall of words all turned to ice. Paul had to chip the ice from around Bill's shoulders, tie a rope to him, and have Babe pull him out.

Paul Moves West

The greatest logging job Paul ever did was in North Dakota, where some of the trees were so tall it took a man a whole day to see up to their tops. Shortly after Paul had finished logging off most of the white pine, spruce, and hemlock in Minnesota, he began looking around for an even bigger job. Most of the land nearby had been logged over, and there weren't many large forests left. Paul decided to go west to the Pacific Ocean. There were trees there so huge, called the Big Trees, that it took a day to walk around them. There were redwood trees and Douglas fir trees so tall they were bent over from pressing against the sky.

Paul told his friends goodbye and he and Babe started out for the West Coast. On the way, Paul happened to let his peavey, a pole with a sharp spike on the end, drag along behind him. This made a rut that is now called the Grand Canyon. Farther on, heading through Oregon and Washington, Babe trampled some hills in the way, and that made the passes in the Cascade Mountains.

When Paul Bunyan started lumbering in the West, the fir and redwoods began to fall like grass. He built one big camp after another and invented all sorts of ways to make the lumbering business go faster. When the biggest part of the job was done, he grew restless again. He would go and sit on a hill with the Blue Ox and think about the old days. Even though there was gray in his beard now—and gray mixed in with the blue hairs on Babe's coat—Paul felt almost as young as ever.

"We've had a good life, eh, Blue Babe?"

Babe's soft blue eyes would shine, and he would push his damp muzzle against Paul Bunyan's cheek.

"Yes, sir, Babe, old friend," said Paul on one of those starlit nights with the wind crooning in the sugar pines, "it's too good a life to leave. So I guess we'll just keep on going as long as there's a toothpick of a tree left anywhere."

Apparently, that is what Paul Bunyan and his blue ox did. They just kept on going. The last time anyone saw them they were up in Alaska. People there say, when the wind is right, they can still hear Paul whirling his sky-bright axe and sending the shout of "T-I-M-B-E-R-R-R!" booming across the air.

Developing Comprehension Skills

1. Paul Bunyan's size is not the only thing he is known for. Here is a list of personality traits. Which ones describe Paul?

selfish	lazy	kind
polite	proud	careless
energetic	generous	

2. Select two of Paul's personality traits that you chose above. Find examples in the story that prove to you that your choices are right.

3. When Babe the Blue Ox was a calf, Paul saved him from freezing. How did Babe feel about Paul when he recovered? How do you know this?

4. Each of the following sentences tells why something happened or didn't happen. Identify the cause and the effect. Then tell the clue words that helped you find this relationship.

   a. Since there wasn't anyone his size around, Paul never got into fights.
   b. Babe strained so hard that his eyes nearly turned pink.

5. Look at this list of jobs. If Paul Bunyan could choose one, which do you think it would be? Tell how Paul and Babe would do the job.

   Rebuild an old part of the city.
   Create a shopping mall on the Mississippi River.
   Make an ice skating rink in the desert.

Reading Literature: Folklore

1. **Recognizing Setting.** What is the setting of this tall tale? How are Paul Bunyan's remarkable deeds related to the setting?

2. **Enjoying Hyperbole.** As you know, hyperbole is wild exaggeration that puts an instant picture in your mind. Find at least three examples of hyperbole in this story. Tell why you think the examples are funny.

3. **Understanding Personification.** In the fables chapter, there were many examples of personification in which animals had human qualities. Personification can also give human characteristics to plants. In the following description, what things are being personified? What attitude do they have that some people have?

The trees marched up mountains and down again. They followed rivers and creeks. They massed up together in purple canyons and shoved each other out of the way on the shores of lakes.

Developing Vocabulary Skills

Arranging Words in Alphabetical Order. Find the following words or groups of words in the story. Write them in alphabetical order.

1. The things that people made out of the trees that Paul cut down. They are listed on page 58, column 2, paragraph 3.

2. The states where Paul and the blue ox did their logging work. They are reported on page 60, column 2, paragraph 3.

3. All the words beginning with *s* on page 62, paragraph 1.

Developing Writing Skills

1. **Finding Facts.** Even though a story may include a great deal of nonsense, it must still make some sense for us to understand it. Even made-up characters must be enough like real people for us to believe in them, if only for a while. In "Paul Bunyan," for example, all the details about Paul's breakfast make it seem almost real. Paul's loneliness because of being different is a feeling we all have shared.

   Write about details in "Paul Bunyan" that make the story, or at least parts of it, seem real.

2. **Writing Hyperbole.** Write a hyperbole of at least three sentences about some problem in your life. If you like, you may use one of the sentence starters below. Make sure your exaggeration is funny.

   The noise in the cafeteria is so loud that _____.
   We don't say the bus is crowded until _____.
   Some tests are hard, but the worst ever was _____.

3. **Writing a Tall Tale.** Make up a tall tale about a modern hero or heroine of tremendous size and strength. Tell how your character solves a problem by using his or her special abilities. Your story may use names of real places. Use hyperbole in your story.

When Paul Bunyan Was Ill

WILLIE READER

What would you do for a superhero who got sick, just like an ordinary person? See how this writer answers the question. Can you come up with a better suggestion?

When Paul Bunyan was ill
we sent
twelve long-stemmed sequoias.

Developing Comprehension Skills

1. Sequoias are the tallest and widest trees that grow in North America. Why would it be fitting to send twelve sequoias to Paul Bunyan?

2. To what is this poem comparing the sequoias? (What do we usually send to people who are sick?)

3. Make up three more endings to the poem. Leave the first two lines as they are. Just change the last line.

Reading Literature: Folklore

1. **Appreciating Folklore.** To enjoy this poem, a reader must first know who Paul Bunyan is. Explain why this statement is true.

2. **Appreciating Hyperbole.** How does hyperbole make this poem funny?

The Ballad of John Henry

SOUTHERN FOLK BALLAD

When the American railroads began, workers hacked tunnels through mountains with pick-axes and hammers. Then the steam drill was invented. As you read, see why John Henry became a folk hero.

When John Henry was about three days old,
A-sittin' on his pappy's knee,
He gave one loud and lonesome cry:
"The hammer'll be the death of me,
The hammer'll be the death of me."

Well, the captain said to John Henry one day:
"Gonna bring that steam drill 'round,
Gonna take that steam drill out on the job,
Gonna whop that steel on down,
Gonna whop that steel on down."

John Henry said to the captain:
"Well, the next time you go to town
Just bring me back a twelve-pound hammer
And I'll beat your steam drill down,
And I'll beat your steam drill down."

John Henry said to the captain:
"Well, a man ain't nothin' but a man,
And before I let a steam drill beat me down
Gonna die with the hammer in my hand,
Gonna die with the hammer in my hand."

John Henry went to the tunnel,
And they put him in the lead to drive,
The rock so tall and John Henry so small,
He laid down his hammer and he cried
He laid down his hammer and he cried.

John Henry said to his shaker:
"Shaker, why don't you sing?
For I'm swingin' twelve pounds from the hips
      on down,
Just listen to that cold steel ring,
Just listen to that cold steel ring."

10 Lb. Hammer, 1965, THOMAS HART BENTON.
Private collection.

John Henry told his captain:
"Look-a yonder what I see—
Your drill's done broke and your hole's
    done choke',
And you can't drive steel like me,
And you can't drive steel like me."

Well, the man that invented the steam drill,
He thought he was mighty fine,
But John Henry drove his fifteen feet,
And the steam drill only made nine,
And the steam drill only made nine.

John Henry looked up at the mountain,
And his hammer was striking fire,
Well, he hammered so hard that he broke
    his poor old heart,
He laid down his hammer and he died,
He laid down his hammer and he died.

They took John Henry to the graveyard,
And they laid him in the sand,
Three men from the east and a woman
    from the west
Came to see that old steel-drivin' man,
Came to see that old steel-drivin' man.

They took John Henry to the graveyard,
And they laid him in the sand,
And every locomotive comes a-roarin' by
Says: "There lies a steel-drivin' man,"
Says: "There lies a steel-drivin' man."

Developing Comprehension Skills

1. What did John Henry cry when he was a baby? How did it come true?

2. Was John Henry a giant like Paul Bunyan? How do you know?

3. Can you find any ways in which John Henry and Paul Bunyan were alike?

4. Why do people still like the story of John Henry? He was not the only worker whose job was threatened by a machine. What makes his reaction to this problem special?

Reading Literature: Folklore

1. **Studying Form.** "The Ballad of John Henry" is a folk tale in poem form. It has been set to melodies so that it can be sung. Look at the way the words are arranged on the page. You can immediately see differences in form between this poem and the story about Paul Bunyan. Tell what some of those differences are. What might be some of the reasons for a song having a form different from that of a spoken story?

2. **Identifying Setting.** The ballad does not give much description of the setting. Name the four places where the story takes place.

3. **Recognizing Mood. Mood** is the feeling a story gives the reader. What do these two lines tell you about the mood of this ballad?

   He gave one loud and lonesome cry:
   "The hammer'll be the death of me."

Developing Vocabulary Skills

Finding Out Where To Divide a Word into Syllables. Probably you already know the meaning of most of the words you read. You do not need to look them up in a dictionary to understand them. However, a dictionary can help you to use them in writing. As you write a long word on your paper, you may not be able to fit it all on one line. You will need to break it into two parts. Each entry word in the dictionary shows where the word is broken into syllables. When you are not sure where to break a word, refer to the dictionary. Remember not to separate a single letter from the rest of a word, even if it is a separate syllable.

Each of the following words appears in "The Ballad of John Henry." Show all of the correct ways to divide each word at the end of a line.

Example: hammer, ham-mer

1. lonesome
2. captain
3. tunnel
4. shaker
5. nothing
6. graveyard
7. mighty
8. locomotive

Developing Writing Skills

1. **Taking a Stand.** Was John Henry right to challenge the steam drill? If he had known it was dangerous, should he have avoided the race? Should the captain or John Henry's friends have stopped the race when he looked tired? John Henry felt it was more important to prove himself than it was to stay alive. Do you agree with him? State your opinion and explain why you feel that way.

2. **Changing a Song to a Story.** Rewrite this song as a story. (Review your answer to Reading Literature: Folklore, 1, for differences.) You should include more description of the setting and characters, and you may change the mood if you like.

Developing Skills in Study and Research

1. **Using Audio-Visual Resources.** Many libraries have record collections of folklore, including songs, rhymes, and tales told by experienced storytellers. Investigate your public or school library to see what is available. If possible, find a record that has "John Henry" on it, in story or ballad form. Report on how you found it.

2. **Relating Reading with Music Resources.** See if you can find sheet music for "The Ballad of John Henry." Look in the library or your school's music department. If you cannot find "John Henry," report on what is available. If you can find it, learn to sing it or to play the melody on the piano, guitar, or other instrument. If you find several versions, choose one to work with.

Pecos Bill: America's Greatest Cowboy

TRADITIONAL AMERICAN FOLK TALE
Retold by Adrien Stoutenburg

In the old West, white, black, and Mexican-American cowboys worked hard and faced many dangers. Still, they liked to tell stories, sing songs, and make up jokes—especially about themselves.

There aren't as many coyotes in Texas now as there were when Pecos Bill was born. But the ones that there are still do plenty of howling at night, sitting out under the sagebrush like thin, gray shadows, and pointing their noses at the moon.

Some of the cowboys around the Pecos River country claim that the oldest coyotes remember the time when Bill lived with them and are howling because they are lonesome for him. It's not often that coyotes have a boy grow up with them like one of their own family.

Bill was pretty unusual from the start. When he was only a few days old, he raised such a fuss about having to drink ordinary milk that his mother had to go and take milk from a mountain lion who was raising baby cubs. Bill's mother was rather unusual in her own way. Borrowing milk from a wild mountain lion was no problem for her.

Bill had over a dozen older brothers and sisters for playmates, but they were ordinary boys and girls and no match for him. When Bill was two weeks old, his father found a half-grown bear and brought the bear home.

"You treat this bear nice, now," Bill's father said.

The bear didn't feel friendly and threatened to take a bite out of Bill. Bill wrestled the bear and tossed it around until the bear put its paws over its head and begged for mercy. Bill couldn't talk yet, but he patted the bear to show that he didn't have any hard feelings. After that, the bear followed Bill around like a big, flat-footed puppy.

Pecos Bill's father was one of the first settlers in the West. There was lots of room in Texas, with so much sky that it seemed as if there couldn't be any sky left over for the rest of the United States. There weren't many people, and it was lonesome country, especially on nights when the wind came galloping over the land, rattling the bear grass and the yucca plants and carrying the tangy smell of greasewood. However, Bill didn't feel lonely often, with all the raccoons, badgers, and jack rabbits he had for friends. Once he made the mistake of trying to pet a skunk. The skunk sprayed Bill with its strong scent. Bill's mother had to hang Bill on the clothesline for a week to let the smell blow off him.

Bill was a little over one year old when another family of pioneers moved into the country. The new family settled about fifty miles from where Bill's folks had built their homestead.

"The country's getting too crowded," said Bill's father. "We've got to move farther west."

So the family scrambled back into their big wagon and set out, the oxen puffing and snorting as they pulled the wagon toward the Pecos River. Bill was sitting in the rear of the wagon when it hit some rocks in a dry stream bed. There was a jolt, and Bill went flying out of the wagon. He landed so hard that the wind was knocked out of him, and he couldn't even cry out to let his folks know. It might not have made any difference if he had, because all his brothers and sisters were making such a racket and the wagon wheels were creaking so loudly that no one could have heard him. In fact, with so many other children in the family besides Bill, it was four weeks before Bill's folks even missed him. Then, of course, it was too late to find him.

Bill Joins the Coyotes

Young Bill sat there in the dry stream bed awhile, wondering what to do. Wherever he looked there was only the prairie and the sky, completely empty except for a sharp-shinned hawk floating overhead. Bill felt more lonely than he ever had in his life. Then, suddenly, he saw a pack of coyotes off in the distance, eating the remains of a dead deer. The coyotes looked at Bill, and Bill looked at them. These coyotes had never seen a human baby before, and they didn't know quite what to think. Apparently, they decided Bill was some new kind of hairless animal, for one of the female coyotes took a hunk of deer meat in her teeth and trotted over to Bill with it. She put it in front of him and stood back, waiting for him to eat it.

Bill had not eaten much raw meat before, but he knew that the female coyote meant well, and he didn't want to hurt her feelings. So he picked the meat up and began chewing on it. It tasted so good that he walked over and joined the other coyotes.

From that time on, Bill lived with the coyotes, going wherever they went, joining in their hunts, and even learning their language. Those years he lived with the coyotes were happy ones. He ran with them through the moonlit nights, curled up with them in their shady dens, and howled with them when they sang to the stars.

By the time Bill was ten years old, he could out-run and out-howl any coyote in the Southwest. Since he had not seen any other human beings in all that time, he thought he was a coyote himself.

He might have gone on believing this forever if one day a cowboy hadn't come riding through the sagebrush. The cowboy stopped, stared, and rubbed his eyes, because he could scarcely believe what he saw. There in front of him stood a ten-year-old boy, as naked as a cow's hoof, wrestling with a giant grizzly bear. Nearby sat a dozen coyotes, their tongues hanging out. Before the cowboy could say, "Yipee yi-yo!" or plain "Yipee!" the boy had hugged the bear to death.

When Pecos Bill saw the cowboy, he snarled like a coyote and put his head down between his shoulders, ready to fight.

"What's your name?" the cowboy asked. "What are you doing out here?"

Since Bill didn't know anything but coyote talk, he naturally didn't understand a word.

The cowboy tossed Bill a plug of tobacco. Bill ate it and decided it tasted pretty good, so when the cowboy came up close, Bill didn't bite him.

The cowboy stayed there for three days, teaching Bill to talk like a human.

Then he tried to prove to Bill that Bill wasn't a coyote.

"I must be a coyote," Bill said. "I can howl the moon out of the sky. And I can run a deer to death."

"All Texans can howl," the cowboy said. "In order to be a true coyote, you have to have a bushy tail."

Bill looked around and realized for the first time that he didn't have a nice bushy, waving tail like his coyote friends. "Maybe I lost it somewhere."

"No siree," the cowboy said. "You're a human being, sure as shooting. You'd better come along with me."

Bill Becomes a Cowboy

Being human was a hard thing for Bill to face up to, but he realized that the cowboy must be right. He told his coyote friends goodbye and thanked them for all that they had taught him. Then he straddled a mountain lion he had tamed and rode with the cowboy toward the cowboy's ranch. On the way to the ranch, a big rattlesnake reared up in front of them. The cowboy galloped off, but Bill jumped from his mount and faced the snake.

"I'll let you have the first three bites, Mister Rattler, just to be fair. Then I'm going to beat the poison out of you until you behave yourself!"

That is just what Bill did. He whipped the snake around until it stretched out like a thirty-foot rope. Bill looped the rattler-rope in one hand, got back on his

lion, and caught up with the cowboy. To entertain himself, he made a loop out of the snake and tossed it over the head of an armadillo plodding along through the cactus. Next, he lassoed several Gila monsters.

"I never saw anybody do anything like that before," said the cowboy.

"That's because nobody invented the lasso before," said Pecos Bill.

Before Pecos Bill came along, cowboys didn't know much about their job. They didn't know anything about rounding up cattle, or branding them, or even about ten-gallon hats. The only way they knew to catch a steer was to hide behind a bush, lay a looped rope on the ground, and wait for the steer to step into the loop.

Pecos Bill changed all that the minute he reached the Dusty Dipper Ranch. He slid off his mountain lion and marched up to the biggest cowboy there.

"Who's the boss here?" he asked.

The man took one look at Bill's lion and at the rattlesnake rope and said, "I was."

Young though he was, Bill took over. At the Dusty Dipper and at other ranches, Bill taught the cowboys almost everything they know today. He invented spurs for them to wear on their boots. He taught them how to round up the cattle and drive the herds to railroad stations where they could be shipped to market. One of the finest things Bill did was to teach the cowboys to sing cowboy songs.

Bill made himself a guitar. On a night when the moon was as reddish yellow as a ripe peach, though fifty times as large, he led some of the fellows at the ranch out to the corral and set himself down on the top rail.

"I don't want to brag," he told the cowhands, "but I learned my singing from the coyotes, and that's about the best singing there is."

He sang a tune the coyotes had taught him, and made up his own words:

"My seat is in the saddle,
and my saddle's in the sky,
And I'll quit punchin' cows
in the sweet by and by."

He made up many more verses and sang many other songs. When Bill was through, the roughest cowboy of all,

Hardnose Hal, sat wiping tears from his eyes because of the beauty of Bill's singing. Lefty Lightning put his head down on his arms and wept. All the cowboys there vowed they would learn to sing and make up songs. And they did make up hundreds of songs about the lone prairie, and the Texas sky, and the wind blowing over the plains. That's why we have so many cowboy songs today.

Pecos Bill invented something else almost as useful as singing. This happened after a band of cattle rustlers came to the ranch and stole half a hundred cows.

"You boys," said Bill, "have to get something to protect yourselves with besides your fists. I can see I'll have to think up a six-shooter."

"What's a six-shooter?" asked Bronco-Busting Bertie. (Bill had taught horses how to buck and rear so that cowboys could learn bronco busting.)

"Why," said Bill, "that's a gun that holds six bullets."

Bill sat down in the shade of a yucca tree and figured out how to make a six-shooter. It was a useful invention, but it had its bad side. Some of the cowboys started shooting at each other. Some even went out and held up trains and stage-coaches.

One of the most exciting things Bill did was to find himself the wildest, strongest, most beautiful horse that ever kicked up the Texas dust. He was a mighty, golden mustang, and even Bill couldn't outrun that horse. To catch the mustang, Bill had the cowboys rig up a huge slingshot and shoot him high over the cactus and greasewood. When Bill landed in front of the mustang, the horse was so surprised he stopped short, thrusting out his front legs stiff as rifle barrels. The mustang had been going so fast that his hoofs drove into the ground, and he was stuck. Bill leaped on the animal's back, yanked on his golden mane, and pulled him free. The mustang was so thankful for being pulled from the trap that he swung his head around and gave Pecos Bill a smacking kiss. From then on, the horse was as gentle as a soft wind in a thatch of Jimson weed.

No one else could ride him, however. Most of the cowboys who tried ended up with broken necks. That's why Bill called his mustang Widow-Maker.

Bill and Widow-Maker traveled all over the western range, starting new ranches and helping out in the long cattle drives. In stormy weather they often holed up with a band of coyotes. Bill would strum his guitar and the coyotes would sing with him.

Bill the Rainmaker

Then came the year of the Terrible Drought. The land shriveled for lack of water, and the droves of cattle stood panting with thirst.

The cowboys and the ranch bosses from all around came to Bill, saying, "The whole country's going to dry up and blow away, Bill, unless you can figure out some way to bring us rain."

"I'm figuring," Bill told them, "but I've never tried making rain before, so I'll have to think a little."

While Bill thought, the country grew so dry it seemed that there would be nothing but bones and rocks left. Even cactus plants, which could stand a lot of dryness, began to turn brown. The pools where the cattle drank dried up and turned to cracked mud. All the snakes hid under the ground in order to keep from frying. Even the coyotes stopped howling, because their throats were too dry for them to make any sound.

Bill rode around on Widow-Maker, watching the clear, burning sky and hoping for the sight of a rain cloud. All he saw were whirls of dust, called dust devils, spinning up from the yellowing earth. Then, toward noon one day, he spied something over in Oklahoma that looked like a tall whirling tower of black bees. Widow-Maker reared up on his hind legs, his eyes rolling.

"It's just a cyclone," Pecos Bill told his horse, patting the golden neck.

But Widow-Maker was scared. The mighty horse began bucking around so hard that even Bill had a time staying in the saddle.

"Whoa there!" Bill commanded. "I could ride that cyclone as easy as I can ride you, the way you're carrying on."

That's when Bill had an idea. There might be rain mixed up in that cyclone tower. He nudged Widow-Maker with his spurs and yelled, "Giddap!"

What Bill planned to do was leap from his horse and grab the cyclone by the neck. But as he came near and saw how high the top of the whirling tower was, he knew he would have to do something better than that. Just as he and Widow-Maker came close enough to the cyclone to feel its hot breath, a knife of lightning streaked down into the ground. It stuck there, quivering, just long enough for Bill to reach out and grab it. As the lightning bolt whipped back up into the sky, Bill held on. When he was as high as the top of the cyclone, he jumped and landed astraddle its black, spinning shoulders.

By then, everyone in Texas, New Mexico, Arizona, and Oklahoma was watching. They saw Bill grab hold of that cyclone's shoulders and haul them back. They saw him wrap his legs around the cyclone's belly and squeeze so hard the cyclone started to pant. Then Bill got out his lasso and slung it around the cyclone's neck. He pulled it tighter and tighter until the cyclone started to choke, spitting out rocks and dust. All the rain that was mixed up in it started to fall.

Down below, the cattle and the coyotes, the jack rabbits and the horned toads, stuck out their tongues and caught the sweet, blue falling rain. Cowboys on the ranches and people in town ran

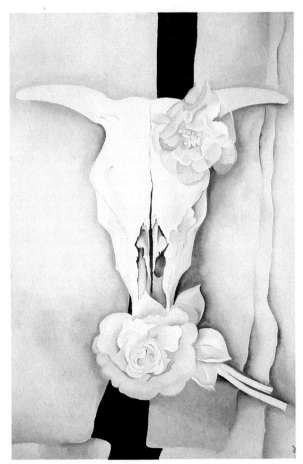

Cow's Skull with Calico Roses, 1931, GEORGIA O'KEEFFE. The Art Institute of Chicago.

around whooping and cheering, holding out pans and kettles to catch raindrops.

Bill rode the cyclone across three states. By the time the cyclone reached California, it was all out of steam and out of rain, too. It gave a big sigh, trembled weakly, and sank to earth. Bill didn't have time to jump off. He fell hard, scooping out a few thousand acres of sand and rock and leaving a big basin below sea level. That was what made Death Valley.

Bill's Family

Bill was a greater hero than ever after that. Yet at times, he felt almost as lonely as on the day when he had bounced out of his folks' wagon and found himself sitting alone under the empty sky. Widow-Maker was good company most of the time, but Bill felt there was something missing in his life.

One day, he wandered down to the Rio Grande and stood watching the brown river flow slowly past. Suddenly, he saw a catfish as big as a whale jumping around on top of the water, its whiskers shining like broomsticks. On top of the catfish was a brown-eyed, brown-haired girl.

Somebody beside Bill exclaimed, "Look at Slue-Foot Sue ride that fish!"

Pecos Bill felt his heart thump and tingle in a way it had never done before. "That's the girl I want to marry!" he said. He waded out into the Rio Grande, poked the catfish in the nose, and carried Slue-Foot Sue to a church. "You're going to be my bride," he said.

"That's fine with me," said Sue, looking Pecos Bill over and seeing that he was the biggest, boldest, smartest cowboy who had ever happened to come along beside the Rio Grande.

That was the beginning of a very happy life for Bill. He and Sue raised a large family. All of the boys grew up to be cowboys, and the girls grew up to be cowgirls. The only time Bill and Sue had any trouble was when Bill wanted to adopt a batch of baby coyotes who were orphans.

"We're human beings," Sue said, "and we can't be raising varmints."

"I was a varmint once myself," said Bill. He argued so much that Sue agreed to take the coyotes in and raise them as members of the family. Eventually, several of them were elected to public office.

Pecos Bill grew old, as everyone and everything does in time. Even so, there wasn't a bronco he couldn't bust, or a steer he couldn't rope, or a bear he couldn't hug to death faster and better than anyone else.

No one knows, for sure, how he died, or even if he did die. Some say that he mixed barbed wire in his coffee to make it strong enough for his taste, and that the wire rusted in his stomach and poisoned him. Others say that one day he met a dude cowboy, all dressed up in fancy clothes, who didn't know the front end of a cow from the side of a boxcar. The dude asked so many silly questions about cow punching that Pecos Bill lay down in the dust and laughed himself to death.

But the cowboys back in the Pecos River country say that every once in a while, when the moon is full and puffing its white cheeks out and the wind is crooning softly through the bear grass, Pecos Bill himself comes along and sits on his haunches and sings right along with the coyotes.

Developing Comprehension Skills

1. Put the following events from Pecos Bill's life in time order.

   a. grew up with coyotes
   b. got married and had many children
   c. taught the cowboys everything they knew
   d. rode a mountain lion
   e. wrestled a half-grown bear

2. For a while, Bill thought that he was a coyote. Tell one thing he did that proves this.

3. Explain the thinking of the cowboy in this part of the story.

   > Pecos Bill slid off his mountain lion and marched up to the biggest cowboy there.
   > "Who's the boss here?" he asked.
   > The man took one look at Bill's lion and at the rattlesnake rope and said, "I was."

4. Are Bill's mother and father like real parents? Do they act like real people? Give reasons for your answer.

5. Tell one important way in which Paul Bunyan and Pecos Bill are alike. Tell one important way in which they are different.

Reading Literature: Folklore

1. **Recognizing Hyperbole.** Find five sentences at the beginning of the story that convince you this is a tall tale.

2. **Understanding Comparisons.** In a **comparison**, the writer asks the reader to find something in common between two unlike things. When you look for some quality that one object has in common with another, you see the first object better. In each of the following examples, tell what is being compared to what. Then explain how the comparison made the description clearer.

   a. From then on, the horse was as gentle as a soft wind in a thatch of Jimson weed.
   b. Then, toward noon one day, he spied something over in Oklahoma that looked like a tall whirling tower of black bees. "It's just a cyclone," Pecos Bill told his horse.

c. Just as he and Widow-Maker came close enough to the cyclone to feel its hot breath, a knife of lightning streaked down into the ground.

d. Everyone saw Bill grab hold of that cyclone's shoulders and haul them back. They saw him wrap his legs around the cyclone's belly and squeeze so hard the cyclone started to pant.

3. **Using Dialog.** Conversation between characters in a story is called **dialog.** In a written story, the exact words in a dialog are set off by quotation marks (" "). "Pecos Bill" uses dialog to tell the reader what is happening. Find an example.

4. **Identifying Point of View.** An author decides which character will tell the story. This narrator can be one of the following:

   a. a character in the story, using "I" and "me"
   b. a person outside the story who tells only what one character can see and hear
   c. a person outside the story who knows and tells all.

From which point of view was this story written?

Developing Vocabulary Skills

Using a Pronunciation Key. When you read a word, you do not need to pronounce it. However, you may want to talk about what you read. Then you may need to know the correct pronunciation of a new word. The **respelling** after each entry word in the dictionary can help you.

Look up the following words in a dictionary. On your paper, copy each word and its respelling. In the respelling, you will find a heavy mark like this: ′. It is called the **accent.** It shows which syllable gets the most stress when you say the word. If the word has more than two syllables, it may have two accents. The heavy one is then called the **primary accent.** The second, lighter one is called the **secondary accent.** A syllable marked with a secondary accent gets less stress than one with the primary accent.

In each word below, which syllable is marked with a dark accent mark? Find the vowel symbol of that accented syllable in the pronunciation key. Then, on your paper, write the sample word for that vowel symbol next to the respelling.

Example: woman (wŏŏm′ ən), took

1. yucca   2. shrivel   3. ordinary   4. cyclone   5. armadillo

Using the Schwa. The vowel sound in an unaccented syllable often has a sound called the **schwa** sound. It is shown in the pronunciation key as an upside-down *e*. The schwa is the sound of the *e* in *pocket* and the *o* in *bacon*. The schwa sound always comes in an unaccented syllable.

Copy each of the words above, and its respelling, a second time. Underline each of the syllables in which the vowel sound is a schwa.

Example: wo<u>man</u> (wo͞om′ ən)

Pronouncing a New Word. Now look up the vowel symbol for any unaccented syllable that does not have the schwa sound. Combine what you have learned about the vowel sounds in each word. Pronounce the complete word.

Developing Writing Skills

1. **Creating Characters.** In "Pecos Bill," we do not learn much about what Bill or any other character looks like or sounds like. However, we find out what Bill acts like. Choose one of the other characters: Hardnose Hal, Lefty Lightning, Bronco-Busting Bertie, or Slue-Foot Sue. Write a short tall tale about this character solving a problem. Show what this character acts like.

2. **Writing a Poem.** Review the poem "When Paul Bunyan Was Ill," on page 67. Then write a similar poem, beginning "When Pecos Bill was ill." Make sure your present or presents are especially fitting for Pecos Bill and no one else.

Developing Skills in Speaking and Listening

Telling a Tale. The story of "Pecos Bill" is divided into five parts. Choose one part and prepare to tell it to a group. Read the part several times, till you are familiar with it. Make a list or time line of the important events, and think about how they are related.

When you tell the story, tell what happens in your own words. However, try to use some of the hyperbole in the book. Remember that the narrator is pretending that the story is true. It would spoil the story to laugh or to show in any other way that you don't believe what you are saying.

Davy Crockett

MICHAEL GORHAM

Unlike the other heroes in this chapter, Davy Crockett was a real person. However, were the stories he told about himself concerned with real events?

The best way to get acquainted with Davy Crockett is to listen to what he said about himself.

"I'm a screamer," Davy said. By that he meant that he could out-shout and out-talk anybody on the whole Kentucky frontier, and there were plenty of screamers there—take my word for it.

"My father can lick anyone in Kentucky," Davy said, "and I can lick my father. I can run faster, dive deeper, stay under longer, and come out drier than anyone this side of the Mississippi. I can carry a steamboat on my back and wrassle a lion. I can walk like an ox, run like a fox, swim like an eel, yell like an Indian and fight like a devil."

Now Davy was being modest when he said all this. He could do everything in the list and a lot more, too, as you shall see.

In the days when Davy lived on the frontier in Kentucky and Tennessee, along about 1825, a man had to be a hunter if he wanted to eat. Davy was such a good shot that he never missed, and so he always had plenty of bear and deer and raccoon. But round lead bullets and powder for his muzzle-loading rifle were scarce. So Davy invented a way of getting raccoons without shooting them.

One day Davy had a raccoon up a tree. It looked so solemn that Davy couldn't help laughing. He just stood there on the ground and grinned. And the first thing he knew, he'd grinned that raccoon right out of the tree. He had done it without firing a shot.

Well, after that Davy never lacked for meat. On a moonlit night he just went out and grinned raccoons. He even got so good that he could grin a panther out of a tree.

Then one day Davy met another hunter in the woods. This fellow was taking aim at something in a black gum tree.

"Wait a minute," Davy said. "Don't waste your powder. I'll grin that raccoon down for you."

Davy braced himself against a log, so his own grin wouldn't knock him over backward, and went to work. But nothing happened.

Now the other hunter was tickled pink. The great Davy Crockett couldn't do what he'd bragged about.

After a while Davy said, "I never saw such a spunktiliferous animal in all my days." Then he climbed the tree to look into the matter. When he got up there, he found he'd been grinning at a knot that *looked* like a raccoon. But he didn't feel too bad about it. He'd grinned every bit of bark off that tree.

About the time Davy was really famous in the woods, he had a strange experience. That was the day his dog Rattler treed a raccoon, and Davy got himself all set and braced and ready. But before he could let fly with his grin, the raccoon lifted a paw to catch Davy's attention and said politely, "Is your name Crockett?"

"You are right for once," Davy answered. "My name is Davy Crockett."

"In that case, don't trouble yourself," the raccoon said. "I know I might just as well come down without any argument." And down he came.

Davy watched the critter, who had considered himself dead, and he felt kind of flattered.

"I've never had such a compliment in my life," he said, patting the raccoon on the head. "I hope I may be shot before I hurt a hair of your hide."

"Thank you," said the raccoon. "Seeing as you feel that way, I'll just take a little walk. Not that I doubt your word—but in case you change your mind."

One of the things Davy liked best in the world was a good thunderstorm. He said, "A regular, round-roaring, savage peal of thunder is the greatest treat in all creation. It sets everything but a coward shouting in his very heart and soul, till he swells so eternally big with natural glorification that he feels as if he could swallow the entire creation at one gulp."

Well, one day Davy was out in a storm, feeling full of thunder glory, and he just stood stock-still with his mouth open. Right then a teetotal thunderbolt came along, and he swallowed it. That streak of lightning was so powerful it blew off his hip pockets, and it heated up his insides something remarkable. For a month after that, Davy ate raw food, and the leftover lightning cooked·it as it went down.

Now Davy was a mighty fine shot, but one particular day he hadn't seen anything to shoot at. Instead of going home empty-handed, he decided to sleep out on a hillside and try for better luck tomorrow. He leaned his rifle up against a tree and hung his powder horn on a branch.

Next morning he shouldered his gun, but there was no powder horn in sight. Davy looked around everywhere for it. He looked all day. He was still looking when night came and the new moon started skimming toward him through the sky above the hill. There, on one sharp point of the moon, hung Davy's powder horn. The new moon had come by the night before while Davy was asleep and just accidentally hooked the powder horn off the tree above him. Naturally, Davy grabbed the horn, and after that he shot three bears, two catamounts, and a rabbit. But from that day to this he never hung his powder horn on a tree again.

Developing Comprehension Skills

1. Identify the cause and the effect described in these sentences.

    One day Davy had a raccoon up a tree. It looked so solemn that Davy couldn't help laughing.

2. Which of these personality traits describe Davy Crockett? Find proof for your answer in the story.

    shy   brave   boastful   lazy
    cheerful   unfriendly   crabby   lonely

3. What do you think Davy Crockett meant when he made each of the following statements?
   a. "I'm a screamer."
   b. "My father can lick anyone in Kentucky, and I can lick my father."

4. A lie is defined as "anything that gives or is meant to give a false impression." Are Davy's stories lies? Why or why not?

5. Compare the character of Davy Crockett in this story with one of these heroes: Pecos Bill, John Henry, Paul Bunyan. How are the characters similar? How are they different? Give examples showing how they act, think, and feel about themselves or others.

Reading Literature: Folklore

1. **Examining Setting.** The stories of Paul Bunyan and Davy Crockett are both set in the woods. However, the stories present the woods in noticeably different ways. Point out some of the differences. Can you think of any reasons for these differences?

2. **Examining Dialect.** People living in one part of the United States may use certain words that other Americans do not know. Sometimes they use the same words but with different meanings. The variety of language spoken in a particular area is called the **dialect** of that area. The story of Davy Crockett uses some of the dialect of the frontier. Use context clues or the dictionary to find the meaning of these words.

   critter   tickled pink
   stock-still   teetotal

3. **Recognizing Hyperbole.** Find at least three examples of hyperbole in this story.

Developing Vocabulary Skills

Using the Definition. Imagine that you have come across an unfamiliar word in your reading. You stop to look it up in the dictionary. How do you use what the dictionary tells you? A good way to understand the meaning of the new word is to replace it in the sentence with its definition.

Often the dictionary will provide a **synonym**, or word that has a similar meaning. For example, one of the definitions given for *solemn* is "serious, grave, deeply earnest." The word *serious* can replace the word *solemn* in the sentence "The raccoon looked so solemn that Davy couldn't help laughing."

Other times you will have to rearrange the words in the definition or in the sentence. Sometimes only part of the definition is necessary. For example, the meaning of *lumbering* is "the business of cutting or preparing timber for use." Try to use that definition in the sentence "Paul

Bunyan started lumbering in the West." The sentence could say "Paul Bunyan started cutting timber in the West."

Different sentences use different meanings of a word. Therefore, for each sentence you must decide which part of a definition can be used. If you are not sure, try one meaning at a time in the sentence in place of the unfamiliar word.

Read the following sentences from the story of Davy Crockett. Locate each underlined word in your dictionary or glossary. Decide which definition best fits the idea of the sentence. Then rewrite the sentence using words of the definition in place of the underlined word. Rearrange words if necessary.

1. Now Davy was being modest when he said all this.
2. He shouldered his gun, but there was no powder horn in sight.
3. Right then a teetotal thunderbolt came along, and he swallowed it.
4. He just stood stock-still with his mouth open.
5. Davy found he'd been grinning at a knot that looked like a raccoon.
6. A regular, round-roaring, savage peal of thunder is the greatest treat in all creation.
7. That was the day his dog Rattler treed a raccoon.
8. Powder for his muzzle-loading rifle was scarce.

Developing Writing Skills

1. **Reporting the Facts.** Look up Davy Crockett in an encyclopedia. Write a short report about what he really did. Include a few important dates and places, such as those of his birth and death.

2. **Writing Dialog.** Write a dialog between Davy Crockett and Pecos Bill. Have them boast to each other about their inventions. Use hyperbole in the conversation. Be careful to use punctuation, especially quotation marks and commas, correctly.

Developing Skills in Speaking and Listening

Interpreting a Character. Choose one of the parts of this story and tell what happened as if you were Davy Crockett. Use the words in the book and simply change "Davy," "he," and "him" to "I" and "me."

They Tell Yarns

CARL SANDBURG

This poem by Carl Sandburg is not a folk tale itself. Instead, it is about folk tales. Can you recognize in it any tales you have already read?

They have yarns
Of a skyscraper so tall they had to put hinges
On the two top stories so to let the moon go by,
Of one corn crop in Missouri when the roots
Went so deep and drew off so much water
The Mississippi riverbed that year was dry,
Of pancakes so thin they only had one side,
Of "a fog so thick we shingled the barn and six
    feet out on the fog,"
Of Pecos Bill straddling a cyclone in Texas and
    riding it to the west coast where "it rained out
    under him,"
Of the man who drove a swarm of bees across
    the Rocky Mountains and the Desert "and
    didn't lose a bee,"
Of a mountain railroad curve where the engineer
    in his cab can touch the caboose and spit in
    the conductor's eye,
Of the boy who climbed a cornstalk growing so
    fast he would have starved to death if they
    hadn't shot biscuits up to him,
Of the old man's whiskers: "When the wind was
    with him his whiskers arrived a day before
    he did,"

Of the hen laying a square egg and cackling
  "Ouch!" and of hens laying eggs with the
  dates printed on them,
Of the ship captain's shadow: it froze to the deck
  one cold winter night,
Of mutineers on that same ship put to chipping
  rust with rubber hammers,
Of the sheep counter who was fast and accurate:
  "I just count their feet and divide by four,"
Of the man so tall he must climb a ladder to
  shave himself,
Of the runt so teeny-weeny it takes two men and a
  boy to see him,
Of mosquitoes: one can kill a dog, two of them a man,
Of a cyclone that sucked cookstoves out of the
  kitchen, up the chimney flue, and on to the
  next town,
Of the same cyclone picking up wagon-tracks in
  Nebraska and dropping them over in the
  Dakotas,
Of the hook-and-eye snake unlocking itself into
  forty pieces, each piece two inches long, then
  in nine seconds flat snapping itself together again,
Of the watch swallowed by the cow—when they
  butchered her a year later the watch was
  running and had the correct time,
Of horned snakes, hoop snakes that roll
  themselves where they want to go, and
  rattlesnakes carrying bells instead of rattles on
  their tails,
Of the herd of cattle in California getting lost in a
  giant redwood tree that had hollowed out,
Of the man who killed a snake by putting its tail in
  its mouth so it swallowed itself,
Of railroad trains whizzing along so fast they reach
  the station before the whistle,

Of pigs so thin the farmer had to tie knots in their
    tails to keep them from crawling through the
    cracks in their pens,
Of Paul Bunyan's big blue ox, Babe, measuring
    between the eyes forty-two axe-handles and a
    plug of Star tobacco exactly,
Of John Henry's hammer and the curve of its
    swing and his singing of it as "a rainbow
    round my shoulder."

        "Do tell!"
        "I want to know!"
        "You don't say so!"
        "For the land's sake!"
        "Gosh all fish-hooks!"
        "Tell me some more.
    I don't believe a word you say
        but I love to listen
        to your sweet harmonica
        to your chin-music.
    Your fish stories hang together
        when they're just a pack of lies:
        you ought to have a leather medal:
        you ought to have a statue
        carved of butter: you deserve
        a large bouquet of turnips."

Developing Comprehension Skills

1. What does Carl Sandburg mean when he says "yarns"? In the title of this poem, who are "they"?

2. Some of the characters in "They Tell Yarns" should have sounded familiar. Find at least two references to tall tales you have read.

3. In the first part of the poem, after the line "They have yarns," all the lines start with "of." The last part, starting with "Do tell," is different. How are the two parts of the poem related?

4. Explain whether this part of the poem is logical:

   Of the sheep counter who was fast and accurate: "I just count their feet and divide by four."

   Why is the sheep counter funny?

5. This collection of yarns does not develop characters, setting, or plot. Instead, it jumps to the joke part of each of the yarns it mentions. Did you enjoy reading the yarns this way? Why or why not? Why do you think the poet wrote the poem in this style?

Reading Literature: Folklore

1. **Appreciating Hyperbole.** "Yarns" is a long series of hyperbole.
   a. Pick out three exaggerations that seem funniest to you. Tell why you chose them.
   b. Usually hyperbole brings an instant picture to your mind. Sandburg uses some exaggerations that are impossible to picture. Find two of these. Explain why they can't be pictured.

2. **Recognizing the Speaker.** There are at least two speakers, or two groups of speakers, in "They Tell Yarns." Where does the second speaker, or group of speakers, begin to talk? How can you tell?

3. **Relating Mood and Meaning.** Read the last six lines of the poem again. A "fish story" is a story someone might tell after losing a fish he or she was trying to catch. The fish in the story is a lot bigger than the fish was in real life. If you called a story a fish story, would you believe the story?

   Is it possible to award a leather medal? Can a statue be carved of butter? Would anyone appreciate a bouquet of turnips?

Is the speaker of the last six lines serious?

Now read the last eleven lines again. What do you think the speaker means by "chin-music"? What is the speaker really saying in these last eleven lines?

Developing Vocabulary Skills

Recognizing Homographs. In the dictionary you may have noticed two entry words that look the same. Sometimes, as with the word *bow*, the word is used for three separate entries.

bow[1] (bou) *v.*, bend the head or body in greeting, respect, or worship.

bow[2] (bō) *n.*, weapon for shooting arrows

bow[3] (bou) *n.*, the forward part of a ship, boat, or airplane

Other words, however, are given only one entry. Their definitions may be much longer than the combined definitions for *bow*. Why are the words treated differently?

Sometimes a word becomes popular. It is used for many reasons, and soon it has many meanings. However, all the meanings started from one word. The dictionary will list all the meanings in one entry. For examples, look up *line*, *make*, or *run* in any dictionary.

Other times, the English language takes two different words, with different meanings, and gives the words the same spelling. Sometimes the two words sound the same. Often they sound different. Still, because spelling in English does not always make sense, the words are spelled the same. Words like this are called **homographs**. They look the same, but they have nothing else in common. Each homograph is given a separate entry in the dictionary.

In each of the following sentences from tall tales you have read, find the underlined word. Look it up in the dictionary. On your paper, write whether it is a homograph or not. If it is, write how many separate entries your dictionary gives for that spelling. Then tell the number of the entry that defines the word in the sentence.

1. They have yarns of a skyscraper so tall they had to put hinges on the two top stories to let the moon go by.

2. They were ordinary boys and girls and no match for Paul.

3. All of Bill's brothers and sisters were making a racket.

4. Davy had grinned every bit of <u>bark</u> off that tree.

5. They have yarns of the <u>watch</u> swallowed by the cow.

6. John Henry drove his fifteen feet, and the steam <u>drill</u> only made nine.

7. Bill saw a <u>pack</u> of coyotes.

8. With four strokes Paul would lop all the limbs and bark off a tree, making it a tall, square <u>post</u>.

Developing Writing Skills

1. **Presenting Your Opinion.** Imagine that Carl Sandburg is arrested and charged with telling lies in this poem. Is he innocent or guilty? Explain your answer. Be sure to define what a lie is.

2. **Writing a Modern Yarn.** Carl Sandburg wrote more than fifty years ago. This poem uses examples of hyperbole based on life in America up to his time. Write a poem like "They Tell Yarns," using examples from modern life. You might choose to write hyperbole relating to things like cars, airplanes, space craft, television, or computers. Your poem should have at least four examples of hyperbole in it.

3. **Creating Dialog.** Draw a cartoon that shows two people talking, using sentence balloons. Write a short "yarn" in one balloon and a reply in the other. If you like, use one of the replies from the last part of "They Tell Yarns."

Developing Skills in Study and Research

Using the Card Catalog. Go to your school or local library and look up Carl Sandburg in the card catalog. List all the books he wrote himself. Count the books that are written about him by others. Would you suppose he is considered an important American author?

Developing Skills in Speaking and Listening

Interpreting a Poem. Prepare to read this poem aloud to a group. Decide on the best way to read the exaggerations and dialog. If you can work with a group, members should take turns reading the different lines. Try to make the second part sound different from the first. (See question 3 under Developing Comprehension Skills.)

The Snakebit Hoe Handle

APPALACHIAN FOLK TALE

Paul Bunyan, John Henry, Pecos Bill, and Davy Crockett were all larger-than-life heroes. This tall tale is about an average person. As you read, try to picture the small farm and the strange events that occur on it.

One day, like any other day, I was out hoeing my corn. From the corner of my eye, I saw something moving across the ground. It was a huge copperhead snake. He was heading straight at me.

I began hitting him with the hoe. He thrashed around. He bit the hoe handle a couple of times. Finally, I killed him. I hung him on the fence.

Then I went back to hoeing my corn. Before long my handle felt thicker. I looked it over. Sure enough, it was swelling. The poison from the snakebite was working through it.

I tried hoeing with it a little longer. The handle was growing fatter and fatter. Suddenly, the head of the hoe popped right off!

I didn't think too much about it at the time. I just wanted to get my work done. I threw that handle over the fence and got another hoe from the shed. I finished hoeing my corn about dark.

Two weeks passed. One day I took a walk through my cornfield. A huge new log lay at the end of my fence. I looked closer. It was that hoe handle! The poison had made it as big as a tree trunk.

I took the log to the sawmill. It made twenty or thirty boards. There was just

enough lumber to build a new chicken house.

First I nailed the boards together. Then I mixed my paint with some turpentine. I painted the chicken house a beautiful red, from top to bottom.

Early the next morning, I walked over to admire my new chicken house. All I could see was an empty field. I ran down the corn rows toward the fence. There was my chicken house, snug against a fencepost. It was no bigger than a shoebox!

I finally figured out what happened. During the night my chicken house had shrunk. The turpentine in the paint must have cured the snakebite. It had taken out all the swelling.

I guess I was pretty lucky. What if I had already put my chickens in that new house?

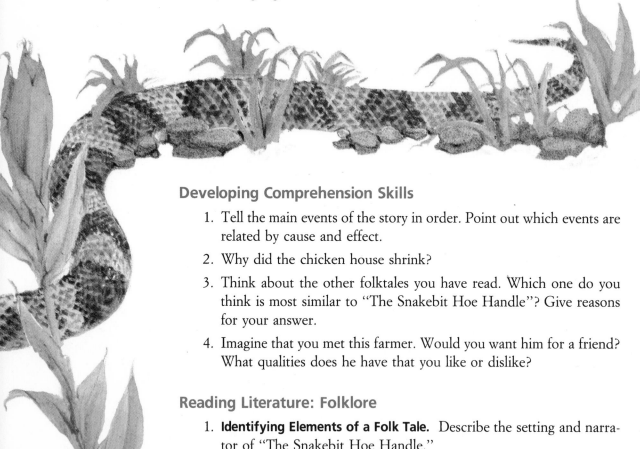

Developing Comprehension Skills

1. Tell the main events of the story in order. Point out which events are related by cause and effect.

2. Why did the chicken house shrink?

3. Think about the other folktales you have read. Which one do you think is most similar to "The Snakebit Hoe Handle"? Give reasons for your answer.

4. Imagine that you met this farmer. Would you want him for a friend? What qualities does he have that you like or dislike?

Reading Literature: Folklore

1. **Identifying Elements of a Folk Tale.** Describe the setting and narrator of "The Snakebit Hoe Handle."

2. **Using Hyperbole.** This entire story is built upon one main hyperbole. What is it? How does it lead to the other events?

Developing Vocabulary Skills

Recognizing the Part of Speech. After the respelling of a dictionary entry you will find a part of speech listed. One of these abbreviations will be used: *n.* (noun), *v.* (verb), *adj.* (adjective), *adv.* (adverb), *conj.* (conjunction), *prep.* (preposition), *pro.* (pronoun), *interj.* (interjection).

Some words are used as only one part of speech. Only one of these abbreviations will appear in the definition.

Many words, however, are used as two or more parts of speech. Usually the dictionary entry will group all the meanings for one part of speech together. A different abbreviation will appear before each group of meanings. Most dictionaries will start numbering the meanings in each group with 1.

Look up each of the following words in your dictionary. Can it be used as two or more parts of speech? On your paper, list those parts of speech. Then write how the word is used in the given sentence.

1. handle: He bit the hoe handle a couple of times.

2. head: He was heading straight towards me.

3. hit: I began hitting him with the hoe.

4. hoe: One day, like any other day, I was out hoeing my corn.

5. house: There was just enough lumber to build a new chicken house.

Developing Writing Skills

1. **Comparing Stories.** Compare "The Snakebit Hoe Handle" with one or more of these tales: "Paul Bunyan," "Pecos Bill," and "Davy Crockett." Discuss the setting, narrator, and use of hyperbole.

2. **Writing a First-Person Narrative.** Write a tall tale about an imaginary experience of your own. Write it in the **first person**, that is, using *I* and *me* and telling events as if they happened to you. Base the story on one major exaggeration. Everything else in the story should relate to that impossible event. Use this story starter: "One day, like any other day, I was _____."

How To Tell Bad News

COLONIAL FOLK TALE

Here is another folk tale without a hero. However, it certainly has a lot of bad news! As you read about each disaster, can you guess the disaster that caused it?

(Mr. H. and the Foreman are talking.)

Mr. H. Ha! Foreman, how are you, my old boy? How do things go at home?

Foreman. Bad enough, your honor; the dog's dead.

Mr. H. Poor dog! So he's gone. How came he to die?

Foreman. Overate himself, sir.

Mr. H. Did he? A greedy dog. Why, what did he get he liked so well?

Foreman. Horseflesh, sir. He died of eating horseflesh.

Mr. H. How came he to get so much horseflesh?

Foreman. All your father's horses, sir.

Mr. H. What! Are they dead, too?

Foreman. Aye, sir. They died of overwork.

Mr. H. Why were they overworked, pray?

Foreman. To carry water, sir.

Mr. H. To carry water! And what were they carrying water for?

Foreman. Sir, to put out the fire.

Mr. H. Fire! What fire?

Foreman. Oh, sir, your father's house is burned to the ground.

Mr. H. My father's house burned down! And how came it to be set on fire?

Foreman. Sir, I blame the torches.

Mr. H. Torches! What torches?

Foreman. At your mother's funeral.

Mr. H. My mother dead!

Foreman. Ah, poor lady! She never looked up, after it.

Mr. H. After what?

Foreman. The loss of your father.

Mr. H. My father gone, too?

Foreman. Yes, poor gentleman! He took to his bed as soon as he heard of it.

Mr. H. Heard of what?

Foreman. The bad news, sir.

Mr. H. What! More miseries! More bad news!

Foreman. Yes, sir. Your bank failed, and your credit is lost, and you are not worth a penny in the world. I made bold, sir, to wait for you about it, for I thought you would like to hear the news.

Fire Engine Weathervane, 1875–1885, CUSHING AND WHITE.
The Edison Institute, Henry Ford Museum and Greenfield Village, Dearborn, Michigan.

Developing Comprehension Skills

1. Tell the causes of these three events.

   a. the death of the horses
   b. the burning of the house
   c. the illness of the father

2. Put the following events in the order in which they happened. (Do not follow the order in which the Foreman told about them.)

   mother dies   horses are overworked   bank fails
   father dies   house burns down   horses die
   dog dies

3. The Foreman told Mr. H. a lot of bad news. Some of the news was worse than the others. In which order did the Foreman tell Mr. H. the news: bad to better, or bad to worse?

4. What did the Foreman think was the worst news? How can you tell?

5. This story is full of terrible news. Still, it is funny. What do you think makes it funny?

Reading Literature: Folklore

1. **Recognizing the Effects of Form.** This story is written in the form of dialog, that is, two people talking to each other. Do you think the use of dialog makes it funnier or more interesting than if it were told by a narrator? Give a reason for your answer.

2. **Using Understatement.** Understatement is the opposite of hyperbole. In **understatement**, you tell about an object or event as if it were small or dull when it is actually great and exciting. Discuss how "Bad News" uses understatement.

3. **Recognizing Setting.** This tale never describes the setting where the two men are talking. Can you suggest a fitting place?

Developing Vocabulary Skills

Recognizing Subentries and Idioms. You have probably noticed certain phrases at the end of a dictionary entry. These phrases are printed in dark type. The entry word appears somewhere in each phrase. The special meaning, or meanings, of the phrase are listed after it. Each of these phrases is called a **subentry**.

Sometimes these phrases include idioms. An **idiom** is a phrase or expression that many people use to mean something different from what it says. For example, in "How To Tell Bad News" the Foreman says that the mother "never looked up" after the father died. What he means is that she became depressed and lost interest in life. He means almost the same thing when he says that the father "took to his bed."

Each idiom in the following sentences uses a word from "Bad News." Then, each idiom is used in a sentence. Look up the underlined word in your dictionary. Look at the subentries following the definition of the word. See if the idiom is explained. If it is, copy the dictionary definition on your paper, and then write the meaning of the sentence in your own words. If it isn't, try to guess the meaning from the rest of the sentence. Write your guess.

1. like a <u>house</u> on fire: Jim worked on his project like a house on fire.

2. to put one's <u>house</u> in order: Before she could run for class office, Dorothy had to put her house in order.

3. to make <u>news</u>: Lila's crazy hairdo made news at school today.

4. to <u>burn</u> oneself out: If he's in good shape, Van won't burn himself out early in the game.

5. to <u>water</u> down: The comic book tells a watered-down version of the story.

Developing Writing Skills

1. **Setting a Scene.** Imagine you were producing "How To Tell Bad News" as a play. Write a description of the scenery and costumes you would use. Explain why you think the play should be done your way.

2. **Writing a Dialog.** Write a story that uses dialog to tell the story. Follow the pattern of "How to Tell Bad News," and use understatement in the story. Choose *a* or *b*.
   a. Fill in your own bad news, such as losing or breaking something belonging to a friend.
   b. Fill in good news, such as winning a prize in an unexpected way.

Developing Skills in Critical Thinking

Organizing Information. A simple and effective way to organize information about the American tall-tale heroes is to make a chart. Draw four lines down your paper to form five columns. Write these headings above the columns: (1) Name of character; (2) Where the character lived; (3) What he did for a living; (4) What made him special; and (5) Some great achievements. In the first column, list these names: Paul Bunyan, John Henry, Pecos Bill, and Davy Crockett. Then fill in the other columns with information about each hero.

You may want to read in the library about other heroes and heroines, such as Johnny Appleseed and Calamity Jane. If time is available, add these names to the chart and fill in the information.

Developing Skills in Speaking and Listening

Interpreting a Scene. With a partner, prepare a performance of "How To Tell Bad News" for your class. One of you should be the Foreman, and the other should be Mr. H. Read the scene several times. Thinking about the cause and effect relationships will help you to remember the words. See if you can perform the scene without reading from the book.

Yankee Exaggerations

FOLKLORE
From the 1800's

To people of the American South, Yankees are Northerners. To many Northerners, Yankees are people in New England. To Europeans, Yankees are all Americans. In which sense does this title use Yankee?

A man from Virginia has grown so tall that hot soup freezes before it gets down to his stomach. There is a boy out west who grew so fast his shadow couldn't keep up with him. Another man out west is so tall that he has to stand on a ladder to shave himself.

There is a man in Ohio so short that he has to stand on his own head to kiss his wife.

They have a man in Mississippi so thin he makes no shadow at all and a rattlesnake struck at his leg six times in vain and retired in disgust. There is a man in Indiana so thin that when the sheriff was after him he crawled into his rifle barrel and hid.

There was this politician with a mouth so big that one of his opponents threatened to go and live in it if he didn't close it.

There is a man who had a nose so big that he couldn't blow it without using gunpowder.

There is a family in Ohio so lazy that it takes two of them to sneeze, one to throw his head back and the other to make the noise.

There is one man who has such a good disposition that he rents himself out in the summer to keep people cool.

There is a man out west so cheap that he stands on one foot at a time, for fear that he'll wear out his shoes too quickly.

There is a grocer so cheap that when he sees a fly on his counter he holds him up and looks into the cracks of his feet to see that he hasn't been stealing sugar.

A shoemaker in Massachusetts said that he made so many pairs of shoes in one day that it took him two days to count them. And a mason in New Hampshire built so many miles of stone wall one day that it took him two days to get home again.

A man from Missouri is so successful as a fisherman that he can tie a hook and line to each foot and dive into the river and bring up a fish on each foot.

A Californian says they have fireflies so large that they use them to cook by.

One winter a cow floated down the Mississippi on a piece of ice and caught such a cold that she yielded nothing but ice cream ever after. And one time snowflakes fell so large in Oregon that the ladies put handles on them and used them for umbrellas.

Another time it rained so hard in Arkansas that people had to jump into the river to keep from drowning.

It is said that in some towns in the west it is so healthy that the folks have to shoot a man to start a cemetery.

There is this lake in Minnesota that is so clear that by looking into it you can see them making tea in China.

Uncle Sam Whirligig, 19th Century.
Courtesy of Museum of American Folk Art, New York.

Developing Comprehension Skills

1. What happened to make the cow give ice cream instead of milk?

2. Reread this sentence: "There is one man who has such a good disposition that he rents himself out in the summer to keep people cool." On the surface it seems as though disposition, or personality, has nothing to do with being cool in summer. Yet the sentence seems to make sense. Explain how the idea of a good disposition relates to staying cool in summer.

3. "Yankee Exaggerations" is very similar in some ways to "Yarns." What is the main difference between the two? Which style do you like better? Give a reason for your answer.

Reading Literature: Folklore

1. **Examine Setting.** Many locations are mentioned in this selection. Are these different settings important to what happens? Why are the different locations reported?

2. **Identifying Characteristics of American Folklore.** Which of the following are found in "Yankee Exaggerations"? Give examples.
   a. dialect   b. hyperbole   c. understatement

Developing Vocabulary Skills

Using the Dictionary. Using the dictionary skills you have learned, answer the following questions about some words that appear in this selection.

1. *Stomach* can be used as more than one part of speech. In which ways can it be used? How is it used in paragraph 1?

2. How many syllables are in *umbrella*? Which syllable is accented? Which sample word in the pronunciation key has the same vowel sound?

3. Match the words with their respellings. On your paper, copy the word. After it write the letter of its respelling.

yield	a. dis′ pə zish′ ən
cemetery	b. ə pō′ nənt
opponent	c. yēld
disposition	d. sem′ ə ter′ ē

4. Find the word *retired* in paragraph 3. Which dictionary meaning would best fit the sentence?

5. What are two ways to pronounce *close*? Write the respellings. What do we call words that are spelled alike but have different meanings and, sometimes, different pronunciations?

Developing Writing Skills

1. **Writing a Definition.** You have been looking for and discussing hyperbole throughout this chapter. In your own words, write a paragraph telling what hyperbole means. Describe the effect it has in folklore. Refer to "Yankee Exaggerations" or any other selection in this chapter to explain your ideas.

2. **Writing Hyperbole.** Using "Yankee Exaggerations" as a pattern, write five original exaggerations. These ideas may help you:

   a. Two joggers ran so fast that _____.
   b. A man's pocket was so full that _____.
   c. A television screen was so large that _____.
   d. There was a wind so strong that _____.
   e. The classroom was so hot that _____.

CHAPTER **2** **R**eview

Using Your Skills in Reading American Folklore

Read the following paragraph from Adrien Stoutenberg's "Paul Bunyan." Identify the setting and the characters. Find an example of hyperbole and explain why it is funny.

> One night he [Paul's father] had wakened to find his bed down on the floor. There beside it sat Baby Paul, a crosscut saw in one hand. In the other hand he held one of the sawed-off legs of the bed. He was chewing on it to help his teeth grow.

Using Your Comprehension Skills

Here is a paragraph from James Thurber's "Many Moons," which you will soon read. It contains at least two examples of cause and effect. Identify at least one effect and its cause. Then identify any key words that helped you.

> The King shook his head from side to side. "If the Princess wore dark glasses, she would bump into things," he said, "and then she would be ill again." So he called the Royal Wizard.

Using Your Vocabulary Skills

The following sentences are from stories you will read in Chapter 4. Look up each underlined word and give the following information:

a. Can the word be divided when it is written at the end of a line? If so, show a way. If not, write **Not divided**.
b. Write the respelling, including symbols and accents.
c. Write the definition that best fits the sentence. Be sure to test each meaning given to find the best one.

1. She had no way of being known in <u>society</u>.
2. That dreadful <u>debt</u> must be paid.

3. They were now weaving as fast as they could, but without thread or shuttle.

4. This was the year Pony Pony was going to bake her first squash pie all by herself.

5. Three corners of the room are empty, and in the fourth the servants are waiting to serve the next course.

6. Then the King rang a gong and summoned the Royal Mathematician.

7. Tassai lived on the top of a mesa that looked far out over the Painted Desert.

8. The open place in the town was bright with color. It was like a fair.

Using Your Writing Skills

Choose one of the writing assignments below. Follow the directions.

1. Choose either "Pecos Bill" or "The Snakebit Hoe Handle." Discuss parts of the story that make it seem real. If you like, you may use this beginning sentence: "Even though _____ is a tall tale, some parts of it could really happen."

2. Write a new tall tale using one of the following narrators. Be sure to identify the setting clearly and to use hyperbole. The main character may be a superhero or an ordinary person.

   a. The narrator is someone outside of the story, telling what happened.

   b. The narrator is someone in the story, telling what happened to himself or herself.

Using Your Skills in Study and Research

Read the questions below. For which of them could you find answers in the library? Discuss how you would look for the answers.

1. Has Adrien Stoutenburg written any complete books?

2. Do other countries have folklore heroes?

3. Are there any songs about other American heroes besides John Henry? How do their melodies go?

CHAPTER 3

How Writers Write

The Letter, 1891, MARY CASSATT.
National Gallery of Art, Washington, D.C.; Rosenwald Collection.

Using the Process of Writing

A writer does not decide to write a story and immediately sit down and write one. He or she thinks about such a project for some time. Usually the writer goes through four main steps:

prewriting or planning
drafting
revising which includes proofreading
sharing

Together, these four steps are called the **process of writing**.

Phenomena Mount Olive, 1983, PAUL JENKINS. Courtesy of Samuel Stein Fine Arts Gallery, Chicago.

Understanding the Process of Writing

Imagine that a friend takes you to your first basketball game. As you watch the game, you enjoy the action and excitement. However, you realize that you do not understand everything that is happening. The next day you borrow a basketball. Your friend plays with you, explaining the rules of the game as you go along.

Very likely, the next game that you see will give you more enjoyment. You will see more clearly what is happening. You will know what plays to look for. You will appreciate the good moves that players make.

Reading a story can be compared to watching a basketball game. You can enjoy the story even though you may not know everything that went into it. However, you can enjoy it more if you know what the writer is doing. You can appreciate his or her good moves.

In this chapter, you will look at what a writer does. You will see some of the ways a writer can make his or her writing clear, lively, and readable. You will even practice some of those ways. After finishing this chapter, you should be able to get more out of the next story you read.

Prewriting

The first stage of the process of writing is called **prewriting**. It includes all the thinking and planning that a writer does before putting a single word of a story or other writing on paper. Before you write, follow these five pre-writing steps.

1. Choose and limit a topic. Think of things that interest you. Make a list of any ideas that come to mind. Then go over the list more carefully. Which of the ideas seem most interesting to you? Which do you know something about? Which would you like to know more about?

Robert McClung, an author of books on animals, told about his own lists:

> When a particular subject or idea appeals to me as a possible book, I start a file folder on that subject. I add related references, thoughts, and plans as they come. Sometimes months or years go by before I finally develop the idea and do something about it—or perhaps discard it.

After choosing the topic, make a second list. What are some of the things you could say about the topic? How many of them belong in your story or poem or other writing? Limit your topic to the ideas you think you can handle well in the space available.

In order to choose and limit your topic intelligently, you must know both your purpose and your audience.

2. Decide on your purpose. Do you want to teach a lesson, as in a fable, or do you want simply to entertain, as in a tall tale? Do you want to inform the reader of facts? Or will you try to lead him or her to think about the topic in a certain way? Perhaps you wish the reader to see what is around him or her with new eyes. For each of these purposes, you would treat your topic in a different way.

3. Decide on your audience. Suppose you like bikes. Do you want to write about biking for first-grade children? Or for cyclists in competitions? Knowing your audience will help you narrow your topic.

Your purpose and audience will also affect the language you use. For young readers, for example, you would use short words and sentences. For your friends, you might use slang and an informal style. For adults, your language would be more formal.

4. Gather supporting information. After you have decided on your topic, purpose, and audience, you can begin to gather information. List everything you know about the topic that may be useful. Then list your questions, and use every resource you can to find the answers. Take notes on all the information you find.

Ann Petry, author of a biography of Harriet Tubman, reported the following about her pre-writing activities:

> When I begin to research a book, I usually read widely about the period first. Then I begin to look for detail—what kind of houses people lived in, the kind of clothing they wore, the kind of food they ate. I build a file based on the material.
>
> The research is so detailed and widespread that in the case of *Harriet Tubman*, for example, I could make my way on foot from the eastern shore of Maryland to Philadelphia, following the same route that Harriet followed.

Ms. Petry was writing about real people, so she needed to find facts. Matt Christopher, author of over thirty sports books for young people, writes about imaginary people. Therefore, he must make up all of his supporting information.

> After I get a story idea, I dream up the people who are part of the life of my young hero. These are often his family, his close friends, and the boys on the teams he plays against. On a separate sheet of paper, I write the names of the people and how they look and act.
>
> Since my books tell about league play, I name the teams and draw up schedules for the entire playing season, complete with wins and losses. For my baseball books I go a step further—I draw up complete box scores of the games I plan to write about.

As you gather the information, you will probably begin to see ways in which the facts relate to each other. Author Pura Belpré noted the following about her research:

> As the research continued, the characters developed. Problems the characters had to solve also fell into place. When I saw these things happening, I found it was time to begin organizing and outlining the material.

5. Organize your ideas. Now you have a topic and a list of details that may be useful. It is time to put some order into your materials. Read through your details and cross out any that seem unrelated to your topic. You may find, however, that your new information is more interesting than your original topic. You may decide to keep those details and change your topic instead.

When you have settled on your topic and crossed out unwanted details, choose a logical order for the details that remain. If you are telling a story, you may arrange the events in time order. If you are writing a description, arrange the details in the order in which they might be noticed. If you are trying to convince your reader to think a certain way, you might arrange your reasons in order of importance.

As you organize your facts and ideas, you may find that you need even more information. If so, go back to step 4 and continue your research. Then use your new facts to improve your outline.

There are many different ways to outline your writing. Author Keith Robertson described his approach this way:

> After I decide upon the general theme or plot of my book, I outline it chapter by chapter in considerable detail.

Another author, Elizabeth Coatsworth, uses a less detailed plan:

> When a general idea emerges, I sometimes make a rough outline of the story, with the scenes or chapters and, under each chapter heading, some of the incidents likely to occur. Usually the outline changes as I work.

You must decide on some method of outlining that makes sense to you.

Drafting

The important idea in writing a draft, or version, is to get all your thoughts down on paper quickly. You should follow your outline as much as possible. However, change the outline if you get better ideas as you write. Leave space between the lines of your draft for later corrections and changes.

Here is what three authors have said about the drafting stage:

Writing my first draft is the phase of writing that I most enjoy. This part is fun. I am a poor typist and I make many mistakes. I do not worry about these in my first draft. Frequently, I will type so fast that I omit words. I make no attempt to correct as I go along because I know I must go over the manuscript word for word later. I am busy telling a story and I do not want to interrupt it with details.

    —Keith Robertson

When writing the first draft of a story with many chapters, I do not think of each chapter at this time. I build up my plot and work on shaping the characters. As I write, I put down everything that comes into my mind, much more than I am going to need for a final story. Later, I keep only the parts which mean exactly what I want to say, but I have lots to choose from because I have written much.

    —Mary Lewis

Often characters grow and change as the book progresses, and then perhaps the plot must change too. This means reorganizing and rewriting.

    —Carol Ryrie Brink

Revising and Sharing

Your completed draft is far from a finished piece of writing. Read it over carefully with these questions in mind:

1. Is the writing interesting? Will others want to read it?
2. Did I stick to my topic? Are there any unnecessary details? Should any other details be added?
3. Is the organization clear and easy to follow? Do the ideas flow together smoothly?
4. Does every sentence express a complete thought? Is every word the best word to express my idea?

Mark your corrections on your draft. Draw lines through the words you are dropping. Write in the words and sentences you are adding. In the example on page 117, note how Jean Lee Latham marked up her first draft as she revised her work.

Whenever the paper gets messy and hard to read, rewrite it. Author Mary Lewis noted the following:

> Often, parts of a story are rewritten many, many times. I find that a messy page distracts from the flow of the story as it is read. So, as margins are filled with notes and there is more written between the lines than can be comfortably read, it is time to copy a page over.

Sometimes you may decide that your organization is poor. Then you may need to make a new outline and start writing again. Experienced writers have these problems, too.

> Although I rework constantly as I go along, once a piece of work is finished, I start back through it again. Often I find that I must discard large portions of my first draft, as I strive for three things: to make the story interesting, to make everything clear, and to make my language vivid.
>
> Making it interesting may mean cutting out a lot of "fat"—the words and paragraphs that slow the story.

Author Jean Lee Latham shows how she corrected a page of her own manuscript while writing her novel, *This Dear-Bought Land*.

David suddenly had had enough of his meat. He laid it down and x

went toward the ſound of his father's voice. ~~If only I weren't such~~

~~a poor escuse of a Warren, he thought.~~ W~~h~~en Father ~~was~~ fifteen, he was

~~sailing with Drake!"~~

As usual, Gran ~~xkx~~ sat stiffly erect, stabbing at her needlework

with anger jerks; ~~as usual~~ Uncle Rupert slumped in his chair, his to

~~elbows, resting on the arms, making his shoulders hunch, his long~~

~~face blank,~~ his pale eyes staring over the peak of his matched finger

tips! ~~As usual,~~ Father strode up and down, frowning one minute, laugh-

ing the next, bellowing.

He saw David, smiled, then turned back to his argument. "Mother,

you know I can't stay ~~home!~~ her! Every ship that ever sailed for the glory

of England has carried a Warren!"

Gran's needle stabbed; the thread rasped. "The more fools they,"

~~If you~~ she said. "And you're the worst of the lot!"

~~Father's rumble interrupted.~~ grinned. "Started young enough, didn't I? ~~Clear back in 1553, when Sir Hugh~~

~~Willoughby sailed to find a northeast passage to China, my Uncle David~~

~~Warren sailed with him."~~

~~"And died with him," Gran said. "Froze to death somewhere in~~

that God-forsaken north. ~~Three~~-fourths of the men on that expedition

die~~d~~."

Uncle Rupert stirred. His thin voice complained. "But we can't

call it failure, Madam. Out of that venture we founded the Muscovy

Company. A very Kprofitable enterprise. Now that Portugal holds the

Cape of Good Hope, and Spain holds ~~the~~ Cape Horn and the passage

~~across Panama---"~~ Sailed before the mast with Drake

"Spain didn't hold Cape Horn when I sailed with Drake! Clear

around the world ~~with him! xSailed before the mast!~~ No older than

David when we started, but when we got back I was a man!"

Making everything clear means trying to forget that you know what you mean, and putting yourself in the place of the reader, who does not.

Making language vivid involves largely an act of the imagination and recall.

All of this is hard work, but the reward comes when I finish the work and feel it is about as good as I can make it—that it has the "feel" I want; that the characters show a little spirit, something beyond what I consciously fed into them.

—Frank Bonham

Proofreading. After you have marked all your changes concerning ideas and organization, reread your writing once more. This time, look for errors in grammar, spelling, punctuation, and capitalization. It is also helpful to read the paper aloud, as Robert McClung does: "I read aloud to myself, and discover awkward words or phrases that had escaped me when I read them silently."

Preparing and Sharing the Final Copy. Write out, or type, your writing one last time. Make this copy as neat and correct as possible. Be sure to make every correction you marked on the earlier drafts. Then proofread the final copy.

Mary Lewis describes this stage as follows:

At last the story seems finished. Every extra word has been crossed out. Dull words are replaced by interesting words. Each sentence has been made to read as smoothly as possible. The transitions are smooth, which means that each part of the story leads to the next part easily. It seems by now that the story surely has been rewritten and reread a zillion times. Now I will let someone else read it.

Practicing the Process of Writing

When you do any writing, keep in mind the ideas discussed in this chapter. Also refer to the Process of Writing section in your Handbook for Reading and Writing. There you will find guidelines for the process of writing, for revising, and for proofreading.

Using the Sounds of Language

A good writer arranges his or her words in a logical way that will appeal to the reader's reason. The good writer also tries to appeal to the reader's senses. By using the sounds of language, a writer keeps the reader alert and interested. Sometimes the sounds even help to make the writer's meaning clear.

In this chapter, you will learn about these uses of language:

alliteration	rhythm
rhyme	onomatopoeia

Whaam! (detail), 1963, ROY LICHTENSTEIN. Tate Gallery, London, England.

Alliteration

Alliteration is the repetition of a consonant sound at the beginnings of words.

Example: pretty as a picture

Alliteration in Prose. We use alliteration frequently in phrases such as "bread and butter," "live and let live," and "smooth as silk." Tongue twisters like "Round the rugged rock the ragged rascal ran" are fun to say because of the repetition of sounds.

Writers of prose use alliteration for special emphasis. It makes phrases easier to remember. As you read the following examples, notice how the letters repeated at the beginnings of words are often repeated within words as well.

These are the times that try men's souls. The summer soldier and the sunshine patriot will, in this crisis, shrink from the service of their country; but he that stands it now, deserves the love and thanks of man and woman.

—Thomas Paine, "The Crisis"

It is a far, far better thing I do than I have ever done.

—Charles Dickens, *A Tale of Two Cities*

A great, dusty golden square of sunshine lay on the fireplace wall, where the brass pendulum of the clock at every swing blinked into sudden brilliance.

—Joan Aiken, "Searching for Summer"

Alliteration in Poetry. Alliteration can be found in almost any poem. Here are just a few examples.

Let us walk in the white snow
    In a soundless space;
With footsteps quiet and slow,
    At a tranquil pace
    Under veils of white lace.

     —Elinor Wylie, "Velvet Shoes"

"The time has come," the walrus said,
    "To talk of many things:
Of shoes—and ships—and sealing-wax—
    Of cabbages—and kings."

     —Lewis Carroll, *Through the Looking Glass*

Exercises: **Using Alliteration**

A. Find alliteration in each of the following samples of poetry and prose. Identify each consonant sound repeated at the beginning of words.

1. Sweet and low, sweet and low,
    Wind of the western sea.

    —Alfred, Lord Tennyson, "The Princess"

2. The lake rippled red as fire beneath the awful beating of Smaug's
    wings.   —J.R.R. Tolkien, *The Hobbit*

3. If at first you don't succeed, try, try again.

4. This Kansas boy who never saw the sea
    Walks through the young corn rippling at his knee.

    —Ruth Lechlitner, "Kansas Boy"

5. You could fairly feel the fierce energy suddenly burning in him.
       —Jack Schaefer, *Shane*

B. Write three sentences about the clothes you or others in the room are wearing today. Use alliteration in each sentence. For example, you might write about a "blue blouse with bright white buttons."

C. Make a list of commonly-used phrases that have alliteration in them.

Rhyme

> **Rhyme** is the repetition of sounds at the ends of words.
>
> Example: Red sky at night,
>   Sailors' delight.
>
> In poetry, rhyme most often comes at the ends of lines.

Rhyme in Prose. Writers do not often use rhyme in prose. They save it for special effects, such as for slogans, advertising, and newspaper headlines.

> Now in that same place far in the south was a little girl with two braids of hair twisted down her back and a face saying, "Here we come—where from?"
> —Carl Sandburg, "Pig Wisps"

Rhyme in Poetry. In some poems the lines that rhyme come one after another.

> I sprang to the stirrup, and Joris, and he;
> I galloped, Dirck galloped, we galloped all three.
>   —Robert Browning, "How They Brought the
>   Good News from Ghent to Aix"

Not all poems are like that, however. For instance, in this example only the second and fourth lines rhyme.

> THE CAMEL
> The camel has a single hump;
> The dromedary, two;
> Or else the other way around.
> I'm never sure. Are you?
>   —Ogden Nash

Here is a stanza of a poem. Can you find the pattern of rhyme in this poem?

"To-night will be a stormy night—
You to the town must go;
And take a lantern, Child, to light
Your mother through the snow."
　　　　　—William Wordsworth, "Lucy Gray"

The different patterns in which rhyme can be used are called **rhyme schemes**. Since rhyming words are not always spelled the same, we can use a code to show the rhyme scheme in a poem clearly. A different letter of the alphabet stands for each different ending sound. Here are the rhyme schemes for the three examples you have just read:

HOW THEY BROUGHT THE GOOD NEWS	THE CAMEL	LUCY GRAY
	a	*a*
	b	*b*
a	*c*	*a*
a	*b*	*b*

Compare the letter patterns to the sound patterns. Did you notice that "Lucy Gray" uses only two letters when "The Camel" uses three? In the "Lucy Gray" poem, there are two sets of rhymes.

Exercises: Using Rhyme

A. Examine the poetry samples on page 121. Write the rhyme scheme for each sample.

B. Write as many rhymes as you can think of for each word below. Then write a two- or four-line poem using one or two pairs of rhyming words. You may use any rhyme scheme you like.

cat　　　bird　　　wagon
dog　　　car　　　tree
horse　　bike

Rhythm

Rhythm is the pattern of accented and unaccented syllables in a sentence or line of poetry. It can be shown by marking each syllable with one of these marks:

/ for accented, or stressed syllables

ᵕ for unaccented, or light syllables

Example: Twinkle, twinkle, little star
How I wonder what you are.

Rhythm in Prose. A fast or slow rhythm in the sentences of a story or other writing helps to express mood. In this example, note how the excitement is built by the gradual speeding up of the rhythm.

Yet the sound increased—and what could I do? It was a low, dull, quick sound—much such a sound as a watch makes when enveloped in cotton. I gasped for breath—and yet the officers heard it not. I talked more quickly—more vehemently; but the noise steadily increased. I arose and argued about trifles, in a high key and with violent movements; but the noise steadily increased. Why would they not be gone? I paced the floor to and fro with heavy strides, as if excited to fury by the observations of the men—but the noise steadily increased. Oh God; what could I do? I foamed—I raved—I swore! I swung the chair upon which I had been sitting and grated it upon the boards, but the noise arose over all and continually increased. It grew louder—louder—*louder!*

—Edgar Allan Poe, "The Tell-Tale Heart"

Rhythm in Poetry. Usually a poem has a regular rhythm. Changes in the rhythm give more emphasis to the words involved. As you read the following poem, listen for a change in rhythm. The accent marks will help you.

A diamond is a brilliant stone,
    To catch the world's desires;
An opal holds a fiery spark;
    But a flint holds fire.

—Christina Rossetti, "Precious Stones"

After the poet has established a regular rhythm of light-heavy beats, she puts three heavy beats in a row in the last line. This forces the reader to give special attention to that line.

Exercises: **Using Rhythm**

A. Copy this poem, adding the accent marks.

Everyone grumbled. The sky was gray.
We had nothing to do and nothing to say.
We were nearing the end of a dismal day,
And there seemed to be nothing beyond,
        THEN
Daddy fell into the pond!

—Alfred Noyes, "Daddy Fell Into the Pond"

B. As you read this prose sample, decide what mood the author means to express. Be able to read the sample aloud.

Every time, just before I take off in a race, I always feel like I'm in a dream, the kind of dream you have when you're sick with fever and feel all hot and weightless. I dream I'm flying over a sandy beach in the early morning sun, kissing the leaves of the trees as I fly by. And there's always the smell of apples, just like in the country when I was little and used to think I was a choo-choo train, running through the fields of corn and chugging up the hill to the orchard. But once I spread my fingers in the dirt and crouch over the Get on Your Mark, the dream goes and I am solid again and am telling myself, Squeaky, you must win, you must win, you are the fastest thing in the world.

—Toni Cade Bambara, "Raymond's Run"

Onomatopoeia

> **Onomatopoeia** is the use of words that imitate sounds.
>
> Examples: boom, hiss, crunch

Onomatopoeia in Prose.   In the first example below, a single word imitates an animal. In the second, listen for traffic.

> The wolf pups were barking their excited 'yipoo' that rang out the hour at the end of the hunt.
> —Jean Craighead George, *Julie of the Wolves*

> Stretched out on his cot, he listened sleepily to the diesels blatting by, the cars passing with a rising and falling whoosh.
> —Frank Bonham, *Durango Street*

Onomatopoeia in Poetry.   In this example, notice how the many *b*'s, *d*'s, and *p*'s in this poem suggest the sounds of swiftly-moving water.

> I chatter over stony ways,
> In little sharps and trebles,
> I bubble into eddying bays,
> I babble on the pebbles.
> —Alfred, Lord Tennyson, "The Brook"

Exercises: Using Onomatopoeia

A. What sound is suggested by this line? Is it soft or loud?

> Over the cobbles he clattered and clashed in the dark inn-yard.
> —Alfred Noyes, "The Highwayman"

B. Write a sentence that suggests the sound of one of these: radio static, water dripping from a faucet, bacon frying, or bees.

Using Figures of Speech

Writers use language in special ways. Some of the special uses of language are called **figures of speech**. The figures of speech used most often are these:

simile	personification
metaphor	hyperbole

In this section you will learn about these four figures of speech. Using figures of speech is called using **figurative language**.

Girl, Back to Piano, 1932, JOHN SLOAN. Courtesy of Sordoni Art Gallery, Wilkes College, Wilkes Barre, Pennsylvania.

Simile

A **simile** is a comparison that uses *like* or *as*. It points out how two unlike things have something in common.

Examples: The clouds were like cotton candy stuck on the sky.
His beard was as white as the snow.

Similes in Prose.   The goal of a simile is to make us think in a new way of the things being compared. We must find in what way the things are alike. For instance, in the first example above, the reader must think of how cotton candy looks, feels, tastes, sounds, and smells. Then he or she must decide in which ways the clouds are like candy. The reader will probably decide that the clouds look fluffy and sticky.

In everyday speech, people often use similes, as in "My hands are as cold as ice." A simile that is used too often becomes a cliché. It loses its ability to make us see the two unlike things in a new way. Writers try hard to avoid clichés.

In each of these comparisons, can you tell what the two unlike things have in common?

Silence dropped like a curtain around them.
—Norton Juster, *The Phantom Tollbooth*

Helen is like a little safe, locked, that no one can open. Perhaps there is a little treasure inside.
—William Gibson, *The Miracle Worker*

His left hand was as tight as the gripped claws of an eagle.
—Ernest Hemingway, *The Old Man and the Sea*

Similes in Poetry.   Notice how these writers combine sounds and images. Look for both alliteration and similes.

How dreary to be somebody!
How public, like a frog,
To tell your name the livelong day
To an admiring bog.

        —Emily Dickinson, "I'm Nobody! Who Are You?"

The sun shines warm on seven old soldiers
    Paraded in a row,
Perched like starlings on the railings.

        —Robert Graves, "The Oldest Soldier"

Exercises: **Using Simile**

A. In each item below, identify the two things being compared. Then identify what they have in common.

1. Like silent, hungry sharks that swim in the darkness of the sea, the German submarines arrived in the middle of the night.
    —Theodore Taylor, *The Cay*

2. Arithmetic is where numbers fly like pigeons in and out of your head.   —Carl Sandburg, "Arithmetic"

3. There came a wind like a bugle.
    —Emily Dickinson, "There Came a Wind Like a Bugle"

4. Ichabod's sharp elbows stuck out like grasshoppers; and as his horse jogged on, the motion of his arms was not unlike the flapping of a pair of wings.   —Washington Irving, "The Legend of Sleepy Hollow"

5. The freeways dipped and swerved above one another like roller coasters.   —Frank Bonham, *Durango Street*

B. Write three or more similes of your own. If you like, begin with these phrases.

1. The couch was as lumpy as _____.
2. The heavy snow was like _____.
3. The bar of soap was as slippery as _____.

Metaphor

> A **metaphor** is a comparison that says one thing is another, unlike thing. It suggests how the things are alike.
>
> The black rolling clouds are elephants going down to the sea for water.

Metaphor in Prose. Find the metaphor in this sentence. It describes a wolf watching over his cubs on the tundra, the treeless plain near the North Pole.

> The great wolf's eyes softened at the sight of the little wolves, then quickly hardened into brittle yellow jewels as he scanned the flat tundra. —Jean Craighead George, *Julie of the Wolves*

By calling the wolf's eyes jewels, the metaphor makes you think of them as hard, bright, and beautiful.

This next sentence describes a girl worried about a hungry but proud neighbor. Notice how the words *wheeled* and *circled* suggest that her mind is a hunting animal or bird.

> Her mind wheeled and circled around the problem of this person, this human being, who had to eat and would not eat.
> —Leland Webb, "Point of Departure"

This metaphor did not state "The girl's mind was a bird." Instead, it told what her mind did like a bird.

Metaphor in Poetry. Sometimes a poem will use several metaphors.

> The wind was a torrent of darkness among the gusty trees,
> The moon was a ghostly galleon tossed upon cloudy seas,
> The road was a ribbon of moonlight across the purple moor.
> —Alfred Noyes, "The Highwayman"

Other poems may depend completely on one metaphor. As in the second prose sample on page 130, the writer may expect the reader to figure out what two things are being compared.

> A silver-scaled Dragon with jaws flaming red
> Sits at my elbow and toasts my bread.
> I hand him fat slices, and then, one by one,
> He hands them back when he sees they are done.
>
> —William Jay Smith, "The Toaster"

Exercises: Using Metaphor

A. In each of these metaphors, identify the two things being compared. Then explain in what way, or ways, they are alike.

1. The fog comes
   on little cat feet.   —Carl Sandburg, "Fog"

2. The Moon's the North Wind's cooky.
   He bites it, day by day,
   Until there's but a rim of scraps
   That crumble all away.
   > —Vachel Lindsay, "The Moon's the North
   > Wind's Cooky"

3. The rumor of what she was doing dropped down the stair well, hit, and spread ripples through the rooms, out doors and windows, and along the street of elms to the edge of the green ravine.
   > —Ray Bradbury, "Goodbye, Grandma"

4. Morning is
   a new sheet of paper
   for you to write on.   —Eve Merriam, "Metaphor"

B. Answer the questions below, and then write three metaphors about yourself. Each metaphor should suggest what you have in common with the answers to the question.

1. If I were an animal, which animal would I be?

2. If I were a plant, which plant would I be?

3. If I were a color, what color would I be?

Personification

> **Personification** is the giving of human qualities to an object, an animal, or an idea.
>
> Examples: Money talks.
>
> The wind moaned and screeched.

Personification in Prose. By using personification, a writer can share a feeling with the reader quickly.

> The road, finally making up its mind, plummeted down, as if anxious to renew acquaintance with the sparkling blue stream that flowed below.
> —Norton Juster, *The Phantom Tollbooth*

> There was no sound or movement but the play of leaves and the play of the water and its continual song.
> —Ursula K. LeGuin, *The Farthest Shore*

Personification can make an idea more easily understood. In this example, the power and wealth of a character are obvious.

> The cold regions of the north sent him their tribute in the shape of furs; hot Africa gathered up the ivory tusks of her great elephants out of the forests; the East came bringing him the rich shawls, and spices, and teas, and the splendor of diamonds, and the gleaming purity of large pearls.
> —Nathaniel Hawthorne, "The Great Stone Face"

Personification in Poetry. Notice how each example of personification below refers to a different characteristic of people.

> Swaying daisies sing a lazy song beneath the sun.
> —John Lennon, "Mother Nature's Son"

When you let proud words go, it is not easy
    to call them back.
They wear long boots, hard boots; they walk off proud;
    they can't hear you calling.
Look out how you use proud words.
                    —Carl Sandburg, "Primer Lesson"

Exercises: Using Personification

A. In each of these examples of personification, identify what is being compared to humans. Explain how it is like humans.

1. The small, dry, crumbling houses were collapsing from sheer discouragement.   —Frank Bonham, *Durango Street*

2. Reflections on the water, like shadows on my mind,
    Speak to me of passing days and nights and passing time.
                    —John Denver, "Fall"

3. Every rose on the little tree
    Is making a different face at me!
    Some look surprised when I pass by,
    And others droop—but they are shy.
                    —Rachel Field, "The Little Rose Tree"

4. In the wind it was good to sing, the wind drowned song, sang a song of its own, saved a man from feeling that miles of quiet woods were listening.   —Elliot Merrich, "Without Words"

5. Who has seen the wind?
        Neither you nor I.
    But when the trees bow down their heads,
        The wind is passing by.
                    —Christina Rossetti, "Who Has Seen
                    the Wind?"

B. Use personification to describe each of the things listed below. Suggest some action or attitude in which the thing could be like people. If you can, let your figure of speech suggest a feeling or mood.

1. A skyscraper   2. A noisy clock

Hyperbole

> **Hyperbole** is exaggeration that puts an image into the reader's mind. Usually it is funny.
>
> Example: I've eaten so much I could burst.

Hyperbole in Prose. Hyperbole is a favorite figure of speech in tall tales. In Chapter 2 of this text, many examples of hyperbole are pointed out. Here is one of them:

> That same winter, men's words froze in front of their mouths and hung stiff in the air.   —Adrien Stoutenburg, "Paul Bunyan"

Hyperbole is also used in other kinds of stories and writing.

> He was tall and exceedingly lank, with narrow shoulders, long arms and legs, hands that dangled a mile out of his sleeves, feet that might have served as shovels, and his whole frame most loosely hung together.
> —Washington Irving, "The Legend of Sleepy Hollow"

Hyperbole in Poetry. The effect of these hyperboles is very much like that in a tall tale.

> Then from the gladdened multitude went up a joyous yell;
> It bounded from the mountaintop and rattled in the dell;
> It struck upon the hillside and recoiled upon the flat,
> For Casey, mighty Casey, was advancing to the bat.
> —Ernest Lawrence Thayer, "Casey at the Bat"

> WEATHER
> It is a windy day.
> The water's white with spray.
> And pretty soon, if this keeps up,
> The world will blow away.   —Marchette Chute

Exercises: **Using Hyperbole**

A. Identify which of the following use hyperbole.

1. He had collapsed shoulders almost meeting under his chin, and his hair looked as if each separate strand had been carefully glued into place, ready for church.
   —Peter Jones, "Wheldon the Weed"

2. The wind came drawing out of the blackness with a great draft. It hissed through the grass, sucked and tore at the wagon sheet, and whistled through the spokes.
   —Conrad Richter, *Early Marriage*

3. They had good food to eat, rice and vegetables, and very fine fish and chicken and pork, and certainly the best eggs.
   —Pearl S. Buck, "Little Red"

4. The geese flying south
   In a row long and V-shaped
   Pulling in winter.
   —Sally Andresen, "Fall"

5. Finally, Paul went to sleep. He snored so loudly the gulls went flapping toward land for they thought a thunderstorm was coming.
   —Adrien Stoutenburg, "Paul Bunyan"

6. This particular stalk, the farmer said, happened to be popcorn, and when the ears got up so close to the sun, the heat was so great that all the kernels popped and fell all over his hayfield. He said a mule that was standing hitched to a hayrake in that field mistook all those white popcorn kernels for a June snowstorm and just naturally lay down and froze to death.
   —Carl Carmer, "How the Educated Bulldog Said Too Much"

B. Write a hyperbole beginning with one of these phrases.

1. The room was so crowded that _____.
2. My cooking is so bad that _____.
3. My friend is so lazy that _____.
4. The sun was so hot that _____.

R*eview*

Understanding the Process of Writing

Below are statements by three writers about their writing habits. About which stage in the process of writing—pre-writing, writing, or revising—is each one speaking?

1. I can't understand how anyone can write without rewriting over and over again. I scarcely ever reread my published writings but, if by chance I come across a page, it always strikes me: all this must be rewritten; this is how I should have written it.
   —Leo Tolstoy

2. When I am working on a book or a story I write every morning as soon after first light as possible. There is no one to disturb you and it is cool or cold, and you come to your work and warm as you write. You read what you have written and, as you always stop when you know what is going to happen next, you go on from there.
   —Ernest Hemingway

3. Even if a writer had nine lives, there would never be days enough nor years enough to make use of all the ideas that come his way. In my case, story ideas come from many places and many people—a sentence tucked away in the back pages of a newspaper, or a glowing account from a traveler returned from the Palio of Spain or the Spanish Riding School of Vienna.
   —Marguerite Henry

Understanding Sounds of Language

As you read each sample below, consider each of these sounds of language:

alliteration	rhythm
rhyme	onomatopoeia

Identify which sounds you find in the samples. If you can, tell how the use of sound helps the reader to understand the samples.

1. The lion, ruler over all the beasts,
   Triumphant moves upon the grassy plain
   With sun like gold upon his tawny brow
   And dew like silver on his shaggy mane.

   He gazes down into the quiet river,
   Parting the green bulrushes to behold
   A sunflower-crown of amethyst and silver,
   A royal coat of brushed and beaten gold.
   —William Jay Smith, "Lion"

2. I was the only kid in town with a cat like Harry. I tied a piece of old throw rug over the rear carrier of my bike. Harry would ride along, hanging on with his claws dug into the rug like a bundle of fishhooks. He'd turn his head and hiss at passing cars. Other times we guys would form a circle and hiss at him. Harry would stand up on his hind legs, double up his front paws, and jab away like a heavyweight.
   —A. R. Swinnerton, "Harry the Heavyweight"

Understanding Figures of Speech

Read the samples above a second time. Identify any of these figures of speech.

simile   personification
metaphor   hyperbole

If you find a comparison, tell what two things are being compared and in what way they are alike.

CHAPTER 4

Short Stories

The Front Parlor, 1913, WILLIAM McGREGOR PAXTON.
The St. Louis Art Museum. Cora E. Ludwig Bequest, by exchange,
and Edward Mallinckrodt, Sr., by exchange.

Reading Literature: Short Stories

What Is a Short Story?

A **short story** is a story so short that it can be read at one sitting. It is a work of **fiction**. That is, it comes from the writer's imagination.

In one sense, people have always told short stories. Many folk tales and fables were short. However, these tales were not written. They are part of the **oral tradition**, passed on by storytellers. They have no one author. They can change with each retelling.

What we call a short story is written down by one person, the author. It is printed in this book in the same words the author used. Short stories may not be changed with each retelling.

The author of a short story chooses the words carefully. Short story writers also make sure that all the parts of their stories—the setting, the characters, and the events—work together.

The History of the Short Story

The short story as a form of writing began in the nineteenth century. Writers in many countries began experimenting with it.

One of the first masters of the short story was the French writer Guy de Maupassant. He spent years learning to write good stories. During that time he observed people carefully. Later, he used what he had learned to write realistic stories about everyday situations. One of his stories begins this chapter.

The short stories in this chapter are divided into two groups. The first group presents great classic stories. They are some of the most skillfully-made and best-loved short stories ever written.

The second group is made up of great modern stories. These stories are newer than the classics. They are good short stories, too. Perhaps people in the future will call them classic stories.

The Elements of a Short Story

Setting. The setting, as you know, tells when and where the story takes place. The writer usually describes the setting early in the story to help you picture the action.

Characters. The characters are the people or animals who take part in the story. Characters can be major or minor.

A **major character** is a main character in the story. You learn a lot about the major characters, and the action could not happen without them. The story is really about them.

A short story may also have **minor characters**. The story doesn't focus on these characters. It isn't really about them.

Plot. The plot is the series of events that takes place in the story. The plot usually includes the following parts:

Introduction: The setting and characters are introduced.
Rising Action: It becomes clear that the characters face a problem. This struggle is called the **conflict**.
Climax: The climax is the most exciting part of the story. Usually it involves an important discovery, decision, or event. It is the turning point of the story.
Falling Action: The story draws to a close.
Resolution: The loose ends are tied up.

How To Read a Short Story

1. Read carefully. Every word in a short story is important.
2. Decide who is telling the story. Is it a narrator outside the story or a character in the story?
3. Try to picture the setting.
4. Pay close attention to what is said about the characters. You may also get to know them through their words or actions.
5. Look for cause and effect relationships in the plot.

Making Inferences, or Reading Between the Lines

Imagine a frog coming to his pond. He finds an elephant sitting in the pond. The frog glares at the elephant and yells angrily, "Hey, you. . . . Out!"

How could you describe the character of the frog? Would you use words such as *shy* and *quiet* to describe him? It is more likely that you would describe him as *bossy*, *pushy*, and *loud-mouthed*. No one had to tell you these things about the frog. You could figure out what he was like by what he did and said.

Would you call the frog and elephant friends? Think about the clues that are given. Would a friend say "Hey, you. . . . Out!"? Would friends glare at each other? Probably not. So, given a few clues, you can guess how the characters feel about each other.

Using clues in this way is called reading between the lines or **making inferences**. You **infer** what the writer hasn't said from what he or she has said.

Predicting Outcomes

Think of the frog story again. That tiny frog expects the huge elephant to follow his order. What will the elephant really do? You can make a reasonable guess about what will happen next.

You can **predict outcomes** as you read longer stories just as you did with the frog story. Writers set up situations for you to think about. They explain the conflict, or problem. They describe the setting and the characters. They try to build suspense in your mind. What will the character do? How can he or she solve the problem? What would I do? What will happen next?

It's fun to predict what will happen. When you find out what really happens, you may feel proud that you guessed correctly. Of course you may be surprised at the outcome. Good readers find that just guessing helps them understand what happens.

Use every possible clue to predict outcomes.

1. Use what you know about the characters. How do they think? How do they act? What do other characters tell you about them?
2. Use what you know about the plot so far. What would be a logical next step? Where are all the events leading?
3. Use what you know about the setting. Would some outcomes be more natural in this setting than others?
4. Use what you know about your life. If you were in the story, what would you do? What would your friends do?

Just one word of warning: Don't be disappointed if your guesses are wrong. After all, why would you read a story if you were sure about the outcome before you read it?

Exercise: **Making Inferences and Predicting Outcomes**

In the short story "The Necklace," a man wants to buy his wife a dress for a ball. He asks her how much the dress will cost.

She thought for several seconds. How much could she ask for without getting a quick refusal? How much would he agree to, and how much would make him angry?

"I don't know, exactly," she finally replied, "but I think I could manage it with four hundred francs."

He grew a little pale. Four hundred francs was just what he had saved up to buy a gun. He had planned to do a little shooting with some friends in the spring.

But he said, "All right. I'll give you four hundred francs. And try to have a pretty dress."

1. How would you describe the husband, based on his words and actions?
2. How does he feel about his wife?
3. From what you know about the wife, do you think she will be satisfied with the dress?

Vocabulary Skills: Context Clues

Using Context Clues to Unfamiliar Words

Often, writers use words that are new to you. As you read, you find these new words **in context**. **Context** means the sentence or paragraph in which you find a word. Some writers know you might not understand the new word. Therefore, they give you clues to its meaning. These clues are called **context clues**. One kind of context clue is the definition or restatement clue.

Definition or Restatement Clues. In a **definition or restatement** clue, the writer tells the meaning of the new word. The writer may include a phrase that directly defines the word, as in a dictionary. Or the writer may restate the word—that is, say the idea again in a different way.

1. The dress cost four hundred *francs*. A franc is a unit of French money.
2. The King called his *chamberlain*, the person who managed his palace.

The writer often gives signals to tell you that a clue is included in the context. Common signals for definition or restatement clues include the following key words and punctuation marks:

is	that is	dashes
who is	in other words	commas
which is	or	parentheses

In the following examples, notice the clue words from the list. The meaning of the new word follows the clue word.

1. One morning, the *Sultan,* who is the ruler of an Eastern country, was resting in his palace.

2. Two *rogues*, or rascals, said they were weavers.
3. Two tears *descended*, that is, came down her face.
4. The weavers were *deceitful*. In other words, they told lies.

In sentences with dashes or parentheses, read the words between those marks for the meaning.

1. A *cobra*—a very poisonous snake—crawled into the room.
2. He thought the moon was made of *molten* (melted) copper.

Exercises: Using Context Clues

A. Each sentence below is about a story you will read. The sentence contains a definition or restatement of a new word. Identify the word and the meaning given. Then identify the clue words in each sentence.

1. The muscles of the hostess's face contracted slightly. That is, they drew together.

2. Late at night, he copied manuscripts for a pittance. A pittance is a small amount of money.

3. The servants held up the king's train, which was the part of the robe that trailed behind.

4. Tommie answered Margie's question nonchalantly. That is, he appeared unconcerned.

5. One day Lenore felt ill because of a surfeit of raspberry tarts. In other words, she had eaten too many tarts.

B. Each of these sentences contains a definition or restatement of the underlined word. Identify the clue word or punctuation that helped you find the meaning. Then explain the underlined word.

1. They paid back the loan plus the <u>interest</u> (money paid for the use of money).

2. The Emperor was always in his <u>wardrobe</u>, the room where his clothes were kept.

3. The boy placed the bowl of milk on the <u>veranda</u>, or porch.

4. "No one can help me," he said <u>mournfully</u>, or sadly.

5. Margie didn't want to <u>dispute</u>—argue about—that idea.

Great Classic Stories

Short stories can take you to far-away places and long-ago times. They can take you to places that never existed. Even more important, they can point out truths inside yourself and others that you might never see otherwise.

The selections in this section, "Great Classic Stories," will give you an idea of the power of short stories. These tales have been read and enjoyed by many people, for many years.

Camel and Keeper (detail), 1556–57, SHEYKH MUHAMMED. Smithsonian Institution, Freer Gallery, Washington, D.C.

The Necklace

GUY de MAUPASSANT

Guy de Maupassant wrote about the struggles of common people. He was an expert at using the right details to help us know his characters. As you read, notice how much you learn about the characters from each detail.

She was one of those pretty and charming girls who are sometimes, as if by a mistake of fate, born into a family of quite ordinary people. She had little money and less hope. She had no way of being known in society. There was just no chance for her to meet and marry any rich and handsome man. So she married an office worker in the Department of Education.

She dressed plainly because she could not dress well. Feeling herself born for the best that life had to offer, she suffered endlessly. She suffered from the poverty of her apartment. The walls were dirty. The chairs were worn out. The curtains were ugly. All these things another young bride might not have minded at all. But not she! Her surroundings tortured her and made her angry. She dreamed often of luxuries, of candlelight dinners, of servants. She thought of huge rooms filled at five o'clock with good friends talking together. She imagined herself in conversation with the famous and powerful.

Yet her own husband was hardly a famous or a powerful man. He would come home for dinner and lift the lid on the pot. "Ah, the good soup!" he would say. "I don't know of anything better than that." Then she would think of dainty dinners, of shining silverware. Rows of expensive plates would flash through her mind. On them would be the pink flesh of a trout or the wings of a quail.

She had no fine dress, no jewels, nothing. She loved nothing but things like these. She felt made for them! She would so have liked to please. She wanted to be envied, to be charming, to be a popular hostess.

She had a friend, a former schoolmate, who was rich, but she went to see this friend less and less. She suffered so much when she came back to her own house.

One evening, her husband came home with a smile on his face. He held a large envelope in his hand.

"Here," he said, "this is something for you."

She tore the paper quickly. In the envelope was a printed card with these words:

> The Secretary of Education
> and Mme. Georges Ramponneau
> Request the Honor of Your Company
> in the Grand Hall
> on Monday Evening,
> January 18th.

She threw the invitation on the table with a heavy sigh. Her husband was surprised. He had expected her to be delighted.

"What do you want me to do with that?" she murmured.

"But, my dear, I thought you would be glad. You never go out, and this is a good chance. I had awful trouble getting it. Everyone wants to go, but not many of the office staff have been invited. It is a great honor for us. All the important people in Paris will be there."

She looked at him with troubled eyes. "And what do you want me to put on my back?"

He had not thought of that. "Why," he stammered, "the dress you always go out in. It looks very fine to me." He stopped, seeing that his wife was crying. Two great tears descended slowly from the corners of her eyes to the corners of her mouth.

"What's the matter?" he asked. "What's the matter?"

She wiped one wet cheek with the back of her hand. Soon she had won the battle with her tears. "Nothing," she replied in a calm voice. "Only I have no dress. That means I can't go to this ball. Give your card to some friend whose wife is better equipped than I."

He was in despair. "Come, let's see, Mathilde," he stuttered. "How much would it cost? A suitable dress. Something very simple that you could wear on other occasions."

She thought for several seconds. How much could she ask for without getting a quick refusal? How much would he agree to, and how much would only make him angry?

"I don't know, exactly," she finally replied, "but I think I could manage it with four hundred francs."

He grew a little pale. Four hundred francs was just what he had saved up to buy a gun. He had planned to do a little shooting with some friends in the spring.

But he said, "All right. I'll give you four hundred francs. And try to have a pretty dress."

The day of the ball grew near. Mathilde Loisel's dress was ready, but she seemed sad, uneasy, anxious. Her husband said to her one evening, "What's the matter? Come, you've been so quiet these last few days."

"It annoys me," she said, "not to have a jewel. Not a single stone, even. Nothing to put on. I shall look so out of place. I'd almost rather not go at all."

"You might wear flowers," he suggested. "They're in style this time of year. For ten francs you can get two or three roses."

She was not at all sure. "No," she sighed. "There's nothing worse than to look poor among other women who are rich."

"There's your friend Mme. Forestier!" he cried. "Ask her to lend you some jewels. You're still good friends enough for her to do that."

"That's true," she said, smiling. "I never thought of that."

The next day she went to her friend and explained her problem.

Mme. Forestier went to a closet with a glass door. She took out a large jewel box, opened it, and brought it back.

"Choose, my dear," Mme. Forestier said.

Mathilde first of all saw some bracelets. Then a pearl necklace. A cross of gold and precious stones. She tried on the jewelry standing before the mirror. Everything looked so beautiful! It was impossible for her to make up her mind. She kept asking, "Have you any more?"

"Why, yes, take your time. I don't know what you like."

All of a sudden she discovered, in a black satin box, a superb necklace of diamonds. Her heart began to beat with desire. Her hand trembled as she took it. She fastened it around her throat. Her eyes would not move from the mirror.

"Can you lend me this?" she gasped finally. "Only this?"

"Why yes, certainly."

She sprang up and kissed her friend with joy. Then she fled with her treasure.

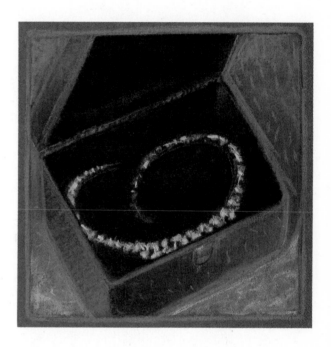

The day of the ball arrived. Mathilde Loisel made a great success. She looked prettier than them all. She was brilliant, smiling, and crazy with joy. The important men looked at her, asked her name. All wanted an introduction, a chance to dance. She danced and danced, made wild by pleasure. In the glory of success, she forgot all. She danced in a cloud of

happiness, for the whole ball seemed to belong to her. She had a sense of complete victory.

She turned away from the ball at about four o'clock in the morning. Her husband had been sleeping since midnight. She found him in a little coat room, with three other gentlemen whose wives were having a very good time.

"Wait a bit," he said, wiping sleep from his eyes. "You'll catch cold outside. I'll go and call a cab."

But she did not listen. They rapidly descended the stairs. When they got to the street, there was no cab to be seen. Shivering with cold, they began to search for one. It took a long time.

Finally, they arrived at their door. Feeling sad, they climbed up the stairs. All was ended for her. As for him, he groaned that he must be at work at ten o'clock.

She removed her coat before the mirror. This would be her last chance to see herself in all her glory. But suddenly she cried out. She no longer had the necklace around her neck!

Her husband was half-undressed. "What's the matter?" he demanded.

She turned madly toward him, "I have—I have—I've lost Mme. Forestier's necklace!"

"What? How? Impossible!" He stood up, alarmed.

They looked in the folds of her dress. In the folds of her coat. In her pockets. Everywhere. They did not find it.

"You're sure you had it on when you left the ball?" he asked.

"Yes. I felt it, coming down the stairs."

"But on the street we would have heard it fall. You must have lost it in the cab."

"Yes, probably. Did you notice the number?"

"No. And you?"

"No."

They looked at one another, horrified. At last Loisel put on his clothes. "I'll go back on foot," he said. "I'll go over the whole route. Maybe I can find it."

He went out. She sat waiting on a chair in her ball dress, overwhelmed, without fire, without a thought. She lacked the strength to go to bed.

Her husband came back about seven o'clock. He had found nothing.

He went to Police Headquarters. He went to the newspapers, to offer a reward. He went to the cab companies.

She waited all day, in the same state of mad fear.

Loisel returned at night with a hollow, pale face. He had discovered nothing.

"You must write to your friend," he said. "Tell her that you have broken the clasp of the necklace. You are having it fixed. That, at least, will give us some time."

She wrote at his dictation.

At the end of a week they had lost all hope. Loisel, who had aged five years, declared, "We must find a way to replace that necklace."

The next day they took the box that had held the necklace. They went to the jeweler whose name was found inside. He examined his records.

"It was not I who sold that necklace," the jeweler finally announced. "I must simply have sold the case."

Then they went from jeweler to jeweler, searching for a necklace just like the other. Both were sick with worry and fear. At last they found a string of diamonds that seemed just right. As far as they remembered, it was exactly like the one that had been lost. The jeweler said it was worth forty thousand. They could have it for thirty-six.

They begged the jeweler not to sell it for three days. Then they faced the question of finding the money. Loisel had a little that his father had left him. He would borrow the rest.

He did borrow, asking for a thousand here, five hundred there. To everyone he gave signed promises to repay, even to criminals. He risked all the rest of his life and then signed away another life. All that mattered was to get the thirty-six thousand together. It took time, but on the afternoon of the third day they were able to put the money down on the jeweler's counter.

Immediately, Mme. Loisel left for her friend's with the necklace. She did not find her friend in a good mood.

"You should have returned it sooner," Mme. Forestier said icily. "I might have needed it."

Mme. Forestier did not open the case, as her friend had feared. If she had noticed a difference, what would she have thought? What would she have said? Would she not have taken Mme. Loisel for a thief?

Mme. Loisel now began to know the horrible existence of the needy. That dreadful debt must be paid. And, she declared, she would help pay it. They gave up their small apartment and moved into a small attic under a roof.

She soon came to know what heavy housework meant. She learned the hated cares of the kitchen. She washed dishes, using her rosy nails on greasy pots and pans. She washed dirty clothes. She carried out garbage. She went shopping, insulting storekeepers and looking for bargains.

Each month they had to pay some debts. Others they managed to renew, gaining more time.

Her husband worked in the evening, doing anything and everything that would bring in a little money. Late at night he often copied manuscripts for a pittance per page.

This life lasted ten years.

At the end of ten years they had paid back everything. They had paid back the thirty-six thousand and, almost as much, the high interest on the money.

Mme. Loisel looked old now. She had become strong and hard and rough. With messy hair and dirty skirt and red hands, she talked loudly while washing floors with great swishes of water. But sometimes, when she sat home alone, unable to find work, her thoughts went back in time. Sitting next to the window, she thought of that brilliant evening of long ago. She dreamed again of that ball where she had been so beautiful.

What would have happened if she had not lost that necklace? Who knows? Who knows? Life is strange and full of changes. How little a thing can make the difference? How little a thing is needed for us to be lost or to be saved?

One Sunday, Mme. Loisel wanted to refresh herself from the labors of the week. She decided to go for a walk. She soon found herself on the Champs Élysées, the finest street in Paris. In front of her she noticed a woman leading a child. It was Mme. Forestier, still young, still beautiful, still charming.

Mme. Loisel felt thrilled. Was she going to speak to her? Yes, certainly. Now that she had paid for losing the necklace, she was going to tell her all about it. Why not?

She went up.

"Hello, Jeanne."

The other was astonished to hear her first name spoken by a common stranger. She did not recognize Mathilde at all, and stammered, "But—I do not know—You must be mistaken."

"No. I am Mathilde Loisel."

Her friend cried out. "Oh! My poor Mathilde! How you have changed!"

"Yes, I have had bad days since I last saw you."

"Oh? How so?"

"Do you remember that diamond necklace you once lent me?"

"Yes. Well?"

"Well, I lost it."

"What do you mean? You brought it back."

"I brought you back another just like it. We have been ten years paying. You can understand that it was not easy for us. At last it is ended, and I am very glad."

Mme. Forestier had stopped.

"You say that you bought a diamond necklace to replace mine?"

"Yes. You never noticed it, then! We thought they were exactly alike." Mme. Loisel smiled with a proud joy.

Mme. Forestier, strongly moved, took her friend's hands in hers.

"Oh, my poor Mathilde! Why, my necklace was made of glass—a clever fake. It was worth at most five hundred francs."

Developing Comprehension Skills

1. At the beginning of the story, Mathilde Loisel thought she and her husband were poor. Was she correct? How do you know whether they actually were or not?

2. When Madame Loisel received news of the invitation to the ball, she was not overjoyed. Why was she upset?

3. Examine the following quotations about events that occurred very close in time: "She danced, in a cloud of happiness, for the whole ball seemed to belong to her. She had a sense of complete victory." "Finally, they arrived at their door. Feeling sad, they climbed the stairs. All was ended for her." What has happened to Mme. Loisel between the first event and the second?

4. What would have happened if Mme. Loisel had not lost her necklace? Would she have been happy? Would her life have been different than it was before she went to the ball? Refer to your answer to question 3 before answering.

5. Do you think Mme. Loisel acted like a real person? Did she seem real to you? Do you think she deserved sympathy, either before or after the ball?

Reading Literature: Short Stories

1. **Recognizing Irony.** Irony is an important element in this story. In **irony**, what appears to be true is the opposite of the truth. Tell what ironic situation is revealed at the end of this story.

2. **Finding Character Traits.** A **character trait** is a quality that a character shows. For example, important traits of John Henry were his determination and his pride. Tell what character traits you learned about Mathilde by reading the first four paragraphs of the story. Identify the sentences that led you to believe she had those qualities. Then tell what you learned about her in the rest of the story.

3. **Writing the Moral.** Imagine that this story was written as a fable. What might its moral or morals be?

4. **Diagraming the Plot.** You have learned that a plot can be divided into five parts: introduction, rising action, climax or turning point, falling action, and resolution. In Chapters 1 and 2, you learned that

the events of a fable or folk tale can be shown on a time line. Below, you see a special kind of time line for a short story. It lists the main events that fall into the five parts of the plot. This is called a **plot diagram**.

The plot diagram below is partly filled in. It shows the main events in three parts of "The Necklace." Tell what events belong in the climax and the falling action.

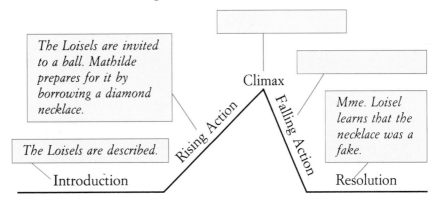

Developing Vocabulary Skills

1. **Using Context Clues in Sentences.** The underlined words in the sentences below appear in "The Necklace." Each sentence contains a **definition or restatement** clue. On your paper, write the following:

    (1) The clue words or clue punctuation that helped you find the meaning of the word
    (2) The meaning of the underlined word

  a. She dreamed of <u>luxuries</u>—costly food and dress—and huge rooms filled at five o'clock with good friends.
  b. She had no way of being known in <u>society</u>. In other words, there was no chance for her to meet any rich and powerful people.
  c. On the plates would be the pink flesh of trout or the wings of a <u>quail</u>, which is a kind of game bird.
  d. All of a sudden she discovered, in a black satin box, a necklace of diamonds that was <u>superb</u>, splendid!
  e. She went shopping, <u>insulting</u> storekeepers. That is, she treated them rudely.

f. Mme. Loisel now began to know the horrible existence, the unhappy life, of the needy.

g. His wife's tears caused him to be in despair—without hope.

h. He wanted her to buy a suitable dress—a dress that would fit the occasion.

2. **Using Context Clues Within a Paragraph.** Read how Mme. Loisel feels as she sits in the cold house after the ball (page 151). What is the meaning of *overwhelmed*? What clues helped you figure out the meaning?

Developing Writing Skills

1. **Discussing Meaning.** Here are three sentences from "The Necklace" that describe M. Loisel when he borrows the money to buy the replacement for the necklace:

   To everyone he gave signed promises to repay, even to criminals. He risked all the rest of his life and then signed away another life. All that mattered was to get the thirty-six thousand together.

   What does the statement that Loisel "signed away another life" mean? Write a paragraph about what these three sentences tell concerning M. Loisel's action and feelings.

2. **Changing the Point of View.** This story is written from the point of view of the all-knowing narrator. Try looking at the story from a different point of view, that of M. Loisel, Mathilde's husband. Write his thoughts when he learns that Mathilde wants a new dress. The story gives you a hint in the line "Four hundred francs was just what he had saved up to buy a gun."

3. **Writing About a Character.** Review question 2 in Reading Literature: Short Stories, above. Then think of a different character. You may create one or choose someone you know. Decide on one or two character traits that are most important in this person. Then write two or three paragraphs describing your character. Let your reader know the character's important traits.

Appointment in Baghdad

TRADITIONAL STORY
Retold by Edith Wharton

This is a traditional story retold by Edith Wharton, an American writer. Notice how she creates an atmosphere, or mood, of suspense in the story. Watch for the surprise ending that adds to this mood.

Bijar Rug, Late 19th Century. Collection of Joseph W. Fell.

One morning the Sultan was resting in his palace in Damascus. Suddenly the door flew open, and in rushed a young man, out of breath and wild with excitement. The Sultan sat up alarmed, for the young man was his most skillful assistant.

"I must have your best horse!" the youth cried out. "There is little time! I must fly at once to Baghdad!"

The Sultan asked why the young man was in such a rush.

"Because," came the hurried reply, "just now, as I was walking in the palace garden, I saw Death standing there. When Death saw me, he raised his arms in a frightening motion. Oh, it was horrible! I must escape at once!"

The Sultan quickly arranged for the youth to have his fastest horse. No sooner had the young man thundered out through the palace gate, than the Sultan himself went into the garden. Death was still there.

The Sultan was angry. "What do you mean?" he demanded. "What do you mean by raising your arms and frightening my young friend?"

"Your Majesty," Death said calmly, "I did not mean to frighten him. You see, I raised my arms only in surprise. I was astonished to see him here in your garden, for I have an appointment with him tonight in Baghdad."

Developing Comprehension Skills

1. Why did the young man ask the Sultan for his best horse?

2. How does the Sultan act when he meets Death? In other words, what tone does he use with him?

3. Compare the young man's and the sultan's reaction to Death. How are they like or unlike people you know, or have heard of, who are facing death?

4. Is there any way that the young man could have avoided Death?

5. If a story tells the exact words a character uses, the words are set off by quotation marks (" "). This means that the writer has used a **direct quotation**. Here is a direct quotation from this story:

   "I must have your best horse!"

   Sometimes the story tells the main idea of what the character said but does not give the exact words. Then the writer has used an **indirect quotation**. Here is an indirect quotation from this story:

   The Sultan asked why the young man was in such a rush.

   Each of the following passages uses a direct quotation. Restate each passage, using an indirect quotation.

   a. The Sultan was angry. "What do you mean?" he demanded.
   b. "Your Majesty," Death said calmly, "I did not mean to frighten him."

Reading Literature: Short Stories

1. **Appreciating Personification.** In this story Death is one of the characters. How does the personification of death add to the story?

2. **Recognizing Irony.** As you know, the term **irony** describes a situation in which what appears to be true is the opposite of the truth. What is ironic in this story?

3. **Understanding the Main Idea.** Almost every story has a main idea. The author is telling the reader one of his or her own ideas about life. The author believes that this idea is true for all people of all ages. What do you think is the main idea of "Appointment in Baghdad"? Write the main idea in a complete sentence.

Developing Vocabulary Skills

Reviewing Word Parts. Review the prefixes and suffixes and their meanings on pages 6 and 7 in Chapter 1. You have probably noticed that these word parts have been used in many words in this chapter. Write the words from "The Necklace" and "Appointment in Baghdad" that mean the following:

1. without end
2. full of power
3. not possible
4. opposite of dressed
5. not easy
6. full of beauty
7. to take wrongly
8. not able
9. full of skill
10. to make new

Developing Writing Skills

1. **Describing a Personal Experience.** Most of us have known some experience that we strongly wished to avoid. It might have been a visit to the dentist, a test, a problem with a friend. Write several paragraphs describing an experience that you wished you could have avoided.

2. **Using Personification.** Write a short, short story using personification of a concept such as nature, life, love, hate, fear, or envy. The concept you select must be used as a character in your story.

Developing Skills in Speaking and Listening

Interpreting a Short Story. With a partner, prepare an oral reading of "Appointment in Baghdad." One person should read the narrator's words. The other should read all the quotations—the words of all three characters. Make your voices agree with the descriptive words in the story, such as "alarmed," "angry," and "calmly."

How the Camel Got His Hump

RUDYARD KIPLING

This nonsense story was written for fun, to be read to children. Imagine you are reading it to a younger brother or sister. Watch for clues that show that the writer is not serious.

In the beginning of years, when the world was so new-and-all, and the Animals were just beginning to work for Man, there was a Camel, and he lived in the middle of a Howling Desert because he did not want to work; and besides, he was a Howler himself. So he ate sticks and thorns and tamarisks and milkweed, most 'scruciating idle; and when anybody spoke to him he said "Humph!" Just "Humph!" and no more.

Presently the Horse came to him on Monday morning, with a saddle on his back and a bit in his mouth, and said, "Camel, O Camel, come out and trot like the rest of us."

"Humph!" said the Camel, and the Horse went away and told the Man.

Presently the Dog came to him, with a stick in his mouth, and said, "Camel, O Camel, come and fetch and carry like the rest of us."

"Humph!" said the Camel, and the Dog went away and told the Man.

Presently, the Ox came to him, with the yoke on his neck, and said, "Camel, O Camel, come and plough like the rest of us."

"Humph!" said the Camel, and the Ox went away and told the Man.

At the end of the day, the Man called the Horse and the Dog and the Ox together and said, "Three, O Three, I'm very sorry for you (with the world so new-and-all); but that Humph-thing in the Desert can't work, or he would have been here by now, so I am going to leave him alone, and you must work double-time to make up for it."

That made the Three very angry (with the world so new-and-all), and they held a palaver,[1] and an indaba,[2] and a punchayet,[3] and a powwow[4] on the edge of the Desert; and the Camel came chewing milkweed most 'scruciating idle, and laughed at them. Then he said "Humph!" and went away again.

---

1. **palaver** (pə lav′ ər), from the Portuguese, meaning a conference or discussion
2. **indaba** (in dä′ bä), from Zulu, meaning a council or conference
3. **punchayet** (pən chī′ ət), from Hindi, an Indian village council or board that makes laws
4. **powwow** (pou′ wou′), from native American, Algonquin, a conference or gathering

Presently there came along the Djinn in charge of All Deserts, rolling in a cloud of dust (Djinns always travel that way because it is Magic), and he stopped to palaver and powwow with the Three.

"Djinn of All Deserts," said the Horse, "is it right for any one to be idle, with the world so new-and-all?"

"Certainly not," said the Djinn.

"Well," said the Horse, "there's a thing in the middle of your Howling Desert (and he's a Howler himself) with a long neck and long legs, and he hasn't done a stroke of work since Monday morning. He won't trot."

"Whew!" said the Djinn, whistling, "that's my Camel, for all the gold in Arabia! What does he say about it?"

"He says 'Humph!'" said the Dog, "and he won't fetch and carry."

"Does he say anything else?"

"Only 'Humph!' and he won't plough," said the Ox.

"Very good," said the Djinn. "I'll humph him if you will kindly wait a minute."

The Djinn rolled himself up in his dust-cloak, and took a bearing across the desert, and found the Camel most 'scruciatingly idle, looking at his own reflection in a pool of water.

"My long and bubbling friend," said the Djinn, "what's this I hear of your doing no work, with the world so new-and-all?"

"Humph!" said the Camel.

The Djinn sat down, with his chin in his hand, and began to think a Great Magic, while the Camel looked at his own reflection in the pool of water.

"You've given the Three extra work ever since Monday morning, all on account of your 'scruciating idleness," said the Djinn; and he went on thinking Magics, with his chin in his hand.

"Humph!" said the Camel.

"I shouldn't say that again if I were you," said the Djinn, "you might say it once too often. Bubbles, I want you to work."

And the Camel said "Humph!" again; but no sooner had he said it than he saw his back, which he was so proud of, puffing up and puffing up into a great big lolloping humph.

"Do you see that?" said the Djinn. "That's your very own humph that you've brought upon your very own self by not working. Today is Thursday, and you've done no work since Monday, when the work began. Now you are going to work."

"How can I," said the Camel, "with this humph on my back?"

"That's made a-purpose," said the Djinn, "all because you missed those three days. You will be able to work now for three days without eating, because you can live on your humph; and don't you ever say I never did anything for you. Come out of the Desert, and go to the Three, and behave. Humph yourself!"

And the Camel humphed himself, humph and all, and went away to join the Three. And from that day to this the Camel always wears a humph (we call it "hump" now, not to hurt his feelings), but he has never yet caught up with the three days that he missed at the beginning of the world, and he has never yet learned how to behave.

Developing Comprehension Skills

1. Why are the Horse, Dog, and Ox angry at the beginning of the story?

2. The man states that "the Humph-thing in the Desert *can't* work, or he would have been here by now." Explain the Man's thinking. Was he correct?

3. The camel's idleness is always referred to as *'scruciating*. The apostrophe in *'scruciating* shows that some letters have been left out. The full word is *excruciating*, which means painful. For whom is the camel's idleness painful?

4. The Three held "a palaver, and an indaba, and a punchayet, and a powwow" on the edge of the desert. What were they doing? (See the footnotes on page 161.)

5. Make a time line showing the events in this story. Use a straight line. Which event do you think is the turning point? Why do you think so?

6. Do you think that Djinn's punishment for the Camel was just? Explain your answer.

Reading Literature: Short Stories

1. **Finding Common Elements.** How is this story like a fable? Can you write a moral for it?

2. **Recognizing the Setting.** Tell the setting of the story.

3. **Analyzing Character.** You can analyze, or examine, a character by taking a careful look at three things:

   a. What the character says
   b. What the character does
   c. What the other characters say about him or her

   Using these three ways of finding out about a character, describe the camel.

Developing Vocabulary Skills

Using Context Clues and Reviewing Dictionary Respellings. In the story "How the Camel Got His Hump," there are several words that are probably new to you. The sentences below provide context clues for five of them. However, each sentence shows the new word in its dictionary respelling.

Read each sentence. Sound out the respelling, and on your paper write that word in its correct spelling. (Choose from the list above the sentences.) Then write the meaning of the word.

excruciating   idle   yoke
tamarisk   palaver

1. The camel ate thorns, milkweed, and *tam'ə risk,* which is a kind of shrub.

2. The camel living in the middle of a Howling Desert was *ī'd'l*—that is, he refused to work.

3. That made the Three very angry, and they held a *pə lav'ər,* or conference.

4. The ox came to him with a *yōk*—a bar or frame made of wood—on his neck.

5. The animals complained that their work was most *iks krōō'shē āt'ing.* In other words, it was intensely distressing or painful.

Developing Writing Skills

1. **Developing a Character.** Imagine a person who might use the expression "humph." Describe the person's age, occupation, and physical characteristics. What mood would this person usually be in?

2. **Writing a Story Explaining Nature.** Write a story explaining how a particular animal's special feature came to be. If you can't think of a topic, try one of the following:

   > How the Turtle Got Its Shell
   > How the Monkey Got Its Tail
   > How the Giraffe Got Its Long Neck
   > How the Snake Lost Its Legs
   > How the Raccoon Got Its Mask

Developing Skills in Study and Research

1. **Using Footnotes.** In question 4 of Developing Comprehension Skills, you were directed to the footnotes on page 161. A **footnote** is a note of explanation in a text, usually at the foot, or bottom, of the page. Examine page 161. What signal in the text tells the reader that there is an explanation at the bottom of the page? When there is more than one footnote, how does the reader know which footnote explains each word or phrase in the text?

2. **Using the Card Catalog To Find Books.** Almost all people have wondered why things came to be as they are. Long ago, different groups of people made up stories to explain nature. These stories are called **myths**. In the library, books about myths are grouped together. Use the card catalog in your library to find out how books about myths are grouped, or classified, there. (Libraries may choose among at least two methods.) Choose one or more titles about myths from the card catalog. Locate at least one of those books in the shelves.

   Report on the following:

   a. The title of each book you found
   b. How you found the book or books
   c. How books on myths are arranged in your library

The Emperor's New Clothes

HANS CHRISTIAN ANDERSEN

This well-known story reminds us that clothes are important. The story isn't talking only about clothing, however. As you read, try to discover what the author is telling you about people.

Many years ago there lived an Emperor who was so exceedingly fond of fine new clothes that he spent all his money on rich robes. He did not care for his soldiers, nor for the theatre, nor for driving about, except for the purpose of showing his new clothes.

He had a robe for every hour of the lay. As they say of a king, "He is in Council," they always said of him, "The Emperor is in his Wardrobe."

Well, the great town in which he lived was very busy. Every day a number of strangers arrived.

One day two rogues came along, saying they were weavers and that they knew how to weave the finest cloth one could imagine. Not only, said they, were the colors and designs exceedingly beautiful, but the clothes that were made of their material had the wonderful quality of being invisible to everybody who was either unfit for his or her position or was extraordinarily stupid.

"They must be splendid clothes," thought the Emperor. "By wearing them I could easily discover what persons in my kingdom are unfit for their posts. I could distinguish the wise from the stupid. I must have that cloth woven for me at once!" So he gave the two rogues a large sum of money, in order that they might begin their work without delay.

The rogues put up two looms and pretended to be working, but they had nothing at all in the frames. Again and again they demanded the finest silks and the most magnificent gold thread, but they put it all into their own pockets. Then they worked at their empty looms late into the night.

"Now, I should like to know how far they have got on with that cloth," thought the Emperor. He felt quite uncomfortable when he remembered that those who were stupid or unfit for their positions could not see it. He did not think for a moment that he had anything to fear for himself. Nevertheless, he would rather send somebody else first to see how the weaving was getting on.

Everybody in the town knew what a remarkable quality the cloth possessed, and each was anxious to see how bad or how stupid his neighbors were.

"I will send my honest old minister to the weavers," thought the Emperor. "He can judge best how the cloth looks, for he is intelligent, and no one is better fit for his office than he."

So the clever old minister went out into the hall, where the two rogues were sitting at work on their empty looms.

"Goodness me!" he thought, and he opened his eyes wide. "I cannot see anything." But he did not say so. Both of the rogues begged him to be so kind as to step nearer. They asked him was it not a pretty design and were not the colors beautiful, and they pointed to the empty looms.

The poor old minister kept on opening his eyes wider and wider. He could not see anything, for there was nothing there.

"Goodness me!" he thought. "Am I really stupid? I never thought so, and nobody must know it. Am I really unfit for my office? No, I must certainly not tell anybody that I cannot see the cloth."

"Well, what do you think of it?" asked the one who was weaving.

"Oh, it is beautiful! most magnificent!" replied the old minister and looked through his spectacles. "What a pattern!

What colors! Yes, I must tell the Emperor that I like it very much indeed."

"Ah! We are very glad of that," said both weavers. Then they described the colors and explained the strange patterns.

The old minister listened attentively, so as to be able to repeat it all when he returned to the Emperor, and this he did.

The rogues now asked for more money and for more silk and gold thread, which they required for weaving. They put everything into their pockets, and not a thread went on the frames. Nevertheless, they continued to work at the empty looms.

Soon afterwards the Emperor sent another clever statesman to see how the weaving was getting on and whether the cloth was nearly ready. The same thing happened to him as to the minister. He looked and looked, but, as there was nothing on the empty frames, he could not see anything.

"Now, is not that a beautiful piece of cloth?" said both rogues. Again they described the beauty of the pattern, which did not exist at all.

"I am not stupid," thought the statesman, "so it must be that I am unfit for the high position I hold. That is very strange, but I must not let anybody notice it." So he praised the piece of cloth, which he could not see, and said how pleased he was with the beautiful colors and the pretty pattern.

"Oh! It is really magnificent!" he said to the Emperor.

All the people in the town were talking about the beautiful cloth, and the Emperor himself wished to see it while it was still on the loom. With a whole suite of chosen courtiers, among whom were the two honest old statesmen who had been there before, the Emperor went to the two cunning rogues. They were now weaving as fast as they could, but without thread or shuttle.

"Well! Is it not magnificent?" cried the two clever statesmen. "Does your majesty recognize how beautiful is the pattern, how charming the colors?" And they pointed to the empty looms, for they thought that the others could see the cloth.

"What?" thought the Emperor. "I cannot see anything! This is terrible! Am I stupid? Or am I not fit to be Emperor? This would be the most dreadful thing that could happen to me!"

"Yes, it is very beautiful," he said at last. We give our highest approbation." He nodded as if he were quite satisfied, and gazed at the empty looms.

He would not say that he saw nothing. The whole of his suite looked and looked, but, like the others, they were unable to see anything. So they said, just like the Emperor, "Yes, it is very pretty." They advised him to have some clothes made from this magnificent cloth and to wear them for the first time at the great procession that was about to take place. "It is magnificent! Beautiful! Excellent!" they said to one another. They were all so exceedingly pleased with it that the Emperor gave the two rogues a decoration to be worn in the buttonhole, and the title "Imperial Weavers."

The rogues worked throughout the whole of the night preceding the day of the procession. They had over sixteen candles lighted, so that people should see how busy they were in preparing the Emperor's new clothes.

They pretended to take the cloth off the looms, cut it in the air with great scissors, and sewed with needles without

thread. At last they said, "See! Now the clothes are ready!"

The Emperor, followed by his most distinguished courtiers, came in person. The rogues lifted their arms up in the air, just as if they held something, and said, "See! Here are the trousers, here is the coat, here is the cloak," and so forth. "It is all as light as a cobweb. One might imagine one had nothing on, but that is just the beauty of it!"

"Yes," said all the courtiers, but they could not see anything, because there was nothing.

"Will your imperial highness please undress?" said the rogues. "We will then dress your majesty in the new clothes, here, in front of the mirror, so you can see how becoming they are."

"Oh! How well they look! How beautifully they fit!" said everyone. "What a pattern! What colors! It is indeed a magnificent costume."

"They are standing outside with the canopy that is to be carried over your majesty in the procession," announced the Master of Ceremonies.

"Well, I am ready," said the Emperor. "Does it not fit me well?" Then he turned again to the mirror, for he wanted it to appear that he was admiring his rich costume.

The chamberlains who were to carry the train fumbled with their hands on the floor, just as if they were holding the train up. They raised their hands in the air but dared not let anybody notice that they saw nothing. So the Emperor went in procession beneath the magnificent canopy, and all the people in the street and at the windows said, "Oh! How beautiful the Emperor's new clothes are! What a splendid train, and how well everything fits!"

People would not admit that they could see nothing, for that would have shown that they were either unfit for their posts or very stupid. None of the Emperor's robes had ever been so much admired.

"But he has nothing on at all!" said a little child.

"Just hear the voice of the innocent!" said his father. Then each one whispered to the other what the child had said. " 'He has nothing on,' says a little child. 'He has nothing on!' "

"But he has nothing on," cried the whole of the people at last. The Emperor shivered, for it seemed to him that they were right.

But he thought to himself, "I must go through with the procession," and he walked with even greater dignity than before. The chamberlains followed, carrying the train that did not exist at all.

Developing Comprehension Skills

1. The Emperor's love for clothes led to problems. First, having a lot of clothes is expensive. Name another problem caused by the Emperor's concern over dressing well.

2. Several people react to the empty loom. Tell how each of these people react: the old minister, the statesman, the Emperor. Why did they react in this way?

3. Why do you suppose that a child is the one who comes out and says that the Emperor is naked?

4. What does the Emperor do when he discovers that he has no clothes on? Why? What does this tell us about his character? Was this an intelligent action, under the circumstances? Why or why not?

5. Decide what events belong in each part of the plot diagram below.

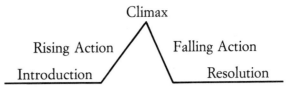

Climax

Rising Action   Falling Action

Introduction   Resolution

6. As you remember, a direct quotation uses the exact words of a character and is set off by quotation marks. An indirect quotation only tells the main idea of what the character said. It does not use the character's exact words and is not set off by quotation marks.

Each of the following passages from "The Emperor's New Clothes" uses an indirect quotation. Imagine what words the character might have used. Restate each passage, using a direct quotation.

a. One day two rogues came along, saying they were weavers and that they knew how to weave the finest cloth one could imagine.

b. The rogues now asked for more money and for more silk and gold thread, which they required for weaving.

Reading Literature: Short Stories

1. **Identifying Character Traits.** The rogues in this story counted on the weaknesses of others. Those weaknesses enabled the rogues to succeed. What character traits in the Emperor make this story possible? What character traits in his officials allowed him to be tricked?

2. **Identifying the Author's Purpose.** In an attempt to deliver his message, Hans Christian Andersen uses many important people as characters: an emperor, a minister, a statesman, courtiers, and chamberlains. Why did he select people of high rank for characters?

3. **Determining the Main Idea.** Although this story deals with clothes, the message goes much deeper. Can you write this message in a sentence or paragraph? Make sure that your statement is broad enough to apply to many different people and situations. Consider why people are afraid to "speak up."

4. **Recognizing Reasons for Enjoying a Story.** "The Emperor's New Clothes" is written as if it were a fairy tale for children. However, for over a hundred years it has been popular with adults. It is so well

known that the phrase "the Emperor's new clothes" is used by itself, like a proverb. It can refer to any foolish idea or practice that no one challenges. Can you suggest reasons for the popularity of this story?

Developing Vocabulary Skills

Finding Word Meanings. You have learned the following ways of learning the meaning of unfamiliar words:

a. **Using Word Parts.** Separate a word into its base word and prefix or suffix. Then combine what you know about the meaning of each part to figure out the meaning of the whole word.

b. **Using Context Clues.** Look for clue words or clue punctuation that signals a definition or restatement of a new word. Then use that information to figure out the meaning of the word.

c. **Using the Dictionary or Glossary.** Look up a new word in your dictionary or glossary. Find the meaning that makes the most sense in the sentence.

Read the following sentences about events in the story. Find out the meaning of the underlined word. Use any of the three methods to determine the meaning of the word. Choose the quickest method that will give you the correct meaning. On your paper, write the word and its meaning. Then write **word part**, **context clue**, or **dictionary** to tell which method you used.

1. The material had the wonderful quality of being invisible to everybody who was <u>unfit</u> for his position.

2. They are standing outside with the <u>canopy</u> that is to be carried over your majesty in the procession.

3. "The clothes are splendid, <u>magnificent</u>," cried the King.

4. The Emperor gave his highest <u>approbation</u>. In other words, he told everyone that he was completely satisfied.

5. The Emperor went to the two <u>cunning</u> rogues, who were now weaving as fast as they could.

6. The Emperor walked with great <u>dignity</u> as the many chamberlains followed.

7. The weavers described the beauty of the <u>pattern</u>, or design, which did not exist at all.

8. People who were <u>extraordinarily</u> stupid could not see the cloth.

9. With a whole <u>suite</u>, or company, of courtiers, the Emperor went to the weavers.

10. Not a thread went on the frames. Nevertheless they continued to work at the empty <u>looms</u>.

Developing Writing Skills

1. **Telling About a Personal Experience.** Have you seen people afraid to criticize something foolish? Perhaps everyone else was doing something silly or dangerous, and you wanted to be part of the group. Tell about an experience you have had that is like "The Emperor's New Clothes."

2. **Showing an Attitude in a Description.** Are clothes important or unimportant to you? Write a paragraph describing how you dress. Do not state directly how you feel about clothes. Show by your selection of details whether you consider clothes important.

Developing Skills in Study and Research

Using the Encyclopedia Index. This story uses several terms connected to courts: *emperor, minister, chamberlain, courtiers,* and others. A dictionary will explain each title but it will not explain the job. One reference source that might help you find out more about these officials is an encyclopedia.

Encyclopedias with many volumes usually have an index. The index is a section or volume that lists many topics in alphabetical order. After each topic, it lists all the entries in that encyclopedia related to the topic.

Look in the indexes of two or more different encyclopedias. Find out if any of them lists articles on the titles above. Also look up any related terms that you think of or discover in the index such as *courts, court life, kings,* or *royalty*. Is one encyclopedia more helpful in this area than the others? Or would you need to find other reference books in the library to learn about jobs with the court?

The Huckabuck Family and How They Raised Popcorn in Nebraska and Quit and Came Back

CARL SANDBURG

Carl Sandburg is well known for his poetry. In his stories he chooses words as carefully as he does in his poetry. As you read this story, listen in your mind to the sounds of the words.

Jonas Jonas Huckabuck was a farmer in Nebraska with a wife, Mama Mama Huckabuck, and a daughter, Pony Pony Huckabuck.

"Your father gave you two names the same in front," people had said to him.

And he answered "Yes, two names are easier to remember. If you call me by my first name Jonas and I don't hear you, then when you call me by my second name Jonas maybe I will.

"And," he went on, "I call my pony-face girl Pony Pony because, if she doesn't hear me the first time, she always does the second."

And so they lived on a farm where they raised popcorn, these three, Jonas Jonas Huckabuck, his wife, Mama Mama Huckabuck, and their pony-face daughter, Pony Pony Huckabuck.

After they harvested the crop one year, they had the barns, the cribs, the sheds, the shacks, and all the cracks and corners of the farm, all filled with popcorn.

"We came out to Nebraska to raise popcorn," said Jonas Jonas, "and I guess we got nearly enough popcorn this year for the popcorn poppers and all the friends and relations of all the popcorn poppers in these United States."

And this was the year Pony Pony was going to bake her first squash pie all by herself. In one corner of the corn crib, all covered over with popcorn, she had a secret, a big round squash, a fat yellow squash, a rich squash all spotted with spots of gold.

She carried the squash into the kitchen, took a long sharp shining knife, and then she cut the squash in the middle till she had two big half squashes. And inside just like outside it was rich yellow spotted with spots of gold.

And there was a shine of silver. And Pony Pony wondered why silver should be in a squash. She picked and plunged with her fingers till she pulled it out.

"It's a buckle," she said, "a silver buckle, a Chinese silver slipper buckle."

She ran with it to her father and said, "Look what I found when I cut open the golden yellow squash spotted with gold spots—a Chinese silver slipper buckle."

"It means our luck is going to change, and we don't know whether it will be good luck or bad luck," said Jonas Jonas to his daughter, Pony Pony Huckabuck.

Then she ran with it to her mother and said, "Look what I found when I cut open the yellow squash spotted with spots of gold—a Chinese silver slipper buckle."

"It means our luck is going to change, and we don't know whether it will be good luck or bad luck," said Mama Mama Huckabuck.

And that night a fire started in the barns, cribs, sheds, shacks, cracks, and corners, where the popcorn harvest was kept. All night long the popcorn popped. In the morning the ground all around the farm house and the barn was covered with white popcorn so it looked like a heavy fall of snow.

All the next day the fire kept on and the popcorn popped till it was up to the shoulders of Pony Pony when she tried to walk from the house to the barn. And that night in all the barns, cribs, sheds, shacks, cracks, and corners of the farm, the popcorn went on popping.

In the morning when Jonas Jonas Huckabuck looked out of the upstairs window he saw the popcorn popping and coming higher and higher. It was nearly up to the window. Before evening and dark of that day, Jonas Jonas Huckabuck,

Grandpa Eating Popcorn, 1935, GRANT WOOD.
The Warner Collection of Gulf States Paper Corporation, Tuscaloosa, Alabama.

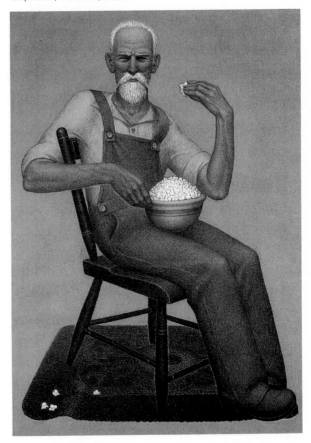

and his wife Mama Mama Huckabuck, and their daughter Pony Pony Huckabuck, all went away from the farm saying, "We came to Nebraska to raise popcorn, but this is too much. We will not come back till the wind blows away the popcorn. We will not come back till we get a sign and a signal."

They went to Oskaloosa, Iowa. And the next year Pony Pony Huckabuck was very proud because, when she stood on the sidewalks in the street, she could see her father sitting high on the seat of a coal wagon, driving two big spanking horses hitched with shining brass harness in front of the coal wagon. And though Pony Pony and Jonas Jonas were proud, very proud all that year, there never came a sign, a signal.

The next year again was a proud year, exactly as proud a year as they spent in Oskaloosa. They went to Paducah, Kentucky, to Defiance, Ohio; Peoria, Illinois; Indianapolis, Indiana; Walla Walla, Washington. And in all these places Pony Pony Huckabuck saw her father, Jonas Jonas Huckabuck, standing in rubber boots deep down in a ditch with a shining steel shovel shoveling yellow clay and black mud from down in the ditch high and high up over his shoulders. And though it was a proud year, they got no sign, no signal.

The next year came. It was the proudest of all. This was the year Jonas Jonas Huckabuck and his family lived in Elgin, Illinois, and Jonas Jonas was watchman in a watch factory watching the watches.

"I know where you have been," Mama Mama Huckabuck would say of an evening to Pony Pony Huckabuck. "You have been down to the watch factory watching your father watch the watches."

"Yes," said Pony Pony. "Yes, and this evening when I was watching father watch the watches in the watch factory, I looked over my left shoulder, and I saw a policeman with a star and brass buttons, and he was watching me to see if I was watching father watch the watches in the watch factory."

It was a proud year. Pony Pony saved her money. Thanksgiving came. Pony Pony said, "I am going to get a squash to make a squash pie." She hunted from one grocery to another; she kept her eyes on the farm wagons coming into Elgin with squashes.

She found what she wanted, the yellow squash spotted with gold spots. She took it home, cut it open, and saw the inside was like the outside, all rich yellow spotted with gold spots.

There was a shine like silver. She picked and plunged with her fingers and pulled and pulled till at last she pulled out the shine of silver.

"It's a sign; it is a signal," she said. "It is a buckle, a slipper buckle, a Chinese silver slipper buckle. It is the mate to the

Young Corn, 1931, GRANT WOOD.
Courtesy of Cedar Rapids Museum of Art, Cedar Rapids School District Collection.

other buckle. Our luck is going to change. Yoo hoo! Yoo hoo!''

She told her father and mother about the buckle. They went back to the farm in Nebraska. The wind by this time had been blowing and blowing for three years, and all the popcorn was blown away.

"Now we are going to be farmers again," said Jonas Jonas Huckabuck to Mama Mama Huckabuck and to Pony Pony Huckabuck. "And we are going to raise cabbages, beets and turnips; we are going to raise squash, rutabaga, pumpkins, and peppers for pickling. We are going to raise wheat, oats, barley, rye. We are going to raise corn such as Indian corn and kafir corn—but we are not going to raise any popcorn for the popcorn poppers to be popping."

And the pony-faced daughter, Pony Pony Huckabuck, was proud because she had on new black slippers, and around her ankles, holding the slippers on the left foot and the right foot, she had two buckles, silver buckles, Chinese silver slipper buckles. They were mates.

Sometimes on Thanksgiving Day and Christmas and New Year's, she tells her friends to be careful when they open a squash.

"Squashes make your luck change good to bad and bad to good," says Pony Pony.

Developing Comprehension Skills

1. Jonas Jonas Huckabuck believed that having "two names the same in front" was good for two reasons. What were his reasons?

2. This story has several settings. List them in the order in which the Huckabucks moved to them.

3. Why did the Huckabucks leave the farm?

4. The Huckabucks saw each Chinese slipper buckle as a sign that their luck was going to change—either to good or to bad. Tell whether each change was good or bad.

5. Do you believe that the events in this story could happen? Explain your answer.

6. At the end of the story, Jonas Jonas lists the crops that the family will raise. He finishes by saying, "but we are not going to raise any popcorn for the popcorn poppers to be popping." How do you think he said these words? What was his tone of voice?

Reading Literature: Short Stories

1. **Identifying Tone.** The **tone** of a story is the author's attitude toward what he or she is saying. For example, the tone in "The Necklace" was critical. The tone in "How the Camel Got His Hump" was joking. Tell what the tone of this story is. What details from the story helped you decide on your answer?

2. **Identifying Alliteration.** In poetry a writer usually pays great attention to sound. This story is written in prose, but it sounds like poetry because of its attention to sound. One sound effect found throughout

is alliteration. **Alliteration** is the repetition of beginning sounds in two or more words, for example, "**s**ilver **s**lipper buckle." Find other examples of alliteration in the story.

3. **Identifying Repetition.** A second strong sound effect in "The Huckabuck Family" is **repetition** of words. Point out examples of repetition in which the same words, such as "Pony Pony," are repeated without change. Then point out other examples in which the repeated phrase grows, as in this example: "a buckle, a silver buckle, a Chinese silver slipper buckle." What effect does this repetition have on the story? Why do you think Sandburg used it?

4. **Identifying Imagery.** The term **imagery** refers to a certain kind of description. This description makes an object or an experience seem so real that we can imagine it with our senses—sight, hearing, touch, smell, or taste. In this story, an example of imagery is the description on page 176 of Jonas Jonas Huckabuck shoveling clay. What sense or senses does this description appeal to? Identify the words in the description that prove your answer.

Developing Vocabulary Skills

Using Your Skills. The following questions are about words used in "The Huckabuck Family." Use context clues, your dictionary or glossary, or the information in Chapter 1 on word parts to answer the questions.

1. Read all the definitions of *relation* in your dictionary. Write the meaning that is used in this sentence:

> We have enough popcorn for all the friends and relations of all the popcorn poppers.

2. In which of these words is *-er* a suffix: *farmer, remember, daughter?* What does the suffix *-er* mean?

3. Write two meanings for *watch* as it is used in the sentence below. Use your own understanding of the word to make up the definitions.

> Jonas Jonas was a watchman in a watch factory watching watches.

4. On the last page of the story, read the list of vegetables the Huckabucks are going to grow. What is a *rutabaga*? What helped you figure out what it is?

5. Write the words in the first list below in syllables. Mark each accented syllable. Use a dictionary. Then find a word in the second list that has the same vowel sound as the accented syllable. Write that word after the word from the first column.

   a. relations   chalk
   b. Nebraska   crack
   c. daughter   care
   d. stairway   charm
   e. harvest   cake

6. Read these sentences:

   On her slippers Pony Pony Huckabuck had two silver buckles that were mates. That is, they were two matching buckles.

   What type of context clue helped you figure out the meaning of *mate*? What clue words are used?

Developing Writing Skills

1. **Presenting an Opinion.** There are many reasons to enjoy "The Huckabuck Family," including the silly characters and plot, the funny effects of all the alliteration and repetition, and the clear images of the descriptions. Tell what your favorite part of the story is. Give at least one reason for your choice.

2. **Writing a Description.** Write a description of a food. Include details that will appeal to as many of your reader's senses as possible.

3. **Writing a Humorous Story.** Write a short story about something silly. Use alliteration, as Sandburg did in "The Huckabuck Family." Also use repetition of words in the two ways described in question 3 under Reading Literature: Short Stories. Make sure that your tone is light. In other words, your reader should not take your characters and their actions seriously.

Developing Skills in Speaking and Listening

Interpreting a Short Story. With a group, read "The Huckabuck Family" aloud. Three members of the group should take the parts of Jonas Jonas, Mama Mama, and Pony Pony. Everyone else in the group should take turns reading the narrator's words. Let your listeners hear the alliteration, repetition, and rhythm in this story.

Great Modern Stories

Some of the stories in the first part of this chapter took you far into the past. One story in this part will take you far into the future. There is no limit to the time in which a story can be set.

In the same way, there is no limit to the problems that a story can consider. As you read the selections in "Great Modern Stories," notice how the characters face their problems—and sometimes solve them.

The City from Greenwich Village, 1922, JOHN SLOAN. National Gallery of Art, Washington, D.C.; Gift of Helen Farr Sloan 1970.

More About the Elements of a Short Story

You know that in a short story three important elements are its setting, characters, and plot. You know, also, that the plot tells how the characters react to a problem, called the conflict.

Conflict. The struggle or clash between opposing forces is called **conflict**. It can be either external or internal.

External conflict is a struggle between a character and outside forces. For example, one character may oppose another character, as in "How the Camel Got His Hump." Sometimes a character must struggle with nature, fighting against a force such as a blizzard or a flood. In each case, only one force can win.

Internal conflict is a struggle within a character. Maybe the character can't decide what to do next. Perhaps the character must fight himself or herself to do the right thing. Sometimes the conflict is a struggle between a character and his or her own feelings. Internal conflict would be shown, for example, in a story about a student tempted to cheat on a test.

As you read a short story, you will be looking for information about the setting, characters, conflict, and plot. Also, keep these questions in mind: What idea is the story about? How do I feel reading the story? How much information am I being told?

Theme. Think about "The Necklace" again. Madame Loisel could have led a happy life if she had not desired impossible riches. You could say that the whole story is about the importance of valuing what you have or the foolishness of wanting things you can never have. These are examples of theme.

The **theme** of a short story is the main idea about life that the writer shares with the reader. Every story has a theme. However, you won't find any sentence in the story that says "The theme of this story is. . . ." You need to think about the whole story, the characters, and the plot to decide on the theme. The same story may have more than one theme, as "The Necklace" does.

Mood. One of the greatest American short story writers was Edgar Allan Poe. He once said that during the time a person is reading, the writer has control over him or her. A story can make you feel hopeful, nervous, thoughtful, or terrified. The feeling the writer creates in you is called the **mood** of the story.

Writers create the mood of a story by careful choice of words. They know that certain words make you feel certain emotions. Let's look at "Appointment in Baghdad." Notice the words that suggest fright: *suddenly, flew, rushed, wild, excitement, alarmed, cried.* For contrast, look at "How the Camel Got His Hump." You will find none of those words in this easy-going tale. Instead, notice the words that suggest calmness: *just beginning, most 'scruciating idle, presently, so new-and-all.* The first story has an anxious mood; the mood of the second is relaxed.

Point of View. In Chapter 2, you learned that the narrator is the person who is telling the story. The writer chooses a narrator for every story. The narrator can tell the story from either the first-person or the third-person point of view.

In the **first-person** point of view, the narrator uses the pronouns *I* and *we.* The narrator can be either the writer or a character in the story. The reader learns only as much as the narrator can see or hear about characters or events.

A story written in the **third person** is told by an outsider who is not part of the story. Characters are referred to as *he* or *she.* There are two types of third-person point of view.

A story may be written from the **omniscient**, or all-knowing, third-person point of view. In this case, the narrator knows everything that happens, including what characters are thinking. "The Emperor's New Clothes" is an example of this type.

In a story written from a **limited** third-person point of view, the narrator tells only what one character sees and thinks. The first story in this section, "The Dinner Party," is an example.

The Dinner Party

MONA GARDNER

An uninvited guest shows up at this dinner party. As you read the story, think about how you might have reacted if you had been at the party.

The country is India. A colonial official and his wife are giving a large dinner party. They are seated with their guests—army officers, and government attachés with their wives, and a visiting American naturalist—in their spacious dining room. It has a bare marble floor, open rafters, and wide glass doors opening onto a veranda.

A spirited discussion springs up between a young girl who insists that women have outgrown the jumping-on-a-chair-at-the-sight-of-a-mouse era and a colonel who says that they haven't.

"A woman's unfailing reaction in any crisis," the colonel says, "is to scream. And while a man may feel like it, he has that ounce more of nerve control than a woman has. And that last ounce more is what counts."

The American does not join in the argument but watches the other guests. As he looks, he sees a strange expression come over the face of the hostess. She is staring straight ahead, her muscles contracting slightly. With a slight gesture, she summons the native boy standing behind her chair and whispers to him. The boy's eyes widen, and he quickly leaves the room.

Of the guests, none except the American notices this or sees the boy place a bowl of milk on the veranda just outside the open doors.

The American comes to with a start. In India, milk in a bowl means only one thing—bait for a snake. He realizes there must be a cobra in the room. He looks up at the rafters—the likeliest place—but they are bare. Three corners of the room are empty, and in the fourth the servants are waiting to serve the next course. There is only one place left—under the table.

His first impulse is to jump back and warn the others, but he knows the commotion would frighten the cobra into striking. He speaks quickly, the tone of

his voice so arresting that it sobers everyone.

"I want to know just what control everyone at this table has. I will count to three hundred—that's five minutes— and not one of you is to move a muscle. Those who move will forfeit fifty rupees.[1] Ready!"

The twenty people sit like stone images while he counts. He is saying "two hundred and eighty" when, out of the corner of his eye, he sees the cobra emerge and make for the bowl of milk. Screams ring out as he jumps to slam the veranda doors safely shut.

"You were right, Colonel!" the host exclaims. "A man has just shown us an example of perfect control."

"Just a minute," the American says, turning to his hostess. "Mrs. Wynnes, how did you know the cobra was in the room?"

A faint smile lights up the woman's face as she replies. "Because it was crawling across my foot."

---

1. **rupee** (rō͞o pē′, rō͞o′pē), the unit of money of Asian countries such as India, Pakistan, and Sri Lanka.

Developing Comprehension Skills

1. What is the setting of this story? How are these parts of the setting important to the story?

   a. The country in which it is set

   b. The room in which the action takes place

2. At the dinner party, about what do the young girl and colonel disagree?

3. What event lets the American know there is a cobra in the room? What effect does that knowledge have on his words and actions?

4. What characteristics does Mrs. Wynnes have, as shown by her actions? How do her actions settle the argument between the guests?

5. Think up another title for this story. Choose a title that suggests the theme, or statement the story makes.

6. The story tries to build a mood of suspense from the first sentence until the point at which the American slams the veranda doors. Does it succeed? Did you feel tense as you read it? If so, can you identify some sentences that helped to build the mood?

Reading Literature: Short Stories

1. **Making a Plot Diagram.** Diagram the plot of this story. Identify the events that belong in each of the parts of the following diagram.

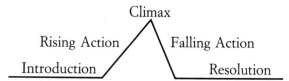

2. **Appreciating Point of View.** The events of this story are told in the third person as they are seen by one character in the story. This is called **limited** third-person point of view. How does the point of view in "The Dinner Party" help to build the suspense in the story?

3. **Recognizing Conflict.** In "The Dinner Party," several conflicts develop at the same time. One external conflict is between the cobra and the people, especially Mrs. Wynnes and the American. One internal conflict is within the American. Part of him wishes to jump up and get away, while another part insists that he remain calm. Can you name another external conflict in the story? Another internal conflict?

Developing Vocabulary Skills

1. **Making Use of Context Clues.** Read these two sentence groups, and look for context clues that give the meaning of certain words. Then answer the questions following the sentences.

    (1) He knows the commotion, or disturbance, would frighten the cobra into striking.

    (2) Those who move will forfeit—give up—fifty rupees. A rupee is a unit of money used in India.

    a. What type of context clue is provided in each sentence? What clue words and punctuation are used for each of these context clues?

    b. What is a synonym for *commotion*?

    c. If a rupee is worth 6¢, how much would a person who moved have to *forfeit*?

2. **Making Use of the Dictionary and Glossary.** Use your dictionary or glossary to answer the following questions about words from the story. Be sure you know the meaning of each word.

    a. In the second paragraph, what does the word *era* mean? How many syllables does the word have?

    b. What does a *naturalist* do? What base word gives a clue to the meaning of the word?

    c. How is the word *colonel* pronounced?

    d. How many syllables are in the word *reaction*? Which syllable is accented?

    e. The word *contract* is a homograph. Remember that a homograph is a word with the same spelling as another but with a different meaning. It comes from a different source and often has a different pronunciation. Write the two ways the word *contract* can be respelled. Which word best fits the context of the sentence in the fourth paragraph of the story? What does the word mean?

    f. Is the *a* in *native* pronounced like the *a* in *age* or the *a* in *clap*?

    g. Write a word that begins with the same sound as the *g* in *gesture*.

    h. What is a synonym for the word *summons* as it is used in the fourth paragraph of the story?

    i. Which word in the first paragraph is pronounced this way— kə lō′nē əl?

Developing Writing Skills

1. **Presenting an Argument.** In the story, the American naturalist and Mrs. Wynnes present a strong argument that proves the colonel wrong. Think about a person with whom you strongly disagree on a particular subject. Write a paragraph to persuade the person to change his or her opinion. In your paragraph, be sure to state your opinion clearly and give specific examples or reasons to back up your decision.

2. **Describing a Personal Experience.** Think of a time when you had to "keep your cool." If you can't think of a personal experience, write about someone you have observed or make up such an experience.

Developing Skills in Speaking and Listening

Taking Part in a Debate. In a **debate**, two or more groups take sides and argue on an issue or problem where there is a lot of disagreement. This type of arguing is more controlled than most, however. First, one group gives its opinion. Second, the other group presents its view on the issue. The first group is then allowed to refute, or give reasons against, the argument of the second group. After that, the second group can give its reasons against the first group's argument. Last, a judge who has listened to the entire debate decides whose statements and reasons were stronger.

Work with a group or your whole class to hold a debate on the issue discussed in "The Dinner Party." One subgroup should be composed of those who think that a woman is less able than a man to handle a crisis. Another subgroup would be made up of those who think that a woman is as good as, or better than, a man at handling a crisis. Those who cannot decide on the issue can act as judges of the debate.

Many Moons

JAMES THURBER

"Many Moons" may seem much like a fairy tale. But don't be fooled! Watch for parts of the story that are taken from fairy tales. Then see what the author adds or changes to make something quite different — and funny.

Once upon a time, in a kingdom by the sea, there lived a little Princess named Lenore. She was ten years old, going on eleven. One day Lenore fell ill of a surfeit of raspberry tarts and took to her bed.

The Royal Physician came to see her and took her temperature and felt her pulse and made her stick out her tongue. The Royal Physician was worried. He sent for the King, Lenore's father, and the King came to see her.

"I will get you anything your heart desires," the King said. "Is there anything your heart desires?"

"Yes," said the Princess. "I want the moon. If I can have the moon, I will be well again."

Now the King had a great many wise men who always got for him anything he wanted, so he told his daughter that she could have the moon. Then he went to the throne room and pulled a bell cord, three long pulls and a short pull, and presently the Lord High Chamberlain came into the room.

The Lord High Chamberlain was a large, fat man who wore thick glasses which made his eyes seem twice as big as they really were. This made the Lord High Chamberlain seem twice as wise as he really was.

"I want you to get the moon," said the King. "The Princess Lenore wants the moon. If she can have the moon, she will get well again."

"The moon?" exclaimed the Lord High Chamberlain, his eyes widening. This made him look four times as wise as he really was.

"Yes, the moon," said the King. "M-o-o-n, moon. Get it tonight, tomorrow at the latest."

The Lord High Chamberlain wiped his forehead with a handkerchief and then blew his nose loudly. "I have got a great many things for you in my time, your Majesty," he said. "It just happens that I have with me a list of the things I have got for you in my time." He pulled a long scroll of parchment out of his pocket. "Let me see, now." He glanced at the list, frowning. "I have got ivory, apes, and peacocks, rubies, opals, and emeralds, black orchids, pink elephants, and blue poodles, gold bugs, scarabs, and flies in amber, hummingbirds' tongues, angels' feathers, and unicorns' horns, giants, midgets, and mermaids, frankincense, ambergris, and myrrh, troubadours, minstrels, and dancing women, a pound of butter, two dozen eggs, and a sack of sugar—sorry, my wife wrote that in there."

"I don't remember any blue poodles," said the King.

"It says blue poodles right here on the list, and they are checked off with a little check mark," said the Lord High Chamberlain. "So there must have been blue poodles. You just forget."

"Never mind the blue poodles," said the King. "What I want now is the moon."

"I have sent as far as Samarkand and Araby and Zanzibar to get things for you, your Majesty," said the Lord High Chamberlain. "But the moon is out of the question. It is thirty-five thousand miles away and it is bigger than the room the Princess lies in. Furthermore, it is made of molten copper. I cannot get the moon for you. Blue poodles, yes; the moon, no."

The King flew into a rage and told the Lord High Chamberlain to leave the room and to send the Royal Wizard to the throne room.

The Royal Wizard was a little, thin man with a long face. He wore a high red peaked hat covered with silver stars, and a long blue robe covered with golden owls. His face grew very pale when the King told him that he wanted the moon for his little daughter and that he expected the Royal Wizard to get it.

"I have worked a great deal of magic for you in my time, your Majesty," said the Royal Wizard. "As a matter of fact, I just happen to have in my pocket a list of the wizardries I have performed for you." He drew a paper from a deep pocket of his robe. "It begins: 'Dear Royal Wizard: I am returning herewith the so-called philosopher's stone which you claimed'— no, that isn't it." The Royal Wizard brought a long scroll of parchment from another pocket of his robe. "Here it is," he said. "Now, let's see. I have squeezed blood out of turnips for you, and turnips out of blood. I have produced rabbits out of silk hats, and silk hats out of rabbits. I have conjured up flowers, tambourines, and doves out of nowhere, and nowhere out of flowers, tambourines, and doves. I have brought you divining rods, magic wands, and crystal spheres in which to behold the future. I have compounded philters, unguents, and potions to cure heartbreak, surfeit, and ringing in the ears. I have made you my own special mixture of wolfbane, nightshade, and

eagles' tears to ward off witches, de-
mons, and things that go bump in the
night. I have given you seven-league
boots, the golden touch, and a cloak of invisibility—"

"It didn't work," said the King. "The
cloak of invisibility didn't work."

"Yes, it did," said the Royal Wizard.

"No, it didn't," said the King. "I kept
bumping into things, the same as ever."

"The cloak is supposed to make you
invisible," said the Royal Wizard. "It is
not supposed to keep you from bumping
into things."

"All I know is, I kept bumping into things," said the King.

The Royal Wizard looked at his list again. "I got you," he said, "horns from Elfland, sand from the Sandman, and gold from the rainbow. Also a spool of thread, a paper of needles, and a lump of beeswax—sorry, those are things my wife wrote down for me to get her."

"What I want you to do now," said the King, "is to get me the moon. The Princess Lenore wants the moon, and when she gets it, she will be well again."

"Nobody can get the moon," said the Royal Wizard. "It is a hundred and fifty thousand miles away, and it is made of green cheese, and it is twice as big as this palace."

The King flew into another rage and sent the Royal Wizard back to his cave. Then he rang a gong and summoned the Royal Mathematician.

The Royal Mathematician was a bald-headed, nearsighted man with a skullcap on his head and a pencil behind each ear. He wore a black suit with white numbers on it.

"I don't want to hear a long list of all the things you have figured out for me since 1907," the King said to him. "I want you to figure out right now how to get the moon for the Princess Lenore. When she gets the moon, she will be well again."

"I am glad you mentioned all the things I have figured out for you since 1907," said the Royal Mathematician. "It so hap-pens that I have a list of them with me."

He pulled a long scroll of parchment out of a pocket and looked at it. "Now let me see. I have figured out for you the distance between the horns of a dilemma, night and day, and A and Z. I have computed how far is *Up*, how long it takes to get to *Away*, and what becomes of *Gone*. I have discovered the length of the sea serpent, the price of the priceless, and the square of the hippopotamus. I know where you are when you are at *Sixes* and *Sevens*, how much *Is* you have to have to make an *Are*, and how many birds you can catch with the salt in the ocean— 187,796,132, if it would interest you to know."

"There aren't that many birds," said the King.

"I didn't say there were," said the Royal Mathematician. "I said if there were."

"I don't want to hear about seven hundred million imaginary birds," said the King. "I want you to get the moon for the Princess Lenore."

"The moon is three hundred thousand miles away," said the Royal Mathematician. "It is round and flat like a coin, only it is made of asbestos, and it is half the size of this kingdom. Furthermore, it is pasted on the sky. Nobody can get the moon."

The King flew into still another rage and sent the Royal Mathematician away. Then he rang for the Court Jester. The

Jester came bounding into the throne room in his motley and his cap and bells, and sat at the foot of the throne.

"What can I do for you, your Majesty?" asked the Court Jester.

"Nobody can do anything for me," said the King mournfully. "The Princess Lenore wants the moon, and she cannot be well till she gets it, but nobody can get it for her. Every time I ask anybody for the moon, it gets larger and farther away. There is nothing you can do for me except play on your lute. Something sad."

"How big do they say the moon is," asked the Court Jester, "and how far away?"

"The Lord High Chamberlain says it is thirty-five thousand miles away and bigger than the Princess Lenore's room," said the King. "The Royal Wizard says it is a hundred and fifty thousand miles away and twice as big as this palace. The Royal Mathematician says it is three hundred thousand miles away and half the size of this kingdom."

The Court Jester strummed on his lute for a little while. "They are all wise men," he said, "and so they must all be right. If they are all right, then the moon must be just as large and as far away as each person thinks it is. The thing to do is find out how big the Princess Lenore thinks it is, and how far away."

"I never thought of that," said the King.

"I will go and ask her, your Majesty,"
said the Court Jester. And he crept softly into the little girl's room.

The Princess Lenore was awake, and she was glad to see the Court Jester, but her face was very pale and her voice very weak.

"Have you brought the moon to me?" she asked.

"Not yet," said the Court Jester, "but I will get it for you right away. How big do you think it is?"

"It is just a little smaller than my thumbnail," she said, "for when I hold my thumbnail up at the moon, it just covers it."

"And how far away is it?" asked the Court Jester.

"It is not as high as the big tree outside my window," said the Princess, "for sometimes it gets caught in the top branches."

"It will be very easy to get the moon for you," said the Court Jester. "I will climb the tree tonight when it gets caught in the top branches and bring it to you."

Then he thought of something else. "What is the moon made of, Princess?" he asked.

"Oh," she said, "it's made of gold, of course, silly."

The Court Jester left the Princess Lenore's room and went to see the Royal Goldsmith. He had the Royal Goldsmith make a tiny round golden moon, just a little smaller than the thumbnail of the Princess Lenore. Then he had him string

it on a golden chain so the Princess could wear it around her neck.

"What is this thing I have made?" asked the Royal Goldsmith when he had finished it.

"You have made the moon," said the Court Jester. "That is the moon."

"But the moon," said the Royal Goldsmith, "is five hundred thousand miles away and is made of bronze and is round like a marble."

"That's what you think," said the Court Jester as he went away with the moon.

The Court Jester took the moon to the Princess Lenore, and she was overjoyed. The next day she was well again and could get up and go out in the gardens to play.

But the King's worries were not yet over. He knew that the moon would shine in the sky again that night, and he did not want the Princess Lenore to see it. If she did, she would know that the moon she wore on a chain around her neck was not the real moon.

So the King sent for the Lord High Chamberlain and said: "We must keep the Princess Lenore from seeing the moon when it shines in the sky tonight. Think of something."

The Lord High Chamberlain tapped his forehead with his fingers thoughtfully and said: "I know just the thing. We can make some dark glasses for the Princess Lenore. We can make them so dark that she will not be able to see anything at all through them. Then she will not be able to see the moon when it shines in the sky."

This made the King very angry, and he shook his head from side to side. "If she wore dark glasses, she would bump into things," he said, "and then she would be ill again." So he sent the Lord High Chamberlain away and called the Royal Wizard.

"We must hide the moon," said the King, "so that the Princess Lenore will not see it when it shines in the sky tonight. How are we going to do that?"

The Royal Wizard stood on his hands and then he stood on his head and then he stood on his feet again. "I know what we can do," he said. "We can stretch some black velvet curtains on poles. The curtains will cover all the palace gardens like a circus tent, and the Princess Lenore will

not be able to see through them, so she will not see the moon in the sky."

The King was so angry at this that he waved his arms around. "Black velvet curtains would keep out the air," he said. "The Princess Lenore would not be able to breathe, and she would be ill again." So he sent the Royal Wizard away and summoned the Royal Mathematician.

"We must do something," said the King, "so that the Princess Lenore will not see the moon when it shines in the sky tonight. If you know so much, figure out a way to do that."

The Royal Mathematician walked around in a circle, and then he walked around in a square, and then he stood still. "I have it!" he said. "We can set off fireworks in the gardens every night. We will make a lot of silver fountains and golden cascades, and when they go off they will fill the sky with so many sparks that it will be as light as day and the Princess Lenore will not be able to see the moon."

The King flew into such a rage that he began jumping up and down. "Fireworks would keep the Princess Lenore awake," he said. "She would not get any sleep at all and she would be ill again." So the King sent the Royal Mathematician away.

When he looked up again, it was dark outside and he saw the bright rim of the moon just peeping over the horizon. He jumped up in a great fright and rang for the Court Jester. The Court Jester came bounding into the room and sat down at the foot of the throne.

"What can I do for you, your Majesty?" he asked.

"Nobody can do anything for me," said the King mournfully. "The moon is coming up again. It will shine into the Princess Lenore's bedroom, and she will know it is still in the sky and that she does not wear it on a golden chain around her neck. Play me something on your lute, something very sad, for when the Princess sees the moon, she will be ill again."

The Court Jester strummed on his lute. "What do your wise men say?" he asked.

"They can think of no way to hide the moon that will not make the Princess Lenore ill," said the King.

The Court Jester played another song, very softly.

"The wise men know everything," he said, "and if they cannot hide the moon, then it cannot be hidden."

The King put his head in his hands again and sighed. Suddenly he jumped up from his throne and pointed to the windows. "Look!" he cried. "The moon is already shining into the Princess Lenore's bedroom. Who can explain how the moon can be shining in the sky when it is hanging on a golden chain around her neck?"

The Court Jester stopped playing on his lute. "Who could explain how to get the moon when your wise men said it was too large and too far away? It was the Princess Lenore. Therefore, the Princess Lenore is wiser than your wise men and knows more about the moon than they do. So I will ask *her*." And before the King could stop him, the Court Jester slipped quietly out of the throne room and up the wide marble staircase to the Princess Lenore's bedroom.

The Princess was lying in the bed but she was wide awake and she was looking out the window at the moon shining in the sky. Shining in her hand was the moon the Court Jester had got for her. He looked very sad, and there seemed to be tears in his eyes.

"Tell me, Princess Lenore," he said mournfully, "how can the moon be shining in the sky when it is hanging on a golden chain around your neck?"

The Princess looked at him and laughed. "That is easy, silly," she said. "When I lose a tooth, a new one grows in its place, doesn't it?"

"Of course," said the Court Jester. "And when the unicorn loses his horn in the forest, a new one grows in the middle of his forehead."

"That is right," said the Princess. "And when the Royal Gardner cuts the flowers in the garden, other flowers come to take their place."

"I should have thought of that," said the Court Jester, "for it is the same way with the daylight."

"And it is the same way with the moon," said the Princess Lenore. "I guess it is the same way with everything." Her voice became very low and faded away, and the Court Jester saw that she was asleep. Gently he tucked the covers in around the sleeping Princess.

But before he left the room, he went over to the window and winked at the moon, for it seemed to the Court Jester that the moon had winked at him.

Developing Comprehension Skills

1. Why did the King ask the wise men to get the moon?

2. What did the Lord High Chamberlain, the Royal Wizard, and the Royal Mathematician have in common? How were they all alike?

3. Which of these events do you think is the climax of "Many Moons"? Give reasons for your choice.

    a. The Jester gives the golden moon on a chain to Princess Lenore.
    b. The Jester asks Lenore how the moon can be both in the sky and on a chain at the same time.
    c. Lenore gives an explanation.

4. Why do you think that Thurber has the Court Jester solve the problem rather than the wise men?

5. The title of a story should relate to the meaning of the story and help to make it clear. Is "Many Moons" a good title for this story? Tell why or why not.

Reading Literature: Short Stories

1. **Identifying Parody.** In Chapter 1, you read two versions of "The Fox and the Crow." The second version, by James Thurber, made both the fox and the crow funnier. It was a parody of the first version. A **parody** is a funny imitation of something serious.

    In "Many Moons," Thurber has written another parody. This time he has parodied or imitated a whole group of stories—fairy tales. Here is a list of facts about fairy tales. Discuss how Thurber makes fun of each fact in this story.

    a. Things usually come in threes, such as three daughters, as in "Cinderella"; three wishes, as in "The Magic Fish"; and three tasks or chances, as in "Rumplestiltskin."
    b. The characters are often grand kings and queens or romantic princes and princesses.
    c. Often there are powerful witches or wizards, and dangerous magic.
    d. There is usually some impossible challenge that the hero or heroine must conquer.

Besides these, can you find other facts about fairy tales that Thurber has parodied in "Many Moons"?

2. **Enjoying Repetition.** This story was written to give the reader some fun. One way Thurber lets you know that is by playing with words. Repetition is one way of playing with words. For example, the King repeats himself:

> "I will get you anything your heart desires," the King said. "Is there anything your heart desires?"

The narrator repeats himself:

> The Lord High Chamberlain was a large, fat man who wore thick glasses which made his eyes seem twice as big as they really were. This made the Lord High Chamberlain seem twice as wise as he really was.

The characters repeat the actions of other characters. For example, each advisor reads a list of things he has done for the King. Two of the advisors accidentally read their wives' lists as well.

How many other examples of repetition can you find in the story? Do any of your examples show something getting bigger or sillier as it is repeated?

3. **Appreciating Humor.** Besides repetition, Thurber uses other ways of playing with words. One way is using important-sounding words to make unimportant statements. For example, in the first paragraph, the narrator says Lenore "fell ill of a surfeit" of tarts. He means she ate too much and got a stomach ache. Also, each of the advisors reads a long list of great things he has done for the King. However, none of these things makes much sense. Nothing in any list has anything to do with what the King wants. Why does each advisor read the list? What does he mean to tell the King by reading it?

4. **Identifying Theme.** The theme of a story, as you know, is the statement the writer is making about life. Review your answer to question 4 under Developing Comprehension Skills. Then state what you think is the theme of "Many Moons."

5. **Identifying Mood.** The mood of a story is the feeling the reader gets while reading it. What do you think is the mood of "Many Moons"?

Using Other Context Clues. You have learned how to use definition and restatement clues to get meanings from contexts. There are also several other types of context clues.

An **antonym**, or word with the opposite meaning, may be given in the same sentence as the new word. Sometimes it is in a nearby sentence. Look for a word or phrase in a neighboring sentence that is in the same position as the unfamiliar word.

The metal was *not solid* after the fire. It was *molten.*

In this example, both the word *molten* and the phrase *not solid* appear after the verb *was*. This clue lets you know that *molten* means the opposite of *solid.*

In other sentences, context clues may be picked up from different parts of the sentence. An unfamiliar word that is the subject of a sentence, for example, may be explained by the predicate.

The unicorn dipped its single, long horn into the pool.

From this sentence you can guess that a unicorn is an animal with one horn.

What you know of prefixes and suffixes can lead you to context clues. For example, in this sentence, how does the suffix *-er* help you to figure out the meaning of *jester?*

If you want good jokes at your court, hire a good jester.

The *-er* ending tells you that a *jester* is someone who does something. From the sentence, you might suppose that what he or she does is tell jokes or play jokes on others.

Read each sentence below and look for any of these types of context clues. Figure out a likely meaning for the underlined word. On your paper write the word and a possible meaning.

1. "I don't want to hear about seven hundred million <u>imaginary</u> birds," said the King. "I just want a solution to the real <u>problem.</u>"

2. "If you don't want to be seen, wear this cloak of <u>invisibility,</u>" said the Royal Wizard.

3. The <u>conjurer</u> used his powers of magic to produce rabbits out of silk hats, and flowers and doves out of nowhere.

4. The king was full of sorrow as he <u>mournfully</u> put his head in his hands.

5. The sparkling <u>cascades</u> of fireworks will remind the princess of real waterfalls.

6. When Princess Lenore ate too many of the raspberry tarts, she became ill from the <u>surfeit</u> of desserts.

Developing Writing Skills

1. **Comparing Stories.** How does the court in "Many Moons" compare with the court in "The Emperor's New Clothes"? What is similar about the wise men in the two stories? If the Emperor had had a Court Jester, might his story have turned out differently? Write from one to five paragraphs comparing "Many Moons" and "The Emperor's New Clothes."

2. **Writing an Original Parody.** Write your own parody of a fairy tale. Keep in mind the four facts about fairy tales listed in question 1 under Reading Literature: Short Stories. Make fun of each fact through the characters and events in your story. The story should end quickly after the climax, when the hero or heroine conquers the challenge.

Developing Skills in Speaking and Listening

Acting Out a Dialog. In "Many Moons," there are many scenes in which two people talk together. Such a scene is called a **dialog**.

Work this activity with a partner. Choose one of the scenes listed below. Each partner should practice saying the words of one of the characters. He or she should speak and move as the text tells or suggests. Present your dialog to a group.

1. The King with the Lord High Chamberlain (page 189)

2. The King with the Royal Wizard (page 190)

3. The King with the Royal Mathematician (page 192)

4. The King with the Court Jester—first discussion (page 193)

5. The King with the Court Jester—second discussion (page 196)

6. The Court Jester with Princess Lenore—both discussions (pages 193 and 196)

Keplik, the Match Man

MYRON LEVOY

Some people seem to be just naturally satisfied with their lives. Keplik is one of these people. However, is there a limit to the patience even of these people? What does this story suggest?

There once was a little old man who lived in a big old tenement on Second Avenue. His name was Mr. Keplik and he had once been a watchmaker. In the window of his tiny watch-repair shop he had put up a sign that read:

> When Your Wrist Watch
>   Won't Tick,
> It's Time for Keplik.

Keplik loved watches and clocks and had loved repairing them. If a clock he was repairing stopped ticking, he would say to himself, "Eh, eh, eh, it's dying." When it started ticking again he would say, "I am *gebentsht*. I am blessed. It's alive."

Whenever an elevated train rumbled by overhead, Keplik would have to put down his delicate work, for his workbench and the entire shop would shake and vibrate. But Keplik would close his eyes and say, "Never mind. There are worse things. How many people back in Lithuania wouldn't give their right eye to have a watch-repair shop under an el train in America."

While he worked Keplik never felt lonely, for there were always customers coming in with clocks and watches and complaints.

"My watch was supposed to be ready last week," a customer would say. "I need my watch! Will you have it ready by tonight, Keplik?"

Keplik would answer, "Maybe yes, maybe no. It depends on how many el trains pass by during the rush hour," and he would point his finger up toward the el structure above.

But when Keplik grew very old, he had to give up watch repairing, for he could no longer climb up and down the three flights of stairs to his apartment. He became very lonely, for there were no longer any customers to visit him and complain. His hands felt empty and useless for there were no longer any gears or pivots or hair-springs or mainsprings to repair. "Terrible," said Keplik, to himself. "I'm too young to be old. I will take up a hobby. Perhaps I should build a clock out of walnut shells. Or perhaps I should make a windmill out of wooden matchsticks. I'll see what I have in the house."

There were no walnuts, but there were lots and lots of burned matchsticks, for, in those days, the gas stoves had to be lit with a match every time you wanted a scrambled egg or a cup of hot cocoa. So Keplik started to build a little windmill out of matches.

Within a month's time, the windmill was finished. Keplik put it on his kitchen table and started to blow like the east wind. The arms turned slowly, then faster, just like a real windmill. "I'm *gebentsht*," said Keplik. "It's alive."

Next, Keplik decided to make a castle, complete with a drawbridge. But the matches were expensive; he would need hundreds and hundreds for a castle. So he put a little sign outside his apartment door, and another in his window:

Used Matchsticks Bought Here,
A Penny for Fifty,
If You Have a Matchstick,
Sell It to Keplik.

The word spread up and down the block very quickly, and soon there were children at Keplik's door with bags and boxes of used matches. Keplik showed them the windmill on the kitchen table and invited them to blow like the east wind. Keplik was happy, because he had visitors again and work for his hands.

Day after day, week after week, Keplik glued and fitted the matches together. Finally the castle stood completed, with red and blue flags flying from every turret. The children brought toy soldiers and laid siege to the castle, while Keplik pulled up the drawbridge.

Next, Keplik made a big birdcage out of matches and put a real canary in it. The bird sang and flew back and forth while the delicate cage swung on its hook. "Ah ha," said Keplik. "The cage is alive. And so is the canary. I am double *gebentsht*."

Then he made little airplanes and jewelry boxes from matchsticks and gave them to the boys and girls who visited him. The children began calling him "the Match Man."

One day, Keplik decided that it was time for a masterpiece. "I am at my heights as an artist," Keplik said to himself. "No more windmills. No more birdcages. I am going to make the Woolworth Building. Or the Eiffel Tower. Or the Brooklyn Bridge. Eh . . . eh . . . but which?"

After much thought, he decided that a bridge would be better than a tower or a skyscraper, because if he built a bridge he wouldn't have to cut a hole in the ceiling. The Brooklyn Bridge would be his masterpiece. It would run across the living room from the kitchen to the bedroom, and the two towers would stand as high as his head. "For this I need matches!" Keplik said aloud. "Matches! I must have matches."

He posted a new sign:

Match for Match,
You Cannot Match
Keplik's Price for Used Matches.
One Cent for Fifty.
Hurry! Hurry! Hurry!

Vincent DeMarco, who lived around the corner, brought fifty matches that very afternoon, and Cathy Dunn and Noreen Callahan brought a hundred matches each the next morning. Day after day, the matches kept coming, and, day after day, Keplik the Match Man glued and fixed and bent and pressed the matches into place.

The bridge was so complicated that Keplik had decided to build it in separate sections, and then join all the sections afterward. The bridge's support towers, the end spans, and the center span slowly took shape in different parts of the room. The room seemed to grow smaller as the bridge grew larger. A masterpiece, thought Keplik. There is no longer room for me to sit in my favorite chair. But I must have more matches! It's time to build the cables!

Even the long support cables were made from matchsticks, split and glued

The Bridge, 1920–22, JOSEPH STELLA.
The Newark Museum, Newark, New Jersey.

and twisted together. Keplik would twist the sticks until his fingers grew numb. Then he would go into the kitchen to make a cup of coffee for himself, not so much for the coffee, but for the fact that lighting the stove would provide him with yet another matchstick. Sometimes, as he was drinking his coffee, he would get up and take a quick look at his bridge, because it always looked different when he was away from it for awhile. "It's beginning to be alive," he would say.

Then one night, it was time for the great final step. The towers and spans and cables all had to be joined together to make the finished structure. A most difficult job, for everything was supported from the cables above, as in a real bridge, and all the final connections had to be glued and tied almost at the same moment. Nothing must shift or slip for a full half hour, until the glue dried thoroughly.

Keplik worked carefully, his watchmaker's hands steadily gluing and pressing strut after strut, cable after cable. The end spans were in place. The center span was ready. Glue, press, glue, press. Then suddenly, an el train rumbled by outside. The ground trembled, the old tenement shivered as it always did, the windows rattled slightly, and the center span slid from its glued moorings. Then one of the end cables vibrated loose, then another, and the bridge slipped slowly apart into separate spans and towers. "Eh, eh, eh," said Keplik. "It's dying."

Keplik tried again, but another train hurtled past from the other direction. Again the bridge slowly slipped apart. I am too tired, thought Keplik. I'll try again tomorrow.

Keplik decided to wait until late the next night, when there would be fewer trains. But again, as the bridge was almost completed, a train roared past, the house shook, and everything slipped apart. Again and again, Keplik tried, using extra supports and tying parts together. But the bridge seemed to enjoy waiting for the next train to shake it apart again.

Ah me, thought Keplik. All my life those el trains shook the watches in my hands, down below in my shop. All my life I said things could be worse; how many people back in Lithuania wouldn't give their left foot to have a watch-repair shop under an el train in America.

But why do the el trains have to follow me three flights up? Why can't they leave me alone in my old age? When I die, will there be an el train over my grave? Will I be shaken and rattled around while I'm trying to take a little, well-deserved snooze? When I reach heaven, will there be an el train there, too, so I can't even play a nice, soothing tune on a harp without all this *tummel*, this noise? It's much too much for me. This is it. The end. The bridge will be a masterpiece in parts. The Brooklyn Bridge after an earthquake.

At that moment, another el train roared by and Keplik the Match Man called toward the train, "One thing I'll never do! I'll never make an el train out of matches! Never! How do you like that!"

When the children came the next afternoon, to see if the bridge was finished at last, Keplik told them of his troubles with the el trains. "The bridge, my children, is *farpotshket*. You know what that means? A mess!"

The children made all sorts of suggestions: hold it this way, fix it that way, glue it here, tie it there. But to all of them, Keplik the Match Man shook his head. "Impossible. I've tried that. Nothing works."

Then Vincent DeMarco said, "My father works on an el station uptown. He knows all the motormen, he says. Maybe he can get them to stop the trains."

Keplik laughed. "Ah, such a nice idea. But not even God can stop the Second Avenue el."

"I'll bet my father can," said Vincent.

"Bet he can't," said Joey Basuto. And just then, a train sped by: raketa, raketa, raketa, raketa, raketa. "The trains never stop for nothing," said Joey.

And the children went home for dinner, disappointed that the bridge made from all their matchsticks was *farpoot* . . . *farbot* . . . whatever that word was. A mess.

Vincent told his father, but Mr. DeMarco shrugged. "No. Impossible. Impossible," he said. "I'm not important enough."

"But couldn't you try?" Vincent pleaded with his father.

"I know one motorman. So what good's that, huh? One motorman. All I do is make change in the booth."

"Maybe he'll tell everybody else."

"Nonsense. They have more to worry about than Mr. Keplik's bridge. Eat your soup!"

Mr. DeMarco thought to himself that if he did happen to see his friend, the motorman, maybe, just for a laugh, he'd mention it . . .

Two days later, Vincent ran upstairs to Keplik's door and knocked. Tonight his father had said! Tonight at one A.M.! Keplik couldn't believe his ears. The trains would stop for his bridge? It couldn't be. Someone was playing a joke on Vincent's father.

That night, Keplik prepared, just in case it was true. Everything was ready: glue, thread, supports, towers, spans, cables.

A train clattered by at five minutes to one. Then silence. Rapidly, rapidly, Keplik worked. Press, glue, press, glue. One cable connected. Two cables. Three. Four. First tower finished. Fifth cable connected. Sixth. Seventh. Eighth. Other tower in place. Now gently, gently. Center span in position. Glue, press, glue, press. Tie threads. Tie more threads. Easy. Easy. Everything balanced. Everything supported. Now please. No trains till it dries.

The minutes ticked by. Keplik was sweating. Still no train. The bridge was holding. The bridge was finished. Then, outside the window, he saw an el train creeping along, slowly, carefully: cla . . . keta . . . cla . . . keta . . . cla . . . keta . . . cla

. . . keta . . . Then another, moving slowly from the other direction: cla . . . keta . . . cla . . . keta. . . .

Keplik shouted toward the trains, "Thank you, Mister Motorman! Tomorrow, I am going to start a great new masterpiece! The Second Avenue el from Fourteenth Street to Delancey Street! Thank you for slowing up your trains!"

First one motorman, then the other, blew his train whistle as the trains moved on, into the night beyond. "Ah, how I am *gebentsht*," said Keplik to himself. "In America there are kind people everywhere. All my life, the el train has shaken my hands. But tonight, it has shaken my heart."

Keplik worked for the rest of the night on a little project. The next morning, Keplik hung this sign made from matches outside his window, where every passing el train motorman could see it:

Developing Comprehension Skills

1. In the first six paragraphs of the story, the author tells much about Mr. Keplik. How does he tell the reader that Mr. Keplik feels that he has been blessed? What little stories are given to show how Mr. Keplik reacts to problems?

2. Why does Mr. Keplik start to make models out of matchsticks?

3. On page 205, why does Mr. Keplik call to the el train and say, "I'll never make an el train out of matches"?

4. At the end of the story, Mr. Keplik says that the el train has shaken his heart. What does he mean by that? How does he feel?

5. The setting and the characters of "Many Moons" were not realistic. That is, the author did not expect the reader to believe that a Royal Mathematician or Wizard ever lived in "a kingdom by the sea." Are the setting and characters of "Keplik, the Match Man" realistic? Could you imagine that Mr. Keplik actually lived in a New York apartment? Give reasons for your opinion.

Reading Literature: Short Stories

1. **Identifying Conflict.** The one problem Mr. Keplik cannot solve is the rumble of the el train. Identify two problems Mr. Keplik did solve satisfactorily.

2. **Suggesting Other Outcomes.** Imagine that the el train motormen had not been able to help Mr. Keplik. Can you think of any other way that he might have finished the assembly of the Brooklyn Bridge?

3. **Making Inferences.** What do you learn about Mr. Keplik's past life when he says, "How many people back in Lithuania wouldn't give their left foot to have a watch-repair shop under an el train in America?"

4. **Identifying Changes in Mood.** Reread the three paragraphs near the end of the story that begin with these sentences:

   That night, Keplik prepared, just in case it was true.
   A train clattered by at five minutes to one.
   The minutes ticked by.

   Do you get any special feeling reading the first paragraph? Do you get a special feeling reading the second? How is it different from the feeling you get reading the third paragraph?

   Compare the sentence lengths in these three paragraphs. How do the different sentence lengths express the different moods of the three paragraphs?

   Did the author do anything else unusual with the words in the second and third paragraphs? How do these unusual words or phrases stress the mood of their paragraph?

Developing Vocabulary Skills

1. **Defining Familiar Words Used in Unexpected Ways.** What does Keplik mean when he says that a watch he has worked on is alive? He says

that his windmill, the birdcage, and the bridge are alive, too. What does he mean in each of these cases?

2. **Understanding Foreign Words.** Three Yiddish words are used in the text. Each one has a context clue. Find the words in the text and write them on a piece of paper. Then find the meaning in the text.

3. **Understanding Words That Stand for Sounds.** What is the difference between an el train that is saying, "raketa, raketa, raketa" and one that is saying, "cla . . . keta . . . cla . . . keta . . . cla . . . keta. . ."?

Developing Writing Skills

1. **Retelling a Story.** Write a short version of this story, leaving out the less important events. Use your own words. Be sure to include every happening or fact that the reader must have to understand the story.

2. **Expressing a Mood.** Reread the paragraph near the end of the story beginning "A train clattered by at five minutes to one." Think of an occasion when you have tried to pull everything together on time— putting a big sandwich together, for instance, or trying to get all your books and pencils and homework together to go to school. Write about the occasion, showing haste and suspense and care. You may use the ways this paragraph did to express mood. (See question 4 under Reading Literature: Short Stories.)

Developing Skills in Study and Research

Making Use of Pictures. Sometimes you can understand a story better if you have a better idea of its setting. When the setting is a real place, such as New York, it is possible to find pictures to help you. You might find useful pictures in an encyclopedia, in a book about the places mentioned in the story, or in a library picture file.

In "Keplik, the Match Man," there are references to the el, the Woolworth Building, and the Brooklyn Bridge. These let you know that the city is New York. Can you find any pictures of the New York el, either in reference books or in a picture file in your library? What headings could you look for in a book index or the card catalog? Ask the librarian for help if necessary. Show the best of the pictures you find to your class. Be able to explain how you found them.

The Jar of Tassai (tə sī′)

GRACE P. MOON

Tassai is another happy person who loves the life she lives. As you read her story, find ways that Tassai's life on the mesa is different from Mr. Keplik's life next to the el train in New York City.

Tassai lived on the top of a mesa that looked far out over the Painted Desert. The air was clear as thin ice. It made even the farthest mountains and blue hills look nearer than they really were. Tassai was a Pueblo Indian girl, brown as a nut that has dried in the sun. She liked to lie on the edge of the mesa and look over the desert and dream long dreams.

But Tassai did not often have time for dreams. There was too much work for her to do. It was not hard work, and it had magic in it. It had the magic of watching green things spring up out of the ground where only brown earth had been before.

For Tassai worked with her mother in the little fields at the foot of the mesa.

Tassai brought water, too, from the spring at the foot of the mesa, carrying it up the steep trail in jars. For hours each day she ground the red and blue and yellow grains of corn. She cooked when her mother needed her help, and she knew where to find the grasses that her mother wove into baskets.

There was one thing Tassai did that no one knew about, for she did it only at times when no eyes were watching. She was making a jar from clay that she had found in a secret place, where the earth was smooth as honey to the touch and rich and dark in color. Not even her mother knew that Tassai was working at this jar. She had a very special reason for making it.

She shaped and smoothed it just as she had seen her mother do, until one day the most beautiful jar of all seemed to form itself in her hands. She could hardly believe her own eyes, it was so beautiful. And when she had added a design of little black lines and baked it a golden brown, she thought again that never had a jar been so lovely as this one. She wrapped it in a piece of blanket and hid it away carefully until the time should come for her to show it.

All through the hours when she worked in the fields, Tassai thought of her jar. In her thoughts a little song sang itself over and over again until her feet danced to the music of it:

> It is so beautiful,
> My big, round jar!
> So round and beautiful!
> Only the Moon,
> When it walks on the edge of
>   the world
> At harvest time
> Is like my jar.
> Round and smooth it is,
> And has a shine that sings!
> Maybe the Moon has come to me
> To be my jar!

Not long before Tassai had made her jar, the Governor of the Pueblo called the people of the town together in the little open place where meetings were held. He told them that the people of three towns were going to meet for a time of dancing and feasting. He asked that each man, woman, and child bring to the feast something he or she had made. This was because a great white man who had visited the Indian towns had said that the Indians could not make any good things. The white man had also said that, since this was so, the Indian children would have to go away to the white man's school to learn the white man's ways.

The Indians did not want their children to be sent away. They planned to show all the finest things that they could make so that the white man would change his mind. Prizes would be given for the best things brought to the feast.

There was much excitement at the governor's news and much talking and planning of what should be done. Tassai was excited from the first. She could hardly wait for the time to come.

The Big Day

The day itself was wonderful. There was a feel in the air that was different. Tassai felt that she could not walk or talk or even breathe as she did on other days. The open place in the town was bright with color. It was like a fair.

There were good smells and different sounds everywhere. There were baskets and pottery and woven things all spread

out for everyone to see. There were silver bracelets and rings and belts. There were bright blankets and things of leather and wood. There were great pumpkins and squashes and ears of corn that were bigger than any Tassai had ever seen before. There were beaded moccasins and sandals for the feet and nets for carrying things. There were fruits piled high in baskets and little cakes made of pine nuts and seeds. There was good food cooking.

Tassai was one of the very last to come into the open place on that big day. She had been busy since dawn, helping her mother make their home ready for strangers to see. When at last she was free, she picked up the blanket in which her jar was wrapped and ran to the open place. There she stood, holding tightly to her bundle.

The old Governor of the Pueblo, with two white men from the big white school, moved from place to place. They looked long and closely at each of the many things that had been brought. These three men were to say which were the best of all and to give the prizes.

A little white girl, daughter of one of the men, danced ahead of them as they walked. She looked at everything with bright, eager eyes. Her father looked at her proudly as often as he looked at the shining things the Indians had made.

When the men had seen everything else, Tassai came close with her bundle and touched the blanket with trembling fingers. She was frightened now. Perhaps they would not think her jar was beautiful. Others crowded close. They had not known that Tassai would have anything to show.

"Maybe it is not very good," she said in a voice that was so low no one heard her. "Maybe it—" Then her words would not come at all, for when she opened her bundle the beautiful jar was not there. She had not noticed that there were two bundles of blankets in the room of her home. The one she had picked up in her excitement held only an old corncob doll.

There was a big laugh from those who stood near. The words of Tassai, explaining her mistake, were lost. Quickly she pushed her way through the laughing crowd and ran home. She did not know that the little white girl, eager to see again that strange doll, was following close behind her.

The house of Tassai was the last one in the little town, on the very edge of the mesa top. She ran into the door and did not notice that the little white girl who had followed her had stopped suddenly just outside the doorway. The child was watching, with wide, frightened eyes, a snake that lifted its head from beside a big stone. It was a rattlesnake, and it moved its flat, ugly head closer and closer to the little girl. She gave one sharp cry as Tassai

came out of the door with the jar in her arms. Tassai had thrown aside the blanket and held the jar unwrapped in her arms.

There was no time to think. There was no time to call for help. Tassai did the only thing she could do. With all her strength she threw the jar at the snake. It broke into many pieces on the rock, and the snake lay flat and still.

The little girl did not make another sound. Her father, who had heard her first cry, came running. He held her tightly in his arms.

For the first moment Tassai thought only that the snake was dead. Then she thought of her jar. No one would call it beautiful now. She picked up a little broken piece. One of the white men took it from her hand.

"It must have been a mighty pretty jar," he said. "Did you make it?"

Tassai nodded her head.

The father of the little white girl looked at the piece of jar, too, and then at Tassai.

"That was a beautiful jar," he said slowly. His voice shook a little so that he

had to clear his throat. "I am sorry that we cannot give the prize for a broken jar— but—" He cleared his voice again. "For what you have done for me I will give you anything else you ask." He closed his arms more tightly around his little girl.

At first Tassai could not answer. In her surprise the words would not come. Then she said, "There is nothing I wish but to stay here in the pueblo. Could it be that we need not go far away to learn the ways of the white men?"

The man smiled. "You will not have to go away," he assured Tassai. "The white teachers are coming here to learn from the Indians instead. Today your people have shown what beautiful things they can make—like your jar. There will be a school here where the Indians and the white teachers will work together."

Tassai was very happy now. It did not matter that her jar was broken. She could make another, even more beautiful.

Developing Comprehension Skills

1. What kinds of work did Tassai do?

2. How old do you suppose Tassai was? What details in the story make you think that?

3. A major conflict in this story is the Indians' struggle to keep their children home. Why did the white man want to send the children away to a white school? Explain how the feast might end that threat.

4. The other important conflict in this story is Tassai's desire to win praise for her jar. Why did she keep the jar a secret?

5. Make a plot diagram for "The Jar of Tassai." Be careful when you decide which event is the climax. The event should be a turning point in both the Indian/white man conflict and Tassai's efforts to win a prize.

6. Three stories in this chapter have presented girls as characters: Pony Pony Huckabuck in "The Huckabuck Family," Princess Lenore in "Many Moons," and now Tassai. Think about which of these three characters seems most like a real girl to you. What were some of the ways the author of that story made her seem real? Then make at least one suggestion that will tell other writers how to make their characters seem more real.

Reading Literature: Short Stories

1. **Identifying the Narrator.** From what point of view is this story written? Does the author know everything? Give examples from the story that tell you whether the narrator is omniscient—all-knowing—or has limited knowledge.

2. **Making Inferences.** When the father of the little white girl talked to Tassai, his voice shook. Why? How did he feel at that time?

3. **Understanding a Character.** What kinds of things made Tassai happy?

4. **Predicting Outcomes.** When Tassai saw the rattlesnake, it was close to the little white girl. The text says that "There was no time to think. There was no time to call for help. Tassai did the only thing that she could do."

   Imagine that, when Tassai saw the snake, it was a bit further away. Would she call for help and wait, doing nothing, till someone else came? Would she run for help? Would she think about the matter and decide that her jar was more important than the little girl?

   Keep in mind all you know about Tassai. Tell what you think she would have done.

5. **Identifying Theme.** What do you think is the theme, or statement about life, in "The Jar of Tassai"?

Developing Vocabulary Skills

Identifying and Using Clue Words and Punctuation. Each of these sentences contains a definition or a restatement of a word from this selection. Find and write the word that is defined or restated; then write its meaning. Finally, write the clue words and punctuation that helped you find the meaning of the word.

1. Tassai lived on top of a mesa. A mesa is a flat-topped hill with steep sides.

2. Tassai brought water from the spring, a small stream coming from the earth.

3. The Indians had made beaded moccasins, which are soft leather shoes.

4. Many people were showing off their pottery (pots, bowls, dishes, and other things made from clay and hardened by baking).

5. The pueblo, or Indian town, was full of excitement.

Developing Writing Skills

1. **Writing a Description.** Read the description of the open place, in the second paragraph under the subtitle "The Big Day." What words show the atmosphere and color of the place?

   Write a description of a place you have been. Write about a place that had as much color and life in it as Tassai's open place. First make a list of the things you could see there. Add to the list adjectives that describe these things. Decide in what order you will tell about the things. Then write your paragraph of description. Begin with an introductory sentence that covers what you are describing, like the first sentence in the paragraph you have read: "There were good smells and different sounds everywhere."

2. **Creating Possible Plots.** Suppose that the first time Tassai ran to the open space, she had picked up the blanket that held her jar. Could this have been made into a short story? Can you think of other things that might have happened to Tassai that would have made as good a story?

   List three or more different ideas for new stories about Tassai. Suggest things she could have done, or things that could have happened at the feast. Write a few sentences telling what you think might happen in each new story.

Developing Skills in Critical Thinking

Identifying Generalization. In "The Jar of Tassai," there is a reference to a certain white man. He had visited the Indian towns and did not see anything that he thought was good. Therefore, he decided that no Indians were able to make good things. He made a general statement, or generalization, based on his experience. What was wrong with his generalization? Could you make any suggestions for making better generalizations?

The Fun They Had

ISAAC ASIMOV

In many of his stories, Isaac Asimov gives us a view of the future. This view helps us see the present more clearly. See if you can figure out what Asimov is saying here about both the present and the future.

Margie even wrote about it that night in her diary. On the page headed May 17, 2157, she wrote, "Today Tommy found a real book!"

It was a very old book. Margie's grandfather once said that when he was a little boy, his grandfather told him that there was a time when all stories were printed on paper.

They turned the pages, which were yellow and crinkly. It was awfully funny to read words that stood still instead of moving the way they were supposed to—on a screen, you know. And then, when they turned back to the page before, it had the same words on it that it had had when they read it the first time.

"Gee," said Tommy, "what a waste. When you're through with the book, you just throw it away, I guess. Our television screen must have had a million books on it, and it's good for plenty more. I wouldn't throw it away."

"Same with mine," said Margie. She was eleven and hadn't seen as many tele-books as Tommy had. He was thirteen.

She said, "Where did you find it?"

"In my house." He pointed without looking, because he was busy reading. "In the attic."

"What's it about?"

"School."

Margie was scornful. "School? What's there to write about school? I hate school."

Margie always hated school, but now she hated it more than ever. The mechanical teacher had been giving her test after test in geography, and she had been doing worse and worse. Her mother had shaken her head sorrowfully and sent for the County Inspector.

He was a round little man with a red face and a whole box of tools with dials and wires. He smiled at Margie and gave her an apple, then took the teacher apart.

Margie had hoped he wouldn't know how to put it together again, but he knew how all right. After an hour or so, there it was again, large and black and ugly, with a big screen on which all the lessons were shown and the questions were asked.

That wasn't so bad. The part Margie hated most was the slot where she had to put homework and test papers. She always had to write them out in a punch code that they had made her learn when she was six years old, and the mechanical teacher calculated what her mark was in no time.

The Inspector had smiled after he was finished and patted Margie's head. He said to her mother, "It's not the little girl's fault, Mrs. Jones. I think the geography sector was geared a little too quick. Those things happen sometimes. I've slowed it up to an average ten-year level. Actually, the overall pattern of her progress is quite satisfactory." And he patted Margie's head again.

Margie was disappointed. She had been hoping they would take the teacher away altogether. They had once taken Tommy's teacher away for nearly a month

From Day to Day to Eternal, 1976–78. YAACOV AGAM. Private Collection.

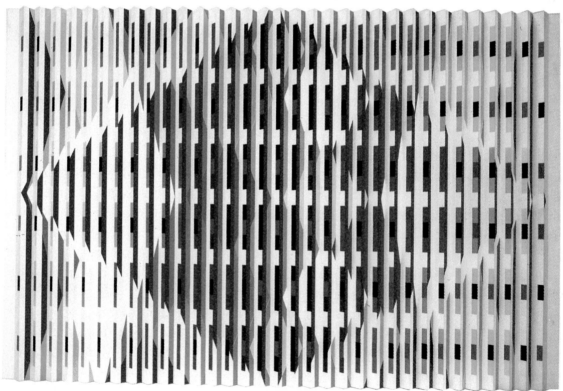

because the history sector had blanked out completely.

So she said to Tommy, "Why would anyone write about school?"

Tommy looked at her with very superior eyes. "Because it's not our kind of school, stupid. This is the old kind of school that they had hundreds and hundreds of years ago." He added loftily, pronouncing the word carefully, "Centuries ago."

Margie was hurt. "Well, I don't know what kind of school they had all that time ago." She read the book over his shoulder for a while, then said, "Anyway, they had a teacher."

"Sure they had a teacher, but it wasn't a regular teacher. It was a man."

"A man? How could a man be a teacher?"

"Well, he just told the boys and girls things and gave them homework and asked them questions."

"A man isn't smart enough."

"Sure he is. My father knows as much as my teacher."

"He can't. A man can't know as much as a teacher."

"He knows almost as much, I betcha."

Margie wasn't prepared to dispute that. She said, "I wouldn't want a strange man in my house to teach me."

Tommy screamed with laughter. "You don't know much, Margie. The teachers didn't live in the house. They had a special building, and all the kids went there."

"And all the kids learned the same things?"

"Sure, if they were the same age."

"But my mother says a teacher has to be adjusted to fit the mind of each boy and girl it teaches, and that each kid has to be taught differently."

"Just the same, they didn't do it that way then. If you don't like it, you don't have to read the book."

"I didn't say I didn't like it," Margie said quickly. She wanted to read about those funny schools.

They weren't even half-finished when Margie's mother called, "Margie! School!"

Margie looked up. "Not yet, Mamma."

"Now!" said Mrs. Jones. "And it's probably time for Tommy, too."

Margie said to Tommy, "Can I read the book some more with you after school?"

"Maybe," he said nonchalantly. He walked away whistling, the dusty old book tucked beneath his arm.

Margie went into the schoolroom. It was right next to her bedroom, and the mechanical teacher was on and waiting for her. It was always on at the same time every day except Saturday and Sunday, because her mother said children learned better if they learned at regular hours.

The screen was lit up, and it said, "Today's arithmetic lesson is on the addition of proper fractions. Please insert yesterday's homework in the proper slot."

Margie did so with a sigh. She was thinking about the old schools they had when her grandfather's grandfather was a little boy. All the kids from the whole neighborhood came, laughing and shouting in the schoolyard, sitting together in the schoolroom, going home together at the end of the day. They learned the same things, so they could help one another on the homework and talk about it.

And the teachers were people.

The mechanical teacher was flashing on the screen, "When we add the fractions ½ and ¼—"

Margie was thinking about how the kids must have loved it in the old days. She was thinking about all the fun they had.

Developing Comprehension Skills

1. Approximately how many years into the future is Isaac Asimov taking us in this story?

2. Identify at least two ways in which Margie's schooling is like yours. Then think of the ways in which it is different. Name two or more things that Margie thinks are better about your school.

3. Remember that, in irony, a situation is not what it seems to be. What is the ironic situation at the end of this story?

4. Is Asimov making any comment on our present day educational system? What do you think he is saying?

5. Do you agree or disagree with Margie's statement that a man can't be as smart as a computer?

Reading Literature: Short Stories

1. **Evaluating the Setting.** Good science fiction carries us into a believable future. In many cases it seems to predict the future. Find several events and things in the story that are "new" or that we don't recognize as part of our present day society. Then tell whether or not you think these things or events are believable or could happen.

2. **Finding the Author's Message.** Frequently a new invention will thrill people. They will be so excited by the powers of the invention that they believe it will solve many problems. They fail to see its limitations, or the new problems that it may cause. Science fiction writers often caution us about ourselves and our inventions. In "The Fun They Had," what is the danger that Isaac Asimov is warning us about?

3. **Identifying Flashbacks.** The events in this story are not told in the order in which they occurred. Instead, we find out about some of the events in **flashbacks**, passages that tell about actions that happened before. For example, Margie's statement "I hate school" leads into a flashback about the County Inspector's visit. That visit occurred before Margie's discussion with Tommy, but it is not described until the middle of their discussion.

   List these events from the story in the order in which they occurred.

   a. Margie writes in her diary.
   b. Tommy finds the real book.
   c. Margie's mother sends for the County Inspector.
   d. Tommy explains to Margie about old schools.
   e. Margie has her arithmetic lesson.

4. **Diagraming the Plot.** The major conflict in "The Fun They Had" is Margie's struggle to learn about and understand the "old-fashioned" school. The climax is her decision that the old-fashioned system was fun. Draw a plot diagram to fit this story.

Developing Vocabulary Skills

1. **Choosing the Best Definition for the Context.** Look up the word *proper* in a dictionary and read all the definitions. Choose the definition that fits each of these sentences.

   a. Today's arithmetic lesson is the addition of *proper* fractions.
   b. Please put yesterday's homework in the *proper* slot.

2. **Using the Prefix Tele-.** In this story, the word *telebook* is used to describe a book seen on a television screen. Some other common words containing the prefix *tele-* are *telephone* and *telegraph*. Tele-

means "far" or "at a distance." Match the following words in column A with the definitions in column B. Check the dictionary if necessary.

A	B
a. telephonic	(1) method of photographing distant objects with a camera
b. telethon	(2) an instrument used to make distant objects appear nearer and larger
c. telescope	(3) having the ability to convey sound across a distance
d. telephotography	(4) an apparatus for indicating the temperature of a distant point
e. telepathy	(5) a long television program, usually to ask for money for a charity
f. telethermometer	(6) apparent communication from one mind to another without speech or signs

Look up the words in column A in your dictionary and write the respelling of each word. Note that *tele-* in the word *telepathy* is pronounced differently from *tele-* in all other words.

Developing Writing Skills

1. **Expressing an Opinion.** Do you like the school you are in now better than the one described in the story? Why or why not? Write a paragraph listing the reasons for your answer.

2. **Writing Science Fiction.** Write several paragraphs about what you think schools will be like in 100 years or so. What subjects will be taught? How will the teachers look? What kind of buildings will schools be in? If you like, you could tell about the adventures of one of the students in a typical school day.

The Great Detective

STEPHEN LEACOCK

Tone is the author's attitude toward the subject. Because this story is so short, the author must make his tone clear quickly. What is Stephen Leacock's attitude toward this story? What clues let you know?

The murder had now reached its climax. First, the man had been undoubtedly murdered. Secondly, it was absolutely certain that no conceivable person had done it.

It was, therefore, time to call in the great detective.

He gave one searching glance at the corpse. In a moment, he whipped out a microscope.

"Ha! Ha!" he said, as he picked a hair off the lapel of the dead man's coat. "The mystery is now solved."

He held up the hair.

"Listen," he said, "we have only to find the person who lost this hair and the criminal is in our hands."

The chain of logic was complete.

The detective set himself to the search.

For four days and nights he moved, unobserved, through the streets of New York, scanning closely every face he passed, looking for a person who had lost a hair.

On the fifth day he discovered a man, disguised as a tourist, his head enveloped in a steamer cap that reached below his ears. The man was about to go on board the ship *Gloritania*.

The detective followed him on board.

"Arrest him!" he said, and then drawing himself to his full height, he held aloft the hair.

"This is his," said the great detective. "It proves his guilt."

"Remove his hat," said the ship's captain sternly.

They did so.

The man was entirely bald.

"Ha!" said the great detective, without a moment of hesitation. "He has committed not one murder but about a million."

Developing Comprehension Skills

1. What are the events and the judgments that lead to the sentence "The chain of logic was complete"? Have those events and judgments been logical so far?

2. How does the detective explain his error, when it is obvious that he has chosen the wrong person as the murderer?

3. What was the author's purpose in writing this story? Is this an ordinary detective story? Give reasons for your answer.

Reading Literature: Short Stories

1. **Identifying the Narrator.** Who tells this story, the detective? Or does someone else who is a character in the story? Or is it the all-knowing author? Suggest some ways that the story would differ if it were told by the detective in the first person.

2. **Identifying Tone.** What is the writer's attitude, or tone, toward his subject? What clues led you to the answer?

3. **Identifying Parody.** Think of a detective story you read recently or have seen on TV or in a movie. Usually a detective story stresses these ideas:

   The brilliance of the detective
   His or her ability to solve a mystery because of a clue everyone else has overlooked

   How does "The Great Detective" parody these ideas? Can you identify any other ideas in detective stories that are parodied here?

4. **Evaluating a Character.** Is the detective a believable character? Explain your answer. Do you think the author intended to make him believable? Why or why not?

Developing Vocabulary Skills

Reviewing Ways of Learning Word Meanings. The following sentences contain words from the story whose meanings can be figured out by one of these methods:

   a. using a dictionary or glossary
   b. recognizing context clues that restate or define the word
   c. knowing base words with prefixes and suffixes

Write the definition of each underlined word. Then write which method you used to obtain that meaning.

1. The crime had now reached its climax, or highest point.
2. First, the man had been undoubtedly murdered.
3. He gave one searching glance at the corpse.
4. He picked a hair off the lapel of the dead man's coat. A lapel is the part of the collar that is folded back.
5. For days and nights he moved, unobserved, through the streets.
6. Without a moment of hesitation, the detective accused the man of murder.

Developing Writing Skills

1. **Classifying Stories.** Review the stories in this chapter briefly. Then choose one of the topics below. Pick out two or three stories that you think fit with that topic. Write several paragraphs explaining why you chose those stories.

funniest stories	most exciting plots
most realistic character	themes worth thinking about
most realistic settings	stories for children
best images or sounds	stories I wish I'd written

2. **Writing a Detective Story.** Rewrite this story from the sixth sentence on. Use the character of the great detective. Identify a clue. Solve the mystery. The story can be serious or funny as you wish. Before you write, plan a plot line with the introduction (the first paragraph of this story), rising action, climax, falling action, and resolution.

Developing Skills in Study and Research

Conducting a Survey. Take a survey of about a dozen members of your class. Ask each what his or her favorite mystery story is. If several students like the same story, make a list of the ten favorite mysteries, like the list of the ten best selling books in the Sunday newspaper. Rank the most popular stories first.

If you prefer, ask each student to name his or her favorite story in this chapter, or a favorite character. Make a chart showing the stories or characters named, in the order of their popularity.

Review

Using Your Skills in Reading Short Stories

The following paragraph is the beginning of a short story named "Little Red," by Pearl Buck. Read it and answer the questions below.

> Little Red was called Little, because his father was Big Red, and he was called Red because, like his father, he always wore something red. Big Red and Little Red, father and son, had always lived, since they were born, in a village on the edge of a lake in the mountainous country of Lu, in the province of Kiangsi, in China.

1. What does this paragraph tell you about the setting of the story?

2. What have you learned about the characters?

3. Has the rising action of the plot begun yet?

4. Does the story use the first-person or the third-person point of view?

Using Your Comprehension Skills

Read the following lines from the poem "74th Street" in Chapter 5. State what you can infer about the little kid. What is she like?

> Hey, this little kid gets roller skates.
> She puts them on.
> She stands up and almost
> flops over backwards.
> She sticks out a foot like
> she's going somewhere and
> falls down.
>
> She brushes off the dirt and the
> blood and puts some
> spit on it and then
> sticks out the other foot
> *again*.

Using Your Vocabulary Skills

This sentence is from the introduction to Chapter 5, "Reading Poetry." Find the word defined by context clues. Tell what kind of clue is used. Then tell the meaning of the word.

> Ancient Greeks and Romans, for example, believed that the gods spoke to humans through human messengers called oracles.

Using Your Writing Skills

Choose one of these writing assignments. Follow the directions.

1. Choose one of the characters listed below. In one or more paragraphs, discuss how the writer let you know what kind of person the character was. Give examples from the story. Consider the following: (1) what the writer says about the character; (2) what the character says about himself or herself; (3) what other characters say about this character; (4) what the character does.
   a. Mme. Loisel   c. the Emperor   e. Keplik
   b. the Camel   d. the King   f. Tassai

2. Write your own short story about any topic. It should have at least one paragraph for each of the five parts of the plot:
   a. introduction—introduce the setting and characters
   b. rising action—introduce a problem and show the rising action
   c. climax—tell the turning point in the action
   d. falling action—show the effect of the climax
   e. resolution—settle the problem and end the story

Using Your Skills in Study and Research

Imagine that you wish to read more science fiction, including more writing by Isaac Asimov. Answer these questions about how you would find what you want.

1. Which of the following sources would you use to find science fiction stories or books in a library?
   a. footnotes   c. the picture file
   b. the card catalog   d. the encyclopedia index

2. What heading or headings would you look up in each source?

CHAPTER 5

Mt. Fuji and Flowers, 1971, DAVID HOCKNEY.
The Metropolitan Museum of Art, New York City.

Reading Literature: Poetry

What Is Poetry?

Poetry is a form of writing that uses words in a special way. It looks different from most writing, with the words arranged in lines rather than sentences. The sounds of the words and the way they are arranged cause you to read slowly. This makes you think about each word and the idea in each line. When people want to write about strong feelings, exciting ideas, or extraordinary experiences, they often choose to write poetry.

The History of Poetry

Poetry is the oldest form of literature. From earliest times, people have used poetry in songs, chants, and prayers.

For thousands of years, poems were used to pass on learning. It was easier to remember facts if they were in a poem. Even today we use the teaching poem that begins "Thirty days has September, April, June, and November." Poems recorded the history of a country, of its heroes and its victories.

Long ago people believed that poets had special powers. They thought that anyone who could use words in a beautiful and powerful way must be blessed by the gods. Ancient Greeks and Romans, for example, believed that the gods spoke to humans through human messengers called oracles. The oracles spoke only in poems.

In modern times, poetry teaches us about ourselves in different ways. In poems, poets share their feelings and thoughts. They tell stories of great events or of common happenings. They create vivid pictures in the reader's mind and experiment with sounds.

At all times, poets stretch language to make their readers think and feel more strongly than before.

The Elements of Poetry

You have learned that both prose and poetry use the sounds of language and figures of speech. Poetry, especially, uses rhythm and rhyme. Another special element of poetry is its form.

Lines and Stanzas. Poetry looks different from other writing. Poets write in **lines**, which may or may not be sentences. A group of lines is called a **stanza**. Each stanza is printed with a little space above and below it. Here is a two-line stanza:

Do I love you?
I'll tell you true.

Rhythm. As you know, **rhythm** is the pattern of stressed and unstressed syllables in a poem. It is sometimes called the **beat** of the poem. Some poems have a regular pattern of beats, as in this sample: "Sticks and stones are hard on bones." Other poems are not limited to any regular pattern.

Rhyme. Probably you remember that words that end with the same sound **rhyme**. *Flower* and *hour* rhyme. Usually, if a poem uses rhyme, the rhyming words are at the ends of lines, as in the sample above. Not all poems use rhyme. Those that do may use different patterns of rhyming words, called **rhyme schemes**.

How to Read a Poem

1. Read the poem aloud or hear it in your mind. The sounds of the words in a poem are as important as the meanings of the words.
2. Read slowly. Take the time to listen to the words. Think about the meanings of the words and the kinds of feelings they give you.
3. Remember that your reaction to the poem is personal and individual. Not everyone likes the same poems.
4. Try to appreciate every poem. The poet can speak to you only if you will listen.

Comprehension Skills: Figurative Language

Understanding Figurative Language

Usually when you read poetry, you must look beyond the poet's words to see what he or she really means. Poets often use figurative language. **Figurative language** is a way of speaking or writing that looks at familiar things in a new way. It gives new meaning to ordinary words. Here are two examples.

Day and night,
      my eyes roam the world.

Do you think the poet wants you to believe that his eyes are traveling all over the world all day and all night? Definitely not. He uses those words to tell you that he's looking for something that he wants very badly.

Your world is as big as you make it.
I know, for I used to abide
In the narrowest nest in a corner,
My wings pressing close to my side.

Does the poet really think that she used to live in a nest and had wings? No. She means that, when she was younger, she felt like a baby bird, afraid to leave its nest.

We can restate a poet's words in everyday language. However, as you can see, when we do that the poem usually loses its beauty and power.

Understanding the Mood of a Poem

Mood is the feeling you get when you read a piece of writing. Poets choose words carefully to create the mood.

The mood of this poem is casual and cheerful. What words help to create that feeling?

> Hey, this little kid gets roller skates.
> She puts them on.
> She stands up and almost
> flops over backwards.

The poet sets an informal mood with her first word, *Hey*. This and the words *kid* and *flops* tell you that the poet is talking to you as a friend might.

Exercises: Understanding Figurative Language and Mood

A. Read these lines from poems. Choose the best restatement for each.

1. Take time to be friendly—
      It is the road to happiness.
   a. Being friendly will help you be happy.
   b. There is a real road to a place called Happiness.

2. We hated one another.
   The afternoon turned black.
   a. The weather became cloudy that afternoon.
   b. We felt so angry with each other that the whole afternoon was ruined.

B. Read these lines from a poem.

> I like to rest on myself
>   really rest
>   and think what's best
>   about myself.

1. In your words, tell what you think the poet is saying.
2. What is the mood of this poem?
      a. mysterious   c. thoughtful
      b. angry   d. funny

Vocabulary Skills: Multiple Meanings

Using Multiple Meanings

Many words have more than one meaning. Some words that we use frequently have ten or more different meanings. This can be confusing. How do you know which meaning the writer wants?

To choose the right meaning of a word, read it **in context**. That is, read the sentences and phrases before and after the word. Try out the possible meanings in the context of the sentence.

Here is an example. The word *break* has several different meanings. Which meaning in the list below makes sense in this sentence?

Never break a promise.

1. come apart, crack, burst
2. fail to keep
3. make known, reveal
4. come suddenly
5. a short interruption in work

Try each of the meanings in the sentence. Number 2 means "fail to keep." Using it would make the sentence read: "Never fail to keep a promise." That makes sense. That must be the meaning the writer wanted to use.

Which meaning in the list above makes sense in this next sentence?

Go inside before the storm breaks.

Test each meaning of *break* in the sentence. You will find that number 4, "come suddenly," fits well. The sentence would read "Go inside before the storm comes." Note that sometimes the exact wording of the definition will not fit the sentence.

Identifying Denotation and Connotation

Before a poet writes any word, he or she thinks of both the dictionary meaning of the word and the ideas and feelings that the word gives to readers. The dictionary meaning is called **denotation**. The **connotation** refers to all the ideas, thoughts, and feelings that come to mind when you read or hear a word.

For example, the word *street* has the denotation of "a public way or road." It has such connotations as neighbors, crowds, excitement, rough activities, and danger. These connotations add new, unstated meanings to the word.

Exercises: Using Multiple Meanings and Connotations

A. Choose the correct dictionary meaning for each underlined word. Find it in the choices under the second sentence in each group.

1. The package was sent by express.

2. I can hardly express my feelings.

    a. a service for sending goods
    b. to put into words; state

3. Take time to read—
   It is the fountain of wisdom.

4. Brad stopped at the fountain before class.

    a. a place to get a drink
    b. source

5. Imagine the world falling through space.

6. Is there space for me on this bench?

    a. area between things, room
    b. the universe, distance extending without limit

B. For each of these words, write five or more ideas, thoughts, or feelings that you think of when you see it. In other words, write the connotations it has for you.

1. school   2. music

Poems About Individual Growth

Often a poem is written as if someone is speaking to the reader. We call that someone the **speaker**. Sometimes, the poet has the speaker say things that are true about the poet. Other times, the poet has the speaker say things that are true about everyone.

This section is about individual growth. As you read each poem, think about who the speaker might be. Is he or she saying things that are true only about one person? Or is the speaker saying things that are true about everyone?

Faraway, 1952, ANDREW WYETH. Private Collection.

Endless Search

As you read the following poem, decide what the speaker is really searching for.

ALONZO LOPEZ

Searching,
    forever searching.
Looking,
    but never finding.
Day and night,
    my eyes roam the world.
Searching,
    not knowing how to end
This search for myself.

Developing Comprehension Skills

1. What does the poet mean by these lines?

   Day and night,
       my eyes roam the world.

2. What is the speaker searching for? Is he looking in the right places?

Reading Literature: Poetry

1. **Identifying Figures of Speech.** Reread lines 5 and 6. Are they an example of simile, metaphor, personification, or hyperbole? Or do they combine two figures of speech? Explain your answer.

2. **Recognizing Mood.** Would you call the mood of this poem happy? unhappy? angry? Can you think of a better word or phrase to describe the feeling that you get from the poem?

One For
Novella Nelson

MYRA COHN LIVINGSTON

In this poem, as in "Endless Search," the speaker is talking about "myself." Is this speaker also searching? If she is looking for something, what is it?

I like to rest on myself,
  really rest
  and think what's best

  about myself,
  what's wrong
  in the song
  that says I'm alone.

Me, I'm not alone.
I've got myself.

Portrait of Frida Kahlo, 1931. IMOGEN CUNNINGHAM.
Courtesy of Imogen Cunningham Trust, Berkeley, California.

Developing Comprehension Skills

1. The idea of resting on yourself is an example of figurative language. The speaker does not actually rest—relax, sleep, lie down—on top of herself. What is another word you could use for "rest" that would get across the poet's meaning?

2. Thinking of yourself as alone in the world can make you feel small and not worth much. The feeling may be what the speaker refers to when she talks about "the song that says I'm alone." If so, how does she convince herself that there is something "wrong in the song"?

3. Why would anyone like to "rest on myself"? How would this be helpful?

4. Would you call this speaker more or less cheerful than the speaker in "Endless Search"? What do you think is the mood of this poem?

Reading Literature: Poetry

1. **Using Rhyme and Repetition.** This poem appears to have a loose organization. Each stanza has a different number of lines. There is not a clear rhyme scheme. The rhythm changes from line to line.

   However, the poet pulls the poem together with two sets of rhyming words and two words that are repeated at the ends of lines. Identify the rhyming words and where each set is found. Identify which words are repeated, and where. Can you describe the pattern that the poet makes with these words? How does this pattern help the reader notice the important ideas in the poem?

2. **Understanding the Theme.** As you remember, the theme of a piece of writing is the general statement the writer is making about life. What do you think is the theme of "One for Novella Nelson"? Does the title help to make the theme clear?

Not in Vain

EMILY DICKINSON

Emily Dickinson lived about a hundred years ago in Amherst, Massachusetts. She rarely left her house and, during her life, did nothing to make herself famous. What does this poem tell about her opinion of fame?

If I can stop one heart from breaking,
I shall not live in vain:
If I can ease one life the aching,
Or cool one pain,
Or help one fainting robin
Unto his nest again,
I shall not live in vain.

Developing Comprehension Skills

1. Explain the phrase "live in vain."

2. The speaker lists four acts that would give meaning to life. Does she mean that these are the only acts that make life worth living? Or are they examples of something more general? If so, what are they examples of? That is, what do they have in common?

3. Which image, or picture, in this poem do you think is the strongest and clearest? Why did you choose this one?

1. **Recognizing Rhyme.** "Not in Vain" has a definite rhyme scheme. Part of it may be less definite to Americans than to British speakers of English. Most Americans say *again* to rhyme with *then*. The British say *again* to rhyme with *rain*. Use the letters *a*, *b*, and *c* to show the rhyme scheme of this poem with the British pronunciation of *again*. Then, use the letters *a*, *b*, *c*, and *d* to show the rhyme scheme with the American pronunciation of *again*.

2. **Recognizing Rhythm.** The rhythm pattern of "Not in Vain" is shown below. Which lines have the same patterns of stressed and unstressed beats? Is this pattern more regular or more irregular?

<pre>
 ˘ / ˘   /   ˘   /   ˘   / ˘
If I can stop one heart from breaking,
 ˘ /   ˘   /   ˘ /
I shall not live in vain;
 ˘ / ˘   /   ˘ /   ˘ / ˘
If I can ease one life the aching,
 ˘   /   ˘   /
Or cool one pain,
 ˘   /   ˘   /   ˘   / ˘
Or help one fainting robin
 / ˘ ˘ /   ˘ /
Unto his nest again
 ˘ /   ˘   /   ˘ /
I shall not live in vain.
</pre>

Developing Vocabulary Skills

Choosing the Right Meaning for the Context. Each of these words has several dictionary meanings. Find the word in the poem listed below. Choose the meaning that best fits the context of the poem. If none of the dictionary meanings seems adequate, write what you think the word means in that poem. You may combine meanings or include connotations that the word has for you.

1. *end*—"Endless Search"
   a. the last part; conclusion (She read us the *end* of the story.)
   b. bring to a stop; finish (Please *end* your complaining.)
   c. purpose; object (The *end* of this program is to send spacecraft to Venus.)
   d. result, outcome (we were unhappy with the *end* of all our work.)
   e. part left over (Give the birds the *end* of that roll.)
   f. a player in football (Jim is our best *end*.)

2. *rest*—"One for Novella Nelson"
   a. be still; sleep (Be quiet so the baby can *rest.*)
   b. be free from work (Stop sweeping and *rest* for a minute.)
   c. support oneself on; place on (Let your feet *rest* on the hassock.)
   d. rely on; depend (Our plans *rest* on your cooperation.)
3. *ease*—"Not in Vain"
   a. make free from pain or trouble (This news will *ease* your mind.)
   b. reduce the strain (When the tests were over, life *eased* up on us.)
   c. move slowly and carefully (The kitten *eased* itself through the crack in the fence.)

Developing Writing Skills

1. **Comparing Poems.** Write a comparison of "Endless Search," "One for Novella Nelson," and "Not in Vain." Show how the poems are alike or unlike in one or more of the following:
   a. theme   c. use of rhythm   e. use of images
   b. mood   d. use of rhyme   f. your reaction

2. **Imitating a Poem.** Rewrite "Not in Vain," changing lines 1, 3, 4, 5, and 6. Instead of the four actions listed there, insert four actions that you consider meaningful. Try to keep the same pattern of rhythm.

Developing Skills in Study and Research

1. **Using the Library.** In the library, books of poetry are grouped together. Find out how your school or local library classifies them.

2. **Using Parts of a Book.** Every book has a **title page**. It lists the title and author of the book and, usually, the publisher. If the book includes the writing of several authors, the title page will list the editor, who collected and arranged the contents. If the title page does not list the publisher, you will find that information and the year when the book was printed—its publication date—on the **copyright page**. That is usually the page following the title page. Pause now in your reading to locate the title page and copyright page of this text. Examine them to find the authors, publisher, and copyright date.

   Almost every book has a **table of contents** at the front. This lists the chapters in a novel, or the titles in a collection of poetry or short stories, or whatever other materials you will find in the book. The list

title page   copyright page   table of contents

is arranged in numerical order according to the pages the material is on. Briefly examine the table of contents of this text to see how the material is organized.

At the back of many books there are a **glossary** and an **index**. The glossary lists, in alphabetical order, unfamiliar words used in the book and gives their meanings. The index of most books lists separate topics discussed in the book. After each topic there is a list of page numbers to let you know where to look in the book for information on the topic. The index is also arranged in alphabetical order.

Pause briefly now to find the glossary and index of this text. You will note that instead of one index, there are several indexes.

Check out from the library a book of poems of your choice. Use the parts of the book to answer the following questions.

a. Who is the author or editor of the book?

b. When was this book published? By what company?

c. How are the poems and other materials, if any, grouped? Are they in chronological order? According to themes or topics?

d. Does the book have a glossary? How long is it?

e. What kinds of indexes does the book have? How is each one arranged?

f. Does the book have a poem by Emily Dickinson? If so, did you find it by looking in the table of contents or an index?

Developing Skills in Speaking and Listening

Interpreting a Poem. Choose one of the three poems you have read in this chapter. Prepare to read it to a group. Let your listeners hear each word clearly. Stress the accented syllables, avoiding sing-song dullness.

Trifle

GEORGIA DOUGLAS JOHNSON

The word trifle *is defined as
"an article or thing of small
value." How is the title of this
poem ironic?*

Against the day of sorrow
Lay by some trifling thing
A smile, a kiss, a flower
For sweet remembering.

Then when the day is darkest
Without one rift of blue
Take out your little trifle
And dream your dream anew.

Developing Comprehension Skills

1. "Against the day" is a phrase that means in preparation for the day. In your own words, restate the line "Against the day of sorrow" so that it has meaning for you.

2. When the speaker tells us to "Lay by some trifling thing," what does she encourage us to do?

3. The first two lines of stanza 2 use figurative language. The poet is describing a dark, cloudy day but really talking about something else. What is she comparing to a dark day?

4. How can you "take out" a trifle like a smile? In the last two lines, what is the speaker advising us to do?

Reading Literature: Poetry

1. **Identifying Rhyme and Rhythm.** Figure out the rhyme scheme of this poem. Write the rhyme scheme, using the letters *a* to *f*. Then, using light and strong claps, figure out the rhythm pattern. Would you call the pattern of rhythm and the pattern of rhyme regular or irregular?

2. **Analyzing Mood.** How would you describe the mood of this poem? Would you call it despairing? happy? thoughtful? sleepy? Can you think of a better word to describe the feeling the poem gives you?

Old English Prayer

TRADITIONAL

In most prayers, we ask for things or for help. In this prayer, however, we are given advice and promised some rewards. Are there any rewards here that you would ask for—or work for?

Take time to work—
　It is the price of success.
Take time to think—
　It is the source of power.
Take time to play—
　It is the secret of perpetual youth.
Take time to read—
　It is the fountain of wisdom.
Take time to be friendly—
　It is the road to happiness.
Take time to dream—
　It is hitching your wagon to a star.
Take time to love and to be loved—
　It is the privilege of the gods.
Take time to look around—
　It is too short a day to be selfish.
Take time to laugh—
　It is the music of the soul.

Developing Comprehension Skills

1. What is meant by "hitching your wagon to a star"?

2. In this poem, figurative language is used in several places. What action is compared to each of the following? What does the poet mean to say by using each of these comparisons?

   a. fountain of wisdom   b. road to happiness
   c. music of the soul

3. Is there a single theme in this poem? If so, how would you state it? If not, name some of the separate themes you find.

Reading Literature: Poetry

1. **Identifying Elements of Poetry.** Which of the following do you find in "Old English Prayer"? If you can't remember the meanings of any of these words, review them on the pages noted in the parentheses.

   simile (pages 128–129)   rhythm (pages 124–125)
   metaphor (pages 130–131)   alliteration (pages 120–121)
   rhyme (pages 122–123)   onomatopoeia (page 126)

2. **Recognizing Form.** What is the form, or organization, of this poem? Is there a pattern in the repetition of phrases?

Your World

GEORGIA DOUGLAS JOHNSON

One metaphor is used throughout this poem. How does that metaphor help you to feel the theme as well as to understand it?

Your world is as big as you make it.
I know, for I used to abide
In the narrowest nest in a corner,
My wings pressing close to my side.

But I sighted the distant horizon
Where the skyline encircled the sea
And I throbbed with a burning desire
To travel this immensity.

I battered the cordons around me
And cradled my wings on the breeze
Then soared to the uttermost reaches
With rapture, with power, with ease!

Developing Comprehension Skills

1. What metaphor is used in this poem?

2. Tell in your own words the main idea of each stanza. (In the first stanza, ignore line 1 for now.) Do not use the metaphor in your explanation; state the idea that the metaphor stands for.

3. Where did the speaker find the courage to change her life?

4. How did she feel before and after the change?

5. What is the theme of "Your World"?

Reading Literature: Poetry

1. **Examining Imagery.** The speaker has chosen the image of a bird to describe herself. Reread this example of imagery. How well does this image fit with the ideas of fear and freedom?

2. **Identifying Rhyme.** Using three sets of letters for the three stanzas, write the rhyme scheme of "Your World." Would it be possible to use the same set of letters for each of the three stanzas?

3. **Relating Poetry to Personal Experience.** Give an example of how you experienced something similar to what is described in this poem.

Time

TRADITIONAL

"Time" uses a form of repetition similar to "Old English Prayer." As you read, notice where the pattern changes. Decide why it changes.

> Time is
> Too slow for those who wait,
> Too swift for those who Fear,
> Too long for those who Grieve,
> Too short for those who Rejoice;
> But for those who Love
> Time is
> Eternity.

Developing Comprehension Skills

1. *Slow* and *swift* are opposites; *long* and *short* are opposites. Explain how time can be described by each of these opposites.

2. Time passes, and things in time change. Eternity stays the same forever. However, the poem combines these opposites. It seems that the last three lines are saying something impossible. What do they really mean? Can you restate them so that their message sounds possible?

Reading Literature: Poetry

Appreciating Rhythm. Copy "Time" and show its stressed and unstressed syllables with these marks: / and ◡. Which lines have the same rhythm pattern? Do you hear the difference when the pattern changes? How does the change in rhythm help the reader understand the meaning of the poem?

Advice to Travelers

In Chapter 1, Fables, you read several fables, including one in poem form. How is this poem like a fable?

WALKER GIBSON

A burro once, sent by express,
His shipping ticket on his bridle,
Ate up his name and his address,
And in some warehouse, standing idle,
He waited till he like to died.
The moral hardly needs the showing:
Don't keep things locked up deep inside—
Say who you are and where you're going.

Developing Comprehension Skills

1. How did the burro end up in the warehouse?
2. Are you likely to eat a name tag and get lost? Then what does the moral mean to you?

Reading Literature: Poetry

1. **Understanding Figurative Language.** The poet gives advice to travelers. This is an example of figurative language. Who are the travelers he is referring to? Why does he call them travelers?

2. **Recognizing Rhyme.** Using letters of the alphabet, write the rhyme scheme of this poem. In which two pairs of rhyming words do two ending syllables rhyme?

3. **Appreciating Imagery.** To what or whom is the burro being compared? How does using the burro in this comparison make the poem especially strong in delivering its message?

Developing Vocabulary Skills

1. **Choosing Meanings and Identifying Connotations.** The following words were used in the poem "Old English Prayer." Choose the dictionary meaning that you think best fits the context of the poem. Explain why you chose the meaning you did. Then write a definition that describes its connotations for you.

   a. *work* —first line
   (1) to perform as it should; operate (This radio *works* well.)
   (2) to produce results (The potion *works* strange effects.)
   (3) to solve, as a problem (Can you *work* this story problem?)
   (4) to use effort or energy in doing or making something (You must *work* hard to get onto the team.)
   (5) to shape into something (*Work* the clay into a ball.)

   b. *power* —fourth line
   (1) mechanical, electrical, or other energy that can be put to work (We get our *power* from the local utility company.)
   (2) strength or force (She has *power* at bat and skill in the field.)
   (3) ability to control others (The President has immense *power*.)

   c. *play* —fifth line
   (1) to take part in a game against (We *play* South High School next week.)
   (2) to have fun, amuse oneself (Let the children *play* quietly.)
   (3) to perform music on (Can you *play* the piano?)
   (4) to act the part of (Bob *played* the hero of the scene.)
   (5) to move quickly or lightly (The light *played* on the water.)

2. **Choosing Meanings.** The word *power* is also found in the last line of the poem "Your World." Which of the meanings in item b above do you think fits the context of that line?

Developing Writing Skills

1. **Expressing an Opinion.** Choose either your favorite or your least liked poem among the eight studied so far. State whether you think it is great, awful, or somewhere between. Give reasons for your opinion. Express your opinion in such a way that you do not insult someone who disagrees with you. Remember that each person's reaction to a poem is different.

2. **Writing a Poem.** You have read poems with several different forms. Some have been organized by repetition of words, without rhyme or a regular rhythm. Others have had a clear rhyme scheme and a regular rhythm, without repetition of words. The rhyme scheme used most often in the first eight poems has been *abab*.

   Write a poem about yourself. Use one of these organizations — repetition of words or use of rhyme scheme and a regular rhythm. The poem may tell about what you are now, what you wish to be, or what you want or can give to others. It may be serious or joking.

Developing Skills in Speaking and Listening

Developing Choral Interpretation. Work with a group of from three to twelve members. Choose one of the poems listed below. Assign lines to individual speakers or groups of speakers. If you like, assign the lines to speakers or groups as suggested below. Prepare and present a choral reading for the rest of your class.

Make sure that everyone in the group agrees on the theme of the poem, so that the most important words are stressed.

"Trifle": Speaker 1—lines 1, 2, and 4; Speaker 2—line 3; Speaker 3—lines 5 and 6; Speaker 4—lines 7 and 8

"Old English Prayer": odd-numbered lines; even-numbered lines (These could be broken down further.)

"Your World": stanza 1; and the words "With rapture" from line 12; stanza 2 and the words "with power" from line 12; stanza 3, first three lines and "with ease" from line 12

"Time": lines 1, 6, 7, and 8; lines 2, 7, and 8; lines 3, 7, and 8; lines 4, 7, and 8; lines 5, 7, and 8

"Advice to Travelers": lines 1 to 5; line 6; lines 7 and 8

Little Dead

MYRA COHN LIVINGSTON

In the poem "Your World," the speaker compared herself with a bird. In this poem, the speaker is talking to real birds. Is she also speaking to someone or something else, besides?

I've buried so many birds,
so many. I've found them dead:
robins, sparrows, feathers red
and brown. Whispered so many words

of what you say soft to birds
who've fallen. I have said
little bird things, little dead-
of-all-small things. My comfort words

won't bring you back, little birds,
to flying. I'll dig a bed
warm and dark to rest your heads
and keep you singing with my words.

Untitled (Hotel Neptun), 1953–55, JOSEPH CORNELL.
Copyright © Estate of Joseph Cornell.

Developing Comprehension Skills

1. What has the speaker done for the dead birds before burying them? At what point in the poem does she switch from talking about the birds to talking to the birds? What does she promise to do for them after burying them?

2. The mood of this poem is sad, but is that all? How does the end of the poem affect the mood?

3. The speaker talks about two characteristics of birds: they fly and they sing. In the poem "Your World," the flight of the bird **symbolized**, or stood for, the speaker's freedom and joy in life. Suppose that in this poem, also, the flight of birds symbolized something in the speaker, or others, that felt free and joyful. Can you suggest what that might be? Could that thing also be as beautiful as a bird's song?

4. If the birds symbolize hopes or dreams of the speaker or other people, how do you suppose the hopes or dreams died?

5. How can the speaker keep the fallen hopes and dreams "singing with my song"?

Reading Literature: Poetry

1. **Examining Form.** Notice that, until the last line, there are no periods at the ends of the lines in this poem. Not even the last line of stanza 1, or of stanza 2, ends a complete thought. What effect does this have on the organization of ideas? Does it make the stanza divisions more, or less, important?

2. **Recognizing Rhyme.** What is the rhyme scheme of "Little Dead"? What is unusual about the rhyming words?

3. **Understanding Theme.** What do you think the theme of this poem is? State it in such a general way that your sentence will be true both for birds and for dreams.

4. **Recognizing Onomatopoeia.** Imagine that two people are whispering to each other not far from you. Think of the sounds you might overhear. Then read lines 4 to 6, from "Whispered" to "fallen." Which letters are repeated to suggest the sound of whispering?

What really happens in this poem?

Faith

From a sign over an old inn at Bray, England

Fear knocked at the door.
Faith answered.
There was no one there.

Developing Comprehension Skills

1. What happened when the door was answered?

2. How could fear knock at the door? What "door" is the poem talking about?

3. How could Faith answer the door? What "Faith" do you think the poem is talking about? Faith in what?

Reading Literature: Poetry

1. **Recognizing Figures of Speech.** There are two examples of a figure of speech in this poem. Can you identify them? What figure of speech are they?

2. **Understanding Theme.** The theme of this poem is expressed as a general statement. Rewrite it in your own words.

3. **Recognizing Elements of Poetry.** Poems usually have rhyme and rhythm. This poem does not. Why do you think it has been included in this chapter as a poem? Review The Elements of Poetry in the introduction to this chapter, page 231.

74th Street

As you read this poem, keep its title in mind. Can you figure out the poet's reason for choosing this title?

MYRA COHN LIVINGSTON

Hey, this little kid gets roller skates.
She puts them on.
She stands up and almost
flops over backwards.
She sticks out a foot like
she's going somewhere and
falls down and
smacks her hand. She
grabs hold of a step to get up and
sticks out the other foot and
slides about six inches and
falls and
skins her knee.

    And then, you know what?

She brushes off the dirt and the
blood and puts some
spit on it and then
sticks out the other foot

    again.

Developing Comprehension Skills

1. What does the little kid do in this poem? How far does she get?

2. List some of the words and phrases that make the girl and her efforts seem very real.

3. There are two lines printed separately from all the others. This gives them more importance. The last line especially, with only one word, stands out. It stresses the single most important idea about the little kid. What is that idea?

4. How does the poet feel about the little kid?

Reading Literature: Poetry

1. **Understanding Mood.** Usually, our language is more formal in writing than in speaking. The words *hey* and *kid* are used often in speaking, but hardly ever in writing. Why does the poet break this pattern? How do the words *hey* and *kid* establish a relaxed, cheerful mood in this poem? Can you find some other words and phrases that continue that mood? How does the word *and* contribute to the mood?

2. **Understanding Theme.** The poet has presented a very realistic picture of a single little girl. However, the poem also has something to say about life in general. The two lines that are set off by themselves alert us to the theme. State the theme in your own words.

To Satch

SAMUEL ALLEN

*Leroy "Satchel" Paige was a star
pitcher for all-black teams and
then for major league teams. His
career lasted for over thirty
years. How does this poem show
that it is for and about Satchel
Paige?*

Sometimes I feel like I will never stop
Just go on forever
Till one fine mornin'
I'm gonna reach up and grab me
 a handfulla stars
Throw out my long lean leg
And whip three hot strikes burnin'
 down the heavens
And look over at God and say
How about that!

Leroy "Satchel" Paige, Negro League pitcher
and Baseball Hall of Fame member, 1968.
United Press International.

Developing Comprehension Skills

1. Often poems are written to or dedicated to a person. How do we know this one is dedicated to someone?

2. Reread lines 4, 5, and 6 in the poem from "I'm gonna reach . . ." to ". . . down the heavens." What sport is the poet talking about? How do you know?

3. Because the poem pictures Satch pitching in heaven, we can tell that the poet considered him a great baseball player. The poem also pictures Satch saying to God "How about that!" What does this tell you about the poet's opinion of Satch as a person? What would give Satch the right to speak casually to God?

Reading Literature: Poetry

1. **Recognizing Mood.** A very casual, conversational mood is used in this poem. What are some words that establish this mood?

2. **Examining Form.** The form of this poem follows no particular rules. It does not use rhyme. Its rhythm pattern is somewhat irregular, as in conversation. The lines seem to lead naturally into each other. Reread the last line several times. What is different about this line? How does it suggest that the poem is ending?

You Whose Day It Is

NOOTKA INDIAN TRIBE

You whose day it is,
make it beautiful.
Get out your rainbow,
make it beautiful.

Haida Mask, National Museums of Canada,
National Museum of Man, Negative #K-100.

Developing Comprehension Skills

1. In this poem, what does a rainbow represent? Who can have this kind of rainbow?

2. How can we share our rainbows with others?

3. Whose day is it?

4. State in your own words the advice that the poem gives.

Reading Literature: Poetry

1. **Identifying Sounds of Language.** Which of these uses of language do you find in this poem? Where do you find it?

   a. alliteration   b. repetition of words   c. rhyme

   How does it help to make the theme of the poem clear?

2. **Appreciating Figurative Language.** In this poem, what we can do to brighten our lives and the lives of those around us is compared to a rainbow. A real rainbow is beyond the control of human beings. By saying that each of us controls a rainbow, the poem suggests that we have much more power than we think. In what other way does the poem suggest our power—and responsibility? How does this concept strengthen the advice the poem gives?

Developing Vocabulary Skills

1. **Choosing Among Denotations.** Choose the correct meaning for the underlined word in each sentence. Find the meaning in the choices under the second sentence in each group.

   a. I'll throw out my long lean leg.
   b. Many farmers were disappointed with the lean harvest.

   (1) to bend to one side (*Lean* into the wind.)
   (2) producing very little (Last year there was a *lean* corn crop.)
   (3) having little or no fat (I like *lean* meat.)
   (4) to depend on for advice (Her friends *lean* on her for help.)
   (5) to favor a little (He *leans* toward ice cream for dessert.)

   c. The toddler always sticks to his mother.
   d. She sticks out a foot like she's going somewhere.

   (1) keeps close (*Stick* to your friends.)
   (2) pierces with a pointed instrument (Be careful or the pin will *stick* you.)
   (3) puts forward, extends (*Stick* out your tongue and say "ah.")
   (4) fastens; attaches (This tape *sticks* to anything.)

   e. She brushes off the dirt and the blood.
   f. After painting, clean your brushes.

   (1) tools for cleaning, painting, etc. (Use scrubbing *brushes* on the floor.)
   (2) touches lightly in passing (My head *brushes* the leaves as I walk below the branch.)
   (3) remove; wipe away (The giant *brushes* away his enemies easily.)
   (4) smoothes the hair (When she *brushes* her hair, it looks nice.)

2. **Identifying Connotations.** The following words found in the poems are rich in connotative meaning. List five or more ideas, feelings, or thoughts that come to your mind when you read these words.

comfort   fear   faith

Developing Writing Skills

1. **Making Connections.** Review the five poems in this group: "Little Dead," "Faith," "74th Street," "To Satch," and "You Whose Day It Is." Think about their topics and their themes. Write one or more paragraphs explaining why you think the five poems were grouped together. If you feel one of the poems does not belong with the others, take it out of your group but explain why you did so.

2. **Writing a Poem.** Write an original poem, following one of the four sets of directions below. Use alliteration, onomatopoeia, and figures of speech if you can.

   a. Write one or more four-line stanzas, using the rhyme scheme *abcb*. The topic should refer to an animal.
   b. Write a three- to six- line poem in the style of "Faith." Use personification. You may choose one of these titles:

   Pride   Anger   Envy   Patience   Love
   c. Write a poem that presents a picture of someone doing an everyday job. Use strong details to appeal to sight and another sense.
   d. Dedicate your poem to one of your heroes or heroines. The poem should tell about that person. You may speak *to* or *about* the person, or you may use the person as the speaker in the poem.

Developing Skills in Speaking and Listening

Interpreting a Poem. Visit your school or local library and select a poem for this activity. Then read the poem carefully to yourself. Look for figurative language and the sounds of language. Make sure you can state the poem's theme and explain its figures of speech. Then practice reading the poem aloud. Finally, present it before a group. Be careful to speak clearly, with the stresses where they are needed. When you are finished, test how clearly you read the poem by asking someone in your audience to state the theme or mood of the poem.

Poems About the Individual and Others

A poem can be about anything that the poet is interested in. However, it is also important for the topic to be of interest to readers, as well. The poems in this section fit that description. Almost everyone is interested in how to get along with others. Each of these poems has something to say on that subject.

Vincent and Tony, 1969, ALEX KATZ. The Art Institute, Chicago.

More About the Elements of Poetry

Sensory Images. Poems often contain clear, vivid **images**, or pictures made with words. By choosing words carefully, poets can make you see, feel, smell, hear, or even taste the things they describe. The creation of word pictures is called **imagery**.

Here is part of a poem that puts a picture in your mind. The poem, by Edward Leuders, is called "Rodeo."

> Leathery, wry, and rough,
> Jaw full of chaw, and slits
> For eyes—this guy is tough.
> He climbs the slatted fence,
> Pulls himself atop and sits;
> Tilts back his cowboy hat,
> Stained with sweat below
> The crown, and wipes a dirty
> Sleeve across his brow.

Notice how the poet used **sensory details**—details appealing to the senses. Some of them are "jaw full of chaw," "slatted fence," and "sweat below the crown."

Notice also that the poet has used both figurative language and the sounds of language in this poem.

Figurative Language. Any way of speaking or writing that looks at familiar things in a new way can be called **figurative language**. Specific types of figurative language are called **figures of speech**. You already know four figures of speech.

Hyperbole is an exaggeration that puts a vivid picture in your mind. An example is "slits for eyes."

A **metaphor** compares different things that are alike in some way. An example in this chapter is "you are living poems."

A **simile** also compares two different things that have something in common. It uses the word *like* or *as*. If the sample above had said that "you are like living poems," it would have been a simile.

Personification gives human qualities to an object, an animal, or an idea. The poem "Faith" personified faith and fear.

Sounds of Language. The sounds of words are poets' toys and tools. You have already learned about four ways in which poets play with sounds. **Rhyme** and **rhythm** were discussed on page 231.

Alliteration is the repetition of a consonant sound, usually at the beginnings of words. An example in "Rodeo" is "Stained with sweat below the crown." There the *s* sound is repeated.

Onomatopoeia is the use of words that sound like their meanings, such as *crash, clink, bong, quack,* and *buzz*.

A fifth way that poets play with sounds is by **repetition** of words, phrases, or sentences. By repeating part of the poem, the poet emphasizes its importance. Sometimes, too, the repetition gives form to the poem.

In this poem, repetition of "houses in a row" and "squares" stresses the number of squared-off objects in the speaker's life.

SQUARES AND ANGLES

Houses in a row, houses in a row,
Houses in a row.
Squares, squares, squares.
Houses in a row.
People already have square souls,
Ideas in a row,
And angles on their backs.
I myself shed a tear yesterday
Which was—good heavens—square.
              —Alfonsina Storni

Faults

SARA TEASDALE

A fault is a failing or a weakness. In this poem, how does the speaker react to the faults of her friend?

They came to tell your faults to me,
They named them over one by one;
I laughed aloud when they were done,
I knew them all so well before—
Oh, they were blind, too blind to see
Your faults had made me love you more.

Rind, 1974, MAURITS CORNEUS ESCHER. National Gallery of Art, Washington, D.C.; Cornelius Van S. Roosevelt Collection.

Developing Comprehension Skills

1. Who do you think "they" are?

2. What did the speaker do when they told her about the faults of her friend? Why?

3. The speaker says, "Your faults had made me love you more." How is this possible? Wouldn't a person look for perfection in her friends? Can you think of reasons for the speaker to like someone because of her or his imperfections?

Reading Literature: Poetry

1. **Identifying Rhythm.** Copy "Faults," leaving space between the lines, and mark the stressed and unstressed beats with these marks: / and ⌣. Would you call this a regular or irregular rhythm pattern?

   Specific rhythm patterns, or **meters**, have been given names. A meter with one unstressed beat followed by one stressed beat, ⌣ /, is called **iambic**. A meter with two unstressed beats followed by one stressed beat, ⌣ ⌣ /, is called **anapestic**.

   Is this poem written in iambic rhythm or in anapestic rhythm?

2. **Identifying the Rhyme Scheme.** The rhyme scheme of this poem is unusual. What is it? Use letters of the alphabet to show which lines rhyme.

3. **Recognizing the Effect of Sounds.** "Faults" has a warm, caring mood. One characteristic that builds that mood is the repetition of certain letters. The letters *l* and *m* have soft sounds that blend with the sounds around them. Identify all the words in this poem that use the letters *l* and *m*.

A Choice of Weapons

This poem begins like a familiar children's rhyme. However, it goes a step further. According to it, what is the most violent act we can do to each other?

PHYLLIS McGINLEY

Sticks and stones are hard on bones.
Aimed with angry art,
Words can sting like anything.
But silence breaks the heart.

Developing Comprehension Skills

1. According to this poem, how do sticks, stones, and words hurt?

2. The poem moves from the action of throwing hard objects to saying unkind things to behaving in a cold, unfeeling manner. Is this movement from the worst action to the least harmful one? Or is it from the least harmful action to the worst one?

3. In your own words, state the theme of this poem. Do you believe it is true? Why or why not?

Reading Literature: Poetry

1. **Recognizing Alliteration.** Find two places in this poem where alliteration gives the words emphasis.

2. **Identifying Rhythm.** Copy "A Choice of Weapons" and mark the stressed and unstressed beats. Which line begins with an unstressed beat? Do you suppose the poet purposely made it sound different from the others? Why would she do so?

The Quarrel

An argument begins to draw the speaker and her brother into serious difficulties. How is the disagreement finally solved?

ELEANOR FARJEON (fär hā′ ôn)

I quarreled with my brother,
I don't know what about,
One thing led to another
And somehow we fell out.
The start of it was slight,
The end of it was strong,
He said he was right,
I knew he was wrong!

We hated one another.
The afternoon turned black.
Then suddenly my brother
Thumped me on the back,
And said, "Oh, come along!
We can't go on all night—
I was in the wrong."
So he was in the right.

Developing Comprehension Skills

1. What did the two people argue about?

2. After the quarrel, how did they feel about each other? What mood were they in? Which words lead you to the answer?

3. When the brother says "I was in the wrong," the speaker decides "So he was in the right." What does she mean?

Reading Literature: Poetry

Interpreting Figurative Language. In stanza 1, what does "fell out" mean? What are other words that could be used to mean the same thing? In stanza 2, what picture does "the afternoon turned black" create for the reader?

A Love Song

RAYMOND RICHARD PATTERSON

*As you read this poem, watch
how the rhythm and the rhyme
scheme help to establish the
mood. If you understand the
mood, you will understand the
poem!*

Do I love you?
I'll tell you true.

Do chickens have lips?
Do pythons have hips?

Do penguins have arms?
Do spiders have charms?

Do oysters get colds?
Do leopards have moles?

Does a bird cage make
    a zoo?
Do I love you?

Putney Winter Heart, 1971–72, JIM DINE. Collection of Solomon & Co., Fine Art;
Courtesy of Harry N. Abrams, Inc., New York.

Developing Comprehension Skills

1. The speaker begins by asking a question: "Do I love you?" Then he says he will tell the truth, and answers by asking seven more questions. What is the answer to each of the seven questions?

2. Does the speaker love the person?

3. Does the poet have a sense of humor?

Reading Literature: Poetry

1. **Recognizing Irony.** When a writer says one thing but means the opposite, he or she is using **irony**. Frequently, there is humor in irony. What is ironic in the title of this poem?

2. **Appreciating Rhythm and Rhyme.** On your paper, write out the light and strong beats in the five stanzas of this poem. Is the rhythm regular or irregular? Does it seem to you that the beat is slow or fast?
   Write the rhyme scheme of the poem. Is it simple or complicated? How do the rhythm and rhyme help to establish the mood? What is the mood of "A Love Song"?

3. **Examining Form.** What special effect does the poet use in the first and last stanzas to relate them and unify the poem?

While I Slept

This poem is about two kinds of sleeping. What are they? How do you feel at the end of the poem?

ROBERT FRANCIS

While I slept, while I slept and the night grew colder
She would come to my bedroom stepping softly
And draw a blanket about my shoulder
While I slept.

While I slept, while I slept in the dark still heat
She would come to my bedside stepping coolly
And smooth the twisted troubled sheet
While I slept.

Now she sleeps, sleeps under quiet rain
While nights grow warm or nights grow colder
And I wake and sleep and wake again
While she sleeps.

Developing Comprehension Skills

1. How did "she" care for the speaker while he slept?
2. Who do you suppose "she" is?
3. Where does she now sleep? What kind of sleep is referred to?
4. Why do you think the poet wrote this poem?

Reading Literature: Poetry

1. **Examining Form.** The organization of this poem is strong. It achieves a unified effect by several means.

   First, it uses a definite rhyme scheme. Write the rhyme scheme using letters of the alphabet. The rhymes are not as obvious as in most poems. Can you explain why we may not notice the rhymes unless we listen for them?

   Second, the poem uses repetition of certain words and phrases. Find one phrase that is used six times.

   Third, the poem uses practically the same sentence pattern three times, changing only a few words. Notice how much stanza 2 is like stanza 1. The image of the blanket in the cold is simply changed to that of a sheet in the heat. Even stanza 3 is similar. How is the phrase "While I slept" echoed in stanza 3?

2. **Recognizing Sensory Details.** Each stanza suggests an image. Perhaps because the poem tells about the night, and we can't see well at night, the poet does not use words that appeal to sight. However, he uses words that appeal to hearing, to touch, and even to our awareness of hot and cold. Find at least one example of each of these kinds of sensory details.

3. **Understanding Mood.** Even though the idea of death is part of this poem, the mood is not anxious or depressed. How would you describe the mood of the poem? Can you suggest how the unified form of the poem contributes to the mood?

What is the metaphor in this poem?

To Young People

HENRY WADSWORTH LONGFELLOW

You are better than all the ballads
  That ever were sung or said,
For you are living poems
  And all the rest are dead.

Basque Beach, 1958, HELEN FRANKENTHALER.
Hirshhorn Museum and Sculpture Garden, Washington, D.C.

Developing Comprehension Skills

1. A poem can be beautiful and exciting. It can make us think more deeply and feel more strongly. These may be qualities of poetry that the poet also sees in young people. He says young people are "*living* poems." What do you think he means by this?

2. Why are young people better than all the ballads? In your answer, explain how the ballads can be "dead."

3. How does the poet seem to feel about young people?

Reading Literature: Poetry

1. **Examining Rhythm.** If this poem is read mechanically, with a sing-song rhythm, it sounds dull and meaningless. Instead, it must be read with more stress on the words that are important to the meaning. Reading it this way gives the poem a musical quality and makes it interesting. Write the one or two most important words in each line. Consider how you would read the poem aloud.

2. **Identifying Sounds of Language.** Write the rhyme scheme of this poem. Also, identify two examples of alliteration.

Developing Vocabulary Skills

Finding the Best Word. When you are writing, you want to be as careful as other writers. You want each word to be the best word for expressing your meaning. Each word must have the right dictionary meaning, or denotation. Besides, it must have the right connotations.

Frequently you know what you want to say but you can't think of the clearest words with the right connotations. For example, you may want to tell how you felt after a quarrel with a friend. You couldn't concentrate on anything; you couldn't sleep. When you try to write about this experience, the only word that comes to mind is *excited.*

However, you realize that the connotations of *excited* are wrong. A person can be excited about winning a prize or going to a party. Those connotations might confuse your reader. How can you find a better word to describe your experience?

The first help you can refer to is the dictionary. Perhaps the definitions will provide the word you need. However, when you look up *excited*, your dictionary gives the synonyms *aroused* and *agitated.* You don't feel comfortable with either word. You don't normally use these words, and you aren't sure whether they have the right connotations. In such a situation, it is safer not to use those words. You might confuse your reader badly.

A second help you can refer to is a thesaurus. A **thesaurus** is a list of words followed by related words. The related words may be synonyms, words with almost the same meaning but different connotations. The related words may be different parts of speech from the entry word, and may suggest different ways of expressing its meaning. Sometimes the thesaurus also lists **antonyms**, words with meanings opposite from the entry word.

Using a thesaurus, you find the listing for *excited*. It is very long. Among its many related words, you notice these:

> agitated, perturbed, disturbed, troubled, disquieted, upset, unsettled, discomposed, flustered, ruffled, shaken, restless, restive, uneasy, unquiet, unrestful, tense

Again, some of the words are not words you normally use. It's best to avoid these unknown words. Instead, think about all of the words that are familiar to you. Consider their connotations for you. Probably their connotations will be the same for your reader. Then choose the word that best fits the meaning and the mood you want to express. To describe your feelings after you quarrel, *troubled* and *unsettled* would be good choices.

Each thesaurus is organized in a different way. There may be directions at the front of the thesaurus or an index at the back to help you find a particular entry word.

Obtain a thesaurus and find the entry for *excited*. Select five different related words that are listed after *excited*. They may be the same part of speech or different parts of speech. Make sure each has a different connotation. Then write a sentence using each of your chosen words. In each of your sentences, refer to a different kind of excitement.

Developing Writing Skills

1. **Explaining Your Reaction.** All of the poems in this section are about getting along with other people. Some tell about problems we have with each other. Some tell about our feelings for another. Some tell about what we expect from others.

Decide which poem means the most to you. Which one made you think the most? Which gave you the strongest feelings and ideas? Write one or more paragraphs explaining which poem you chose and why you chose it.

2. **Writing an Original Poem.** Write a poem about getting along with others. See question 1, above, for some possible topics. Your poem may use a regular or an irregular rhythm. Try to use at least one example of figurative language and one example of the sounds of language.

Figurative Language	**Sounds of Language**
metaphor	alliteration
simile	onomatopoeia
personification	repetition of certain letters throughout the poem
sensory image	repetition of words, phrases, or sentences
hyperbole	rhyme

Developing Skills in Study and Research

Using Reference Works and Skimming for Information. One type of fast reading is **skimming**. The purpose of skimming is to quickly find specific facts or details.

Find an article about Sara Teasdale and one about Henry Wadsworth Longfellow in an encyclopedia or other reference work. Skim each article to find the answers to these questions:

1. When was the poet born? In what country?

2. When did the poet die? In what country?

3. Did the poet write few or many poems?

4. Does the reference work point out any especially notable poems? If so, what are their titles? Why is each important?

5. Does the reference work explain why the poet is considered important? If so, what reasons does it suggest?

Identify the title, publisher, and copyright date of the reference work you use. If you used a text other than an encyclopedia, also identify the title of the work and its author or editor.

Developing Skills in Critical Thinking

Classifying Poems. Think about the poems in this section:

"Faults," by Sara Teasdale
"A Choice of Weapons," by Phyllis McGinley
"The Quarrel," by Eleanor Farjeon
"A Love Song," by Raymond Richard Patterson
"While I Slept," by Robert Francis
"To Young People," by Henry Wadsworth Longfellow

Classify them in two groups, according to some standard of your choice. The standard must make sense for studying poetry. For example, you could group those that use alliteration as opposed to those that do not. You could group those that are about problems as opposed to those that are not. It would not be sensible to group those that begin with verbs against those that do not.

Write one or more paragraphs explaining your classification. Tell which poems you grouped together and why. Give examples from the poems to support your reason or reasons.

Here are some meaningful topics to consider:

figures of speech   mood
sounds of language   theme

Poems About the World at Large

As you have learned, poetry is an ancient form of literature. However, it is also very modern. The poems in this section could not have been written fifty or even thirty years ago. They use some of our most recent discoveries and inventions to take a new look at our world.

Delineating the Constellations to Simplify Astronomy for the Average Man, 1979, CLAYTON POND.
Serigraph; Courtesy of Van Straaten Gallery, Chicago; Copyright Hadley Art Association.

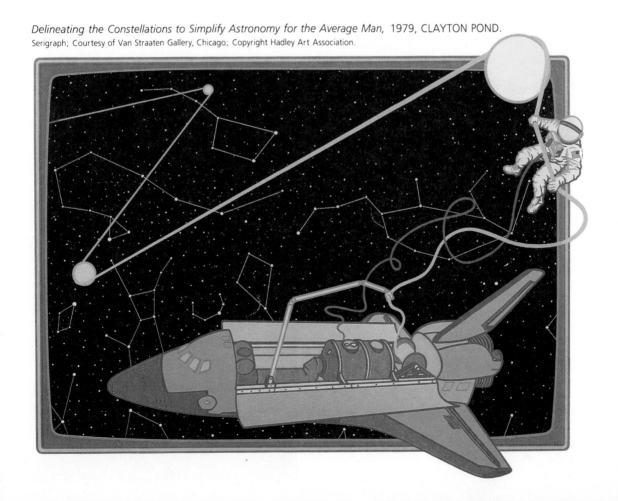

ORBITER 5 SHOWS
HOW EARTH LOOKS FROM THE MOON

There's a woman in the earth, sitting on
her heels. You see her from the back, in three-
quarter profile. She has a flowing pigtail. She's
holding something—some holy jug. Her left arm is thinner,
in her right hand—some holy jug. Her left arm is thinner,
in a gesture like a dancer. She's the Indian Ocean. Asia is
light swirling up out of her vessel. Her pigtail points to Europe
and her dancer's arm is the Suez Canal. She is a woman
in a square kimono, bare feet tucked beneath the tip of Africa. Her tail of long hair is
the Arabian Peninsula.

A woman in the earth.

A man in the moon.

—May Swenson

Note: The first telephoto of the whole earth, taken from above the moon by Lunar Orbiter 5, was printed in the New York Times, August 14, 1967. Poem title is the headline over the photo. NASA.

Developing Comprehension Skills

1. What does the poet see in the photo of the Earth?

2. To what is the poet referring in the line "A man in the moon"?

3. What feeling about the Earth do you get when the poet compares the "woman in the Earth" to the "man in the moon"? Does the comparison make the Earth seem bigger or smaller than it seems in our normal view of it?

Reading Literature: Poetry

1. **Examining Form.** "Orbiter 5 Shows How Earth Looks From the Moon" is a concrete poem. A **concrete poem** is one whose shape suggests a particular figure or design. The way the lines of this poem are arranged suggests the circle of the globe or the swirl of clouds as seen from space. Can you suggest why the poet chose to arrange the poem in this shape? Does it have anything to do with the subject of the poem?

2. **Using Your Imagination.** Try to find the picture of the woman in the photograph illustrating this poem. To what does the poet compare each of these parts of the world?

   a. the Indian Ocean   c. the Suez Canal
   b. Asia   d. the Arabian Peninsula

The First

LILIAN MOORE

"The First" is about the first walk on the moon by a human being. To whom is the speaker addressing the poem?

Moon,
remember
how men left their
planet
in streams of
flame,
rode weightless
in the skies
till you pulled
them down,
and then
in the blinding sunlight
how the first shadow
of an
Earthling
lay
on your
bleak dust?

Developing Comprehension Skills

1. This poem describes three stages in the first U.S. mission to the moon. In your own words, identify those three stages.

2. To what does "streams of flame" refer?

3. Does the speaker expect an answer? Then why does she direct the question to the moon?

Reading Literature: Poetry

1. **Recognizing Personification.** In "Orbiter 5 Shows How Earth Looks from the Moon," the man in the moon was mentioned. This is the person that we imagine seeing in the pattern of hills and valleys on the moon. Is this poem addressed to the man in the moon or to the moon itself? Give a reason for your answer.

2. **Recognizing Repetition of Sounds.** In "The First," the poet does not use rhyme. However, she makes you hear relationships between certain words by repeating consonant sounds in those words. For example, in the phrase "streams of flame," the *m* sound appears at the end of each noun. The *d* and *t* sounds are very close; they are used in the phrase "rode weightless." Can you find two or three consonant sounds repeated in these lines, providing a smooth flow from line to line?

   > till you pulled
   > them down,
   > and then

   What two descriptive words are related by the *bl* beginning? What letter is repeated three times in the last four lines? Can you find other examples in this poem where repetition of letters connects words or phrases?

Earth

OLIVER HERFORD

This poem asks you to look at the Earth from two different points of view. How does this contrast affect your view of yourself and your daily problems?

If this little world tonight
   Suddenly should fall through space
In a hissing, headlong flight,
   Shrivelling from off its face,
As it falls into the sun,
   In an instant every trace
Of the little crawling things—
   Ants, philosophers, and lice,
Cattle, cockroaches, and kings,
   Beggars, millionaires, and mice,
Men and maggots all as one
As it falls into the sun. . . .
Who can say but at the same
   Instant from some planet far
A child may watch us and exclaim:
   "See the pretty shooting star!"

Developing Comprehension Skills

1. This poem pictures an imagined event. What is that event?

2. The poem lists several "little crawling things" that would be destroyed in the event. What are some of those "little things"? Why do you suppose the poet has mixed together such different creatures?

3. If the event should happen, how might someone on another planet observe it?

4. In your own words, state the theme of the poem.

Reading Literature: Poetry

1. **Understanding Punctuation.** This poem uses both a dash and a series of four periods. Frequently a dash is used to set off an explanation. Here is an example:

   The mountain climbers rested at the col—a gap between peaks.

   At other times, it is used between two phrases or sentences to show excitement, as in this example.

   Don't stop climbing—you're almost there—you're at the top!

   How is the dash used in this poem? Explain your answer.

   A series of three periods may be used to suggest that an idea is not finished. If it is used at the end of a sentence, a fourth period, showing the end of the sentence, is added to the series.

   If you're asking my opinion . . . I just don't know. . . .

   In quoted material, the series of three periods suggests that something was left out.

   "Twinkle, twinkle, little star . . . like a diamond in the sky."

   How is the series of periods used in this poem?

2. **Identifying Rhyme Scheme.** Write the rhyme scheme of this poem, using letters of the alphabet. Notice that all sixteen lines of the poem are written as one stanza. Remember that if a word near the middle or end of the poem rhymes with one near the beginning, you must use the same letter as before.

3. **Recognizing Alliteration.** Find at least two instances of alliteration.

4. **Appreciating Irony.** What is ironic about these lines? Also, explain the irony of the last line of the poem.

   . . . the little crawling things—
      Ants, philosophers, and lice,
   Cattle, cockroaches, and kings. . . .

The Computer's First Christmas Card

EDWIN MORGAN

This poem, "The Computer's First Christmas Card," is unusual in several ways.

```
jollymerry
hollyberry
jollyberry
merryholly
happyjolly
jollyjelly
jellybelly
bellymerry
hollyheppy
jollyMolly
marryJerry
merryHarry
hoppyBarry
heppyJarry
boppyheppy
berryjorry
jorryjolly
moppyjelly
Mollymerry
Jerryjolly
bellyboppy
jorryhoppy
hollymoppy
Barrymerry
Jarryhappy
happyboppy
boppyjolly
jollymerry
merrymerry
merrymerry
merryChris
ammerryasa
Chrismerry
asMERRYCHR
YSANTHEMUM
```

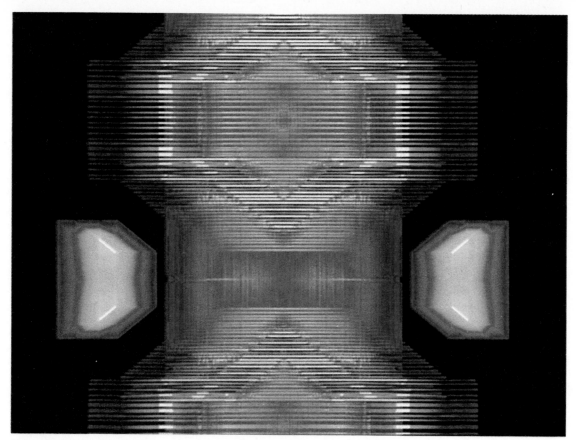

Plug, 1984, MICHAEL ASSANTE. New York Institute of Technology, Computer Graphics Laboratory.
Courtesy of *The International Journal of Typographics.*

Developing Comprehension Skills

1. What is the computer's greeting? (The computer is not the poet.)

2. Do you think the computer intended to give that greeting, and that it has a sense of humor? Or was the greeting an accident or mistake?

3. What seems to be the theme? State it in your own words.

Reading Literature: Poetry

1. **Examining the Form.** What do you notice about almost all of the words on the card?

2. **Evaluating Writing.** Is this really poetry? Give reasons for your answer. Refer to any of the elements of poetry that you have studied so far, including the purposes of poetry.

Developing Vocabulary Skills

Using a Thesaurus. After each of the poems listed below is a word that describes its mood. Look up each of those words in a thesaurus. Read over the related words and see if one of them would describe the mood better than the given word. On your paper, write the word that you think best describes the mood of each poem.

1. "Orbiter 5 Shows How Earth Looks from the Moon"—playful
2. "The First"—thoughtful
3. "Earth"—mocking
4. "The Computer's First Christmas Card"—funny

Developing Writing Skills

1. **Analyzing Poetry.** You have now read several poems that use rhyme schemes and several that do not. Each poet had to decide whether or not to use rhyme. Can you think of some reasons for using rhyme? Are there other reasons not to use rhyme?

   Write two paragraphs. In one, list your reasons for using rhyme. In the other, list your reasons for not using rhyme. Which gives you more fun? Which gives you more challenge?

2. **Writing a Rhymed Poem.** Choose one of the rhyme schemes listed below, and write a poem of one or more stanzas.

   aa   abcb   abab   abba   abcbdd   ababcc

   The poem can be about modern concerns, such as space flight.

3. **Writing a Concrete Poem.** Write an original poem in which the shape of the poem is important. The arrangement of the words and lines may suggest what the poem is about, as in "Orbiter 5 Shows How the Earth Looks from the Moon." The words may form a design, as in "The Computer's First Christmas Card."

Developing Skills in Study and Research

Interviewing for Information. Besides using reference materials, you can find information by talking with informed people. To be most effective, your talk, or interview, should be planned beforehand. You should know something about the background of the person you will interview. It is important to have some idea of what kinds of information he or she can give with authority—that is, what things the person knows the truth about. Then you can decide what questions to ask. You should write your questions ahead of time and keep them with you during the interview. Take notes about the person's answers, either during the interview or immediately after it, before you forget. Then you can use those questions and answers like other reference materials.

All of the poems in this section are about modern concerns, such as space flight and computers. In this activity, you are to learn about what life was like before these topics became important.

Make a list of five to ten questions you can ask an older person about his or her childhood. The questions must be about things the person knew about as a child or teenager. Topics could include school, sports, clothes, and entertainment, such as movies, books, radio, and records.

Then find a person who is willing to answer your questions. Make sure that the person was born no later than 1939. Decide on a time that is good for both of you to talk. At the interview, ask the questions you wrote ahead of time. You should ask additional questions if what the person says is not clear to you. Also ask additional questions if he or she tells about something new to you that you would like to hear more about. Take notes on your interview.

Then write a brief report on your interview or make an oral report about it. Tell who talked to you and why you chose him or her. Then tell about one part of his or her life as a child or teenager that is different from your life.

Developing Skills in Speaking and Listening

1. **Oral Reading for Enjoyment.** By yourself or with a small group, read your choice of the poems in this section. Review the suggestions on page 264 before presenting your reading to a group.

2. **Listening for Information.** If members of your class present oral reports on their interviews above, listen carefully. Take notes on what they say. At the end of his or her report, each speaker may ask a listener a question on the information in the report. A listener may also ask the speaker for additional information.

Using Your Skills in Reading Poetry

Read this poem, "Precious Stones." Look for these elements of poetry in it: simile, alliteration, rhyme, rhythm, theme. Explain how the poet uses each of these elements in the poem.

> An emerald is as green as grass;
> A ruby red as blood:
> A sapphire shines as blue as heaven;
> A flint lies in the mud.
> A diamond is a brilliant stone,
> To catch the world's desires;
> An opal holds a fiery spark;
> But a flint holds fire.
> —Christina Georgina Rossetti

Using Your Comprehension Skills

The following paragraph is from "Jim Thorpe: Indian Athlete" in Chapter 6. It uses figurative language. Find a figure of speech in it. Explain what is meant by the figure of speech.

> On the last lap Jim put on all the speed he had left. Fred Bie, the great athlete from Norway, struggled to catch him. For just a second Bie drew even, but he couldn't match strides with the big Indian. Jim drew ahead. He raced across the finish line, the winner again!
>
> "Oh, that Jim!" Pop Warner was smiling. "Isn't he a horse?"

Using Your Vocabulary Skills

Each pair of sentences about Chapter 6 selections uses a single word with two different meanings. Read the meanings below each pair.

Choose the meaning that best fits the context of each sentence. Then write a sentence using the word with one of the unused meanings.

1. Later, George worked as a ranch <u>hand</u>.
2. Jane stood frowning at her <u>hands</u>, turning her right thumb around to look at it.

   a. part of the arm, including the palm, fingers, and thumb
   b. a farm laborer
   c. the cards held at one time in a card game
   d. assistance, aid, help, as in *to give a hand*

3. Florence tired of the endless <u>round</u> of parties that her mother had insisted on.
4. The astronauts saw the Earth as a <u>round</u> ball floating in darkness.

   a. expressed in even numbers, such as tens, hundreds, and so on
   b. shaped like a ball
   c. any of the timed periods of a boxing match
   d. a series, as of actions or events
   e. a short song for two or more persons or groups

Using Your Writing Skills

Choose one of these writing assignments. Follow the directions.

1. Compare and contrast these three poems: "Advice to Travelers," "A Love Song," and "The Computer's First Christmas Card." Tell how they are alike and how they are different. Consider these topics: form, figurative language, the sounds of language, mood, and theme.

2. Write a poem on a topic of your choice. Use at least one figure of speech—hyperbole, simile, metaphor, and personification. Use at least two sounds of language—rhyme, rhythm, alliteration, onomatopoeia, and repetition of letters, words, or phrases. Choose words with connotations that fit the mood of your poem.

Using Your Skills in Study and Research

Imagine that you are looking in a book of poetry for "Metaphor," by Eve Merriam. What part or parts of the book will tell you whether the poem is included, and where? Tell two ways you can find the poem.

Nonfiction

Reading Literature: Nonfiction

What Is Nonfiction?

Nonfiction is writing that tells about real people, actual places, and true events. It is based on fact. Examples of nonfiction include most of the features in a newspaper. Some of these are world news, sports reports, editorials, letters to the editor, interviews, movie reviews, and how-to-make-something articles. In this chapter you will read three types of nonfiction: biographies, true adventure stories, and essays.

The History of Nonfiction

Biographies. A **biography** is the factual record of a real person's life. The first biographies were written about five thousand years ago in ancient Egypt. When a ruler would die, a record of his or her great deeds was left in the ruler's tomb. These royal biographies never discussed the ruler's faults.

About two thousand years ago, a Greek biographer named Plutarch wrote more realistic biographies. He told about both the good and the bad points of the person's character. However, he often accepted, as fact, stories that people had made up.

Biographers now try to make the subject of the biography seem like someone you might meet. They use small but important details. They try to use only facts. However, depending on which facts they include, they can influence your opinion of the person.

True Adventure Stories. A true adventure story is like a biography but it tells about just one event in someone's life.

Essays. An **essay** is very different from a biography. In it, a writer presents his or her opinions.

The Elements of Nonfiction

Sequence.   In the story of a person's life, the events usually are retold in the order that they happened. In other words, the story is told in **time sequence**. This sequence is also important in true adventure stories. This helps the reader to picture what came first and to see how it led to what came later.

In an essay, the ideas are arranged in a **logical sequence**. The writer presents the ideas in a step-by-step order that leads the reader to understand what the writer thinks and why.

Character.   The characters in a biography or a true adventure story are the real people who took part in the events. The person a biography is written about is called its **subject**. Writers show how their subjects change and grow. When the writer tells you how a character looks or acts, he or she is using **direct description**. A writer can also use **indirect description**. A writer uses indirect description when he or she leads you to an understanding of the character by reporting the character's words, actions, or thoughts, or the reactions of other people to the character.

Setting.   Setting is very important in biographies and true adventure stories. Remember that setting includes both the time and the place in which the story takes place. Setting changes constantly. Even if the events happen in one place, time passes.

An essay may or may not have a setting.

How To Read Nonfiction

1. Keep track of names, places, and years. It is important to be aware of these facts so that you can understand the story.
2. In biographies, look for the reasons why people act as they do. The biographer will either tell you why or give you clues.
3. As you read true adventure stories, try to guess what might happen next. Imagine that you are in the character's position.
4. As you read an essay, decide in what order the writer has arranged ideas. Try to see where the writer is taking you.

Comprehension Skills: Main Idea

Understanding Paragraphs

A **paragraph** is a group of sentences that work together to tell about one idea. This idea is called the **main idea**. Here is an example of a paragraph. As you read it, find the one idea that all the sentences tell about.

> The things that Florence saw in the hospitals were terrible. Sick people were lying in hospitals that were dens of noise and dirt. Even the doctors and nurses were seldom clean. Nobody had ever heard of germs, or of rows of white beds, neat and clean, or of sanitation to prevent disease. Well-to-do people avoided all hospitals, which were meant only for the poor.

The main idea is that the conditions in hospitals were terrible.

Often the main idea of a paragraph is stated in one sentence, called the **topic sentence**. Reread the paragraph above to find the topic sentence. A paragraph may have its topic sentence at the beginning, as in the sample, at the end, or even in the middle. A paragraph may have no topic sentence at all.

With or without a topic sentence, all the sentences in a paragraph should be related to the main idea. Each sentence gives another bit of information, or **detail**, about the main idea. For example, a diagram of the paragraph above would look like this.

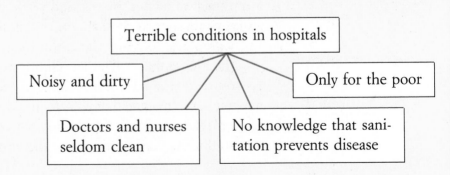

Separating Fact and Opinion

Nonfiction tells about facts. However, not every sentence in nonfiction is a fact. Facts must be connected in a way that makes sense to the writer. He or she wants the reader to understand the facts the same way. Therefore, the writer chooses facts carefully and groups them to fit his or her ideas.

In the sample paragraph about Florence Nightingale, for example, the writer tells four facts about hospitals that Florence saw. The main idea, however, is not a fact. It is an opinion. It tells how the writer feels about the hospitals. This is also how Florence probably felt about hospitals.

Exercise: Understanding the Main Idea and Topic Sentence

Find the topic sentence in each of these paragraphs. Then state the main idea in your own words.

1. Things became more difficult as they left the Ice Shelf behind and reached the glaciers leading to the Polar Plateau. They had to climb a narrow, steep river of ice. The snow was deep and loose, and the dogs had trouble. Again and again, because of impassable chasms or towering ice blocks, the explorers had to turn back and try another path.

2. As he grew older, Neil never lost interest in the sky and flying. He collected and studied issues of *Air Trails*, a magazine about flying. He filled notebooks with scraps of information he found on different airplane makes and designs. Neil especially enjoyed reading about the Wright brothers, who had made the first motor-powered plane flight.

3. All around Jane in the dirty streets swarmed men, women, and children from every country in Europe, shouting and talking in many languages. Many could not speak English at all. They crowded into tenements and into noisy, dark factories and big cattle stockyards where they worked. They all wanted to be Americans, but they did not know how. Chicago was a huge collection of foreign cities flung together without plan.

Vocabulary Skills: Context Clues

Using Comparison and Contrast Clues

Writers often compare one idea with another. They point out how two different things have something in common. Sometimes you will find an unfamiliar word in one part of the comparison. The comparison may give you a clue to the meaning of the word. Here is an example of a **comparison clue**.

> The peak *dominates* the mountain range like a giant among average-size people.

The comparison suggests that *dominates* refers to being larger or more powerful than others.

Certain words tell you to look for a comparison of two things that are similar. Some of these key words are *like, as, similar to, and also,* and *than.* When you find one of these words in a sentence with an unfamiliar word, look for a comparison context clue.

Sometimes you can use a **contrast clue** to get a hint of the meaning of a new word. When writers show a contrast of things or ideas that are opposites, they use a different set of key words. These words signal that an opposing idea is coming: *although, but, however, yet, on the other hand, different from,* and *in contrast.* Use contrast clues here to figure out what *tempted* means.

> George went back to visit the Carvers, who urged him to stay with them and farm their land. George was tempted, but somehow he knew that he must do something more.

The part of the sentence after *but* tells that George knew he had something to do. The word *tempted* is contrasted with that idea. From this you can guess that *tempted* refers to thinking about doing something you should not do.

Inferring Meaning from Context

In Chapter 2, you learned that writers often help you with a difficult word. They provide a definition or a restatement in context. You have also learned about comparison and contrast clues. Sometimes a new word is not defined or restated in context. Nor are there comparison or contrast clues nearby. Still, you have a good chance of understanding it. You can make an intelligent guess based on context clues.

Here is an example:

Florence ran into the gardens between rows of huge rhododendrons bearing pink blossoms above her head.

What has the writer told you about rhododendrons? You find them in gardens; they are huge; they have pink flowers. Even if you never heard of rhododendrons before, you can guess that they are some kind of big flowering plant.

Exercise: Using Comparison and Contrast Clues, and Inferring Meaning from Context

Read these sentences. Figure out the meaning of the underlined word using context clues. Tell what kind of context clue you used: comparison, contrast, or inference. Then find the dictionary meaning of the word.

1. Money was <u>scarce</u> and people had hardly enough to buy food.
2. Dr. Carver got a two-horse plow and went to work himself. Straight <u>furrows</u> stretched out behind him.
3. I jammed my way into this crack, then kicking backwards with my <u>crampons</u> I sank their spikes deep into the frozen snow behind me and levered myself off the ground.
4. While Amundsen was making his triumphant dash to the Pole, <u>tragic</u> events were taking place to the west.
5. Living conditions on the moon are as <u>hostile</u> to us as life on land is to fish.

Biographies

A **biography** is the story of a real person's life. It includes both the important events and the little facts about the person's life — his or her personality, likes, and dislikes. To find out these facts, biographers do a great deal of research. They read letters and journals written by the subject. They read what other people have written about the subject, too. They try to get to know what the person was really like. Then, in their writing, the biographers help their readers get to know the person.

George Washington Carver (detail), 1942, BETSY GRAVES REYNEAU. National Portrait Gallery, Washington, D.C.

Florence Nightingale:
Lady with a Lamp

MAY McNEER *and* LYND WARD

Florence Nightingale changed the way the world saw the nursing profession. As you read of her life, look for the qualities that made her a leader. What set her apart from most people?

Florence glanced up from her Greek book and sighed. Such a long lesson Father had given her! Parthenope, her older sister, learned Greek more easily than she did. Yet, thought Florence with a nod of satisfaction, I can do mathematics much better than she can! At sixteen Florence already knew far more Greek and Latin than most young men. She knew, also, the accomplishments of a rich, young, English lady. She could sing, embroider, paint flowers, and make jellies for the sick.

She jumped up, but paused at the door. If she left her Greek lesson unfinished, she would have to get up at four the next morning and study by cold lamplight. The pause was brief. Florence ran through the large house of the Nightingale family, into the gardens between rows of huge rhododendrons bearing pink blossoms above her head.

Beyond the lodges, stables, and gardens she stepped onto the downs, stretching smooth and green to the hills. As Florence walked, her spirits rose. It was good to be on the downs in spring. Yet why did she have to do so much that she did not want to do? Why did she quarrel so often with Parthe? Florence knew that with her beauty and her bright mind she was her father's favorite. Parthe was jealous, no doubt. Florence enjoyed parties but often tired of the endless round of them that her mother insisted on. What did she want of life? She did not know.

Suddenly, as she came up over a hill, Florence saw a little knot of people. There with them was the pastor. Florence ran toward them calling, "Has someone been hurt?" Then she saw the dog lying on the grass. Old Shepherd Smithers turned and two farm boys nodded respectfully as the daughter of their squire appeared.

"Good morning, Miss Florence," said Reverend Gifford. "See, here is poor Cap, with a broken leg. He will have to be killed, I fear. Smithers' best collie, too."

Florence dropped to her knees. She stroked the rough head gently. Farm dogs were work animals and, like horses, were shot when they couldn't do their job. Florence loved all living creatures, from her old brown pony and her pet pig to the tiny nuthatch swinging on the peach bough. The dog's brown eyes seemed to ask her for help. She turned around and spoke sharply.

"You must not kill Cap, Smithers. Pick him up—carefully now—and bring him to the stables. I will take care of him." There was a ringing tone of command in her voice.

At the stables the dog was made comfortable on a pile of straw. Florence washed the leg and bound it with a piece of wood and clean old rags, and every day she came with food for Cap. It was the talk of the whole estate when the splint was removed and Cap walked on the mended leg again, without a limp.

Florence did not understand her own feelings. She could not read enough and learn enough to suit herself. She also liked parties, and lovely gowns, and she enjoyed being admired for her wit and beauty. Yet there was something else that meant much more to her. She could not forget the suffering eyes of the injured dog. She would always give up a party or miss a lesson to care for the sick children of the farmers. Florence wished that she could take care of all sick people—everywhere.

Florence Finds Her Career

The daughters of Mr. and Mrs. Nightingale were born to riches. Their father, a country squire, was a learned man, and he taught his daughters himself. Their mother was a society leader. Florence had been named for the city of Florence, Italy, where she was born in 1820 during a year of travel for the Nightingales, who often spent months at a time in Europe.

Yet, in the midst of every pleasure, Florence thought about the sick. She had a feeling that she had a mission in life and that she was meant to help sick people.

Florence and Parthé Nightingale, 1836, W. WHITE.
Historical Picture Service, Chicago.

She knew that her parents would not approve, so she sent secretly for every book and pamphlet that she heard of that told how to care for the sick. She read these late at night in her room. When she went traveling to London, Rome, or Paris, she slipped away to visit hospitals. She must see for herself how bad they were.

The things that she saw were terrible. Sick people were lying in hospitals that were dens of noise and dirt. Even the doctors and nurses were seldom clean. Nobody had heard of germs, or of rows of white beds, neat and clean, or of sanitation to prevent disease. Well-to-do people avoided all hospitals, which were meant only for the poor.

After several years of this study, Florence's conversation proved that she knew more about the conditions in such places than almost anyone else did. Her relatives were dismayed. They could not understand her. "Why doesn't Flo marry one of the handsome gentlemen who admire her?" complained Mrs. Nightingale. Mr. Nightingale was worried, too. Why, with her brilliant mind, wasn't Flo happy to be a scholar, as he was? When Florence asked permission to learn nursing, the horrified answer was "No!"

Florence went abroad again with family friends.

A Protestant religious hospital had been established in an ancient town on the River Rhine, in Germany. Florence longed to enter Kaiserswerth and be trained for nursing. Her traveling friends disliked leaving her there, but finally consented. This was something new to Florence—a clean hospital, where decent women nursed the sick. All of the other nurses were working women, but no other nurse had ever learned to care for the sick so quickly and with such eagerness and skill as Florence Nightingale.

At the end of October, Florence went back to England and her angry family. She faced the disgrace firmly. Now she really knew what she wanted to do. She intended to reform the hospitals of England! Yet, for a number of years, she could do nothing. Her mother, or aunts, or cousins begged her to nurse them in their illnesses. She took over the management of her family household and found that she had real talent for handling the many details of such a job. She did not know it at the time, but every one of these jobs helped prepare her for her later work.

Head of a Hospital

Florence heard of a small hospital for women in London that needed a superintendent. She was thirty-three years old when she told her parents that she now meant to make her own decisions. Mrs. Nightingale cried, and Parthe cried, and all of the aunts and cousins cried. Mr. Nightingale argued with Flo and said that such work would probably kill her. He did not actually refuse his permission, and she went to London as she had intended to do, with or without it. When Flo moved into the small hospital, her mother said with a sigh, "At least this is a respectable hospital for sick gentlewomen."

As head of the hospital, Florence worked day and night. First she had the house thoroughly cleaned. Then she put everything in order and replenished supplies. Then she ordered medicines, and when the correct ones were not sent, she spoke to the chemist like a queen to a disobedient subject. When the council of ladies who ran the hospital quarreled, Miss Nightingale brought them to terms. Then—at last—the hospital was running well, and Florence was—at last—doing the work that she wanted to do.

Sometimes she went home for a visit, and she enjoyed the parties as if she had never been away. She loved to be with the many babies and children always visiting there, and in the evening she entertained guests with her mimicry and fun.

War in the Crimea

In the autumn of 1854, England was thrown into excitement by the outbreak of war with Russia. Troops of both England and France were embarking for the Crimea, a peninsula that juts into the Black Sea north of Turkey. Florence Nightingale heard the news with great interest. She read every account of the landing of troops, and of the hospitals being set up at Scutari, across the Straits of Mar-

mora from Constantinople. She read that soldiers were dying by hundreds with wounds untended. She went to the Minister of War, an old friend, and offered to enlist nurses to take to Scutari.

Who had ever heard of such a thing? The Nightingales were so horrified that they could scarcely speak of it. Still, Florence set out with a group of nurses, gathered from the best London hospitals and from some religious orders.

As the dauntless Miss Nightingale stepped ashore in Scutari, followed by her nurses in their ugly brown uniforms and caps, she stood very still for a moment to look the place over. An old Turkish barracks was the principal hospital building. A foul and filthy place it was, and the nurses gasped with dismay as they stared. Wounded and sick men were lying all over the floor. Doctors were not friendly to these "upstart women" invading a man's world, and officers were curt.

The nurses were given a room too small for them but they did not complain. They had no time, for Miss Nightingale was already ordering things done and persuading the doctors and officers to get them done. She asked for a crew of two hundred convalescent men to scrub floors, and she got them. She then hired their wives to wash dirty linen and clothing. She also reorganized the kitchens and added a diet kitchen, for soups and gruel to replace the tough bones, meat, and bread given to desperately sick men. She

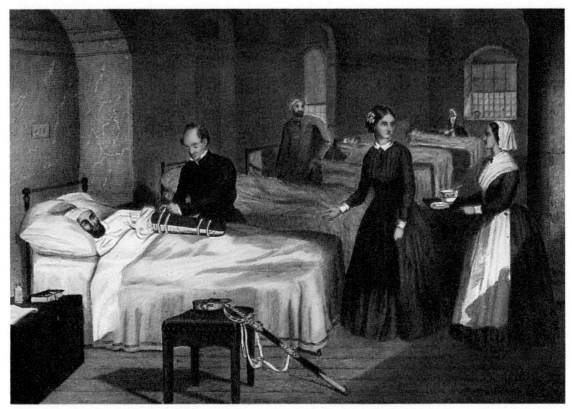

Florence Nightingale in the Hospital at Scutari, 1854. Bettmann Archive, Inc., New York City.

slept on a cot in the kitchen, when she had time to sleep.

Miss Nightingale's voice was soft and kind, yet it was firm and strict, too. After a while many doctors and officers began to trust and respect and, then, to like her. Those who resented her authority called her "the Bird." Nevertheless, the sick men grew to worship Miss Nightingale. At night when the wind shook the old Turkish barracks and rats scurried in the walls, suffering men would look up to see this lady coming down the long rows of cots to find out how they were. She held a lamp before her, to light their faces. To them she was "The Lady with a Lamp." Every night she walked through "our four miles of cots," as she called the hospital. Then she sat down at a kitchen table to write letters.

Florence Nightingale was becoming a heroine not only to the English, but to people everywhere. She received hundreds of letters a week, often containing money for her work, and she tried to answer them all.

In the following spring Miss Nightingale went on shipboard and journeyed to the Crimea itself, to do what she could for the hospitals. The Battle of Balaclava had taken its toll of British wounded. This was the engagement in which the Charge of the Light Brigade took place, made world-famous later by Tennyson's poem. Hospitals were so crowded that men lay in tents pitched all around the harbor. Fever was raging, too.

One day the troops in the front lines looked up to see Miss Nightingale riding out to visit them. She was a good horse-woman, and as she passed the Three Mortar Battery the men broke into cheers. Many were soldiers returned to duty from her hospital.

Then Miss Nightingale fell ill with fever and came close to dying. When the news reached England, even Queen Victoria joined in prayers for her recovery. The whole world rejoiced when the crisis passed and she was better. Doctors urged her to return to England, but she refused. She said that she felt like part of the British army. If they could suffer and endure, then so could she.

When she returned to Scutari, Miss Nightingale decided that the convalescent soldiers should learn to read. "Flo is trying to educate the British army," said Parthenope tartly. At that time soldiers were thought to be closer to brutes than to human beings. There was much talk of not pampering or spoiling them. To Florence Nightingale every person, rich or poor, was a valuable life. Many of these

soldiers remembered that she always stood beside the operation table, with her hands quietly folded, suffering with them as they endured operations without ether or chloroform.

Return to England

When Florence Nightingale returned to England in 1856, she was afraid of the grand celebrations prepared to greet her. She left the ship secretly and walked in on her family at Lea Hurst unannounced. Meetings were held in her honor, nevertheless. With the money collected at them, Florence was able to begin her plans for army hospital reform. She was not well and, as months passed, she did not improve. In spite of this, she intended to carry out her plans. Her next move was to a house in London, where she spent the rest of her life.

At the age of thirty-eight, heroic Miss Nightingale became an invalid. She seldom went out, but spent most of her time on a bed or couch. She worked tirelessly to get better hospitals, better barracks for soldiers, and sanitation reforms in the British colony of India. She also wrote a great deal and saw many people. Everyone thought that she would not live long.

During the Civil War in the United States, Miss Nightingale gave advice on nursing training and on hospitals, at the request of the United States government. She answered thousands of letters, and she directed her household as a general runs an army. Gradually, she lost her fragile good looks and became a stout old lady who looked rather like Queen Victoria. Yet no visitor left her without feeling the great beauty, kindness, and brilliance of her mind and character.

Nursing continued to be her greatest interest. Miss Nightingale directed the training of hospital nurses. In that, she ruled with a strict hand. The young nurses must live like nuns, devoted only to their duty. They had to keep diaries, which she read regularly. When they went out on the street, they had to go "by twos." One of them remarked later that, of course, they always separated at the corner!

Miss Nightingale lived to be ninety years old. She lived so long that she became a legend in her own lifetime. After a while people did not know whether she was really still alive or was only a memory. Those who actually knew her could have remarked, however, that few living people had such a record of accomplishment.

Florence Nightingale is remembered as the great lady who loved people enough to help them by giving her talents, her time, and her strength. She is remembered as a woman walking wearily, yet patiently, through dark rooms, holding up a lighted lamp to see the faces of the suffering people she had come to help.

Florence Nightingale with Nurses at Claydon, 1886. Bettmann Archive, Inc., New York City.

Developing Comprehension Skills

1. Florence Nightingale did not live her life in the way that her family expected her to. What did her family expect her to do with her life? Quote sentences from the text to prove your answer.

2. List at least three of the poor hospital conditions that horrified Florence Nightingale.

3. What do you think were some reasons why the doctors in Scutari changed their attitudes towards Florence?

4. How did Florence Nightingale affect the history of modern medicine?

5. For many years Florence allowed her family to keep her from becoming a nurse. Why did she wait so long? Did she gain anything by this delay? Do you believe that, overall, this delay helped or hurt her? Give reasons for your answer.

Reading Literature: Biographies

1. **Understanding Conflict.** Biographies are often written about people who face a conflict between their own goals and other people's expectations. What kind of conflicts did Florence Nightingale face? Show the differences between her family's ideas and hers and between the doctors' ideas and hers.

2. **Understanding a Character.** How did Florence Nightingale's personality change over the years? Use examples from the story.

3. **Evaluating a Character.** Do the authors of this biography admit that Florence Nightingale had faults? What might these have been? Do you think you would have liked Florence as a classmate? as a teacher? Why or why not?

4. **Understanding Setting.** Paragraph 6 on page 306 describes one of the settings of this biography. What is the main idea of this paragraph? Is there a topic sentence? If so, what is it? List the details about the setting given in the paragraph.

Developing Vocabulary Skills

1. **Using Context Clues.** Read the following sentences about the biography of Florence Nightingale. Use context clues to figure out the

meaning of each underlined word. Then find the dictionary or glossary meaning to see how well you used the clues.

  a. Beyond the lodges, stables, and gardens she stepped onto the downs, stretching smooth and green to the hills.

  b. Florence's father was a learned man, so why wasn't she happy to be a scholar as he was?

  c. Flo was unhappy at home in England, so she went abroad again with family friends to Paris and Switzerland.

  d. Then she put everything in order and replenished supplies that had run out.

  e. In Switzerland she got acquainted with refugees from Italy who told her of the revolution from which they had fled.

  f. Troops from both England and France were going to the Crimea, a peninsula that extends into the Black Sea, north of Turkey.

2. **Recognizing Comparison and Contrast.** For each of the following passages, identify the two ideas presented. State whether they are used in a comparison or contrast. Write the clue word.

  a. Florence enjoyed parties but often tired of the endless round of them that her mother insisted on.

  b. Sick people were lying in hospitals that were dens of noise and dirt. Even the doctors and nurses were seldom clean.

  c. Although Mr. Nightingale said that such work would probably kill her, he did not actually refuse his permission.

  d. Miss Nightingale's voice was soft and kind, yet it was firm.

  e. Doctors urged her to return to England, but she refused.

Developing Writing Skills

1. **Preparing for an Interview.** Imagine that you are a newspaper or television reporter, and that you have an appointment to interview Florence Nightingale. Write five to ten questions that you would ask her. Keep in mind that your interview will last only thirty minutes, so your most important questions should come first. Also, remember that your article or newscast about the interview must give important information that is not easily found in Florence's biography.

2. **Writing a Conversation.** Choose one of the events listed below. Imagine what Florence and the other person might have said to each

other. Write a short conversation. Remember to use quotation marks correctly. Look for guides to correct punctuation in your language arts textbook.

a. Florence tells her mother and father that she is taking the job of superintendent of a small hospital in London.
b. Arriving in Scutari, Florence asks the supervising doctor for a crew of two hundred men to clean the hospital.
c. One night in the Scutari hospital, Florence stops at the bedside of a wounded man to ask how he feels.
d. Florence interviews a young woman applying to become a nurse.

Developing Skills in Study and Research

Using Information from Maps. The biography of Florence Nightingale describes Florence's travels on two continents. To understand her travels and the strain they put on her health, it is helpful to refer to a map.

Look at a map of Europe in an atlas or other reference work. Make sure the map shows England and Turkey as well as France, Italy, and Germany. Use the map to answer these questions.

1. What body of water did Florence cross when she traveled from her home in England to visit in France, Italy, or Germany?
2. What bodies of water did she probably cross on her way from England to Scutari?
3. The city that was called Constantinople during Florence Nightingale's life is now called Istanbul. The modern city of Istanbul includes Scutari. Constantinople was in Europe. Scutari was west of the Bosporus Strait in Asia. Therefore, the city of Istanbul is in two continents, Europe and Asia. On which continent, Europe or Asia, is each of these other cities mentioned in the biography?

   a. London   b. Rome   c. Paris

Developing Skills in Critical Thinking

Evaluating Information. In a story about a person's entire life, there is room for only a small number of facts. A writer must leave out everything that is unimportant to his or her main ideas about the subject. In this biography, the writers were concerned mainly with Florence's mission in life and how she achieved her goals. They left out everything that did not have to do with those concerns.

For answers to each of the questions listed below, skim the selection about Florence Nightingale. On your paper, write your answer and at least two facts in the selection that support your answer. If you cannot find at least two passages that tell about this topic, you do not have enough information to answer the question. On your paper write, "The question cannot be answered."

1. Did Florence get seasick?
2. Was Florence's sister proud of what Florence did in Scutari?
3. Did Florence have determination?
4. Was Florence's father a selfish person?
5. Did Florence demand that other people work hard in hospitals?
6. Did Florence have many boyfriends?
7. When she was a child, was Florence scolded by her mother very often?
8. Did Florence have talent in art or music?

George Washington Carver: Plant Wizard

MAY McNEER and LYND WARD

Everything about George Carver's life seemed to work against him. He was born in slavery, lost his mother, had no money, and was not allowed an education. How could he overcome so many difficulties?

A little boy plodded slowly along a lonely road in Missouri, in the summer of 1874. Over his shoulder swung his belongings, tied in an old shawl, fastened to a stick. He was small and thin, and he did not talk much, for his voice was only a piping squeak. Yet, he seemed to see more than most other people did. As his bare feet moved in the dust, the boy felt his shoes bounce against his chest. New shoes should not be ruined by wear, so he had hung them around his neck by the laces. He was tired and rather hungry, but he smiled as he felt the sun and the breeze on his face. Birds sang, all trees were his friends, and every clump of grass and wild flower seemed to nod to him.

This was George Washington Carver, setting out to seek his fortune. It was astonishing that such a small boy should start out alone to the town of Neosho to learn to read and write; yet it was even more surprising that he was alive at all. Many times he had heard his foster mother tell of a dreadful night during the Civil War. George was a tiny baby then. He could not remember how his sister had been killed, how his older brother had escaped and hidden, and how he and his mother had been stolen by slave raiders. He and his family were slaves and belonged to a German farmer and his wife, named Carver, who were fond of them. Carver had ridden out in pursuit of the thieves and had found tiny, sickly George abandoned by the roadside. His mother had never been heard of again.

Carver had given a good horse to the neighbor who had helped him in the search. Sometimes George looked down at his own spindly legs and wondered if he was worth as much as the horse. There was some doubt about it in his mind.

After a few years George's brother went away, and George did not see him again. George was not strong enough to do farm work, so Frau Carver taught him to cook and wash clothes. He taught himself about trees and plants, for he loved all growing things. He made the Carver garden the finest in the neighborhood.

A farmer friend of the Carvers saw how bright he was, and said that he ought to be taught to read. This farmer gave George a book on plants. Although George did not want to leave the Carvers, and they hated to see him go, he knew that he must learn to read. Now George had a dollar in his pocket to pay for his schooling. As for food and shelter—well, he could work hard. He was on his way to the nearest school for blacks.

Schooling

George reached Neosho by nightfall and crept into an old barn to sleep in the hay. The next morning he found the one-room school and paid his dollar to enter. For several weeks George slept in the barn beside a stray dog. He earned his food by washing dishes or cutting wood. Then, early one morning, the man who owned the barn came in and saw the little boy curled up beside the dog, almost hidden under a mound of hay.

"Well, now, what are you doing in my barn?"

George jumped up in fright and found it impossible to speak. The young man smiled and said, "You look hungry. Come into the house."

Inside the warm kitchen a young wife was frying bacon and eggs and baking corn bread. She gave George some hot food, and then the young couple sat down to hear his story. When he finished, speaking slowly and politely in his squeaky voice, they looked at each other, nodded, and offered him the shed to sleep in. George stayed there for some months and did odd jobs for the young couple, whose name was Martin. As he sat in the kitchen in the evenings, he heard them talk of the West and of how they might join one of the wagon trains rolling through Missouri. He was not surprised when they decided to go. The day that they left, George sat down on the steps and wondered what he was going to do now.

He heard a voice. "Boy, get your things and come with me."

George looked up. There stood Aunt Mariah, an elderly black woman whom he knew. He jumped up, collected his few clothes and the food left him by the Martins, and went to her little house, where he soon felt very much at home.

George lived with Aunt Mariah and Uncle Andy until he was thirteen and had learned far more than his teacher in the school knew. As soon as he could read, he borrowed every book that he could find, and he remembered all that he read. The day came when he knew that, to learn more, he must start out alone on the road again.

George went to Fort Scott, Kansas. He got work in a hotel and was allowed to sleep on a cot on the back porch. He went to school and found that, even here, he knew more about plants than did the teacher. Since George had very little time to go out into the country, he began to draw trees and flowers. He also got a little paint box and painted flowers. He joined the art class of his school and soon became known for his pictures. When he had again learned all that the school could teach him, George was on his way once more. He had grown tall and much stronger, and now his voice was strong, too, though as gentle as ever. He signed up as a laborer on the new railroad that was being built across the western plains and became a camp cook for a while. Later, he picked fruit or worked on ranches. Finally he went to Olathe, Kansas, to go to school again.

College

When George finished high school, he went back to visit the Carvers, who urged him to stay with them and farm their land. George was tempted, but somehow he knew that he must do something more. He wanted more learning. He wanted to go to college.

"College?" asked Frau Carver, folding her hands beneath her big white apron. "*Ja*, you should go to college. But how can you?"

George smiled and nodded. He meant to try. First he applied to Highland College, in Kansas, but was turned down because he was black. Discouraged, he

homesteaded land and tried to make a farm of his own, but the earth was very poor, and he gave it up. One day he wandered into a church in Winterset, Iowa, and joined in singing a hymn. As his rich voice rolled forth, the minister noticed him. Next day Parson Milholland looked George up and invited him to his home. Mrs. Milholland was a musician and was so interested in this talented young man that she gave him music lessons. Mr. Milholland said that he would locate a college that would take George. Simpson College, in Iowa, accepted him, and so once again George set out, this time to enter art school.

Making a living was always a problem, but it was not a new one to George Carver. He found a shed, got permission to use it, and started a laundry service for other students. During his second year

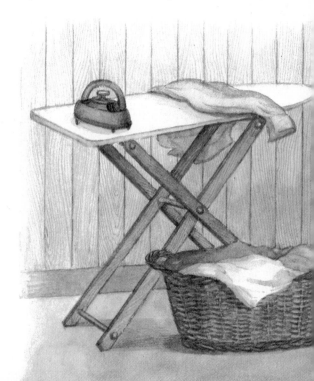

there, as George pushed the hot iron expertly back and forth over shirts, his thoughts were busy with his future. What did he want to do? He liked painting, but he realized now that he did not want to spend all of his time as an artist. Science interested him far more.

The following year George disappointed his art teacher by leaving Simpson College to go to Iowa State College in Ames, to study agriculture and botany. At twenty-seven years of age, this tall, gentle man began the study of plant life. He was soon known as a remarkable student, and he made many friends. George Carver

began to draw attention by his work with plants. After he had been at college a few years, he was called a "plant wizard," for his long fingers could do more than anyone thought possible. He worked day and night, waiting on tables, doing anything to make a simple living. His happiest hours were spent in the greenhouses with plants and flowers.

George Washington Carver received his degree in 1894, and was asked to teach at the college. Now he could smile when he remembered that he had once wondered whether he was worth as much as a horse! Here, in Ames, Iowa, he had great laboratories to work in and every opportunity to do the things that he could do so well. After a few years George had earned another degree, and he was happy in his teaching. It really looked as if this was his place on earth and his wanderings were over.

Tuskegee

Then, one day, up from Alabama came a black man whose name was also Washington. This was Booker T. Washington, an educator who was spending his life trying to improve education for his race. After the Civil War, the slaves were free, but most of them were unable to read and write. Many small schools were started for them, but money was scarce, and people had hardly enough to support themselves. Booker T. Washington had bought a piece of washed-out earth in Alabama.

George Washington Carver (the tallest) instructing students in the laboratory at Tuskegee Institute, Alabama, 1923. Photographer: C. M. Battey.

Here he had taught a few young men to build a schoolhouse of bricks that they made themselves from the red clay of the land.

Carver sat quietly and listened as Washington talked to him about the beginning of the school at Tuskegee. Washington spoke of the black farmers and their wives and children. They had cotton fields and a few other small crops, but they could never grow enough both to feed themselves and to sell a surplus to get cash for clothing and supplies. A man who understood farming was desperately needed to teach young men and women to get better crops from their land.

Dr. Carver listened carefully to the big dark man who talked so earnestly about the needs of his people. He made his decision. Quietly, he told Booker Washington that he would come to Tuskegee to do all that he could. This "plant wizard," with such a brilliant future ahead of him at a fine university, would go to live in the poverty-stricken back country in Alabama.

When he saw the Tuskegee school for the first time, Dr. Carver wondered how he could accomplish anything here at all. The brick building was surrounded by fields overgrown with weeds and washed into gullies by rains. Inside the school he found no laboratory and nothing with which to work. However, George Washington Carver had not been a professor all of his busy years. He had worked with hot irons, wash tubs, cookstoves, axes, hoes, and plows. In his classes he had only a few young men, with little education and no knowledge beyond the cotton fields. They knew poverty as well as he did, and they could be trained to make much of very little. He proposed that he help them make their own laboratory.

He led them on expeditions to the dump heaps around the nearest towns. This was a search that became a treasure hunt. The students went through trash piles in alleys, and asked housewives for broken pans, lamps, and kettles. When they had collected a great pile of cast-off utensils, Professor Carver showed them pictures that he had drawn of laboratory equipment. Long hours the boys worked with broken articles—cleaning, mending, making new things from old ones.

Then Dr. Carver got a two-horse plow and went to work himself. Straight furrows stretched out behind him, and students who had thought of farming as ignorant work, not fit for the educated, felt ashamed. Dr. Carver sent them for bucket after bucket of black muck and leaf mold from swamps and woods and manure from the barns. Then he planted cowpeas! Everybody gasped. Who ever heard of such a thing? Cowpeas were good only for pigs. Cotton was the cash money crop. When the peas were picked, this strange teacher cooked them, and they were so delicious that the students couldn't eat enough.

After that, Dr. Carver planted sweet potatoes, and the earth yielded eighty bushels to the acre. This was unheard of in that country, and now the students, who had not wanted to farm, began to speak of being "agriculturists." After a few years of these crops, Dr. Carver planted cotton in the enriched fields and showed that crop rotation could help the soil.

Nothing was wasted. That was the belief of this man who seemed to have magic in his fingers. Every day he had a whole handful of new ideas, too. He searched the woods and fields and brought home plants, leaves, and roots. Then he took them to his laboratory and made them into useful products, or medicines, or food. He told his students that they must learn to "see." They must always see something good in nature. They must always look for something that would benefit mankind.

Not even a few handfuls of dirt were too humble to interest Dr. Carver. Yet he wanted almost nothing for himself. He wore old clothes and ancient shoes, and he ate the food prepared for the students. He required no luxuries of any kind. His love for flowers was with him, as it had been since he could remember. Instead of painting flowers, Dr. Carver grew them, and he was never seen without a blossom on his coat.

Fame

Far and wide people talked about this gentle, hard-working scientist, who could make something out of nothing. His fame spread, and strangers came to see him. The school began to grow. Yet, as always, money was a problem. Booker T. Washington was often out trying to raise money, lecturing and explaining the needs. Dr. Carver could think of only one way that he could make money for the school. He could play the piano as well as he could paint. A concert tour was arranged, and money came in for new equipment and supplies for the laboratories of Dr. Carver.

There was something else that interested the scientist. He asked himself: How can I reach the poor farmers who need help but cannot come to Tuskegee? A thought struck him: If they cannot come here, why can't I go to them?

A wagon was fitted out, and a program arranged. This was the first mobile school for agriculture, and the first demonstration wagon to go out to the people. There was not a single subject that Dr. Carver didn't know, and not one activity that he couldn't actually do himself. Dr. Carver gave talks on crop rotation, on chicken raising, on the difficult problems of the farmers. Farm wives were told how to make good pickles and preserves and how to can food well. Later on, the wagon carried new types of plows and garden tools. At one time, the demonstration collection included a live cow. Farmers as well as students were learning from Tuskegee.

Slowly, money came in, and Dr. Carver was offered a larger salary. He heard the offer with a smile and asked, "What will I do with more money?"

He had no interest in money for himself, but his interest in the land and its products grew stronger every year. When the boll weevil came eastward from Mexico and Texas, Dr. Carver saw the danger in advance. This bug could destroy cotton plants completely and quickly. He begged farmers to stop planting cotton that year and to plow cotton stalks under to make a cotton-free belt to stop the weevil. Not understanding, they refused. Next, Dr. Carver urged farmers to spray their cotton fields with poison and then to plant peanuts. They refused again, and the boll weevil took over. When the cotton was destroyed, farmers were willing to plant peanuts. Then, because the peanut crop was so large, prices went down.

Dr. Carver set to work in his laboratory. He paid no attention to the things said against him for giving such advice. For many weeks he worked far into the night. When he called people in to see the results, he showed them cheese, milk, and almost two dozen other products made from the peanut. Later he made other things: face powder, printer's ink, soaps, vinegar, creosote, butter, dyes, and many more. Now the farmers had a market for peanuts, and the scientific world was excited. Dr. Carver experimented in the same way with the common sweet potato. Synthetic products could be valuable. Big business was interested in the fact that useful products could be made from so many things that were formerly thrown out as useless waste. Dr. Carver was the great pioneer in this field.

When Booker T. Washington died, Dr. Carver was offered positions with high salaries at other colleges and in manufacturing plants. He chose to stay at Tuskegee because his interest in helping the poor farmer was as strong as ever. He spent more hours in his laboratory and did less teaching. In his spare time he painted flowers, worked in the greenhouses, played the piano, or made fine tapestries.

When visitors asked, "Is that the famous Dr. Carver?" the students thought it a good joke to say, "Yes, and he is still wearing the same suit that he had on when he came to Tuskegee."

Before Dr. Carver died in 1943, he was happy to see a fine new laboratory set up at Tuskegee under his direction. Now he knew that the students could go on to more knowledge under other teachers. He had taught them to see more than others saw, and he tried to teach them to listen well also.

George Washington Carver was a man who never looked down on any kind of hard work, and he was one who used his genius to help his people—those who had so little opportunity. His own love of all things that grow made the work of Dr. Carver an important part of the lives of all people, of all races.

Developing Comprehension Skills

1. What happened to George's mother?

2. Why did George have trouble getting an education?

3. How did Dr. Carver change the attitudes of the Tuskegee students toward farming?

4. Dr. Carver helped people in many ways. Give an example from the text that shows a way in which he helped you.

5. George Washington Carver was talented in art, business, and agriculture. Do you think he made the correct career choice? Why or why not?

Reading Literature: Biographies

1. **Appreciating Details.** Modern biographies include small details about a person's life. This biography mentions that George wondered whether he was worth as much as a horse. Why do you think this detail was included?

2. **Understanding Setting.** Most of Dr. Carver's early life was in the country. How did his experiences there affect his interest in art, his interest in plants, and his ability to understand the needs of the Tuskegee students and nearby farmers?

   Imagine that he had spent his childhood in a city. Do you think his interests and abilities would have developed in the same way? If not, how do you think they would have been different?

3. **Understanding Indirect Description.** The first few paragraphs of this biography provide an indirect description of George Washington Carver's qualities as a child. That is, the paragraphs tell us about his actions and thoughts. From that information, we can figure out his qualities.

   For example, the text does not say "George was brave." However, we learn that from this sentence: "It was astonishing that such a small boy should start out alone to the town of Neosho to learn to read and write."

   What does each of these sentences or groups of sentences tell about George's character? Choose the best statement from the three possibilities listed below the passage.

a. He was tired and rather hungry, but he smiled as he felt the sun and the breeze on his face.
   (1) George got discouraged easily.
   (2) George enjoyed the outdoors.
   (3) George complained a great deal.

b. Sometimes George looked down at his spindly legs and wondered if he was worth as much as the horse. There was some doubt in his mind.
   (1) George was tall.
   (2) George did not like horses.
   (3) George did not brag a lot.

c. He taught himself about trees and plants, for he loved all growing things.
   (1) George was smart.
   (2) George was honest.
   (3) George was friendly.

Developing Vocabulary Skills

Using Example Clues. You have learned about several types of context clues, incuding comparison and contrast clues. Another type of clue that can help you understand the meaning of an unfamiliar word is an example clue. Certain key words or phrases tell you to look for examples in a sentence. Some of these phrases are *an example, for example, one kind, for instance, some types,* and *such as.*

In this sentence the words *such as* give a clue that a loon is an example of a type of bird:

Large web-footed diving birds, such as the loon, have loud, wild cries.

Read the following sentences about Florence Nightingale and George Washington Carver. For each sentence, do the following:

a. Write the meaning of the underlined word.
b. Tell whether the clue was a **definition or restatement clue** or an **example clue**.
c. Write the key words or punctuation that helped you find the meaning of the word.

1. Florence heard much talk about not <u>pampering</u> the soldiers, or spoiling them.

2. Florence's family angrily <u>opposed</u> her decision to learn nursing. That is, they were absolutely against the idea.

3. Hot liquids, such as soups and <u>gruel</u>, were given to desperately sick men.

4. Miss Nightingale brought about worldwide <u>reforms</u>—improvements—in hospital administration and nursing.

5. They endured operations without <u>ether</u> or any other type of anesthetic to ease the pain.

6. George went to Iowa State College to pursue his interest in <u>botany</u>, which is the study of plants.

7. When the <u>boll weevil</u> (a little black beetle) came eastward from Mexico and Texas, Dr. Carver knew this bug could destroy cotton plants completely and quickly.

8. Dr. Carver explained that many oily liquids taken from plants, <u>creosote</u>, for instance, could be useful in medicines.

9. Some examples of wild vegetables that Dr. Carver recommended were clover tops, dandelions, and <u>chicory</u>.

10. Dr. Carver noticed that the poor children from Tuskegee had <u>rickets</u>. This is a disease that comes from a lack of calcium, causing bones to become soft.

Developing Writing Skills

1. **Proving Your Point.** This biography shows that Dr. Carver had many good personal characteristics. He was a hard worker, a considerate man, and a patient teacher. Choose one of these values and write a paragraph proving that Dr. Carver possessed it. Use details from the story to back up your point of view.

2. **Using Indirect Description.** Write a paragraph describing a friend. Tell about one particularly good quality of your subject, but do not state the quality directly. Instead, tell about some action of your subject that suggests he or she has that quality. (See question 3 under Reading Literature: Biographies.)

Developing Skills in Study and Research

Understanding the Information on Maps. A map uses color, different kinds of lines, and different sizes of dots to represent certain kinds of information.

In an atlas, find a map that shows the states where Dr. Carver spent many years: Missouri, Kansas, Iowa, and Alabama. Examine the map and its **legends**, or notes of explanation, at the edges of the map. Find the answers to these questions:

1. Does the map use different colors? What do the different colors stand for?

2. Does the map use different types of lines? What does each type of line stand for?

3. Does the map use dots of different sizes? What does a dot of each size represent?

4. Does the map have a scale of distance? How many miles does one inch represent?

5. Approximately how far is it from the capital of Missouri to the capital of Kansas? from the capital of Iowa to the capital of Alabama?

Next, in the same atlas find a map of Alabama alone. Examine that map and its legends. Answer questions 1 through 4 for that map.

Developing Skills in Speaking and Listening

Giving Directions. On his demonstration wagon, Dr. Carver explained farming methods to his listeners. Think about some short activity you know well and can explain, such as using a tool or appliance, playing a certain game, or preparing a special food. Outline a brief talk to explain the activity. Decide whether you will need pictures or visual aids, such as the tool itself. Prepare your materials and practice your talk. Then present your talk to a group. Be careful to speak slowly and clearly and to look at your listeners as you talk. When you are finished, test whether you gave clear directions by asking one of your listeners to pantomime or explain the activity.

Jane Addams:
Good Neighbor

MAY McNEER *and* LYND WARD

Like Florence Nightingale, Jane Addams left a comfortable life for hard work in uncomfortable circumstances. Can you identify, from the lives of these women, what personal qualities make it possible to live independently?

A little girl stood frowning down at her hands, turning her right thumb around to look at it. She wished that she could see that it was flattening out into a real "miller's thumb," the kind that came from constant rubbing of the wheat between thumb and finger.

She reached into a pile of wheat and slowly rubbed it. Then she turned her hands over and scowled at the backs of them. Why couldn't she have those tiny red and blue marks that millers had? Father still had them on his hands, and he had a miller's thumb, too, even though he was now the owner of the mill instead of a worker. She asked the miller about it, but he only laughed at her. When he ground the millstones and sparks hit his hands and made the tiny red marks, he teased her about wanting to be a miller.

The mill stood among tall elms at the edge of Cedarville in northwestern Illinois. Jane had been born in 1860 in the big house nearby. In the years since the Civil War, her father had become the most important man of the village, for he was wise and thoughtful, as well as a good businessman. He was a Quaker. He had been in the legislature with Abraham Lincoln. Jane was proud of the fact that her father had letters from the martyred president, letters that began jokingly: "My Dear Mr. Double-D Addams."

The Addams children had a wonderful place to play along the little stream that turned the wheel of the flour mill. Jane, who was the youngest, had a spinal curvature that caused her to walk with her toes turned in and with her head slightly to one side. Her mother had died when she was a baby, so Jane had given all of her love and admiration to her handsome father. The other children—Mary, Martha, Weber, and Alice—were much older. Nurse Polly was part of the family also.

Jane was a rather silent girl, playing alone in the mill and under the trees, with kittens and dogs for companions.

One day, when she drove through town with her father, Jane noticed that the laborers lived in poor and ugly houses. She asked her father why this was so. He tried to explain to her that not every child was as fortunate as she.

Jane said thoughtfully, "When I grow up I will live in a beautiful big house, as I do now, but it will be with ugly little houses around it, and I will invite all of the other children to play in my nice yard."

Jane read a great deal in her father's books, for he had a large library. She wanted to understand the books that her father read, and she tried to understand, also, his concern for others. She began to have a strange dream, one that came back to her from time to time for some years. She dreamed that she was alone on earth, and that all by herself, somehow, she had to make a wagon wheel. She knew that the future of the world depended on it. Jane always woke up from this dream terrified. As soon as she could, she went to the village to watch the blacksmith at work. Perhaps she could learn how.

When Jane was about eight, her father married a widow who had two sons. This event started a happier life for Jane, for one of the boys was about her age and now she had a playmate.

The Search for Commitment

At seventeen, Jane entered Rockford Seminary, which was not far from her home town. She was bitterly disappointed because her father wished her to stay close to home and refused to allow her to go East to Smith College. Yet, after a while, she made friends and began to enjoy the life of the school. The girls at Rockford Seminary were serious and studious, and they had such strong religious beliefs that many of them later went into missionary work. Jane, although she was rather religious, refused to become a missionary. Like her father, she made her own decisions and was not swayed by what others did.

When she graduated from Rockford Seminary, she entered the Women's Medical College of Philadelphia. Her spinal trouble grew worse, until she had to have an operation. When Jane was up and well again, she realized sadly that she could not study anything so strenuous as medicine. What was she to do? Her family thought that travel would be good for Jane, so she went to Europe for two years. To her, Europe was a world of lovely landscapes, fine pictures, concerts, and beautiful old buildings. Jane enjoyed them all. Yet there was a different scene that she remembered above all others.

One Saturday night she joined a group of sightseers on a horse-drawn bus in London. The bus rattled into the worst slum in the sprawling city. Jane, who was sitting on top, could look down on a picture that was like a horrible nightmare. By the light of two flaring gas lamps, ragged men, women, and children pushed and fought to buy vegetables and fruit left over from the week's sales. For halfpennies they got rotten cabbages and potatoes, and devoured them, skin and all. All of her life Jane Addams remembered the sight of clawlike hands raised to bid for decaying vegetables.

After that, she visited slums wherever she went in Europe, returning to her own country with more knowledge of social conditions than most travelers ever get. Her health was quite good now, and she was twenty-seven years old. What was she to do? After a time she joined a friend, Ellen Starr, and returned to Europe for another trip. One day in London Jane declared that she was tired of a useless life. Ellen replied thoughtfully that she felt the same. Custom did not permit women of their position to go out to work, except to teach. Ellen was already a teacher, but she and Jane wanted to do something more. They decided to visit Toynbee Hall, in London's East End slums. Perhaps they could get an idea.

Toynbee Hall was the world's first settlement house. As Jane and Ellen walked through it and saw the friendly people who were trying to make this a clubhouse for the neighborhood, they looked at each other and smiled. It was not a "mission" run by a church, but was simply a place where people could come together for classes, clubs, and social life. Suddenly Jane thought: This is a big house in the midst of little ones! This is the kind of house that I have wanted — one that I can share with my neighbors.

Hull House

Jane and Ellen returned to America and at once began to put their plans into action. Jane studied bookkeeping, for her "Big House" must be well run. Ellen had no extra money to put into it, but Jane did have some left to her by her father, who had died several years before. She went to Chicago to find her home among the poor.

Chicago in the eighteen-eighties was a spreading, growing city. People poured in from the East by every train, wagon, and ship. As she walked about, Jane thought that this place was like a great overgrown boy who was shooting up so fast that he could not tell what to do with his feet and hands. All around Jane in the dirty streets swarmed men, women, and children from every country in Europe, shouting and talking in many languages. Many could speak no English. They crowded into tenements and into the noisy, dark factories and big cattle stockyards where they worked. They all wanted to be Americans, but they did not know how. Chicago was a huge collection of foreign cities flung together without plan.

Halsted Street was called the longest straight street in the world, for it ran thirty-two miles. Jane rode slowly along it in a hired carriage, thinking that these

Hull House in the early 1900's. Jane Addams Memorial Collection, University Library, University of Illinois at Chicago. Photographer: Wallace Kirkland.

people must be her neighbors and that here she must find her house. Then she saw it! It was a thirty-year-old mansion, the home of the wealthy Hull family when the street had seen better days. Now it was filled with little flats. A storeroom and a saloon were on the ground floor.

Jane and Ellen Starr found the owner, Miss Helen Culver, and rented part of the house. They had a promise of getting all of it later, when the leases ran out. A friend, Mary Keyser, came to live and work with them, and Jane brought furniture from her old home in Cedarville.

They decided to call it Hull House. It was to be a neighborhood settlement home in the midst of Russians, Germans, Greeks, Poles, Italians, and Irish. The whole neighborhood was dirty, noisy, and filled with smells of all kinds.

They had no sooner cleaned the house and moved in when there was a knock at the front door. A young mother asked if they would keep her baby while she went to work that day. When Miss Addams spoke to her in Italian, her face broke into a delighted smile. The next day more babies arrived at the door, and Hull House had a day nursery. As the three residents wondered what to do with all of these children every day, the problem was unexpectedly solved for them. A young girl from a wealthy family arrived at their door to ask if she could help.

"What can you do?" asked Jane.

"I can look after children," she answered with a smile, looking around at the noisy guests.

Jane Addams soon discovered that there were others, men as well as women, who wanted to do something at Hull House. After a few weeks, evening classes for girls and boys were started, and clubs as well as dances and concerts planned. Carpentry, sewing, and music were taught. More and more men and women came shyly in and were overjoyed to talk to Miss Addams in their native tongues. The whole neighborhood buzzed with the knowledge that Jane Addams could speak several languages. Hull House was open to its neighbors, and its neighbors came.

As the three residents planned and worked and organized, they had many challenges. "Why," asked Jane Addams, "shouldn't these people from countries where they saw so much art, have some to see here?" She started art classes and put pictures on the walls of Hull House.

Problems and Solutions

There were no playgrounds in Chicago at that time, and tenement children had to stay in the dirty streets or be locked in cold rooms while their parents worked. Streets where they played were so filthy that is was difficult to walk in them. Garbage overflowed big wooden boxes placed in the middle of streets.

Early one morning sleepy workmen saw Miss Addams plodding through the ankle-deep refuse. As the sun rose, women hung out of windows to watch. What was the lady doing? She held up her skirts above her shoe tops, out of the dirt, and every now and then she stopped to write something in a notebook. This street was so dirty that it was hard to tell whether it was paved with cobblestones or not. There was a broken pump in a yard here—this she noted down—and a tenement without any pump there. Why were those garbage boxes not emptied? Miss Addams had accepted a job as sanitary inspector for the city and was seeing that the laws were enforced.

One thing led to another. Jane Addams saw that little could be done unless these people had money to live on. She tried to get laws passed for shorter hours and higher wages. She also worked for laws to force landlords to improve tenements. More than anything else, she tried to make those who ran local and national government agencies understand that there must be laws to keep children from working long hours in factories and to send them to school. Hull House organized the first fresh air camps to get children out of the slums in summer.

People in other places talked of Hull House. Many visitors came to see Hull House at work. When they arrived it was not always easy to find Miss Addams, she was doing so many things. Her speaking engagements had a simple message. She asked for understanding of these people and concern for their children.

Yet Hull House continued to have problems. On Halsted Street young girls and boys grew up ashamed of their parents because the old folks could not speak English. The older people had Old-World ways and customs, and they could not understand their American children.

One day as Jane was picking her way through the street refuse, she passed a tenement house where an old woman sat with an ancient loom. Miss Addams stopped to watch as the knobby fingers made delicate woven patterns. She had been searching in her thoughts for some way to help younger people understand the values of the older ones.

She went home and proposed a plan for a "labor museum." A room was fitted out with several looms, benches, and embroidery frames. The neighborhood was searched for women who had these skills. They came to Hull House and made fine laces, weavings, and embroideries. The men did wood carving and other crafts of their native countries. The younger people were invited to watch, and they came away with a new respect for the talents of their old folk.

Jane Addams in 1914.
Bettmann Archive, Inc., New York City.

As the years passed and the circle of activities at Hull House widened, Miss Addams began to put more and more time into studying national laws and improving them. She wrote the story of her life. She was considered an authority on social conditions, and she worked for world peace. In 1931, Jane Addams received the Nobel Peace Prize[1], jointly with a friend.

1. The **Nobel Peace Prize** is given yearly for outstanding work in the cause of peace. Anyone in the world is eligible.

As Hull House grew, the neighborhood around it changed. Central Europeans, Mexicans, and Blacks moved in. Languages changed with changing times. Chicago changed, too. Streets were better and were cleaner; laws were passed to improve tenements, and to provide running water and good sanitary conditions. Children had playgrounds, fresh air camps, and better education. Child labor laws kept them out of factories and in school.

When Jane Addams died at the age of seventy-five, Hull House had grown large. Many buildings had been added to it, and many devoted people worked there. Yet it remained the "Big House" among little ones, the house to which Miss Addams invited her neighbors to come in friendship.

Jane Addams at Hull House in the 1920's. Jane Addams Memorial Collection University Library, University of Illinois at Chicago. Photograph by Wallace Kirkland.

Developing Comprehension Skills

1. Identify one event and one person in Jane Addams' early life that helped her make choices later in life.

2. Why did Jane Addams decide to move to the Halsted Street area in Chicago? If you had been a friend of hers at the time, would you have considered this a wise decision? Why or why not?

3. Jane Addams did much traveling in Europe. Name at least two ways in which this helped her prepare for Hull House.

4. Think about the lives and personal qualities of Florence Nightingale, George Washington Carver, and Jane Addams. Based on their behavior and experiences, draw up a brief test for determining leaders. Your test should have at least three good questions to identify a person who could become a leader.

Reading Literature: Biographies

1. **Using Indirect Description.** In an **indirect description**, we learn about a character's qualities by looking at his or her actions or work. Choose one of Jane Addams' qualities. Identify at least three statements in the selection that prove she had that quality.

2. **Recognizing Time Sequence.** List five important events in Ms. Addams' life in sequence.

3. **Understanding Conflict.** What conflicts did Jane Addams encounter at Hull House? How did she meet these opposing forces?

4. **Appreciating Figurative Language.** Find the simile in each passage below. Identify what two things are being compared. Explain what the two things have in common.
   a. All of her life Jane Addams remembered the sight of clawlike hands raised to bid for decaying vegetables.
   b. As she walked about, Jane thought that this place was like a great overgrown boy, shooting up so fast that he could not tell what to do with his feet and hands.

Developing Vocabulary Skills

Using Context Clues. Each of these sentences explains a word with context clues. Use the context clues for each sentence to figure out the meaning of the underlined word. On your paper, write the meaning and the clue words that helped you find it.

1. Doctors were not friendly to these women invading a man's world, and the officers, also, were <u>curt</u>.
2. Many people <u>resented</u> Miss Nightingale's authority. On the other hand, the sick men grew to trust and appreciate her.
3. Dr. Carver searched for plants that were <u>beneficial</u> to mankind and, also, that would be of help to poor farmers.
4. Besides <u>synthetic</u> soaps, other man-made products included printer's ink, vinegar, butter, and dyes.
5. Jane was not <u>swayed</u> by what others did. On the contrary, she was very independent.
6. Jane's family thought travel in Europe would be easy on her health, unlike the <u>strenuous</u> study of medicine.

Developing Writing Skills

1. **Comparing Biographies.** What similar qualities in Florence Nightingale and Jane Addams impelled each of them to leave a life of comfort to help people? How did these women differ from each other?

   Write one paragraph discussing how the two women were similar. Write a second paragraph explaining how they were different.

2. **Using Your Imagination.** Reread the section of "Jane Addams" that tells about the life of the people who lived around Hull House. Pretend you live in that neighborhood. Write a first-person story about a day in your life.

Developing Skills in Study and Research

Using Almanacs, Books of Records, and Other Reference Books. Besides the encyclopedia and atlas, the reference section of a library contains numerous other reference books. One type is the almanac. An **almanac** is a reference book that is updated and reprinted every year. It tells of the latest events and recent newsmakers who seem important. Some encyclopedia publishers produce an annual almanac to keep their encyclopedias current. Other almanacs may be on special subjects such as sports or medicine.

Books of records are also updated and reprinted every year. They often include information that is not important enough to belong in an encyclopedia, such as the longest baseball game ever played.

Investigate the reference section of your school or local library. List at least three reference books other than dictionaries, the encyclopedia, the thesaurus, and the atlas. For each book identify the title, the authors or editors, the publishing company, and the date of publication. Explain what type of information you can get from that book.

Examine the table of contents of each book and its index, if it has one. Then skim the book to get an idea of how the material is organized and presented. Can you find a reference in the books to any of these topics? For what reason is it included?

Jane Addams	Chicago
Hull House	Nobel Peace Prize

Developing Skills in Speaking and Listening

Persuading an Audience. Imagine that you are scheduled to talk to a group of business people and politicians. You will stand in for Jane Addams, who is trying to get their support and help. Use information from the biography of Ms. Addams, and from other things you know, to speak on one of the following subjects:

1. Why children should not work long hours in factories
2. Why the streets must be cleared of garbage
3. Why Hull House should have classes in art, weaving, sewing, and wood carving

Before presenting your speech, decide on three good reasons you will use. Write out each of your reasons on a note card, and, if you like, refer to the note cards as you speak. When you speak, avoid pauses and such meaningless timekillers as too many *and*s, the word *like,* or the phrase *you know.* Let your voice show interest and enthusiasm.

Jim Thorpe:
Indian Athlete

GUERNSEY VAN RIPER, JR.

Jim Thorpe was one of the world's greatest all-around athletes. However, for many years his name was missing from any list of Olympic winners. Read to find out why.

The sun shown bright and clear over the new Olympic stadium at Stockholm, Sweden. It was July, 1912, the first day for track and field sports at the fifth Olympic games.

Around the cinder track marched hundreds of men and women athletes. They came from twenty-six different countries, from every part of the world. They strode along to the cheers of 30,000 people who had come to watch. The athletes went proudly past the royal box of King Gustav and Queen Victoria of Sweden.

Many other important people were in the box, too, to review the parade. Sitting together were Colonel Victor Balck, president of the Swedish Olympic Commission, and James E. Sullivan of the American Commission.

The American athletes were just coming past the box. In the fourth row marched a tall, powerful-looking American Indian. He had a shock of black hair.

His big square jaw was set firmly. His half-closed eyes stared straight ahead.

"That's Big Jim Thorpe," said Mr. Sullivan. "He comes from our Indian school in Carlisle, Pennsylvania. He's one of the most versatile athletes we've ever had in the United States."

"Indeed!" said Colonel Balck. "I shall look forward to seeing him perform. We think that the champion athlete is one who can do many different things well. So we have the Pentathlon, five different contests, and the Decathlon, ten different contests. The same men will compete in all of the contests."

The colonel didn't have long to wait. The very next day the Pentathlon was held. All over the field, men were warming up.

Jim walked in with Pop Warner, one of the American team's trainers.

"Well, Jim, you're about ready," he said. "But I never expected you to be here when I first saw you at Carlisle. You were a skinny little fellow then!"

Jim smiled. He could hardly believe it himself. In his years at Carlisle he had grown as fast as a milkweed in the spring and as sturdy as one of the oak trees near the Thorpe cabin in Oklahoma.

"Guess I'll jog around a bit to loosen up."

Mike Murphy, the head trainer of the Olympic team, came over to Pop Warner. "I'm eager to see how your big Indian does today. He can beat anybody in the United States, but these are the very best athletes in all the world."

"In every sport I've asked Jim to try, he's always excelled," said Pop.

"You've done a fine job of coaching him," Mike said. "You're about the best there is at training athletes."

Pop laughed. "I didn't do much for Jim. When I found him, all he needed was to grow. Look at him now!"

Mike nodded. "Over six feet tall and a hundred eighty-five pounds of smooth muscle! You know, I've thought he was a little lazy on this trip. He's trotted around a bit. He's hardly practiced at all."

Pop Warner laughed. "Yes, but that's because Jim knows how to save his energy for the races. When he's in top condition, as now, all he needs is to loosen up his muscles. You'll see!"

The judges called for the running broad jump, the first event in the Pentathlon. One by one, the star athletes of the world took their jumps—Fred Bie (bē) of Norway, Frank Lukeman of Canada, Hugo Wieslander (vē′slan dər) of Sweden, and many others. Finally, it was Jim Thorpe's turn.

The big Indian walked slowly away from the take-off board. About twelve yards back, he stood quietly a moment to plan his jump. Then in a flash he was running at top speed. He jumped and soared high in the air. His great speed and the height of his jump carried him far, far out. Legs extended, he reached for every inch as he landed.

"Twenty-three feet, two and seven-tenths inches," one of the judges called.

The stands buzzed with excitement.

Each man got two more jumps, but no one could approach Jim's mark.

"The winner—James Thorpe of the United States," called the judge.

The American athletes set up a shout: "Ray! Ray! Ray! U. S. A.!" There was loud applause from the stands for Jim's fine performance.

He trotted over to the javelin field. When every man had thrown the long wooden spear three times, it was Bie of Norway and Wieslander of Sweden who took the first two places. Jim Thorpe was close behind them for third place!

Then in the 200-meter dash it was Big Jim Thorpe who raced across the finish line in first place. In the discus throw it was Jim Thorpe who tossed the round flat weight the farthest.

Jim Thorpe, Winning the Shot-Put during the 1912 Olympics.
United Press International.

"Wait for the fifteen hundred meters!" shouted one of the Swedes.

Jim toed the mark for the start of this last race, which was almost a mile. *Crack!* went the starting gun. Two men dashed to the front. Around the first turn, they were twenty yards ahead.

"They can't keep that up," Jim said to himself. He held to a steady fast pace.

The second time around the track, the two front runners were exhausted. Jim passed them easily and stayed ahead.

On the last lap he put on all the speed he had left. Fred Bie, the great athlete from Norway, struggled to catch him. For just a second Bie drew even, but he couldn't match strides with the big Indian. Jim drew ahead. He raced across the finish line, the winner!

"Oh, that Jim!" Pop Warner was smiling broadly. "Isn't he a horse, Mike?"

"Winner of the Pentathlon—James Thorpe of the United States," the judge called out. Up went the United States flag on the winner's pole.

The crowds stood and cheered for Jim's great performance. In the royal box Colonel Balck said, "Mr. Sullivan, I've never seen such a man. Four first places, and one third place, of the five events. Nobody will ever come close to that!"

As the days went by, United States athletes won most of the prizes, but all the other nations were certain that the United States would lose in the Decathlon. They still thought Europeans were best in all-around sports.

The Decathlon was held the last three days of the meet. On the first day Jim Thorpe won the shot-put. He made fast time in the 100-meter dash and a good mark in the broad jump. When the judges figured up the points at the end of the day, Jim was far ahead of the other twenty-two contestants.

On the second day he won the hurdle race. Then he won the high jump, and he ran well in the 400-meter race. Again he was far ahead in points at the end of the day.

"He *is* a horse!" said Mike Murphy. "You were right about him, Pop."

"This is nothing," said Pop. "Why, they ought to have some football, baseball, lacrosse, hockey, basketball, tennis, swimming, handball, skating, and target-shooting thrown in! Then Jim could really show them something. He's the best I've ever seen at all those sports!"

On the last day Jim kept up his great records in the discus throw, in the pole vault, and in the javelin throw. Nobody could match his point total now! As in the Pentathlon, the last race was the 1500-meter run. Even Jim was a little tired by now, but off he started with his long easy stride.

"Why, it's only a mile to go," he thought. "I could run ten times that far." Once again he called on all his great strength and energy. Once again he raced across the finish line, the winner.

Panting from his hard race, Jim watched with pride as the United States flag went up on the winner's pole.

In the royal box Colonel Balck held out his hand to Mr. Sullivan. "The greatest performance I have ever seen," he said. "Your Jim Thorpe made eight thousand four hundred twelve points in the Decathlon, where even eight thousand would be sensational. Again he won four first places. Why, it is unbelievable!"

The winning athletes trooped up to the royal box to receive their trophies. The King gave each one a laurel wreath and a gold medal.

Jim Thorpe's turn came. The huge crowd cheered itself hoarse, led by King Gustav himself. The tall, thin monarch shook Jim's hand. "You, sir, are the greatest athlete in the world."

Jim gulped. "Th-thank you," he said.

The King handed Jim his wreath and two gold medals. He also gave Jim a large bronze statue, his own gift, and a silver Viking ship set with jewels, a gift from the Czar of Russia.

Jim couldn't say another word. He just nodded and smiled.

Carlisle Defeats Army

It was the afternoon of November 9, 1912. The stands around the football field at West Point, New York, were jammed. Only 3,000 people could get in, and many were turned away. The cadets of the United States Military Academy had a powerful football team this year. It was one of the strongest teams in the East. This afternoon, Army was favored to win over the Carlisle Braves, led by Captain Jim Thorpe.

However, the Carlisle Braves had a fine record, also. They hadn't lost a game. They had beaten big colleges and smaller schools alike.

The cadets in the stands jumped up and cheered as the Army football players ran onto the field. There were several teams of them. All of the players on the Army teams were big husky youths. They spread out to practice kicking and running to loosen up their muscles.

"Look at that Devore!" observed one cadet. "No wonder he's an All-American tackle. Two hundred forty pounds—and all muscle."

Then the Carlisle players trotted out. There were just sixteen on their squad. With so few reserves, it looked as though they wouldn't have a chance against the many Army players.

"Is that the famous team from Carlisle, Pennsylvania?" exclaimed a tall cadet corporal. "They don't look like much! They're so little."

"You're right," said another cadet. "I read that they average only a hundred seventy pounds per man."

"That must be Jim Thorpe kicking!" cried another. "They say nobody can stop him. He's a team all by himself."

"Well, he's not nearly as big as Devore. I'll bet our boys will chew him up today!"

On the field Pop Warner gave his last instructions to the Carlisle players. He slapped each man on the back. "Go get 'em!" he said.

The players trotted to their positions. Devore kicked off for Army. Thorpe ran over to snatch up the ball. Army players closed in on him, but he pounded ahead for fifteen yards before he was brought down.

"Stop that Thorpe!" chanted the Army cadets.

Jim grinned. He whispered to Gus Welch, the Carlisle quarterback. Welch barked the signals. The ball came back to halfback Alex Arcasa!

Jim led the interference. He plowed into the giant Devore in a powerful block. Arcasa slipped through the line for a fifteen-yard gain.

"Wow!" gasped the tall cadet corporal. "That Thorpe certainly can block. But I thought he'd carry the ball."

Welch called out his signals. Back came the ball to Arcasa again. This time he slipped the ball to Jim on a crisscross play.

"Stop Thorpe!" shouted the Army players.

Two of them tried to tackle him at the line of scrimmage. Still he plunged right ahead, running for all he was worth, knees lifted high. He shook off the tacklers and gained fifteen yards before two more Army men finally brought him down. Thorpe was almost impossible to stop.

Then Possum Powell took the ball for a gain. Next Arcasa was stopped. Jim took the ball on the crisscross again. He dodged and twisted for twenty yards before he was downed.

"Hold that line! Stop that Thorpe!" shouted the cadets.

On the next play the Army charged so hard that a Carlisle player fumbled the ball. Quarterback Pritchard pounced on it for Army.

Left: Jim Thorpe in his Carlisle Braves uniform, 1912. Historical Pictures Service, Chicago.

Below: The Carlisle Braves with Jim Thorpe (circled), 1912. Historical Pictures Service, Chicago.

Right away, Army halfback Hobbs broke loose for a long run. The crowd was yelling, "Touchdown! Touchdown!"

Jim Thorpe cut across from the other side of the field. Running like a deer, he caught the speeding Hobbs. He brought him down with a crashing tackle at the sixteen-yard line.

For a moment, Hobbs just lay on the ground, stunned by the tackle. Jim pulled him to his feet. "Nice run," he said.

Still, Army could not be stopped. Yard by yard the West Point backs pushed the ball across the goal line. Army led 6-0, as Pritchard missed the point after touchdown.

Army kicked off to Carlisle. The Indians could not gain, so Jim Thorpe fell back to kick. He swung his leg into the ball with all his might. High and far it traveled.

There were "Ohs" from spectators at Jim's tremendous seventy-yard kick. Thorpe could do everything better than anyone else!

After this the Army team could not gain. Hobbs punted, and it was Carlisle's ball on Army's forty-four-yard line.

"Come on, fellows, let's play some football now," Jim urged his team.

Arcasa slipped the ball to Thorpe on the crisscross. Jim ripped off seventeen yards before the Army players pulled him down. Arcasa ran for a gain. Then it was Thorpe again for fifteen yards to Army's six-yard line.

"Stop Thorpe! Stop Thorpe!" yelled the cadets. Jim only grinned.

Welch snapped out his signals. The ball came back to Arcasa. Jim led the interference, right through the Army line. He plowed across the goal with Arcasa right behind him. The score was tied 6-6.

The two teams lined up for the try for the point after touchdown. Jim stood ready to kick. Back came the ball to Alex Arcasa. Quickly he set it on the ground for the place kick. Jim's toe met the ball with a smack.

Up the ball went, end over end, right between the goal posts. It sailed off the field, he had kicked so hard. Carlisle led, 7-6, at half time.

Carlisle kicked off to Army to start the second half. Army could not gain. Keyes, the Army fullback, got off a high kick, straight into the arms of Jim Thorpe. The Army ends were ready to pounce on him. However, Jim had started like a flash. He dodged so quickly that the Army ends missed him completely and crashed into each other!

Straight down the field he ran, twisting and turning to avoid tacklers. Big Devore dived at him, but Jim pushed the tackle off with a mighty straight-arm. Two Army men grabbed him at the ten-yard line. But Jim was running so fast and hard they couldn't hang on. Every man on the Army team had tried to tackle him, but no one could stop him. He dashed across the goal line for a touchdown.

Even the Army cadets stood to cheer for Thorpe. On the field the officials blew their whistles and waved their arms. "Carlisle offside! Score doesn't count!" they shouted.

A great moan came from the Carlisle stands.

Down on the field Jim said, "Too bad. That was fun. Come on, Gus, let's get back those points!"

The Carlisle boys did get them back. They plunged and ran and pushed Army all over the field. Twice when the Braves couldn't gain, Jim Thorpe flipped a pass to Arcasa for a first down. Once Army tried a pass, but Jim intercepted. Everywhere it was Thorpe—running, tackling, blocking, kicking, passing.

He made two touchdowns and kicked the points after touchdown. Arcasa made another touchdown. Score: Carlisle 27, Army 6.

When the final gun sounded, the crowd jumped to its feet to cheer Thorpe and his teammates as they jogged off the field.

Several reporters rushed up to Jim. "Congratulations!" said one. "You'd be sure to make All-American again, if you'd played only this one game! Would you call this your best game of the year?"

"Oh, I don't know. I guess we all played pretty well today. But you'll have to ask Pop. My job is playing, not talking!"

Jim felt good about winning, but he wished everyone wouldn't make such a fuss about it! He walked on to the dressing room.

"You've got a great team, Pop!" called another reporter, turning to the coach. "What did you think of Thorpe today?"

"He played a fine game," Pop said. "So did ten other Carlisle boys."

"Jim has a great scoring record," said another sportswriter, "but I never knew he was such a team player, too. Why, he's in every play, and he does more than his share of everything. Is he the best player you've ever seen?"

"Well, I expect to see a lot more football players in my time!" answered Pop with a laugh.

"Quit kidding us, Pop. You act as modest as Thorpe does. I know he's the greatest player I ever saw—or ever will see!"

A Chief Loses with Honor

Back at Carlisle, about two months later, Pop sent for his football star one afternoon. The big Indian youth soon came to the coach's office. "You wanted to talk to me, Pop?" he ventured.

"Yes! Come on in," thundered Pop Warner. He paced the floor angrily.

"Why is Pop so upset?" Jim asked himself. "Did I do something wrong? Maybe it's all those reporters again." He said to Pop, "I—I hope there's not going to be any more fuss."

"You mean because you were chosen All-American halfback again, and scored twenty-five touchdowns and a hundred ninety-eight points last fall? No. It's something else. Jim, did you ever play baseball for money?"

Baseball for money? Jim stopped to think.

"Why—why, yes, Pop. Two years ago, during the summer, down in North Carolina. It wasn't much. They gave us only fifteen a week, but it paid my expenses. I was really playing for the fun of it."

Pop Warner blazed back, "Only a professional takes money for playing. An amateur can't take a cent."

"Wh-what?" Jim stuttered.

"Why didn't you tell me? Don't you know the rule? Didn't you know that fifteen dollars a week made you a professional right then?"

Jim was startled. He had never thought of that. "Why, no, Pop, I didn't know. Other college boys were playing. Everybody knew it."

"But the others didn't use their own names!" Pop Warner exploded. Then he calmed down and smiled. "I've got to hand it to you, Jim, for using your own name honestly. But you should have known the rule."

"But does it make a difference? That was two years ago."

Pop sighed. "It means you shouldn't have been on the Olympic team. It means that the American Amateur Athletic Union says you must return your prizes and trophies."

Jim was taken back. "But, Pop—what does summer baseball have to do with competing on the Olympic team? Nobody ever paid me anything for running or jumping or throwing the discus and javelin."

"It's the rule. You aren't an amateur athlete if you've played any kind of professional sports."

Jim sat and thought. Try as he would, he couldn't see the sense of this. He had gone to North Carolina with a couple of Carlisle boys only for the thrill of playing baseball. He hadn't needed the money. He hadn't even wanted it. The other boys had needed it. Jim had had many big offers for large sums of money, but had never taken any of these.

"They—they want me to give back my prizes?" It was a blow to his pride, after that great day in Stockholm. "All right, Pop," said Jim. "If that's the rule, they can have the prizes back. But I don't understand it. I never meant to do anything wrong."

He was thinking, "I've won lots of things and never bragged much about them. I guess I can lose with honor like Black Hawk[1]."

---

1. **Black Hawk** was a Sauk Indian Chief in what is now northern Illinois and southern Wisconsin. He and his tribe fought the battle of Black Hawk in 1830. They were defeated, and he and his sons were captured. After being held prisoner for three years, he finally agreed to move to a reservation near Des Moines, Iowa.

"I knew you'd see it that way," said Pop. "I'm mighty sorry for you, but we've got to stick to the rules."

"I—I hope they won't blame you for this," Jim said sadly.

Pop exploded again. "Why, you great big galoot, it's you I'm worried about!"

"What do you think I ought to do now?"

"Why I guess you'll just have to accept an offer from one of the major-league baseball teams—the New York Giants, say. And there may soon be professional football. If you want to make your living from sports, there's no better athlete than you."

Jim thought that over for a minute. He still liked sports for the thrill and excitement of competition, but if he could make his living from them, too—"Why, sure, Pop. That's what I'll do. If they say I'm a professional, why, I'll be one."

There was a knock at the door. A messenger brought in a telegram for Pop. He ripped it open and read it. He scowled. Then he grinned. "Well, Jim, this may make you feel better. They tried to offer your prizes to those Scandinavian fellows who won second—you know, Fred Bie and Hugo Wieslander. But they won't take 'em! They say they don't understand our rules, and you won fairly."

This did make Jim feel better. Bie and Wieslander were acting like great chiefs in refusing the awards.

"Even so, I—I guess I'll still have to give up the prizes?" Jim's heart would be heavy for a long time at this unexpected blow.

"Yes," said Pop. "I'll send 'em in to the Amateur Athletic Union. But you're still the greatest athlete. And you'll be a big success in any professional sport you try."

"Thanks, Pop," said Jim. He would be a success, he vowed. He must always prove himself worthy to be called a great chief.

The Medals Return

In a special ceremony at the 1984 Summer Olympics in Los Angeles, a duplicate set of medals was presented to Jim Thorpe's family. Because Jim died in 1953, his daughter Charlotte accepted them for her father. The official record books will not be changed, but Jim Thorpe's name will be added as a footnote.

Developing Comprehension Skills

1. What five contests are included in the Pentathlon? What ten contests are included in the Decathlon?

2. When the King of Sweden gave Jim his prizes and medals, all Jim could say was "th-thank you." What does this show about Jim?

3. Read the description of the football game again. After it is over, why does the reporter say, "I never knew he was such a team player"? Quote specific details from the story to show that Jim was truly a team player.

4. What is Jim Thorpe's reaction when Pop Warner tells him he must return the medals? He has three different thoughts about it. What are they? What does each show about his character?

5. Do you think the American Athletic Union should have asked Jim to return his Olympic prizes and trophies? Did Jim deserve this? Explain your answer.

Reading Literature: Biographies

1. **Understanding Sequence.** Make a time line for the portion of Jim Thorpe's life that you are told about here. Show these events:

   Jim plays baseball professionally one summer in North Carolina.
   Jim wins the Pentathlon and the Decathlon at the Olympics.
   The Carlisle Braves defeat the U.S. Military Academy in football.
   Jim loses his Olympic medals.

   Divide the time line into years and months, and be as accurate as you can in locating the exact dates for these four events.

2. **Identifying Themes.** In nonfiction, just as in fiction and poetry, the writer usually presents a theme in his or her work. That is, he or she makes a general statement about life. A long piece of writing, such as these biographies, may have several themes. For example, in "Florence Nightingale," one theme was that you must be true to yourself. Another was that you must fight for what is worthwhile. Name two or more themes that you find in "Jim Thorpe."

3. **Recognizing Conflict.** Most of this biography is concerned with one kind of external conflict. The selection describes clearly Jim's efforts

in sports against other players. In the final scene in Pop Warner's office, a new kind of external conflict is developed. In addition, the reader is given an idea of Jim's internal conflict due to the bad news. Explain the two kinds of conflict developed in the final scene. You may refer to Chapter 4, page 182, to refresh your memory about internal and external conflicts.

Developing Vocabulary Skills

1. **Understanding Definition and Restatement Context Clues.** In this selection, many words are about sports. To understand what Jim Thorpe does, the reader must know the meanings of these words. Many of these special words are defined by the author in the text. Find five words for which context clues are given. List the five words and their meanings, as given in context. Then tell what kind of context clue you found in each. It doesn't matter whether the word is one you knew before or is one that is new to you.

2. **Using Main Idea for Clues to Word Meaning.** Sometimes the meaning of a new word can be figured out by understanding the main idea of a paragraph or selection. Clues to the meaning of the word are given throughout the paragraph.

   Read the paragraph and look for clues to the meaning of the word *fatigue*.

   > Roger began to feel a strain in his legs at the halfway point. Nine miles later he was barely trotting. His eyes were half shut from *fatigue*. His hands tingled. His joints ached. Each step felt as if someone was pounding his hips with a hammer.

   From the main idea of the paragraph you can tell that *fatigue* means "tiredness." Every sentence tells how weary or tired Roger felt.

   For each word listed below, read the following paragraph or paragraphs from "Jim Thorpe." Find the word and figure out its meaning from the main idea of the paragraph. Write the meaning of each word as it fits into the paragraph.

   a. excelled—paragraph 5, column 1 on page 337
   b. sensational—paragraph 4, column 2 on page 339
   c. monarch—paragraph 6, column 2 on page 339
   d. reserves—paragraph 5, column 1 on page 340

Developing Writing Skills

1. **Identifying a Person's Opinions.** Find two places in this selection where Jim Thorpe compares himself to a great chief. They are at the end of pages 344 and 345. Then think about his actions as described in this biography. What qualities does Jim Thorpe seem to feel a great chief should have? Write a paragraph listing two or three of these qualities. Explain which of Jim's actions led you to choose these qualities.

2. **Writing a Biographical Sketch.** A **sketch** is a short piece of writing. A **biographical sketch** is a short description of a person or of a small part of his or her life.

   Work this assignment with a partner. Interview your partner to find out what he or she did yesterday. Then write a two- to four-paragraph report on the events of the day. Carefully choose the events you will use. Include those events that show one or two important qualities of your subject. Leave out those events that you consider unimportant.

   After both of you are done, exchange biographical sketches. Find out whether you and your subject agreed on which events were important and which were unimportant.

Developing Skills in Study and Research

Applying Research Skills. Use appropriate reference books to find the answers to the questions below. Give the title of the reference book in which you found each answer.

1. From the answer to Developing Comprehension Skills, 1, review the list of the contests that composed the Pentathlon and the Decathlon in 1912, the year of Jim Thorpe's Olympic Games. Then find out which of these events are still contests in the Olympic games. (Note that the running broad jump is now called the long jump.) Are the Pentathlon and the Decathlon still part of the games?

2. Find out all you can about Jim Thorpe's life before and after the portion of it included in this selection.

Developing Skills in Critical Thinking

Recognizing Slanted Writing. A writer carefully chooses words with the connotations he or she wants. The connotations are only suggested and not written. However, the writer knows that the suggested connotations increase the meaning and effect of the written words. Sometimes a writer will use many words with strong connotations. The connotations may lead the reader to feel strongly in favor of the subject. They may lead the reader to feel strongly against it. The reader may not even realize why he feels strongly one way or the other. This kind of writing is called **slanted writing.** It is important for a reader to be aware of the influence of words and to watch for slanted writing.

Here are two reports of the same baseball game. One reporter supports the Greens; the other supports the Blues. Identify which team each writer supports. For each report, make two lists:

    a. words the writer uses to make his or her team look good
    b. words the writer uses to make the other team look bad

1. In this afternoon's game, the Blues leaped back into the winning column with gusto. Smart baserunning in the ninth took advantage of Greens' errors, and power-hitter Chico Figueroa surprised everyone with a timely single dropped neatly into short right field. Loyal fans who had stayed for the happy ending were exuberant.

2. In the most controversial play of the week, Greens' shortstop Woody Anderson barely missed a ninth-inning grounder in today's game. Despite Anderson's impressive effort, he was charged with an error on the play. The next Blues batter just managed to touch the ball, popping it into short right. An unruly fan reaching into the field prevented the Greens' first baseman from catching it. The tainted run gave the Blues the win, finally breaking a dismal string of fourteen losses.

True Adventure Stories

A **true adventure story** is a record of a courageous effort. It may be written by a person who took part in the effort or by an onlooker. Such a story is concerned only with the heroic aspects of the person or persons involved. A true adventure story does not tell a complete story of the person's life, as a biography does. The writer of a true adventure story is interested in suspense. This writer chooses details that will let the reader feel that he or she has joined in and taken part in the adventure.

Columbia Blastoff, 1982. NASA.

First to the South Pole!

WALKER CHAPMAN

The need to be first is a strong urge in people. In this adventure, the desire to be first drives these men to place themselves in incredible danger. Were they foolhardy? Were they heroes? What do you think?

In the Antarctic summer of 1911, two separate expeditions prepared to cross the frozen mountains and vast plains of the world's southernmost continent. A race to the South Pole began between the two parties, one led by Roald Amundsen and the other by Robert F. Scott. It was a race that was to end in glorious victory and tragic defeat.

The South Pole was "second best" for Roald Amundsen. Born in 1872 near Oslo, Norway, he had dreamed since boyhood of exploring the Arctic, and of being the first to reach the North Pole.

By 1909, he had raised money for an expedition and had obtained a specially equipped vessel, the *Fram*. Before he could start, however, news came that an American, Robert Peary, had reached the North Pole in September, 1909!

Amundsen didn't want to be the second man at the North Pole. Here he was, with an outfitted expedition all ready, and Peary had beaten him. Amundsen de-cided to make a voyage anyway—to the unconquered South Pole.

Robert Falcon Scott was just about ready to set out on his second expedition. Amundsen was afraid that if he made his new plan known, Scott might leave earlier. Amundsen wanted the glory of being the first to the South Pole. He began the journey secretly.

Scott had also set out by this time, and Amundsen sent him a telegram. The secret was out—and Scott realized that he was involved in a race with Amundsen to reach the South Pole.

Amundsen's plan for reaching the Pole was simple. Scott was planning to use pony transportation, but Amundsen brought ninety-seven Eskimo dogs with him. He felt certain that with his Arctic experience he could handle dogs.

Dogs were light, and were less likely than ponies to break through the snow bridges over crevasses. Even if they did fall through, they could be pulled out by

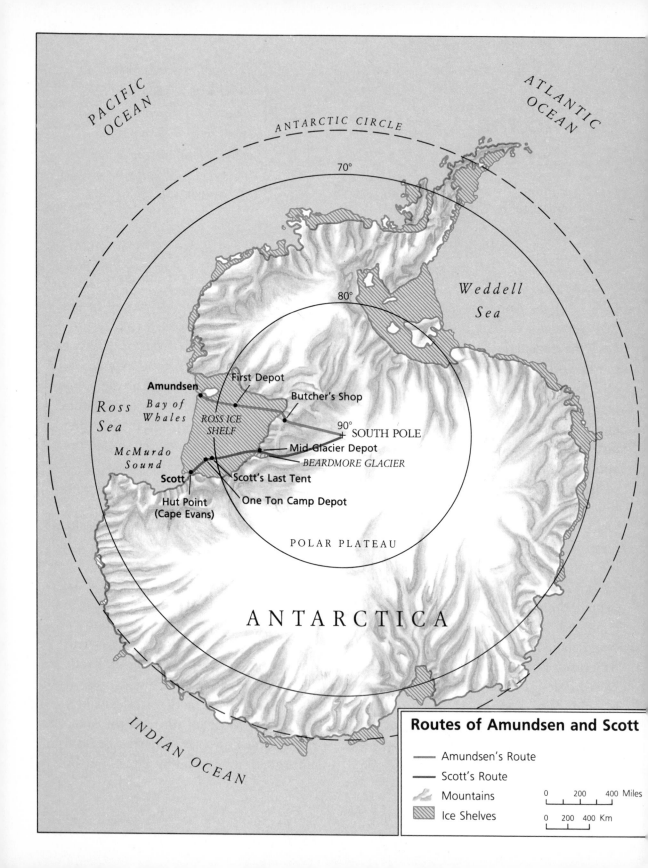

PACIFIC OCEAN

ATLANTIC OCEAN

ANTARCTIC CIRCLE

70°

80°

Weddell Sea

First Depot

Amundsen

Ross Sea

Bay of Whales

Butcher's Shop

ROSS ICE SHELF

90° SOUTH POLE

Mid Glacier Depot

BEARDMORE GLACIER

McMurdo Sound

Scott

Scott's Last Tent

Hut Point (Cape Evans)

One Ton Camp Depot

POLAR PLATEAU

ANTARCTICA

INDIAN OCEAN

Routes of Amundsen and Scott

—— Amundsen's Route

—— Scott's Route

Mountains

Ice Shelves

| 0 | 200 | 400 Miles |

| 0 | 200 | 400 Km |

their harnesses; getting a pony out of a crevasse was almost impossible. Ponies could not climb the glaciers, and would have to be killed. Dog teams could continue on up to the Polar Plateau.

Of course, Amundsen had to find a new base for his camp. Though he had a head start on Scott, it would never do for him to steal Scott's site at Hut Point.

Amundsen was able to put his camp sixty-nine miles closer to the Pole than Scott. Thanks to fair weather, he had an easy journey, landing at the Bay of Whales early in January, 1911. He arrived only a week after Scott reached Hut Point.

Before winter set in, the Norwegians speedily laid down depots for use on their journey the following spring. Dog teams moved at a steady pace of twenty-five miles a day during the depot-laying. Sometimes the Norwegians rode on the sledges; at other times they mounted skis and let themselves be towed along behind. One party, setting up a depot a hundred miles from Amundsen's base, made the return journey in two days. By April, supplies had been stored at the depots. With lighter sledges now, they could move much more rapidly and the dogs would use less energy.

The Norwegians spent a mild winter at their base. Over at Scott's base on the west side of the Ross Sea, the winter was much worse. Scott was held back by severe blizzards, and Amundsen was able to get an early start. He had only nine men.

Scott had fifty-five, and he planned some scientific work. For Amundsen it was simply going to be a dash to the Pole.

Amundsen's Journey to the Pole

Amundsen set out poleward on September 8, 1911, at the first hint of spring. It was too soon; on the way to the first depot, the temperature dropped to −72°, and the dogs could not take it. Amundsen returned to his base. On October 19, he tried again. Four men went with him; three others set out along the coast of the Bay of Whales. The cook remained behind to look after the base.

The polar party had four sledges, drawn by fifty-two dogs. The men were dressed Eskimo style, in light reindeer skin which kept out the cold. The frisky dogs covered ninety miles in the first four days. After a two-day rest at the first depot, they went on. The dogs were tireless, and the men had little to do; they put on skis and let themselves be towed behind the sledges. "And there I stood," wrote Amundsen, "until we reached 85°5′S.—340 miles. Yes, that was a pleasant surprise. We had never dreamed of driving on skis to the Pole!"

Things became more difficult as they left the Ross Ice Shelf[1] behind and

---

1. **Ice shelves** are the outermost fringes of the two-mile thick sheet of ice that covers the continent of Antarctica. They extend, sometimes hundreds of miles, beyond the land. When the water gets deep enough, they float.

reached the glaciers leading to the Polar Plateau. They had to climb a narrow, steep river of ice. The snow was deep and loose, and the dogs had trouble. Again and again, because of impassable chasms or towering ice blocks, the explorers had to turn back and try another path.

By December 4, they thought they had reached the Plateau. According to plan, they killed twenty-four of their weaker dogs. The worst of the hauling was over, and some of the dogs could be used as food for the other dogs and for the men. "It was hard—but it had to be so," wrote Amundsen. He could not bear to watch the slaying of the faithful animals and remained in the tent, hunched over the stove, while the other four carried out the unpleasant work. They named the site the Butcher's Shop, and rested there for two days.

Then it turned out they were not yet on the Plateau at all. Their trail swooped down 2,000 feet, leading them into a tangle of gaping crevasses. They forged onward somehow, even when a blizzard struck. They had eighteen dogs, six to a sledge; the fourth sledge had been left behind at the Butcher's Shop. Frostbitten and weary, the men pushed their way ahead. "Time after time," he wrote, "the dogs fell through, and time after time the men went in. The ground under our feet sounded unpleasantly hollow as we went over it. The drivers whipped their dogs as much as they could, and with shouts and brisk encouragement they went rapidly over the dangerous floor." They crossed the glacier, pushing southward. As they drew closer to their goal, they wondered if they would be first. Would Scott be there ahead of them?

They camped on December 13 at 89°45'S. The weather was fine, except for a few light snow showers. "It was like the eve of some great festival that night in the tent," wrote Amundsen. "I was awake several times during the night and had the same feeling that I can remember as a boy on the night before Christmas Eve."

The next day, the weather was "of the finest, just as if it had been made for arriving at the Pole." The sky clouded over at noon, but, fortunately, it cleared again. At three, the cry of "Halt!" rang out. They were at 90°S.

Of course, it was impossible to find the exact location of the Pole in the blank white desert. To be certain they had been at the Pole, they made a twelve and a half mile circular trek around the camp. Somewhere within that circle, they knew, was the Pole.

They planted the Norwegian flag and held a brief ceremony. They were in no hurry to return, having reached the Pole well ahead of schedule, and they remained there from December 14 to 17. Then, with the temperature at two below zero and a "mild, summer-like wind" blowing, they started back. They left a short message in the tent for Scott.

It was an easy journey back. They found the depots, and they had so much meat that some of the dogs actually gained weight on the homeward trip. On January 25, at four in the morning, they returned to the home base after a ninety-nine day journey of 1,860 miles.

The South Pole had been conquered—easily, by five skillful Norwegians. However, while Amundsen was making his speedy and triumphant dash to the Pole, tragic events were taking place in the west.

Scott's Trip to the Pole

Scott's polar journey began from Cape Evans on November 1, 1911, the earliest that weather would permit. Amundsen was having a milder winter at his base 450 miles to the east. He had been able to get started for the Pole two weeks before.

Scott planned to use motor, dog, and pony transport. Three four-man parties would carry supplies to the foot of Beardmore Glacier. There, the ponies would be shot and the dogs sent back with the Russian boy who was in charge of them. At the top of the glacier, one party of men would turn back; and a second group would be sent back halfway to the Pole, leaving only Scott's team to finish the journey.

The motor sledges had to be left not far from Hut Point. The dogs performed sur-

Hut Point Winter Quarters on McMurdo Sound (Scott) 1904. Courtesy of Popperfoto, London.

prisingly well, reaching their destination and delivering the provisions they hauled. The ponies, one by one, were shot and their meat used for food, though Scott found this a sad task. The returning parties would depend for their nourishment on the caches of pony meat, and on the depots laid down the previous autumn.

The trip across the Ice Shelf was slower than expected. The explorers were held up by blizzards and warm air that melted the snow into slush. From December 4 to December 9 it was impossible to march at all. The same blizzard bothered Amundsen, who was already high on the glacier, but he was able to make some progress where Scott, with his ponies and Siberian dogs, could not.

Scott was racing now, but not against Amundsen. He was racing against the coming winter. Where Amundsen was moving at an easy pace, resting often even when it did not seem necessary, Scott was furiously pushing onward.

On December 22, another depot was set up 8,000 feet up the glacier, and the first supporting party turned back. Many of the men were weakening, less than halfway to the Pole. On January 1, 1912, Scott wrote in his diary: "Only 170 miles to the Pole, and plenty of food."

Three days later, at 87°34'S., 146 miles from the Pole, Scott sent the second support party back, except for one man. The four-man polar team had consisted of Scott, Dr. Wilson, a sailor named Edgar Evans, and an army officer named Lawrence Oates, nicknamed "Titus" or "Soldier." Scott now added a fifth man to the party on the spur of the moment—Bill "Birdie" Bowers.

Bowers was a man of great strength, and Scott thought he would be useful on the man-hauling journey ahead. However, including him had created great problems. Everything—tent, rations, equipment—had been planned for a four-man team. Now the food and living quarters would have to be shared with a fifth. Bowers had left his skis behind at the depot below the glacier, so he would have to plod along through the snow on foot for hundreds of miles, while the others could run on skis.

A blizzard held up the polar team again on January 8, and the soft snow that remained afterward made man-hauling an agony. They made no better than ten miles a day, dropping behind schedule again. On January 12, Scott wrote that he and his men were feeling chilled though the temperature was fairly mild—a sign of growing physical weakness.

Two days later, Scott noted: "I think Wilson, Bowers and I are as fit as possible under the circumstances. Oates gets cold feet," and, soon after, "I don't like the easy way in which Oates and Evans get frostbitten."

On January 15, they were within striking distance of the Pole. "It ought to be a certain thing now," Scott wrote. "Only

Scott with Group at South Pole. Left to right, standing, are Oates, Scott, and Evans. Bowers and Wilson are seated. Bettmann Archive, Inc., New York City.

twenty-seven miles from the Pole. We ought to do it now."

Next day came the shock. "The worst has happened, or nearly the worst," wrote Scott. "Noon sight showed us in Latitude 89°42', and we started off in good spirits." Then sharp-eyed Bowers spotted a black speck ahead. They marched on and "found that it was a black flag tied to a sledge bearer; nearby the remains of a camp; sledge tracks and ski tracks going and coming and the clear trace of dogs' paws—many dogs. This told us the whole story. The Norwegians are first at the Pole. It is a terrible disappointment, and I am very sorry for my loyal companions. . . . Tomorrow we must march on to the Pole and hurry home. All the daydreams must go; it will be a wearisome return."

Scott's Trip Back

On January 17, 1912, there was this entry: "The Pole. Great God! This is an awful place. Now for the run home and a desperate struggle. I wonder if we can do it."

At the Pole, they found Amundsen's tent, with the Norwegian flag flying high, and letters addressed to Scott. There was no time to linger, as the Norwegians had done.

All five men were frostbitten. Evans seemed the worst. On January 23, Scott wrote: "There is no doubt that Evans is a good deal run down—his fingers are badly blistered and his nose is rather seriously congested with frequent frost bites. He is most annoyed with himself, which is not a good sign ... Oates gets cold feet...."

Crossing the Polar Plateau, Wilson strained a tendon, Scott fell and injured his shoulder, Oates' toes began to turn black from frostbite, and Evans' hands were so badly frozen that the fingernails began to drop off. Yet, at the top of Beardmore Glacier, they camped on February 8. "It has been extremely interesting," Scott wrote. They were under sandstone cliffs, from which Wilson "has picked several plant impressions, the last a piece of coal with beautifully traced leaves in layers. . . . In one place we saw the cast of small waves in the sand."

Climbing down the glacier Evans fell twice, injured his head, and became dazed.

On February 17, they were at the bottom of the glacier. All five men were cracking under the strain as their health continued to give way, but now Evans began to drop behind the group, and at lunchtime they had to go back to find him. "He was on his knees with clothing disarranged, hands uncovered and frost-bitten, and a wild look in his eyes," Scott wrote. Evans was brought back to the camp, where he lapsed into a coma. He died that night.

They were saddened by Evans' death, but they could not help admitting that with the sickest man gone, the other four had a better chance of surviving the trip. They struggled along, dragging sledges now weighted with thirty-five pounds of rock specimens. Soon it was Oates' turn to weaken. His hands and feet were frozen, and he could no longer pull the sledges. He simply trudged along beside them. Scott, Wilson, and Bowers, still in fairly good shape, were forced to do extra work. The daily marches became shorter and shorter as they became more exhausted.

When they came to their depots, they found their oil cans had shrunk from cold, and the oil had mostly evaporated. With fuel short, they could have fewer hot meals and would have to cut down on drinking water because they would have less chance to build snow-warming fires. It was well into February, and at night the temperature dropped below −40°. Oates suffered from frostbite. On March 2, Scott wrote: "This morning it took one and a half hours to get our foot gear on. ... The surface is simply awful. Even with a strong wind and full sail we have only done five and a half miles. There is no doubt we cannot do the extra marches and we feel the cold terribly."

The End

There was only one real hope, now: that a relief party would come out from Cape Evans to meet them. However, in those low temperatures and frequent blizzards no relief party was able to set out.

On March 3, the weakening men made only four and a half miles, and the next day, just three and a half. Oates lost strength from hour to hour. On the fifth, Scott wrote that Oates was "nearly done," and a day later put down, with brutal honesty, the statement, "If we were all fit I should have hopes of getting through."

There was no question of leaving him behind. They were about forty miles from the next depot on March 4, and had food for a week, but fuel for only three days. "Shall we get there?" Scott wondered. "Such a short distance it would have appeared to us on the summit!" Cold and hungry, they reached that depot six days later and prepared to go on to the next.

By March 10, Oates himself seemed to realize that he was endangering the life of the entire group, and asked for advice. "Nothing could be said," wrote Scott, "but to urge him to march as long as he could." A day later, Scott figured that they were fifty-five miles from the One Ton Camp depot now and had seven days' food. Since they were doing, at best, six miles a day, "six times seven equals forty-two, leaving us thirteen miles short of our distance, even if things get no worse."

On the seventeenth, Oates came to the end. He had asked to be left behind, and Scott refused. With the party huddled in the tent during a blizzard, and the temperature 40° below zero outside, Oates staggered to his feet and said calmly, "I am just going outside and may be some time." He walked off into the storm and was never seen again. Scott wrote:

"We knew that poor Oates was walking to his death."

The survivors struggled ahead through the terrible cold, like walking corpses, and by March 21 they were within eleven miles of One Ton Depot. To save weight, they had left their camera and other instruments behind, but were still hauling their precious specimens.

A blizzard came up and they had to make camp. Day after day the snow fell, turning the outer world into a blinding landscape of whirling whiteness. It was impossible to move on. For eight days the blizzard pinned them into their tent, and they slowly starved and froze with thousands of pounds of food waiting for them only eleven miles away. As death came nearer, Scott wrote twelve letters, to his wife, to Wilson's wife and Bowers' mother, and to some of his close friends. Now that there was no longer hope of survival, Scott composed a message to the public, explaining why the disaster had occurred. "It was not poor planning," he said, "but the death of many ponies early in 1911, the bad weather on the journey outward, and the unbelievably cold weather on the return."

"I do not think human beings ever came through such a month as we have come through," Scott said. Yet, he insisted, they would have made it if Evans and Oates had not sickened, and if the fuel shortage at the depots had not developed, and if a blizzard had not kept them from reaching One Ton Camp when it was only a two-day march away.

"Had we lived," he concluded, "I should have had a tale to tell of the hardihood, endurance, and courage of my companions which would have stirred the heart of every Englishman. These rough notes and our dead bodies must tell the tale, but surely, surely, a great rich country like ours will see that those who are dependent on us are . . . provided for."

On March 29, 1912, Scott made the final entry in his journal: "Since the 21st we have had a steady gale . . . . We had fuel to make two cups of tea apiece and barely enough food for two days on the 20th. Every day we have been ready to start for our depot eleven miles away, but outside the door of the tent, it remains a scene of whirling drift. I do not think we can hope for any better things now. We shall stick it out to the end, but we are getting weaker, of course, and the end cannot be far.

"It seems a pity, but I do not think I can write more. For God's sake look after our people."

Last Entry in Scott's Diary. Courtesy of Historical Picture Service, Chicago.

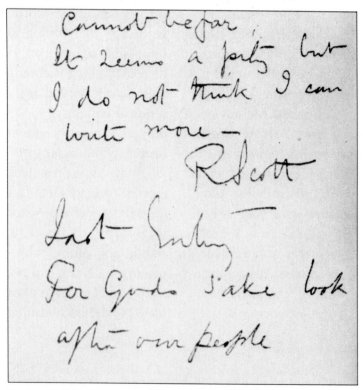

Developing Comprehension Skills

1. Why did Roald Amundsen go to the South Pole?

2. What advantages did the Amundsen party have over the Scott party?

3. What similar qualities in Scott and Amundsen enabled both of them to be as successful as they were in the exploration of these cold regions?

4. How was Scott different from Amundsen? Whom do you like better? Give reasons from the story for your answer.

Reading Literature: True Adventure Stories

1. **Understanding Setting.** Describe what you know of Antarctica after reading this story. Could the story have been the same if Amundsen and Scott had been competing to reach the equator through the Sahara Desert? How might it have been alike? How might it have been different?

2. **Understanding Reasons for Actions.** Does the story give you an idea of what caused Amundsen to take this trip? Can you see why Scott did it? Describe as well as you can the reasons why they were there.

3. **Understanding Sequence.** On a sheet of paper, draw a long straight line and mark an X at each end. Below each X write "Hut Point." Under the first X, mark that it stands for the beginning point of Scott's trek. Under the second, note that it marks the planned ending point. At the center draw a third X. Label that "South Pole."

X————————————————X————————————————X
Hut Point—   South Pole   Hut Point—
Scott's party   Scott's planned
sets out   end point

For every major event reported in the selection, draw another X on the line. Note the date (and place, if possible) of each event. Make a similar chart for the Amundsen expedition.

4. **Understanding Fact and Opinion.** Toward the end of his diary, Scott writes: "It was not poor planning but the death of many ponies early in 1911, the bad weather on the journey outward, and the unbelievably cold weather on the return." Which part of Scott's statement can be proved? Which part is just Scott's idea? Give details from the story

that show that poor planning may have been one of the causes of the disaster.

Developing Vocabulary Skills

Recognizing Context Clues and Reviewing Dictionary Information. Read the following selections about events that occurred in the stories you have read. Figure out the meaning of each underlined word, using context clues. Write the meaning you decide on. Then use your dictionary to answer the questions following each sentence.

1. "In the discus throw it was Jim Thorpe who tossed the round flat weight the farthest." Write the respelling of *discus*. What word in the pronunciation key has the same vowel sound as the vowel in the accented syllable?

2. "Why, they ought to have some football, baseball, lacrosse, hockey, basketball, tennis, handball, and other kinds of sports thrown in." What details in the dictionary definition tell you more about *lacrosse* than the context clues did?

3. "They forged onward somehow, even when a blizzard struck." What are two other dictionary definitions for the word *forge*? Write a sentence to illustrate each of the three meanings.

4. "Rations had been planned for a four-man team. Now the food would have to be shared with a fifth." What are two ways *ration* can be pronounced? Write each respelling.

5. "Several plant impressions were picked, the last a piece of coal with beautiful traces of leaves in layers." Which dictionary definition best fits the meaning of *impression* as it is used in this sentence?

Developing Writing Skills

1. **Presenting an Opinion.** The introduction to this selection asked you to consider whether the explorers of the South Pole were foolhardy or heroic. What did you decide? Write a paragraph or more telling your opinion of the men, and whether the results of their adventure were worth the risk and loss of life. Give reasons for your opinion.

2. **Writing an Adventure.** Write an adventure story about an experience you or someone in your class had. If your class has completed the

activity described under Developing Skills in Speaking and Listening, use your notes for ideas. You may also ask your classmate for further information. Try to use details that will make the experience real for your reader.

Developing Skills in Study and Research

Using the *Readers' Guide to Periodical Literature*. In most public libraries there is a reference book called the *Readers' Guide to Periodical Literature*. This book lists topics that are discussed in magazine articles. It helps you to find material in magazines in the same way as the card catalog helps you to find material in books. To keep the listings up to date, additional booklets are published every two weeks from September through June and once a month in July and August. This reference source can direct you to the latest information on a topic.

Find the *Readers' Guide* in your local library. Your school library may even have a copy. Note that the *Guide* uses abbreviations for the titles of magazines.

Look up the South Pole in the most recent edition of the *Readers' Guide*. On your paper, write the title of every magazine article listed there, along with the name and publication date of the magazine in which the article appears. If the current edition of the *Guide* does not list references to the South Pole, look in older editions until you find one that does.

Developing Skills in Speaking and Listening

Listening for Facts. Each member of the class should prepare a short report on a true adventure of his or her own. The adventure may involve danger, like this selection. It may be sad, or funny, or mysterious.

When you listen to these reports being told by class members, take notes on each one. Record the speaker's name, the main idea of his or her story, and the most exciting or interesting events in the story. As you listen, try to pick out the story you like best. You will not know for sure which is the most interesting story until you have heard them all, so take notes on every one.

Then write out the story you have chosen. Be sure to use your notes. If you remember other things the speaker said which you did not have time to put into your notes, include them in your report. Try to make your report as close as possible to what you heard.

From
The Conquest of Everest

SIR EDMUND HILLARY

High mountains are cold, dangerous, and low in oxygen. Yet people climb them—for fun! Some say that people climb a mountain because "it's there." Does this account explain the challenge better?

For many centuries, Mount Everest, the tallest peak on earth, was unconquered by climbers. Then, in March of 1953, a British expedition led by Sir John Hunt undertook the climb. The group began the ascent together, but it was decided that only two members would attempt the last several thousand feet, the most treacherous of the journey. Here are the words of one of those two, Edmund Hillary (later knighted for his achievement on Everest). His companion was Tenzing Norgay, a Sherpa guide who lived at the foot of the mountain. They reached the top on May 29, 1953.

At 4 A.M. it was very still. I opened the tent door and looked far out across the dark and sleeping valleys of Nepal. The icy peaks below us were glowing clearly in the early morning light, and Tenzing pointed out the monastery of Thyangboche, faintly visible on its dominant spur 16,000 feet below us. It was an encouraging thought to realize that even at this early hour the lamas of Thyangboche would be offering up devotions to their Buddhist gods for our safety and well-being.

We started up our cooker and, in a determined effort to prevent the weaknesses arising from dehydration, we drank large quantities of lemon juice and sugar, and followed this with our last can of sardines on biscuits. I dragged our oxygen sets into the tent, cleaned the ice off them and then completely rechecked and tested them. I had removed my boots, which had become a little wet the day before, and they were now frozen solid. Drastic measures were called for, so I cooked them over the fierce, kerosene,

Mt. Everest from Nepal. Galen Rowell, High and Wild Photo.

flame of the Primus stove and despite the very strong smell of burning leather managed to soften them up. Over our down clothing we donned our windproofs and onto our hands we pulled three pairs of gloves—silk, woolen, and windproof.

Ready To Go

At 6:30 A.M. we crawled out of our tent into the snow, hoisted our thirty pounds of oxygen gear onto our backs, connected up our masks, and turned on the valves to bring life-giving oxygen into our lungs. A few good deep breaths and we were ready to go. Still a little worried about my cold feet, I asked Tenzing to move off and he kicked a deep line of steps away from the rock bluff which protected our tent, out onto the steep powder snow slope to the left of the main ridge. The ridge was now all bathed in sunlight and we could see our first objective, the south summit, far above us. Tenzing, moving purposefully, kicked steps in a long traverse back toward the ridge and we reached its crest just where it forms a great distinctive snow bump at about 28,000 feet. From here the ridge narrowed to a knife-edge and, as my feet were now warm, I took over the lead.

We were moving slowly but steadily and had no need to stop in order to regain our breath, and I felt that we had plenty in reserve. The soft unstable snow made a route on top of the ridge both difficult and dangerous, so I moved a little down on the steep left side. There, the wind had produced a thin crust that sometimes held my weight, but more often than not gave way with a sudden knock that was disastrous to both balance and morale. After several hundred feet of this rather trying ridge, we came to a tiny hollow and found there the two oxygen bottles left on an earlier attempt by the climbers Evans and Bourdillon. I scraped the ice off the gauges and was greatly relieved to find that they still contained several hundred liters of oxygen—sufficient to get us

down to the South pass if used very sparingly. With the comforting thought of these oxygen bottles behind us, I continued making the trail on up the ridge, which soon steepened and broadened into the very formidable snow face leading up for the last 400 feet to the southern summit.

The snow conditions on this face were, we felt, distinctly dangerous. However, as no other route seemed available, we persisted in our strenuous and uncomfortable efforts to beat a trail up it. We made frequent changes of leader on this very trying section; and, on one occasion as I was stamping a trail in the deep snow, a section around me gave way and I slipped back through three or four of my steps. I discussed with Tenzing the advisability of going on and he, although admitting that he felt very unhappy about the snow conditions, finished with his familiar phrase, "Just as you wish." I decided to go on.

The South Peak

It was with some relief that we finally reached some firmer snow higher up and then chipped steps up the last steep slopes and cramponed on to the South Peak. It was now 9 A.M. We looked with some interest at the virgin ridge ahead. Both Bourdillon and Evans had been depressingly definite about its problems and difficulties, and we realized that it could form an almost insuperable barrier. At first glance it was certainly impressive and even rather frightening. On the right, great contorted cornices, overhanging masses of snow and ice, stuck out like twisted fingers over the 10,000-foot drop of the Kangshung Face. Any move onto these cornices could only bring disaster. From the cornices the ridge dropped steeply to the left until the snow merged with the great rock face sweeping up from the Western slope.

Only one encouraging feature was apparent. The steep snow slope between the cornices and the rock precipices seemed to be composed of firm, hard snow. If the snow proved soft and unstable, our chances of getting along the ridge were few indeed. However, if we could cut a trail of steps along this slope, we could make some progress at least.

We cut a seat for ourselves just below the south summit and removed our oxygen. Once again I worked out the mental arithmetic that was one of my main concerns on the way up and down the mountain. As our first partly full bottle of oxygen was now exhausted, we had only one full bottle left. Eight hundred liters of oxygen at three liters per minute? How long could we last? I estimated that this should give us four and a half hours of going. Our equipment was now much lighter, weighing just over twenty pounds, and as I cut steps down off the south summit I felt a distinct sense of freedom and well-being quite contrary to what I had expected at this great altitude.

The First Slope

As my ice ax bit into the first steep slope of the ridge, my highest hopes were realized. The snow was crystalline and firm. Two or three rhythmical blows of the ice ax produced a step large enough even for our oversized high-altitude boots. The most encouraging feature of all was that a firm thrust of the ice ax would sink it halfway up the shaft, giving a solid and comfortable hold for our rope. We moved one at a time. I realized that our margin of safety at this altitude was not great and that we must take every care and precaution. I would cut a forty-foot line of steps, Tenzing belaying me while I worked. Then in turn I would sink my shaft and put a few loops of the rope around it and Tenzing, protected against a breaking step, would move up to me. Then once again as he belayed me I would go on cutting. In a number of places the overhanging ice cornices were very large indeed; and, in order to escape them, I cut a line of steps down to where the snow met the rocks on the west. Scrambling on the rocks and cutting handholds on the snow, we were able to shuffle past these difficult portions. It was a great thrill to look straight down this enormous rock face and to see, 8,000 feet below us, the tiny tents of Camp IV.

On one of these occasions, I noted that Tenzing, who had been going quite well, had suddenly slowed up considerably and seemed to be breathing with difficulty.

Climbers on Mt. Everest with one of the camps below. From *High in the Thin Cold Air* © 1962. Field Enterprises Educational Corporation. Reproduced by Permission of World Book, Inc.

The Sherpas had little idea of the workings of an oxygen set and, from past experience, I immediately suspected his oxygen supply. I noticed that hanging from the exhaust tube of his oxygen mask were icicles, and on closer examination found that this tube, some two inches in diameter, was completely blocked with ice. I was able to clear it out and gave him much needed relief. On checking my own set, I found that the same thing was occurring, though it had not reached the stage to have caused me any discomfort. From then on I kept a much closer check on this problem.

The weather for Everest seemed practically perfect. Insulated as we were in all our down clothing and windproofs, we suffered no discomfort from cold or wind. However, on one occasion, when I removed my sunglasses to examine more closely a difficult section of the ridge, I was very soon blinded by the fine snow driven by the bitter wind and hastily replaced them. I went on cutting steps. To my surprise I was enjoying the climb as much as I had ever enjoyed a fine ridge in my own New Zealand Alps.

The Rock Step

After an hour's steady going we reached the foot of the most formidable looking problem on the ridge—a rock step some forty feet high. We had known of the existence of this step from aerial photographs and had also seen it through our binoculars. We realized that at this altitude it might well spell the difference between success and failure. The rock itself, smooth and almost holdless, was a barrier beyond our strength to overcome.

I could see no way of crossing it on the steep rock bluff on the west, but fortunately another possibility of tackling it still remained. On its east side was another great cornice and running up the full forty feet of the step was a narrow crack between the cornice and the rock. Leaving Tenzing to belay me as best he could, I jammed my way into this crack, then kicking backwards with my crampons I sank their spikes deep into the frozen snow behind me and levered myself off the ground. Taking advantage of every little rock hold and all the force of knee, shoulder, and arms I could muster, I literally cramponed backwards up the crack, with a fervent prayer that the cornice would remain attached to the rock. Despite the considerable effort involved, my progress, although slow, was steady. As Tenzing played out the rope, I inched my way upward until I could finally reach over the top of the rock and drag myself out of the crack onto a wide ledge. For a few moments I lay regaining my breath and, for the first time, really felt the fierce determination that nothing now could stop our reaching the top. I took a firm stance on the ledge and signaled to Tenzing to come on up. As I heaved hard on the rope, Tenzing wriggled his way up the crack and finally collapsed exhausted at the top like a giant fish when it has just been hauled from the sea after a terrible struggle.

I checked both our oxygen sets and roughly calculated our flow rates. Everything seemed to be going well. Probably owing to the strain imposed on him by the trouble with his oxygen set, Tenzing had been moving rather slowly; but he was climbing safely, and this was the major consideration. His only comment on my inquiring of his condition was to smile and wave along the ridge. We were going so well at three liters per minute that I was determined now if necessary to cut down our flow rate to two liters per minute if the extra endurance was required.

Steps to the Top

The ridge continued as before. Giant cornices were on the right, steep rock slopes on the left. I went on cutting steps on the narrow strip of snow. The ridge curved away to the right, and we had no idea where the top was. As I cut around the back of one hump, another higher one would swing into view. Time was passing and the ridge seemed never-ending. In one place where the angle of the ridge had eased off, I tried cramponing without cutting steps, hoping this would save time, but I quickly realized that our margin of safety on these steep slopes at this altitude was too small, so I went on step cutting. I was beginning to tire a little now. I had been cutting steps continuously for two hours, and Tenzing, too, was moving very slowly. As I chipped steps around still another corner, I wondered rather dully just how long we could keep it up. Our original zest had now quite gone and our ascent was turning more into a grim struggle.

I then realized that the ridge ahead, instead of still monotonously rising, now dropped sharply away, and far below I could see the North pass and the Rongbuk Glacier. I looked upward to see a narrow snow ridge running up to a snowy summit. A few more whacks of the ice ax in the firm snow, and we stood on top.

My initial feelings were of relief—relief that there were no more steps to cut—no more ridges to traverse and no more humps to tantalize us with hopes of success. It was 11:30 A.M. The ridge had taken us two and a half hours, but it seemed like a lifetime. I looked at Tenzing and in spite of the balaclava, goggles, and oxygen mask all encrusted with long icicles that concealed his face, there was no disguising his infectious grin of pure delight as he looked all around him. We shook hands and then Tenzing threw his arms around my shoulders and we thumped each other on the back until we were almost breathless.

Sir Edmund Hillary (left) and Tenzing Norgay (right), the day after their climb to the top of Mt. Everest. United Press International.

Developing Comprehension Skills

1. What were some of the things the climbers had to take up the mountain with them that day? What was the purpose of each?

2. During that day Hillary spent much of the time making calculations. What might be some of the talents and skills necessary to master before you might try climbing a mountain? Give specific examples from the story of skills used.

3. At the end, how does Hillary show what an ordeal the climb had been?

4. How does the relationship between Hillary and Tenzing Norgay compare with that between Scott and his companions? How is it similar? How is it different?

5. You have now read about three teams who tried to be the first to accomplish a difficult goal: Amundsen's party, Scott's group, and Hillary and his partner. Can you find any common qualities or attitudes among them? What sets off these explorers from most people?

Reading Literature: True Adventure Stories

1. **Understanding Setting.** Setting is the whole focus of this story. What are some aspects of the setting that makes the story exciting? What were some of the problems that had to be dealt with because of the environment?

2. **Understanding Reasons for Actions.** Compare Hillary's feelings when standing atop Mt. Everest with those of Amundsen when he arrived at the South Pole. To the explorers, are these feelings reason enough to go through what they went through to achieve the goal?

3. **Making Inferences.** This account is drawn from a longer record of the entire expedition. Therefore, a few statements refer to topics that were discussed in earlier parts. As you were reading, you needed to think about those statements. You had to use the context clues to figure out what was missing. Here are three statements of this kind. Read each statement. Answer the questions about it.

   a. "Tenzing pointed out the monastery of Thyangboche, faintly visible on its dominant spur 16,000 feet below us. It was an encouraging thought to realize that even at this early hour the lamas of Thyangboche would be offering up devotions to their Buddhist gods for our safety and well-being."

Had the climbers visited the monastery? Had they talked with the lamas? Did the lamas know that the climbers were on their dangerous journey? What clues suggest that the answer to each of these questions is *yes*?

 b. "We came to a tiny hollow and found there the two oxygen bottles left on the earlier attempt by Evans and Bourdillon."

Did Hillary and Tenzing think that they were the first climbers to go that high? Or did they know about others who had climbed that far? Had the other climbers given complete reports of their expeditions?

 c. "To my surprise I was enjoying the climb as much as I had ever enjoyed a fine ridge in my own New Zealand Alps."

Where had Hillary probably learned mountain climbing? Did he only climb mountains that were difficult and far from his home? Had he expected the climb on Mt. Everest to be fun?

4. **Understanding Fact and Opinion.** At first reading, Hillary's writing seems to be a list of one fact after another. It tells a sequence of events, exactly as they happened, in great detail. As you read more carefully, however, you find many examples of opinions. Hillary tells the reader how he saw things and what he felt about them. For example, in question 3, part *a*, Hillary mentions that he thought of the lamas at the monastery—a fact. He also says that the thought was encouraging—an opinion.

How would you classify each of the following sentences? Is it a fact, an opinion, or a combination of both?

a. The ridge seemed never-ending.

b. I noticed that the tube of his oxygen mask was completely blocked with ice.

c. I was enjoying the climb as much as I had ever enjoyed a fine ridge in my own New Zealand Alps.

d. At first glance the ridge was certainly impressive and even rather frightening.

e. I had been cutting steps strenuously for two hours.

Developing Vocabulary Skills

1. **Understanding Context Clues.** Several words in this selection are special terms used in describing the mountains and mountain climbing. Some examples are *summit* and *cornice*. Other words, such as *depressingly* and *determination*, help describe the personal experiences of the author.

   Read these sentences from the story. Figure out the meaning of each underlined word from the context of the sentence. Also, consider how the word may relate to mountain climbing or to the personal feelings of the author. After writing your definition, find the word in a dictionary and write the exact meaning.

   a. We could see over the top of the main <u>ridge</u> that was now bathed in sunlight.
   b. From there we could see the south <u>summit</u> far above us.
   c. On the right, great contorted <u>cornices</u>, overhanging masses of snow and ice, stuck out like twisted fingers.
   d. A firm thrust of the ice ax would sink it halfway up the shaft, giving a solid and comfortable <u>belay</u>, or secure hold.
   e. I realized that at this point we must take every care and <u>precaution</u>.
   f. For the first time I felt fierce <u>determination</u> that nothing now could stop our reaching the top.
   g. I wondered how long we could keep it up. Our original <u>zest</u> had now quite gone and it was turning more into a grim struggle.
   h. As we reached the top, we felt relief that there were no more ridges to cross, and there were no more humps to <u>tantalize</u> us with hopes of success.

2. **Understanding Affixes.** Prefixes and suffixes added on to a base word are called **affixes**. Several words in this story contain affixes that you learned in Chapter 2. Find the base word in each word listed below. Write the meaning of the base word. If you are not sure of the meaning, check a dictionary. Then write the meaning of the word with its affix or affixes.

   a. unstable
   b. purposeful
   c. uncomfortable
   d. rechecked
   e. discomfort
   f. breathless

Developing Writing Skills

1. **Evaluating Adventure Stories.** Which story interested you more—the race to the South Pole or the conquest of Mt. Everest? State your opinion in one or more paragraphs. Discuss both the topic of the adventure and the way in which the adventure was written.

2. **Writing About an Adventure in the First Person.** Think about the character of Tenzing Norgay, the Sherpa guide. Try to put yourself in his place. What might have been his thoughts as he stood on top of Mt. Everest? Write his thoughts in diary form, as Hillary did.

Developing Skills in Study and Research

1. **Using Graphs.** The graph below compares Mt. Everest with several other notable mountains in the world. It shows the approximate height of each. Every additional 1,000 feet in height makes the temperature about 3° Fahrenheit colder. Use that information and the information on the graph to answer the questions below.

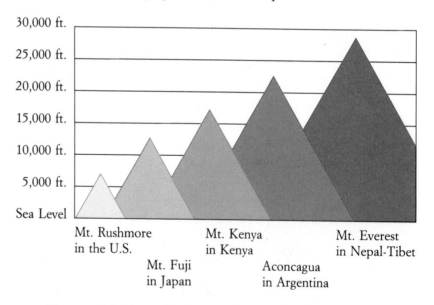

a. How much higher is Mt. Everest than each of the other mountains?

b. Assume that the temperature at the bottom of all six mountains was the same. How much colder would it be at the top of Mt. Fuji than at the top of Mt. Rushmore? How much colder would it be at the top of Mt. Everest than at the top of Mt. Fuji?

2. **Finding and Using Visual Aids.** Unless you are an experienced mountain climber, you may not know about mountain climbing equipment. If you knew what the equipment looked like, you would understand the story better. You can use such reference books as encyclopedias to learn about the equipment.

   Make a list of the special pieces of equipment mentioned in this account, such as a Primus stove, oxygen bottles, oxygen masks, ice axes, and crampons. Find pictures of as many of these as you can. Look in encyclopedias, dictionaries, books about mountain climbing, or catalogs for mountaineering equipment. Draw a sketch of each piece of equipment that you find.

Developing Skills in Speaking and Listening

1. **Delivering a Speech That Persuades.** Imagine that you are the representative of a group that wants to climb Mt. Everest. You need funding from the British government to pay for the climb. You are scheduled to speak to the members of Parliament to ask for their support. Prepare for your speech by listing all the reasons you can think of to support an expedition up Mt. Everest. Arrange them in order from the least important to the most important, or from the most to the least important.

   Read over your notes several times. Think of how you want to express each reason. Remember to choose words with positive connotations. Practice before your family or a mirror. Make sure your voice is loud enough but not too loud. Avoid waving your hands or, if you hold them, playing with your note cards.

   Finally, present your speech to a group. Remember to look at your listeners. Let them see that you want them to listen to you. Let them know that you want their help for your expedition.

2. **Evaluating a Speech That Persuades.** As your classmates present their speeches to the class or to small groups, listen carefully. Note each reason and decide whether you agree with it. See whether the speaker keeps your attention with a well organized, well practiced talk. At the end of each speech, state whether you would support the speaker's project. Be ready to give reasons for accepting or not accepting the speaker's arguments.

Neil Armstrong:
First on the Moon

PAUL WESTMAN

Space travel has been a popular topic of writers for years. When the story is fact, not fiction, it becomes even more fascinating. As you read this, decide what kind of person it takes to become an astronaut.

July 24, 1969. Everyone had waited anxiously for this day to come. In the Pacific Ocean southwest of Hawaii, a rescue ship had been ready for hours. Soon a helicopter began hovering over the blue-green ocean. Swimmers in black rubber suits moved restlessly in the water, staring up into the clouds.

Suddenly, someone saw a dark spot in the sky, far off. Then the *Apollo 11* space-craft came rushing toward the rescue crew, with huge parachutes billowing out behind it. Minutes later the spacecraft splashed safely into the ocean. The waiting was finally over. People throughout the world heard "Splashdown! Apollo has splashdown!" on their televisions and radios.

The President of the United States had come halfway around the world to con-

Apollo 11 Splashdown in the Pacific Ocean at 12:50 p.m., July 24, 1969. NASA.

gratulate the three men who were now bobbing in the ocean. After all, this day had made history. Commander Neil Armstrong and his crew had just returned from the moon!

Practically all his life Neil had been preparing for such a historic trip. Yet he never would have guessed it as a boy. Neil was born August 5, 1930, on his grandfather's farm in northwest Ohio. The closest town, Wapakoneta, was surrounded by woods, rolling hills, and rich farm land.

When Neil was only two years old, his father took him to see the air races in Cleveland, Ohio. Mr. Armstrong boosted Neil up onto his shoulders, high above the crowd. As the planes roared by overhead, little Neil clapped his hands and laughed in delight. He was thrilled at how fast the brightly painted planes could go. Many years later, Neil decided it must have been then when he fell in love with flying.

While Neil was still quite young, his mother spent hour after hour reading to him, and he learned to love books. Neil read 90 books when he was in first grade! He skipped second grade completely, for by that time he could read as well as a fifth grader.

Neil first became interested in building model airplanes after his first plane ride when he was six years old. At first he put together simple models powered by rubber bands. Soon he was building more complicated ones using wood and wire. During the next few years, Neil made hundreds of model planes.

When Neil finished one of his models, he would test it in the grassy park near his house. He even built a wind tunnel in the basement of his house. The wind tunnel had a fan to blow air through it. Neil placed different models in the tunnel to see how well they would fly. Then he chose the designs that worked best.

Neil's interest in experiments showed up in school as well. He particularly liked science and mathematics. One of his teachers, Mr. Crites, helped Neil go on to more difficult studies. He learned calculus, an advanced form of math. Neil also began to read about astronomy. He thought stars and planets were almost as fascinating as airplanes.

One of the Armstrongs' neighbors, Mr. Zint, owned the most powerful telescope in Wapakoneta. Often he let the neighborhood kids look at the night sky through the powerful lens. Neil saw the rings of Saturn and the red planet of Mars. He also gazed at the moon.

As he grew older, Neil never lost interest in the sky and flying. He collected and studied issues of *Air Trails*, a magazine about flying. He filled notebooks with scraps of information he found on different airplane makes and designs. Neil especially enjoyed reading about the Wright brothers. In 1903, Orville and Wilbur Wright had made the first successful motor-powered plane flight in history. They had grown up in a nearby town.

Neil decided that he, too, wanted to be able to fly a plane someday. First he had to take lessons, and they cost nine dollars an hour! He began to do odd jobs around town whenever possible. He worked in a bakery, a hardware store, a grocery store, and, finally, a drugstore. By the time he was 15, Neil had saved enough money to take flying lessons. The day he first soloed, or flew alone, was one of the most thrilling moments of his life. Then, on his 16th birthday, he received his student pilot's license—even before he had his driver's license!

Flight Training

Neil had worked hard to save enough money for flying lessons. Yet, he knew he would have to work even harder to earn enough for college. Neil had read about how the United States Navy offered college scholarships. It seemed like a good way to pay for school, so Neil applied and was awarded one. In return for his schooling, Neil had to agree to serve whenever the navy wanted him.

In the fall of 1947, Neil entered Purdue University in Indiana. He had completed two years there when the navy ordered him to Pensacola, Florida, for flight training. Neil became a naval air cadet.

The Korean War broke out in 1950 while Neil was still at Pensacola. The navy sent Neil and many other pilots to fight in Korea. Neil was the youngest man in his unit.

During the war, Neil flew 78 combat missions. His courage and flying ability won him the respect of his comrades aboard the U.S.S. *Essex*, the aircraft carrier that Neil was stationed on, and the navy awarded him three air medals.

After Neil left the navy in 1952, he went back to Purdue to finish his degree in flight engineering. In his spare time, he taught math courses and delivered the campus newspaper to earn money. He married Janet Shearon in January, 1956.

After college Neil went to work as a research pilot at the Lewis Flight Propulsion Laboratory in Cleveland, Ohio. While he was there, his interest in space flight grew. He told one of the directors at the laboratory, "I think space travel will someday be a reality. When it is, I'd like to take part in it." Few people would have dared to make such a bold prediction in 1955.

Soon Neil took another job as a test pilot at Edwards Air Force Base in California. Most of the other pilots lived in the town of Lancaster, but Neil and Janet bought an old cabin overlooking a beautiful valley in the nearby San Gabriel Mountains. The cabin, which had once belonged to a forest ranger, had no hot water or electricity. The Armstrongs worked hard to fix up the cabin.

Two of their children, Ricky and Karen, were born during these years.

Karen died from a brain tumor when she was only three years old. A second son, Mark, was born later.

In spite of the tragedy of Karen's death, the years at Edwards Air Firce Base were some of the happiest of Neil's life. Much of his time he flew airplanes. Being a test pilot was dangerous work. The planes Neil tested flew faster than the speed of sound. Several times he had close calls. Nevertheless, Neil loved the adventure and excitement of flying and doing important research.

Neil became one of the best pilots in the world while working at Edwards Air Force Base. He was an engineer and experimenter as well. He flew planes to learn more about aircraft design and performance. He contributed much to the development of new methods of flying.

Astronaut

The United States was not the only country experimenting with different forms of air travel. In 1957, the Soviet Union launched the first satellite into outer space. Never before had human beings built a rocket that could fly above the earth's atmosphere. The Russians named their satellite *Sputnik*, meaning "fellow traveler of the Earth."

Because of the success of *Sputnik*, Americans decided to step up their own space program. In 1958 the United States government set up the National Aeronautics and Space Administration (NASA).

All the space research groups in the country, including the one at Edwards, became part of NASA. NASA's purpose was to catch up to the Soviet Union in building rockets and satellites.

Soon United States satellites were being sent into orbit, and people were being trained as astronauts. Neil was eager to participate in the great new adventure of space exploration. While working as a NASA test pilot, he volunteered for the astronaut program. Competition for the few available openings was tough. Applicants had to be jet pilots who had completed at least 1,000 hours of flying time. They had to meet several other requirements as well, including height, weight, age, and health. Applicants also had to have a college degree.

Neil did not think his chances for becoming an astronaut were very good. The people who were already in the training program had begun their careers in the military, but Neil was a civilian. So when his application was accepted in 1962, Neil was both surprised and pleased. He became the first civilian ever admitted to the astronaut program at the NASA Manned Spacecraft Center in Houston, Texas.

The training program proved to be difficult. Neil and the other new men put in many hours of classroom work. They studied outer space and the movements of the sun, moon, and stars. They learned about rockets and how to pilot a space capsule. They also were trained to navigate alone in space with the aid of stars and computers.

Besides classroom work, the new astronauts underwent rugged physical training. They had to accustom their bodies to high pressure, weightlessness, and other conditions they would find in space.

While Neil was in training, NASA was making world headlines. Only three years after it was formed, NASA launched the first American, Alan B. Shepard, into space. Shortly after Shepard's flight, President John F. Kennedy made a famous speech. "Space is open to us now," he said. He urged Americans to join together in an effort to put a person on the moon by 1970.

To carry out President Kennedy's plan, the government established three separate space projects, Mercury, Gemini, and Apollo. Each project was more advanced than the one before it and came closer to the ultimate goal—landing on the moon.

The Mercury Project lasted from May, 1961 to May, 1963. Six tiny Mercury capsules were launched during this two-year period. Each capsule carried one person. The purpose of these six flights was to learn how human beings would react to the new environment of outer space.

In the Gemini Project, 10 flights were made between 1965 and 1966. The Gemini capsule was three times as large as the Mercury one, with room for two people. The Gemini Project was designed to test the effects of long space flights on human

beings and to teach astronauts how to fly their capsules without using computer control from the ground.

In 1966, NASA was preparing to launch *Gemini 8*. The mission of this capsule was to perform the first space docking in history. This meant that *Gemini 8* would connect, or dock, with a second spacecraft that was already in orbit. Neil had just finished his intensive training and was given charge of the historic flight.

Gemini 8 lifted off from the launching pad at Cape Canaveral, Florida, or, as it was then called, Cape Kennedy, on March 16, 1966. Neil and his crewman, David R. Scott, traveled across 105,000 miles of space to reach the orbiting spacecraft.

For the first time, Neil saw what the world looked like from outer space. It resembled a schoolroom globe. The oceans were a vivid blue. Snowy white clouds hid parts of the continents. Space itself was black and empty. Stars looked much brighter and nearer than they did from earth.

Armstrong and Scott caught up to the orbiting spacecraft high above the South Atlantic Ocean. Now it was Neil's job to steer the nose of *Gemini 8* into the docking collar of the other vehicle. Carefully he eased his craft forward. The two connected perfectly.

"As easy as parking a car," he radioed back to earth.

The locked vehicles drifted over the Atlantic Ocean, Africa, and the Indian

Ocean. Then something went wrong. The two crafts began to pitch and spin wildly. Swiftly and skillfully, Armstrong detached the Gemini capsule from the other craft, which floated off into space. Soon *Gemini 8* began spinning faster than ever. It was turning at the rate of one revolution per second! Radio contact between earth and *Gemini 8* crackled and faded.

The NASA crew back on earth waited breathlessly. Was *Gemini 8* lost in space? Then Armstrong's voice came through crisp and clear. He had succeeded in steadying the craft. Armstrong then guided *Gemini 8* to an emergency splashdown in the Pacific Ocean. People everywhere breathed a sigh of relief.

While NASA completed the next two flights in the Gemini Project, Neil went back to test flying. Two years later he had another close call when a jet trainer he was flying crashed. Fortunately, he was able to parachute to safety.

The Apollo Project

Finally, it was time for the Apollo Project, which began in 1968. The twelve Apollo craft launched during this time

Blastoff of Apollo 11, 9:32 a.m., July 16, 1969, Kennedy Space Center, Cape Canaveral, Florida. NASA.

were twice the size of the Gemini capsule and carried three crew members. The purpose of this project was by far the most exciting: to land human beings on the moon. *Apollo 11* would make the historic moon landing. Two of the three people chosen for the *Apollo 11* crew would be the first to walk on the moon. On January 9, 1969, NASA announced the crew. The pilots would be Edwin E. Aldrin, Jr., and Michael Collins. Neil Armstrong was named the commander.

In the months before the flight, the astronauts were kept very busy. They studied moon maps and photographs, spent hours learning about rocks, photography, and weather, and practiced working the controls of their spacecraft. In special laboratories built to resemble the surface of the moon, the astronauts learned to move about in their bulky space suits. Each suit cost $100,000 and had to be sturdily built so tiny space particles called meteoroids could not puncture it. The suit had its own supply of air, water, and electricity. It carried a fan and a refrigeration unit to deal with sharp changes of temperature.

The last ten days before the launch, the astronauts seldom left their crew quarters. They saw few people because doctors feared they might get sick. Even a sore throat would mean delaying the flight for a month.

As launch day approached, excitement grew. People from all over the world arrived at the Cape. Thousands of cars lined the highways. One million people gathered to witness the launch.

On the morning of July 16, 1969, Commander Armstrong and his crew-mates rose before dawn. They ate a hearty breakfast of steak, scrambled eggs, toast, orange juice, and coffee. Then they put on their white space suits, and a truck drove them to the launching pad. An elevator lifted them high into the air, to the very top of the huge Saturn rocket. This rocket was as tall as a 36-floor building. From here the men could see for miles. They saw sand dunes and palm trees, hundreds of boats floating in nearby rivers, and the sparkling blue Atlantic Ocean in the distance.

When it was time, Neil Armstrong, Edwin "Buzz" Aldrin, and Mike Collins boarded the spacecraft. The heavy outer door of the capsule was then sealed shut. The countdown began. "Ten . . . nine . . . eight . . . seven . . . six . . . five . . . four . . . three . . . two . . . one . . . zero!" Millions of people around the world waited tensely. Suddenly orange flames and clouds of smoke shot up around the rocket. There was a mighty roar, and the ground trembled and shook for miles around.

"Lift-off! We have lift-off!" The Saturn rocket shuddered. Ever so slowly it rose into the air. Then it rapidly picked up speed. After ten years of preparation, the voyage to the moon had begun!

The Saturn rocket, also called a launch vehicle, provided the power to send *Apollo 11* to the moon. The rocket had three stages, and each one sent the spacecraft further into outer space. The first stage fueled the lift-off and then dropped off two and a half minutes later. The second stage carried the Apollo craft 116 miles above the earth and dropped off six and a half minutes later. At this point, the third stage sent the spacecraft into orbit around the earth and then to the moon.

The spacecraft had three sections, a command module, a service module, and a lunar module. On the way to the moon, these three sections went through a series of changes. First, the command module, called *Columbia*, and the service module separated from the lunar module, called *Eagle*, and the third stage of the Saturn rocket. Then the command and service modules turned around and docked with the lunar module. Finally, the third stage dropped off, and *Apollo 11* was on its own. Behind it the earth was a beautiful blue green sphere against the blackness.

The Moon

The journey to the moon lasted four days. During that time the astronauts had many important chores to perform. They had calculations to make and instruments to watch. They also broadcast color TV pictures to viewers on earth.

Each crew member had a specific task. Mike Collins was navigator and pilot. His job was to fly the crew from the earth to the moon and back again. Buzz Aldrin was the expert on systems and machines. Neil Armstrong would fly the *Eagle* down to the surface of the moon and lead the expedition outside the craft.

The gray moon seemed to grow larger and larger as *Apollo 11* got closer. The astronauts could see the moon's round shape clearly. "It seemed almost as if it were showing us its roundness, its similarity in shape to our earth, in a sort of welcome," Armstrong said. "I was sure that it would be a hospitable host. It had been awaiting its first visitors for a long time."

Now it was time for the final preparations before reaching the moon. The spacecraft went into orbit around the moon. Armstrong and Aldrin crawled through the narrow passage from the *Columbia* to the *Eagle*, the module that would land them on the moon. Collins remained in the *Columbia*. Then the *Eagle* separated from the command and service modules. "The *Eagle* has wings," Armstrong reported to Mission Control back on earth.

While Collins continued circling the moon in the *Columbia*, Armstrong and Aldrin began their nine-mile descent. If something were to go wrong now, it could spell disaster. One of the *Eagle's* spindly legs could snap. A boulder or a steep slope could cause the craft to fall onto its side. If that happened, the two explorers would be unable to lift off again. They would be stranded on the moon.

The moonscape rushed below them. A computer guided the *Eagle* toward its selected landing site near the Sea of Tranquility. Scientists had selected this site because it looked smooth and safe. However, when Armstrong looked out the window, he was startled. The landing site was actually a crater—a large hole—as wide as a football field and very deep. The ground at the bottom of the crater was covered with huge rocks!

Quickly, Armstrong took control of the *Eagle* from the computer. Guiding the craft by hand, he skimmed over the boulders, looking for flat ground. Flashing red lights warned that fuel was low. Gently he lowered the *Eagle* to the surface. Armstrong's calm voice radioed back, "The *Eagle* has landed."

At Mission Control people started breathing again. In about 30 seconds the *Eagle's* fuel supply would have been gone. One control man turned to another and said, "I think he's the greatest pilot in the whole world."

Armstrong and Aldrin checked all systems on the *Eagle* to be sure nothing had been damaged in landing. They got everything ready for a quick takeoff in case something went wrong. Then they were scheduled to take a nap, but they were too excited! They requested permission to begin exploring the moon, and Mission Control agreed.

Neil Armstrong climbed down the ladder of the *Eagle* and became the first human being to step onto the moon. "That's one small step for a man, one giant leap for mankind," he said. His words were broadcast over radio and TV to listeners and viewers the world over.

As he began to explore the moon, Armstrong saw a desolate area. Rocks and craters littered an empty landscape. Nothing grew at all. The sky appeared to be dark at all times. "But it's very pretty out here," Armstrong radioed back.

There is no air on the moon to make the sky look blue, and no wind or water. Because the moon is unprotected from the sun's deadly rays, the temperature reaches wide extremes. At its hottest it climbs to 250°F. (121°C.) At its coldest it plunges to 280° below zero (−138°C.)

The moon's gravity is much less than that of earth. With full gear Armstrong weighed 360 pounds on earth. On the moon he weighed only 60 pounds. This meant that walking on the moon would be very different from walking on earth. Would Armstrong be able to balance? If he fell and ripped his suit, it could mean sudden death; but Armstrong reported, "It's actually no trouble to walk around."

Soon Aldrin left the *Eagle* and joined Armstrong on the surface. TV viewers a quarter of a million miles away watched the two men walk with slow, bounding strides. After they were used to moving about in very little gravity, the men settled

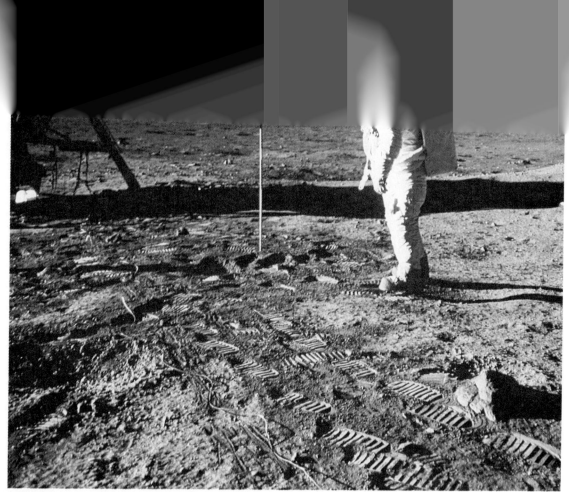

Astronauts' footprints are clearly visible in Neil Armstrong's photograph of Buzz Aldrin on the moon with U.S. flag and lunar module, 1969. NASA.

down to work. In the next two and a half hours they did many things. They planted an American flag and set up TV cameras. They took photographs, gathered moon rocks, and performed several scientific experiments.

Finally Aldrin climbed back aboard the *Eagle*. Armstrong remained outside to collect a few more rocks, which scientists would study back on earth. Then he, too, climbed back into the lunar module. The two astronauts had left large footprints on the moon's soft surface during their work. Because of the moon's environment, those prints may remain undisturbed for hundreds of years.

The next morning Armstrong and Aldrin prepared to blast off. The lower half of the *Eagle* would serve as a launching pad for the upper part.

The rockets fired, lifting the two astronauts away from the moon. Miles above the surface Armstrong docked with the *Columbia*, and they rejoined Collins in the command module. The *Eagle* had completed its task, so it was abandoned.

Four days later the *Columbia* returned to earth. It arched gracefully over Australia and the Coral Sea, splashing down in the Pacific Ocean. Within an hour, Armstrong and his crew were hoisted into a helicopter. They flew to the U.S.S. *Hornet*, a battleship 11 miles away. There they were greeted by the President of the United States, Richard M. Nixon.

"Congratulations, Neil, Buzz, and Mike," the President said. "The response to your accomplishment has been tremendous. In Washington we have received messages and greetings from more than 100 foreign governments. They come from emperors and presidents, prime ministers and kings. You have helped bring the peoples of the world closer together. You have taught man how to reach for the stars."

Armstrong, Aldrin, and Collins were honored in a ticker-tape parade in New York City. Not since aviator Charles Lindbergh flew across the Atlantic had anyone been given such a hero's welcome. The President awarded each the Medal of Freedom, the highest United States civilian award anyone can receive. Later, the men visited 22 nations. Everywhere they were greeted by thousands of people.

Even as a hero, Armstrong remained quiet and shy. People joked that he showed enthusiasm only when speaking of aeronautics or flying. It was true that flying was still his first love.

In 1970, a year after the historic flight to the moon, Armstrong resigned from NASA. He wanted to make room for younger astronauts, and he wanted time to relax.

Now, in his spare time, Armstrong pursues his favorite hobby—gliding. He spends many peaceful hours soaring silently through the blue midwestern skies in his sailplane. Sometimes an early moon floats with him in the sky, a moon whose surface is now marked by human footprints. Above those footprints on that lonely moonscape is a bronze plaque left by the first moon explorers. The plaque was signed by Neil Armstrong, the rest of the *Apollo 11* crew, and the President of the United States. It reads:

HERE MEN FROM THE PLANET EARTH
FIRST SET FOOT UPON THE MOON
JULY 1969, A. D.
WE CAME IN PEACE FOR ALL MANKIND

NEIL A. ARMSTRONG
ASTRONAUT

MICHAEL COLLINS
ASTRONAUT

EDWIN E. ALDRIN, JR.
ASTRONAUT

RICHARD NIXON
PRESIDENT, UNITED STATES OF AMERICA

Plaque on the Moon, left there by Apollo 11 crew, July, 1969. NASA.

Developing Comprehension Skills

1. Pick out as many incidents in Neil Armstrong's early life as you can that influenced him to become an airplane pilot.

2. Neil did not think his chances for becoming an astronaut were very good. Why did he think this? Why do you think he was accepted into the program?

3. Think of three reasons why the United States placed such great importance on the space program.

4. What did Armstrong mean when he said, "That's one small step for a man, one giant leap for mankind"?

5. Today, biographers try to provide a well-rounded picture of their subjects. This story covers most of Neil Armstrong's life. It discusses everything that led up to his walk on the moon. Why do you think it was placed with the True Adventure Stories section instead of Biographies? Why does it not belong under Biographies?

Reading Literature: True Adventure Stories

1. **Understanding Fact and Opinion.** Although this is a true adventure story, some things in it must be considered opinions. One of these is the comment on page 384 that "I think he's the greatest pilot in the whole world." Find three more examples of opinion in the story. Then see if you can find facts that support each of these opinions.

2. **Understanding Setting.** What likenesses are there among the moon, the South Pole, and the top of Mt. Everest? What similar types of special equipment had to be worn and used in each place?

3. **Understanding Sequence.** Make a time line. Write in these events of Neil's life in the correct order. If the events came close together in Neil's life, mark them close together on the time line.

Cleveland Air Races	College
Telescope—astronomy	Korea
Apollo 11, the moon	Test Pilot, Edwards Air Force Base
Pilot's license	Houston, NASA
Skips second grade	*Gemini 8*, space docking
Model airplanes	

Developing Vocabulary Skills

Understanding Context Clues and Affixes. You have learned to find the meaning of unfamiliar words by looking for context clues and knowing word parts. Read these sentences about Neil Armstrong. If the sentence contains a context clue, choose which of these types of clues you used to figure out the meaning of the underlined word: **definition or restatement**, **example**, **comparison**, or **contrast**. If you can determine the meaning of the word by knowing affixes, write **word parts**. After writing what method you used, write the meaning you figured out.

1. At first Neil put together simple models powered by rubber bands, but soon he was building more complicated ones.

2. One of Neil's teachers helped him to learn calculus, an advanced form of math.

3. He also began to read about astronomy, which is the study of stars and planets.

4. The day he first soloed, or flew alone, was one of the most thrilling moments of his life.

5. The people who were already in the training program had begun their careers in the military, but Neil was a civilian.

6. Besides getting used to weightlessness, trainees had to accustom their bodies to high pressure and other conditions they would find in space.

7. This meant that the capsule would connect, or dock, with a second spacecraft that was already in orbit.

8. The NASA crew back on earth waited breathlessly to hear from Armstrong.

9. Each space suit had to be sturdily built so that tiny space particles called meteoroids could not puncture it.

10. The spacecraft had three sections: a command module, a service module, and a lunar module.

11. The men saw that many areas of the moon were covered with large holes, or craters.

12. Miles above the surface Armstrong rejoined Collins in the command module.

Columbia crew, 1983. NASA.

Developing Writing Skills

1. **Presenting an Opinion.** All three of these true adventure stories are based on people who were the first to do something. Why is being first so special and so fascinating? Write one or more paragraphs giving your reasons.

2. **Developing an Argument.** Imagine that the President has announced that he wants to discontinue the space program because of its high cost. Write a letter to him. You can agree with him and back his decision. You can disagree and explain why you feel it is necessary to continue the program.

3. **Writing an Imaginary Adventure.** The time is 2192 and creatures from a different galaxy have just landed on the Earth's moon, right at the site where Armstrong and his party landed. Write a brief composition describing what they see and what conclusions they come to, based on what they see.

Developing Skills in Study and Research

Using the Readers' Guide to Periodical Literature. In order to write this adventure story, the author had to do a great deal of research. He probably referred to the *Readers' Guide to Periodical Literature* many times. He might have used it to find out what was thought and written about the space program over the years.

You can find out for yourself how ideas about space exploration have changed recently. You can do this quickly by looking at three volumes of the *Readers' Guide*. First, look up the terms *astronaut, moon,* and *space* in a volume from 1950 to 1955. Then look up the same terms in a volume from 1965 to 1970. Last, look up the same terms in a volume since 1980. For each volume, count the number of articles listed after each term. How do the totals change from volume to volume? What does that tell you about progress in the space program? What does it tell you about people's interest in the space program?

Write a paragraph or more explaining what you found and your conclusions.

Developing Skills in Critical Thinking

Identifying the Writer's Organization. This story of Neil Armstrong was not simply about one pilot. It was also about the development of the United States space program, especially its efforts to reach the moon. Therefore, the writer needed to do two things. He had to tell about Neil's life. He also had to explain certain parts of the U.S. program.

To organize the information about Neil's life, the writer could use time sequence. However, it was harder to organize the information about the space program. The writer did not want that to interfere with the story of Neil's life. He had to choose places where the information about the space program related to what Neil was doing.

Skim the selection to find where each of these projects or programs is explained. Then choose one of the terms. Explain where and how the writer fit his explanation of the term into the story of Neil's life.

Mercury Project	the Apollo spacecraft design
Gemini Project	facts about the moon that affected
Apollo Project	the *Apollo 11* program

Essays

An **essay** is a special kind of nonfiction writing. In this section you will read two essays about the same topic. What does each of these writers say about our recent exploration of space? What do they think it means to Earth?

The False Mirror, 1928, RENE MAGRITTE. Collection, The Museum of Modern Art, New York City; Purchase. Oil on canvas, 21¼ × 31⅞".

Reading Literature: More About Nonfiction

More About Nonfiction

As you know, nonfiction is writing that tells about real people, places, and events. You have read two types of nonfiction, biographies and true adventure stories. Now you will read a third type of nonfiction, called the **essay**.

You have seen that most of the statements in biographies and true adventure stories are facts. However, some of the statements are opinions. These opinions often help to organize the facts. For example, a biographer might give the opinion "Florence Nightingale was a tireless worker," and then list all the jobs Florence did. In contrast, most of the statements in an essay are opinions. They tell what the writer thinks about certain facts.

What Is an Essay?

An essay is a short piece of writing in which the author tells his or her opinion on a particular topic. The topic can be almost anything—a personal experience, a person, thoughts on watching the news, the joy of skiing, or why strawberry ice cream is the best. The tone can be humorous or serious, casual or formal.

Although essays can be written in the third person, they are most often written in the first person. Reading an essay is like listening to someone think.

The History of the Essay

As a form of writing, the essay started in the 1500's. The name was first used by a French writer, Michel de Montaigne. One meaning of *essay* is "a try" or "an attempt." Montaigne attempted to explain his thinking on personal matters, such as friendship.

The Elements of the Essay

Style.   In an essay, a writer has more freedom than in other kinds of prose writing. An essay is like a poem in many ways. Essayists use figurative language, mood, and tone, just as poets do. Also, like poets, they can use a setting or not, as they please, and they may organize their ideas in any order they choose.

Sequence.   Most essays do not follow a time sequence. Instead, the writer arranges his or her ideas in an order that the reader can follow and understand. The sequence of ideas must be logical.

Each paragraph has a clear main idea, usually stated in a topic sentence. Every detail relates to the main idea. In addition, there is a development from one detail to the next and from one main idea to the next. As you read this first paragraph from an essay on water, watch how one idea leads to the next.

> Are you thirsty? Try a glass of the most valuable drink in the world. We couldn't get along without it. The average person takes in, one way or another, about 16,000 gallons during a lifetime. Animals like it. So do birds. So do plants. If you want, you can swim in it, skate on it, or take a bath in it. You can use it to run powerful machinery, make electricity, or boil an egg. The recipe for this wonderful beverage is simple; you don't even have to mix it yourself. Nature has already done it: two parts of hydrogen and one part of oxygen. We call it water.
>
> —*Cricket Magazine*

The writer states the topic of the essay immediately: the most valuable drink in the world. Then the writer gives the topic sentence of the paragraph: "We couldn't get along without it."

Next, the writer answers three questions: Who likes this drink? What can you do with it? How do you make it? Last, the writer states the main idea of the paragraph and the theme of the essay: water is the most valuable drink in the world.

In this essay, the theme is an opinion; the details are facts that support that opinion.

Morning—The Bird Perched for Flight

ANNE MORROW LINDBERGH

Before Apollo 11 *and Neil Armstrong's moon landing,* Apollo 8 *orbited the moon. Anne Lindbergh watched that liftoff from Cape Canaveral, then called Cape Kennedy. Was she thinking of the moon?*

We wake to the alarm at four thirty and leave our motel at five fifteen. The three astronauts must be already climbing into their seats at the top of their "thirty-six-story" rocket, poised for flight. The pilgrimage of sightseers has started to the Cape. Already the buses have left and lines of cars are on the roads. It is dark, a little chilly, with a sky full of stars. As we approach the Cape, we see again the rocket and its launching tower from far off over the lagoon. It is illumined with searchlights, the newest and most perfected creation of a scientific age—hard, weighty metal.

We watch the launching with some of the astronauts and their families, from a site near the Vehicle Assembly Building. Our cars are parked on a slight rise of ground. People get out, walk about restlessly, set up cameras and adjust their binoculars. The launch pad is about three miles away, near the beach. We look across Florida marsh grass and palmettos.

A cabbage palm stands up black against a shadowy sky, just left of the rocket and its launching tower. As dawn flushes the horizon, an egret rises and lazily glides across the flats between us and the pad. It is a still morning. Ducks call from nearby inlets. Vapor trails of a high-flying plane turn pink in an almost cloudless sky. Stars pale in the blue.

With the morning light, *Apollo 8* and its launching tower become clearer, harder, and more defined. One can see the details of installation. The dark sections on the smooth sides of the rocket, marking its stages, cut up the single fluid line. Vapor steams furiously off its side. No longer stark and simple, this morning the rocket is complicated, mechanical, earth-bound. Too weighty for flight, one feels.

People stop talking, stand in front of their cars, and raise binoculars to their eyes. We peer nervously at the launch site and then at our watches. Radio voices blare unnaturally loud from car windows. "Thirty minutes to launch time . . . fifteen minutes . . . six minutes . . . thirty seconds to go . . . twenty . . . T minus fifteen . . . fourteen . . . thirteen . . . twelve . . . eleven . . . ten . . . nine . . . Ignition!"

A jet of steam shoots from the pad below the rocket. "Ahhhh!" The crowd gasps, almost in unison. Now great flames spurt, leap, belch out across the horizon. Clouds of smoke billow up on either side of the rocket, completely hiding its base. From the midst of this holocaust, the rocket begins to rise—slowly, as in a dream, so slowly it seems to hang suspended on the cloud of fire and smoke. It's impossible—it can't rise. Yes, it rises, but heavily, as if the giant weight is pulled by an invisible hand out of the atmosphere, like the lead on a plumb line from the depths of the sea. Slowly it rises and—because of our distance—silently, as in a dream.

Suddenly the noise breaks, jumps across our three separating miles—a shattering roar of explosions, a trip hammer over one's head, under one's feet, through one's body. The earth shakes; cars rattle; vibrations beat in the chest. A roll of thunder, prolonged, prolonged, prolonged.

I drop the binoculars and put my hands to my ears, holding my head to keep it steady. My throat tightens—am I going to cry?—my eyes are fixed on the rocket, mesmerized by its slow ascent.

The foreground is now full of birds; a great flock of ducks, herons, small birds, rise pell-mell from the marshes at the noise. Fluttering in alarm and confusion, they scatter in all directions as if it were the end of the world. In the seconds I take to look at them, the rocket has left the tower.

It is up and away, a comet boring through the sky, no longer the vulnerable untried child, no longer the earth-bound machine, or the weight at the end of a line, but sheer terrifying force, blasting upward on its own titanic power.

It has gone miles into the sky. It is blurred by a cloud. No, it has made its own cloud—a huge vapor trail, which hides it. Out of the cloud something falls, cartwheeling down, smoking. "The first-stage cutoff," someone says. Where is the rocket itself?

There, above the cloud now, reappears the rocket, only a very bright star, diminishing every second. Soon out of sight, off to lunar space.

One looks earthward again. It is curiously still and empty. A cloud of brown smoke hangs motionless on the horizon. Its long shadow reaches us across the grass. The launch pad is empty. The abandoned launching tower is being sprayed with jets of water to cool it down. It steams in the bright morning air. Still dazed, people stumble into cars and start the slow, jammed trek back to town. The monotone of radio voices continues. One clings to this last thread of contact with something incredibly beautiful that has vanished.

"Where are they—where are they now?" In eleven minutes we get word. They are in earth orbit. They "look good" in the laconic space talk that comes down from over a hundred miles above earth. One realizes again that it is the men above all that matter, the individuals who man the machine, give it heart, sight, speech, intelligence, and direction; and the men on earth who are backing them up, monitoring their every move, even to their heartbeats. This is not sheer power, it is power under control of man.

Another generation will judge what has changed, what is born, what is promised. We, who are here today, can witness only certain very close and tangible miracles that bloomed at this moment for men on earth. Because of the advance in science, mechanics, and electronics, man was able to achieve a giant step beyond himself into space—a step shared by all the world through the marvels of modern communication. From this shared experience in the perceptions of remarkable men, another surprising and human gift came down to us. Along with a new sense of earth's smallness, a fragile, shining ball floating in space, we have a new sense of earth's richness and beauty, marbled with brown continents and blue seas and swathed in dazzling clouds—the only spot of color in a black and gray universe.

No one, it has been said, will ever look at the moon in the same way again. More significantly, can one say that no one will ever look at the earth in the same way? Man had to free himself from earth to see it clearly. Now we perceive both its diminutive place in a solar system and its inestimable value as a life-fostering planet. As earthmen, we may have taken another step into adulthood. We can see our parent earth with detachment, with tenderness, with some shame and pity, but at last also with love. As Elinor Wylie wrote of earth before man circled it:

It is not heaven: bitter seed
Leavens its entrails with despair:
It is a star where dragons breed:
Devils have a footing there. . . .

It balances on air, and spins
Snared by strong transparent space;
I forgive it all its sins
I kiss the scars upon its face.

With adult love comes responsibility. We begin to realize how utterly we are earth's children. Perhaps we can now accept our responsibility to earth, and our heritage from it, which we must protect if we are to survive.

Power over life must be balanced by reverence for life. For life, this rare and delicate essence, seems to be, as far as man's vision now extends, primarily the property of earth, and not simply life of man—life of animals, birds, butterflies, trees, flowers, crops. All life is linked. This is what makes up "the good earth."

As we left the beach at Cape Kennedy the last evening, our eyes followed a lone heron over the marsh, and rose with a cloud of wheeling duck on the horizon. We realized with a new humility, born of a new pride, that without the marsh there would be no heron; without the wilderness, forests, trees, fields, there would be no breath, no crops, no sustenance, no life, no brotherhood, and no peace on earth. No heron and no astronaut. The heron and the astronaut are linked in an indissoluble chain of life on earth.

Through the eyes of the astronauts, we have seen more clearly than ever before this precious earth essence that must be preserved. It might be given a new name borrowed from space language: "Earth shine."

Portions of Africa, Europe, and the Arabian Peninsula as seen from space by the moon-bound *Apollo 11* crew, about 98,000 miles from Earth, 1969. NASA.

Developing Comprehension Skills

1. To Anne Morrow Lindbergh, what does the Apollo rocket look like before liftoff?

2. What does the Apollo rocket look like during and after liftoff? What similes and metaphors does Lindbergh use to describe it?

3. When the noise of the launch hits, Lindbergh describes the effect in the paragraph quoted below. (Remember that *mesmerized* means hypnotized.)

   > I drop the binoculars and put my hands to my ears, holding my head to keep it steady. My throat tightens—am I going to cry?—my eyes are fixed on the rocket, mesmerized by its slow ascent.

   What makes her feel she might cry? What do the paragraphs before this one, and this paragraph, tell you about the experience to explain this feeling?

4. On page 395, the writer says that the rocket is "sheer terrifying force, blasting upward on its own power." Later she says, "This is not sheer power, it is power under control of man." How does she move from thinking the first idea to realizing the second? What has she talked about in the paragraphs between that relates these two statements?

5. Lindbergh believes that sending astronauts into space has given people on earth a new, clearer view of earth. What are some of the facts about earth that she thinks are clearer now?

6. Lindbergh states, "Man had to free himself from earth to perceive both its diminutive place in a solar system and its inestimable value as a life-fostering planet." In other words, there was only one way for man to see how small earth is as part of the solar system and how valuable it is as the source of life. That way was by sending men and women into space.

   In what way is this statement accurate? In what way is it not accurate? Is this statement a fact or an opinion?

Reading Literature: Essays

1. **Understanding the Setting.** This essay is unusual because its setting is very important. Although it begins with its focus on the rocket, the

essay includes description of the natural setting. Gradually, the essay shows how the rocket and nature are related. See how the writer connects them by making a list of every reference to birds that you can find in the selection.

2. **Identifying the Theme.** In your own words, tell the theme of this essay. How does the title of the essay lead the reader to the theme? What is the metaphor in the title?

3. **Recognizing Sequence.** The order of events in this essay is chronological; in other words, the events are described in the order in which they happen. However, besides describing events, the writer also develops the relationship between the launch and our view of the world. At what point does the essay change from chronological sequence to logical sequence? Why is this a good breaking point?

Developing Vocabulary Skills

Choosing the Best Method for Finding Meanings. Read these six sentences with words from the story. Choose the best method you would use to figure out the meaning of each underlined word. Then use that method and write the definition.

1. They "look good" in the laconic space talk that comes down from over a hundred miles above Earth.

   a. restatement clue   b. dictionary   c. word parts

2. We realized that without the wilderness and fields, there would be no sustenance, for instance, no crops or fish or game.

   a. word parts   b. contrast clue   c. example clue

3. As dawn flushes the horizon, an egret rises and lazily glides across the flats between us and the pad.

   a. restatement clue   b. example clue   c. inference clues

4. Perhaps we can now accept our responsibility to Earth, and we can accept our heritage from it.

   a. antonym clue   b. dictionary   c. definition clue

5. Through the eyes of the astronauts, we have seen more clearly than ever before that life on Earth must be preserved, or protected.

   a. restatement clue   b. dictionary   c. comparison clue

6. By sheer terrifying force, the huge rocket is blasting upward on its own <u>titanic</u> power.

    a. contrast clue   b. dictionary   c. antonym clue

Developing Writing Skills

1. **Using Figures of Speech.** Write a poem that deals with this rocket and its liftoff. Use at least one of these figures of speech: simile, metaphor, personification, hyperbole. The essay itself uses several figures of speech to describe the rocket. You may use similes and metaphors from the essay, or you may make up your own.

2. **Writing a Personal Essay.** In this essay, Anne Lindbergh described the Apollo rocket in a personal way. She pictured the rocket as a bird and a star and a weight on a plumb line because the rocket reminded her of those things. Choose something about which you have personal feelings. It may be the sight of a city street during a night rain, or the sound of thunder, or the taste of a food. Write an essay in which you both describe the thing and tell how you feel about it. Use similes and metaphors that show what the thing brings to your mind.

A Great Egret in flight, 1976. Peter B. Kaplan, New York. Photo Researchers, Inc.

Developing Skills in Study and Research

Using Library Resources To Determine an Author's Authority. In an essay, a writer presents his or her opinions about facts. Therefore, it is important for the reader of an essay to know something about the writer. Does the writer know enough about the facts to understand them? Does he or she have any experience with the subjects? Has the writer proved himself or herself to be a thoughtful person?

Use the card catalog, reference books, and the *Readers' Guide to Periodical Literature* to find materials to read about Anne Morrow Lindbergh. You want to find the answers to these questions:

1. Does Lindbergh know anything about space flight or nature?

2. Has she proved herself to be a thoughtful speaker or writer?

Skim the information about Lindbergh to find facts related to these questions. Make a note of any related facts you find. Also, note the reference sources in which you found them.

Developing Skills in Critical Thinking

Separating Fact from Opinion. As you know, an essay uses facts to explain or support the writer's opinion. Reread the paragraphs from Anne Morrow Lindbergh's essay listed below. In each paragraph, find any phrase or sentence that states a fact. On your paper, copy only the phrases and sentences that are facts. Leave out any part of the sentence that sounds like opinion or cannot be proved.

For example, one word in this sentence is an opinion: "Vapor steams furiously off its side." The word *furiously* suggests an attitude. It cannot be proved. Therefore, you would copy only "Vapor steams off its side."

1. Page 394, column 2, paragraph 2 ("With the morning light. . . .")

2. Page 395, column 1, paragraph 2 ("A jet of steam. . . .")

3. Page 395, column 2, paragraph 2 ("It is up and away. . . .")

A Changing Landscape

ARCHIBALD MacLEISH

The astronauts who flew the Apollo 8 mission around the moon in 1968 took photographs of our spaceship, Earth. The poet Archibald MacLeish wrote about this event. How does this essay affect your view of Earth?

For the first time in all of time, men have *seen* the earth: seen it not as continents or oceans from the little distance of a hundred miles or two or three, but seen it from the depths of space; seen it whole and round and beautiful and small . . . And seeing it so, one question came to the minds of those who looked at it. "Is it inhabited?" they said to each other and laughed—and then they did not laugh.

What came to their minds a hundred thousand miles and more into space—"half way to the moon" they put it—what came to their minds was the life on that little, lonely, floating planet: that tiny raft in the enormous, empty night. "Is it inhabited?"

Developing Comprehension Skills

1. Who asks the question, "Is it inhabited?" To what does "it" refer?
2. Why did the question make them laugh?
3. What was it about the question that made them stop laughing?
4. Is the question an important one to ask? Why?

Reading Literature: Essays

1. **Appreciating Setting.** Does setting play an important part in this essay? Could the question "Is it inhabited?" have been asked in any other place?

2. **Understanding Irony.** What was ironic about the question the astronauts asked each other?

3. **Recognizing Figurative Language.** In this selection, find two examples of alliteration and two examples of repetition of words, phrases, or sentences.

4. **Identifying Theme.** What do you think is the theme of this essay?

Developing Vocabulary Skills

Reviewing Connotations. In the first paragraph of this essay, the writer wanted to emphasize how beautiful the earth looked from space. In the second paragraph, he wanted to stress how fragile it looked. Find words in each paragraph that have either a denotation (exact meaning) or a connotation (suggested meaning) that supports the main idea of that paragraph.

Developing Writing Skills

1. **Comparing and Contrasting Selections.** Several of the selections in this text asked you to look at Earth from the viewpoint of space. Choose two of the selections listed below and write a comparison of them. You may write about such matters as theme, tone, mood, organization of ideas, form, figures of speech, and sounds of language. Discuss how the two selections are similar and how they are different. Be sure to use examples from both of the selections to support your statements.

   "Orbiter 5 Shows How Earth Looks from the Moon"—May Swenson
   "Earth"—Oliver Herford
   "Morning–The Bird Perched for Flight"—Anne Morrow Lindbergh
   "A Changing Landscape"—Archibald MacLeish

2. **Writing an Essay.** The introduction to this essay used the term "spaceship Earth." What does this term mean to you? Write a short essay of two or more paragraphs explaining what you think the term means and how you feel about the concept.

Review

Using Your Skills in Reading Nonfiction

Read this paragraph from a biography of Father Damien, who helped lepers in Hawaii. The paragraph describes him as a child. What is the setting? Tell what you learn about Joseph's character. Also, decide whether this paragraph uses direct or indirect description, or both. Give reasons for your answers.

> In Tremeloo the farming people all spoke Flemish, for this was in the northern part of Belgium. So young Joseph spoke Flemish as he grew up, running through the fields after his father and brothers and sisters as they planted and harvested. And he played with the other boys, often getting into trouble in the village for mischief that he thought up.

Using Your Comprehension Skills

In this paragraph from the play "Miss Louisa and the Outlaws," find the topic sentence. Explain how the details are related to the main idea.

> **Miss Louisa.** There are cumulus clouds forming in the west. It is October; showers begin suddenly in the fall. It is a rule of our school that we never allow the American flag to become wet. Therefore, the students must bring in the flag.

Using Your Vocabulary Skills

Use these stage directions from a Chapter 7 selection to infer the meaning of *ad lib.*

> **Sound.** *(Ad lib conversation and footsteps begin as they go from the marketplace together. Noise and talking fade gradually.)*
>
> **Sound.** *(Ad lib goodbyes, good luck, see you in the morning, continue. The voices fade away.)*

All. *(ad lib, exclamations of surprise)* Think of that!

All. *(ad lib)* Thank you!

Using Your Writing Skills

Choose one of these writing assignments. Follow the directions.

1. Write one or more paragraphs comparing the true adventure story about Neil Armstrong with the essay about the launching of Apollo 8. Consider the language, the subject, the theme, the mood, and any other element you choose.

2. Write a short essay about your favorite month. Give your opinions and reasons for feeling as you do. Use figurative language at least once in the essay.

Using Your Skills in Study and Research

Imagine that your teacher alerts you to the fact that in Chapter 7 you will read plays about old Spain and the old American West. You are asked to find out something about the setting of one of the plays. Describe how you would use library resources to learn about either Spain or the old West.

Using Your Skills in Critical Thinking

In this paragraph from the biography of Jane Addams, which sentences state facts? Which one states an opinion?

All around Jane in the dirty streets swarmed men, women and children from every country in Europe, shouting and talking in many languages. Many could speak no English. They crowded into tenements and into the noisy, dark factories and big cattle stockyards where they worked. It seemed that they all wanted to be Americans, but they did not know how.

CHAPTER **7**

The Actor's Mask, 1924, PAUL KLÉE.
Collection, The Museum of Modern Art, New York City;
Gift from Sidney and Harriet Janis Collection.
Oil on canvas mounted on board, 14½ × 13½".

$\mathcal{R}$eading Literature: Drama

What Is Drama?

Drama is writing that tells a story through the words and actions of characters. It is meant to be performed by actors and actresses before an audience. Another word for drama is *play*.

The History of Drama

We do not really know how drama began. Perhaps, after hearing a good story, some cave dweller tried to act it out. Perhaps a hunter decided to show his friends what happened on the hunt instead of telling about it. One thing history tells is that drama is a natural way for people to communicate.

The oldest written plays are from ancient Greece. The Greeks loved plays. They even held contests to see who could write the best plays, and they gave prizes to the winning playwrights.

Until recently, every play was performed by actors and actresses in front of an audience. Since radio was invented, however, this has changed. Playwrights started writing plays to be performed on the radio. These plays included instructions for special sounds, called **sound effects**. Sound effects helped people picture things they could not see or that could not really happen.

Today you can see plays on TV and in movies. You can sometimes hear plays on the radio. Also, of course, you can still see plays performed live by actors and actresses.

The Elements of Drama

A play has many of the same elements as short stories. The three most important elements are **characters**, **setting**, and **plot**. In addition, when you read a play, watch for these features.

Dialog. In most plays, the entire story is told through conversations among the characters, or **dialog**. The reader learns what happens from what characters say to each other. A character's words are printed after the character's name.

Narrator. In some plays, a **narrator** explains parts of the story to the audience. Usually, the narrator is not one of the characters. The narrator knows things the characters do not know. When the narrator speaks to the audience, the actors and actresses playing the characters pretend they do not hear him or her.

Stage Directions. The playwright usually provides short explanations of the action. In this text, they are printed in italic letters inside parentheses. These explanations guide actors in performing the play. They also help the reader to picture how actors might move on the stage. The writer may also suggest which objects, or **props**, should be used on the stage.

Cast of Characters. At the beginning of most plays, the playwright provides a list of all the characters who will appear on stage at any time during the play.

Acts and Scenes. A long play will usually be divided into smaller parts, called **acts**. Each act is further divided into **scenes**. Each scene happens in a single time and place.

How To Read Drama

1. Picture the action. Plays are meant to be performed. Imagine actors and actresses playing the parts of the characters.
2. Remember that anything can happen in a play. Do not expect every play to be realistic. To enjoy drama, you sometimes must accept the impossible.
3. After you finish reading a play, decide what its theme is. Playwrights have themes in mind just as other writers do. Think about what happened in the play. What main idea about life is the playwright sharing with you?

Comprehension Skills: Sentences and Punctuation

Understanding Sentences and Sentence Fragments

Writers usually use complete sentences. If they do not, their writing can be confusing. When this happens, it is important to know what to look for.

A **sentence** is a group of words that tells a complete thought. It has both a subject and a predicate. The **subject** tells who or what did something, or what the sentence is about. The **predicate** tells what the subject did or was. Below, each subject is underlined once. Each predicate is underlined twice.

The old castle was spooky.

The outlaws burst into the room.

A group of words that does not have both a subject and a predicate can make dialog sound more like real conversations.

To understand a sentence fragment, read it in context. The sentence before the fragment will help you. Here is an example from a play you will read.

Maria. Riccardo, you are early!
Riccardo. Not so very.

"Not so very" is a fragment. The context tells what it means. As a complete sentence, the fragment becomes, "I'm not so very early."

Using End Punctuation

In a play, you learn everything from the words of the characters. Therefore, it is especially important to recognize how the characters are speaking. End punctuation can give you clues.

Periods. If a sentence ends in a period (.), the character is making a statement or a request. His or her voice probably will go down at the end of the sentence: "You may sit down now."

Question Marks. If a sentence ends in a question mark (?), the character is asking a question. His or her voice will go up at the end of the question: "What did you say?"

Exclamation Points. If a sentence ends in an exclamation point (!), the character is excited or upset. He or she may be giving a command. The character's voice may be unusually loud or high: "Look out below! I'm coming!"

Exercises: Understanding Sentence Fragments and End Punctuation

A. Number your paper from 1 to 8. Read each word group below. If it is a sentence, copy it on your paper. Underline the subject once and the predicate twice. If it is a fragment, write **Fragment**.

1. The tinker fixed pots and pans.
2. The people of the town were afraid of the ghost.
3. All the better.
4. Showers begin suddenly in the fall.
5. Black hair and beard.
6. That night, Pedro shivered in the cold castle.
7. All clear below?
8. A good coat and vest, though a bit out of fashion.

B. Match each sentence with the way it should be said.

1. Stay where you are!
2. How did you sleep?
3. Pedro made his way into the great hall of the castle.

a. Speak as if you were asking a question.
b. Speak in a normal tone. Lower your voice at the end of the statement.
c. Speak with excitement.

Vocabulary Skills: Levels of Language

Recognizing Different Kinds of Language

Often the meaning of the words we use depends on which kind of English we are using. There are two kinds, or **levels**, of English: standard and nonstandard. **Standard English** follows the rules of the language. It is acceptable everywhere that English is spoken. **Nonstandard English** is language that is not understood or accepted everywhere that English is spoken. Each of these levels of English can be broken down into smaller groups.

Standard English

Formal Standard English. Most writing and most speeches use **formal standard English**. Formal English uses complete and, frequently, long sentences. Its words are chosen carefully. The tone of formal English is usually serious. Here is an example.

> **Narrator.** Pedro made his way into the great hall of the castle. It was dark and musty; bats fluttered around his face. Cobwebs clung to his fingers, and the wind moaned through the empty rooms.

Informal Standard English. The lines in plays are often written in **informal standard English**. Informal English is more like the language people use in conversations. The sentences are of different lengths, and the words are simple. Here is an example.

> **William.** Ha, I'll bet Miss Louisa has never been afraid in her life! All she ever does is scare us to death!

The words used in standard English can usually be found in the dictionary. Their meanings change slowly, if at all.

Nonstandard English

Slang. One type of nonstandard English is **slang**. Slang uses words that are new to the language. It also includes old words that are given new meaning. Slang changes quickly. For example, the word *square* was once slang for "good." Then it was slang for "dull." Today it is not often used in either way.

Most slang words are used for a while and then forgotten. If a slang word is used long enough, it enters standard English. Slang words or meanings may not be in the dictionary. When you read a slang word, try to determine its meaning from its context.

Exercises: Using Standard and Nonstandard English

A. Read each example below. Identify whether it is written in formal standard English or informal standard English.

1. **Gerri.** Do you think we're stupid? Why, the minute those kids leave this room they'll run for the Sheriff.

2. **Narrator.** For many years the people of Toledo pointed out a great stone castle that stood just beyond the city and was haunted.

3. "'No, siree,'" the cowboy said. "'You're human, as sure as shooting.'"

4. He sees a strange expression come over the face of the hostess. She is staring straight ahead, her muscles contracting slightly.

B. Each of these examples contains nonstandard English. Restate each sentence in standard English.

1. Just in case somebody tipped off the Sheriff that we're in town, my pal Dan and me are going to hide out here.

2. So don't anybody get any bright ideas like yelling out the window or running for help, see?

3. Aw, so what if I'm not a good speller.

4. Well, the captain said to John Henry one day:
   "Gonna bring that steam drill 'round,
   Gonna take that steam drill out on the job,
   Gonnna whop that steel on down."

The Tinker of Toledo

NELLIE McCASLIN

"The Tinker of Toledo" was written to be performed on the radio. You will note directions about sound effects and the use of a microphone (mike). Does anything happen here that could not happen on a stage?

CHARACTERS

Narrator
Pedro (pā' drō), *a tinker*
Riccardo (ri kär' dō) ⎫
Estaban (es' tə ban) ⎬ *Men of Toledo*
The Ghost ⎭

Miranda (mə ran' də)
Maria (mə rē' ə) ⎫
Blanca (blan' kə) ⎬ *Women of Toledo*
Costa (kôs' tə) ⎪
Sound-Effects Person ⎭

TIME. *The time is long ago.*

PLACE. *The action takes place in the Spanish town of Toledo.*

Sound. *(winds and low moans, which fade as the narrator begins)*

Narrator. For many years the people of Toledo pointed out a great stone castle that stood just beyond the city and that was said to be haunted. Although no one had actually seen the ghost itself, many had heard the low moans that came from the chimney top and seen the strange light that flared in the windows on moonless nights. Tales were told of adventurers, who, scorning the legend, went to the castle to find out what caused the disturbance. But none of them was ever seen afterward. Since the townsfolk refused to go beyond the courtyard, no one could tell what their fates had been.

One day there came to Toledo a little tinker, Pedro. He drove his donkey through the streets, mending all the pots and pans as he went. Now he was inclined to be talkative. As he stopped at first one door and then another, he soon heard the tales of the haunted castle. Pedro was a brave little fellow and merry, and he could not bear to think of a mystery forever unsolved. So finally he could stand it no longer. He

declared that he would spend the night in the castle and find out who the ghost really was. Of course the folk in the marketplace tried to talk him out of this idea, but he was determined to carry out his plan.

Sound. *(Voices are heard in the marketplace, all talking excitedly together. Above them is the hammering on copper as the tinker works.)*

Miranda *(over the babble of voices)*. But this is All Hallows' Eve. You do not know what may happen.

Maria. No one who's ventured inside those gates has been heard of since.

Blanca. You had better keep on mending pots and pans, Tinker; leave the ghosts to themselves.

Costa. Well, my grandmother once saw—

Miranda *(interrupting rudely)*. We have heard it before, Costa.

Blanca. Many times!

Costa. But the Tinker has not. Wait, let me tell you.

Pedro *(laughing heartily)*. I know what you will say. But whatever has happened before, I am not afraid.

Maria *(in awe)*. He is not afraid!

Blanca *(scornfully)*. So he says.

Pedro *(boldly)*. I fear neither man nor beast. So why should I fear a ghost whom no one has seen or touched?

Miranda. Those who have disappeared in the castle have seen it. Yes, and touched it too, no doubt.

Pedro. Well, I am willing to risk my neck. Here, Señorita, is your pan. Now, have I finished them all?

Miranda. Thank you, Tinker. That is all I have. Here.

Sound. *(sound of a coin being dropped)*

Miranda. Does anyone else have a pot or pan to be fixed?

Costa. I have. This handle's come off. Can you mend it?

Pedro. In two shakes of a donkey's tail. Hand it over.

Sound. *(hammering on copper as the tinker works)*

Blanca. How quickly he works.

Costa. That is good, for it's high time I was home getting the supper.

Maria. Riccardo will be coming along the road any minute. And the beans are not even started.

Blanca. We have spent the whole day here in the marketplace with Pedro the Tinker.

Pedro. To good advantage, Señora. For I have had more business today than in the past month. And who knows, to-night I may have an adventure worth telling.

Riccardo *(fading in)*. Hello there! What are you doing in the marketplace at this time of day?

Maria. Riccardo, you are early!

Riccardo *(coming into the scene)*. Not so very. Ah–hah! The Tinker is here. And so all the pots and pans in Toledo will be shining again.

Estaban *(fading in)*. I thought he must be here from the sound of things. And I'll warrant more gossiping has been done this day than mending.

Blanca. Oh, no, Estaban. But what do you think? We have been telling the Tinker about the ghost in the castle, and he is determined to sleep there tonight.

Estaban. What? He is teasing you.

Pedro. No, Señor Estaban. I am not. These good wives have but whetted my appetite with their stories. And I wish to see this ghost for myself.

Riccardo. If you do, it will be the last thing you ever lay eyes on.

Estaban. Better that you drive your donkey out of Toledo tonight than end your days in the castle. Why, the last man who boasted he would learn the truth was found dead at the gate the next morning.

Maria. And he was twice the size of you, Tinker.

Riccardo. And he carried a sword and a club. But he was found in the courtyard with his own weapons by his side.

Pedro (*airily*). Then I shall go unarmed. Perhaps this ghost prefers a battle of wits.

Blanca. Do not go, Tinker. Believe what they tell you.

Miranda. Forget your boast.

Maria. Do not add your story to these others.

Costa. Yes, Tinker, take your donkey and leave Toledo tonight.

Pedro. No, my good women; my mind is made up. And when my mind's made up, there's no changing it!

Estaban. Very well, fellow, since you insist. Though I must say you don't look as stupid as you are.

Riccardo. To venture inside on just any night would be foolhardy enough, but on All Hallow's Eve—

Pedro (*brightly*). All the better. I should be disappointed if your ghost did not put on his best show. Therefore, I must be going at once. Here, Señora, is your mended pan.

Sound. (*sound of coins being dropped*)

Pedro. I think I shall have supper there as well as my night's sleep. I'll take these coins you have put in my pocket and buy some bread and a slice of bacon.

Sound. (*All talk at once, excitedly. Then—.*)

Miranda. Well, at least let us provide his last meal. I have here a fresh loaf.

Blanca. And my house is yonder. Let me go get a crock of fresh milk and some bacon.

Costa. Wait for me. There will be fresh eggs from our hen.

Sound. (*footsteps going off as the women leave*)

Pedro. So! This is a day of good luck. I find more trade in your city than in all of Spain and am given my supper in the bargain.

Riccardo. Make that boast while you can. For if you can say the same thing tomorrow, Pedro, you are a man of rare fortune.

Estaban. I'll tell you what we'll do. We'll go with you as far as the castle gate. But there we will leave you. Tomorrow morning let us return to see how the Tinker has fared.

All *(ad lib)*. Yes, let us do that. Yes! Yes!

Pedro. You are more than kind. I hope I shall have a tale worth telling.

Sound. *(footsteps as Blanca and Costa return)*

Blanca *(fading in)*. Here is the milk and bacon.

Costa *(fading in)*. And eggs from our hen. Here you are, Tinker.

Pedro. Thank you, thank you! I shall enjoy this supper.

Riccardo *(raising his voice)*. Then let us be getting along. For the Tinker is packed up, and we, too, are hungry.

Sound. *(Ad lib conversation and footsteps begin as townspeople go from the marketplace together. Noise and talking fade as the narrator resumes the tale.)*

Narrator. So Pedro, accompanied by the little band of villagers, went to the castle gate. There they left him to eat his supper and solve the mystery of the ghost.

Sound. *(Ad lib good-byes, good luck, see you in the morning continue. The voices fade away, and the narrator continues.)*

Narrator *(his voice taking on a ghostly quality)*. Pedro made his way into the great hall of the castle. It was dark and musty; bats fluttered about his face.

Cobwebs clung to his fingers, and the wind moaned through the empty rooms.

Sound. *(Wind moans in the distance. It continues through the narrator's next speech.)*

Narrator. Pedro shivered as the dampness settled in. Then as his eyes grew more accustomed to the darkness, he made out a pile of branches on the floor by the great stone fireplace. He lost no

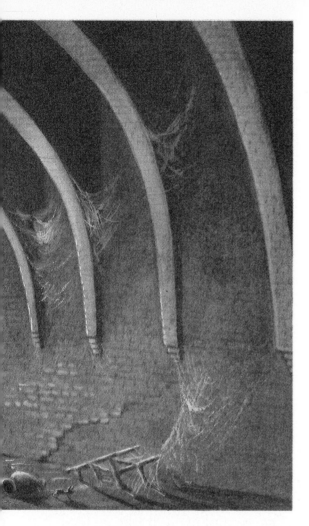

is the bread. A fresh loaf, I'll be bound! And a crock of rich milk. I could not have fared better at the finest inn in Toledo. And all because I am willing to spend the night with their ghost!

Sound. *(Something falls in the distance. The wind begins to moan again, softly and mysteriously.)*

Pedro. What ho! Have I company already? *(There is a pause and no answer but the moaning of the wind.)* Very well, then. I shall proceed with my supper. First to fry the bacon and eggs in my skillet.

Sound. *(There is the sound of frying bacon and then the sound of eggs being broken against the pan. The wind dies.)*

Pedro. How good it smells! But I must have a swallow of milk. *(Raising his voice boldly.)* Here's to you, my friend, whoever you are. I drink the richest milk in all Spain in your honor.

Sound. *(a thump as something falls heavily on the hearth)*

Ghost *(off mike).* Oh—my! Oh, my! Oh, my, oh, my! Oh—!

Pedro. That's not a very jolly welcome, I must say. But hardly frightening to a man who owns a donkey that brays. *(There is a pause, then he continues bravely.)* The bacon is browning nicely. How good it will taste. I'll just dip this piece of bread in the egg as it cooks.

time in lighting them; and soon bright red and yellow flames were leaping high on the hearth. Somehow, in the warmth and firelight, Pedro's uneasiness began to disappear.

Sound. *(Flames crackle in the fireplace. The wind moans once softly and dies.)*

Pedro. Well, I may as well get my supper. A fire is a good cure for one's fears. Let me see, in this basket the good wives packed the bacon and eggs. And in this

(He smacks his lips audibly.) Good wives of Toledo, I thank you!

Ghost (nearer and louder). Dear me! Dear me! Oh, dear me!

Pedro. You sound mighty sad, my friend. What is it?

Ghost. I'm coming down the chimney. Look out!

Sound. (a thump, as something falls heavily on the hearth)

Pedro (startled). What is this? A man's leg? Well, if that's all there is to your ghost—

Ghost. Look out below! I'm coming!

Pedro (assuming bravery). What, again?

Sound. (another thump, as something falls)

Pedro. Another leg? Well, you may just lie there until I finish my supper. Rude of you to interrupt, I must say.

Ghost (louder this time). Here I come! I'm falling!

Pedro (pretending great annoyance). You know, this is getting tiresome. Why not come down all at once instead of a piece at a time?

Sound. (a heavy thud)

Pedro (a bit shaken). So you have a body as well as legs? Hmm . . . A good coat and vest, though a bit out of fashion.

Sound. (two small thumps)

Pedro. Ah-ha! Two arms! I thought they would be coming along. (sighs) Well, there is nothing left but the head. I must admit I am rather curious to see what sort of a head you do have.

Ghost (loud now and much closer). Here I come! All clear below? I'm falling!

Sound. (a final thump)

Pedro (critically). Well, you are not so bad-looking. Black hair and beard. But I do wish you'd stop rolling your eyes.

Sound. (sound of a person scrambling up from the floor)

Pedro (greatly startled). Hold on, there! What are you doing, eh? Well, since you now seem to be in one piece, will you join me at supper?

Ghost (in a sad voice, now on mike). No, I am a ghost and can take no food. Not that I wouldn't like to. But you can do me a favor.

Pedro. Do you a favor? How?

Ghost (going on hopefully). You are the only man who has waited until I could put myself together. All the others either ran away or died of fright before both my legs had come down.

Pedro. Perhaps if they had built a fire and kept their minds on a skillet—

Ghost. Perhaps. But now that you're here—and you look as if you'd stay—I'll tell you what you can do. Out there in the courtyard are three bags of coins. One copper, one silver, one gold. You see, I stole them from some thieves many, many years ago.

Pedro. I see.

Ghost *(going on confidentially)*. I brought them here to my castle and buried them out in the yard. But no sooner were they safe underground than the thieves caught up with me and killed me. *(He sobs as he recalls it.)* They cut me in pieces, but they did not find the bags. All these years I've been waiting to get myself put together again. But not until a brave soul would stay here with me could it be done.

Pedro. Well, now that you're a whole ghost, so to speak, what more can I do for you?

Ghost *(eagerly)*. Come with me to the courtyard. There we shall dig up the coins. The copper you must take to the church. The silver you must give to the poor. And the gold you may keep for your trouble. When this is done, I shall have paid for my sins in full, and I may leave this wretched castle forever.

Pedro. Very well. *(fading out)* Let us go to the courtyard at once.

Sound. *(footsteps as they go out)*

Ghost *(fading in)*. Stop here! The treasure is buried beneath this cypress tree. You will even find the spade I used under that rock.

Pedro. So it is. Let us begin.

Sound. *(soft thuds as the earth is turned)*

Pedro. This has been here a long time!

Ghost. A hundred years I have been waiting for someone brave enough to help get me together.

Pedro. Ho! This looks like something! One more spadeful and— The first bag of coins!

Ghost. Yes, I knew they would be here. This is the copper.

Sound. *(sound of a heavy bag being dragged on the ground)*

Pedro. Now, just a little deeper . . . and . . . we come to the second. Here it is, my friend! Pull it up.

Ghost. This will be the silver.

Sound. *(sound of another heavy bag being dragged)*

Pedro. And the third—right underneath.

Ghost. Just where I put it. Look out, Tinker, here it comes!

Sound. *(sound of the third bag being dragged)*

Pedro (*whistles*). Copper . . . silver . . . gold! I will do as you ask in the morning.

Ghost. One thing more, now that my task is done. I wish to go off and never come back. So will you take my coattails in your two hands and pull?

Pedro (*puzzled*). Of course. But what will that do?

Ghost. Just hold on. You will see. Goodbye, Pedro! You may tell the good folks of Toledo that their castle is haunted no more. Now then, pull! Pull!

Sound. (*a great whirring sound as the ghost disappears*)

Pedro (*in astonishment*). Up in smoke he goes! With me holding onto his coat. I'd say I'd dreamed the whole thing if it weren't for these three bags of coins. Well, there's no use hanging on to some empty clothes. So—(*He yawns loudly.*)—I may as well get me some sleep. This has been a big day.

Narrator. So the little Tinker went back to the castle and stretched out in front of the fire. He fell into a deep sleep almost at once, and it was not until the morning sunshine filled the room that he opened his eyes. When he realized that the folk of Toledo would probably already be at the gate, he hurried outside. There they were, just where he

had left them! And all talking at once!

Estaban *(excitedly).* Not a sign of him. It's too bad. He was a brave little fellow.

Costa. I told him this would come to no good.

Blanca. We shall never know what did happen. Do you suppose he was spirited away?

Riccardo. Look! Look! Here he comes now!

Miranda. So he does! And swinging along as bold as you please. Or do you suppose it's his ghost?

Estaban. Well, we shall soon find out. *(raising his voice)* Tinker, oh, Tinker! Come here!

All. Tinker! Tinker, here we are! Come here!

Pedro *(off mike).* Well, upon my word, you are out early!

Maria. Tell us what happened.

Pedro *(fading in).* What happened?

Miranda. How did you sleep?

Pedro. Sleep? Never better. Of course, the floor was hard, but so peaceful. No noise, no—

Estaban *(cutting in).* Come now, Tinker, don't tell us nothing happened. On All Hallows' Eve the ghost was not quiet.

All *(demanding).* Yes! Tell us, Tinker! What happened?

Pedro *(finally giving in).* Very well. I did see your ghost. *(There is a gasp from his listeners.)* But he was a friendly fellow. Quite nice, in fact, once he pulled himself together. And we reached an understanding in no time at all. He left me these three bags of coins to dispose of. The copper must go to the church. The silver to the poor. And the gold I may keep for myself. You can see where we dug them.

All *(ad lib exclamations of surprise).* Think of that!

Pedro. His duties on earth are now done, so I promise you he will not return.

All *(ad lib).* Thank you!

Estaban. Tinker, the people of Toledo owe you much. Will you not settle down here with your fortune?

Pedro. Settle down here? in Toledo?

Riccardo. Why not? You have wealth. You no longer have to mend pots and pans for a living. And besides, you will have a good name in our city.

Miranda. Yes, Tinker, why not? We all want you to stay.

Pedro. Perhaps I shall. But first I must do your ghost's bidding. Will you help me carry these bags? Just think—the ghost story is ended!

Developing Comprehension Skills

1. What is All Hallows' Eve? Why were the people of Toledo especially afraid of the castle on that night?

2. Early in the play, Pedro says, "I shall go unarmed. Perhaps this ghost prefers a battle of wits." What weapons are needed for such a battle?

3. **Ad lib** comes from a Latin phrase that means "as one pleases." Some stage directions tell actors to speak ad lib. This means they should make up words and sentences that fit the scene. Find one place in this play where stage directions ask for ad lib lines. Tell two phrases or sentences that would fit the scene.

4. In Chapter 4, you learned that every short story has five parts:
   a. the introduction, in which the setting and characters are introduced
   b. the rising action, in which the conflict begins and builds
   c. the climax, which is the most exciting moment of the story and its turning point
   d. the falling action, in which the story moves toward an end
   e. the resolution, which ties up all loose ends

   A play, like a short story, has these five parts. Make a plot diagram of *The Tinker of Toledo*. Tell which events belong in each part.

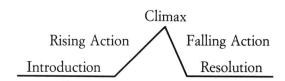

5. Is the conflict in *The Tinker of Toledo* external or internal? Explain your answer. You may refer to Chapter 4, page 182, to review internal and external conflict.

6. There are certain requirements for a good ghost story. One of them is that the reader or listener must **identify** with the hero or heroine. That is, the reader or listener must believe that such a character could exist, and can picture himself or herself in the place of the character. Do you feel that *The Tinker of Toledo* satisfies this requirement? Do you consider Pedro a believable character? Did you identify with him? Give reasons for your answer.

1. **Understanding Dialog.** To make the dialog sound like everyday conversations, the writer of this play used many sentence fragments. Find each of the following fragments in the text. Use the information in the sentence or sentences before the fragment, and restate the fragment as a complete sentence.

   a. And eggs from our hen. (page 418)
   b. Another leg? (page 420)
   c. A good coat and vest, though a bit out of fashion. (page 420)
   d. All clear below? (page 420)
   e. And the third—right underneath. (page 421)

2. **Recognizing Scene Changes.** Because this play was written for radio, the writer presents much information through sound effects. Sometimes the sound effects alone tell what is happening. Other times the narrator describes the action, as well.

   Locate the beginning of the four different scenes in this play. Do sound effects alone inform the listener of the change in scene? Or is the listener informed by the narrator's words in addition to the sound effects? Can you suggest any reasons why the writer gave the information two ways?

3. **Understanding the Characters.** In a short story, a writer can describe exactly how a character feels. In a play, the writer must use dialog to show the character's feelings. In addition, there is one other way the writer can tell about the character. That is through stage directions. In this play, stage directions are particularly helpful. Pedro does not always tell how he feels. When he does tell, he does not always admit the truth. Therefore, the writer has to give clues in the stage directions.

   Read over the scene in the castle, where Pedro is waiting for the ghost. Find three or more stage directions that show that Pedro is putting up a brave front and is really rather afraid.

4. **Appreciating the Possibilities of Radio.** Why did the playwright decide to write this play for radio instead of for the stage?

   If you are not sure of the answer, think of how you would act out each scene on stage. Find out what the problems are, and how radio can solve them.

Developing Vocabulary Skills

Recognizing Levels of Language. Which of these selections are written in formal standard English? Which are written in informal standard English?

1. **Pedro:** Well, I am willing to risk my neck.

2. **Blanca:** Let me go get a crock of milk and some bacon.

3. **Narrator:** So Pedro, accompanied by the little band of villagers, went to the castle gate. There they left him to eat his supper and solve the mystery of the ghost.

4. **Costa:** I told him this would come to no good.

5. **Pedro:** Why not come down all at once instead of a piece at a time?

6. Man had to free himself from earth to perceive both its diminutive place in a solar system and its inestimable value as a life-fostering planet.

7. "No siree," the cowboy said. "You're a human being, sure as shooting. You'd better come along with me."

8. In the royal box Colonel Balck held out his hand to Mr. Sullivan. "That was the greatest performance I have ever seen," he said.

Developing Writing Skills

1. **Contrasting Forms of Literature.** You have seen that a play is like a short story in several ways, but different in a few others. Write at least one paragraph describing the differences between a play and a short story.

2. **Organizing a Play.** Review your answers for Reading Literature: Drama, questions 2 and 4. If you like, reread the stage directions for the play to see how sound effects were used.

   Then choose a simple, familiar story, such as "Little Red Riding Hood" or "The Three Bears." Tell how you would break the story into scenes for a radio play. Describe the time and place of each scene. State in a sentence or two what happens in the scene. Last, tell what sound effects you would use in the scene. Keep in mind that sound effects should give the audience new information.

Developing Skills in Study and Research

Forming Good Study Habits. The word **study** can mean different things. One meaning is "to memorize the exact words." This is what an actor or actress must do when preparing for a play on stage. However, the actor or actress cannot simply put words into his or her memory. He or she must first understand the character and know why the character is saying those words. In the same way, when you study, you cannot simply file words in your memory. You must first understand the material and why it is organized as it is. Memorizing without understanding does not often help you.

The second, more accurate meaning of *study* is "to develop understanding of the material." To do this, you figure out how the material is organized. You decide what the main ideas are and how they are related. If you do this, you do not need to memorize the main ideas. They will make sense to you and will have become part of you. You may still need to memorize many details. However, if you understand how these details are related to the main ideas, it should not be hard to memorize them.

Study *The Tinker of Toledo* according to this second meaning of the word *study*. How is the play organized? Are the main events grouped in any special way? What are the main events?

On your paper, outline the play. Use any form of outline that makes sense to you. Whatever form you use should show the main events and how they are related.

Developing Skills in Critical Thinking

Establishing Standards. Question 6 under Developing Comprehension Skills pointed out that one requirement of a good ghost story is a believable hero or heroine. Can you think of any other requirements? What do you want in a ghost story? List all the requirements you personally would look for in a ghost story.

Miss Louisa and the Outlaws

FRANCES B. WATTS

The following play has a familiar setting—a classroom. On this particular day, what does the teacher, Miss Louisa, teach her class?

CHARACTERS

Narrator
Miss Louisa, *the schoolteacher*
Theodora ⎫
William
Annabelle ⎬ *pupils*
Clara
Reginald ⎭

Gerri the Kid ⎫
Dead-Eye Dan ⎬ *outlaws*
Sheriff
Ed, *his deputy*

Narrator. On an October day, many years ago around the turn of the century, a history lesson is beginning in a little one-room schoolhouse in the West. The teacher is Miss Louisa, and her students, Theodora, William, Annabelle, Clara, and Reginald, are sitting at attention with their hands folded.

Miss Louisa. For our history lesson this afternoon you all were to learn the first three stanzas of "Paul Revere's Ride." Theodora, would you come to the front of the room and recite, please?

Theodora. Uh—uh—Listen, my—uh—children, and you shall hear. Uh—uh—

Miss Louisa (*sternly*). I see that you haven't studied your lesson, Theodora. You will stay after school and learn the lines before you leave this afternoon. Do you understand?

Theodora (*mumbling*). Yes.

Miss Louisa. Remember your manners! Yes what, Theodora?

Theodora (*speaking with respect*). Yes, Miss Louisa.

Miss Louisa. William, let's see how well you have learned the stanzas.

William. Uh—uh. Listen, my children, and you shall hear. Uh—uh. Of the midnight ride of Paul Revere. Uh—uh—

Miss Louisa. Another shirker! William, you will join Theodora after school. Do you understand?

William (*mumbling*). Yes.

Miss Louisa. Yes, what, William?

William (*with respect*). Yes, Miss Louisa.

Miss Louisa (*sighing*). Boys and girls, I realize that this poem may seem a bit long and wordy. But I'm asking you to memorize it in hopes that you will recognize the courage and strength some of our forefathers possessed when they founded our great country. Do you have any idea what courage is?

Class (*after a moment's hesitation*). No, Miss Louisa.

Miss Louisa. Well, courage is behaving bravely when you are most afraid. All of us, at some time, have been afraid. Those who discipline themselves and control fear in times of stress are exhibiting courage. Is that clear?

Class. Yes, Miss Louisa.

William (*in a whispered aside*). Ha, I'll bet Miss Louisa has never been afraid in her life! All she ever does is scare us to death!

Theodora (*aside*). You said it. What does she know about fear? All she has in her veins is ice water!

Miss Louisa. Annabelle, do you think that you can recite the lines for us?

Annabelle. Yes, Miss Louisa. (*reciting*)

> Listen, my children, and you shall hear
> Of the midnight ride of Paul Revere,
> On the eighteenth of April, in
>   seventy-five;
> Hardly a man is now alive
> Who remembers that famous day and
>   year.
>
> He said to his friend, "If the British
>   march
> By land or sea from the town tonight,
> Hang a lantern aloft in the belfry arch
> Of the North Church tower as a signal
>   light,—
> One, if by land, and two, if by sea;
> And I on the opposite shore will be,
> Ready to ride and spread the alarm
> Through every Middlesex village and
>   farm,
> For the country folk to be up and to
>   arm."
>
> Then he said, "Good night!" and with
>   muffled oar
> Silently rowed to the Charlestown shore.

Just as the moon rose over the bay,
Where swinging wide at her moorings lay
The *Somerset,* British man-of-war;
A phantom ship, with each mast and
    spar
Across the moon like a prison bar,
And a huge black hulk, that was
    magnified
By its own reflection in the tide."

Narrator. As Annabelle recites the poem, Gerri the Kid and Dead-Eye Dan, two outlaws, enter the schoolroom with drawn guns.

Gerri. Stay where you are!

Theodora *(fearfully).* Outlaws! It's Gerri the Kid, and Dead-Eye Dan! The ones who robbed Dodge City Bank last week!

William. It is! It is! Their pictures are up in the Post Office. Wanted, dead or alive! A hundred dollars' reward!

Narrator. The children scream with terror, and run to the back of the room. Miss Louisa raps on her desk with a ruler for attention.

Miss Louisa *(sternly).* Back to your seats, everyone! How often have I told you never to leave your seats without permission! Sit down at once!

Dan. Nobody's going to get hurt, kiddies, as long as you set there quiet.

Miss Louisa *(with great dignity).* Watch your grammar in front of my pupils, sir.

The proper expression is—"sit there quietly"—not "set there quiet."

Dan *(baffled).* Huh? Oh. As long as you sit there quietly.

Gerri. Just in case somebody tipped off the sheriff that we're in town, my pal Dan and me are going to hide out here till the two-thirty freight train comes through. Then we'll make our getaway. So don't anybody get any bright ideas like yelling out the window or running for help, see?

Dan. Let's take a load off our feet. We can sit at those two empty desks. May as well be comfortable till train time.

Miss Louisa *(firmly).* Just a moment, Daniel! I believe that is your name. You and Geraldine will kindly wipe your feet on the mat in the doorway before you sit down.

Gerri *(in confusion).* Say, what is this? Dan and me got guns. We don't have to take orders from you.

Miss Louisa. It's "Dan and I have guns," Miss. And as long as you and Daniel take refuge here, I shall insist that you obey the laws and rules of our schoolhouse. Kindly wipe your feet, both of you.

Dan *(grudgingly).* All right. All right. We'll wipe our feet.

Miss Louisa. Mind your manners, please. When I speak to you, you are to

answer, "Yes, Miss Louisa." Do you understand?

Gerri *and* **Dan** *(meekly)*. Yes, we understand, Miss Louisa.

Miss Louisa. All right, you may sit down now.

Gerri *(aside, puzzled)*. I don't know why we let this schoolteacher lead us around by the nose, Dan. By all rights we ought to tie her up in the closet.

Miss Louisa *(brisk and efficient)*. Well, boys and girls, we shall continue our history lesson tomorrow. It is now time for music. Let's have a song. A jolly one. How about "Old MacDonald Had a Farm"?

Reginald. We can't sing, Miss Louisa. We—we're too scared!

Miss Louisa. Afraid, Reginald? Of what is there to be afraid? As far as we are concerned, we simply have two extra pupils in our room. We will follow our usual schedule.

Narrator. Miss Louisa takes her pitch pipe from her pocket and sounds the key. The children begin to sing. Miss Louisa suddenly raps on her desk with the ruler, interrupting the song, and speaks sternly to the outlaws.

Miss Louisa. Geraldine and Daniel, why aren't you singing?

Dan (*bewildered*). Huh? Why should we sing?

Clara (*earnestly*). Because, when we have music in this school, everybody sings.

Annabelle. And that means everybody. It's a school rule.

Miss Louisa. Clara and Annabelle, this is not your affair. (*firmly*) When we start to sing again, you will sing. Do you understand?

Gerri (*mumbling*). Yes.

Miss Louisa. Yes what, Geraldine?

Gerri. Yes, Miss Louisa.

Narrator. Miss Louisa blows on her pitch pipe again and waves her arms as she leads the song. The children's spirits rise as they sing. The faces of the outlaws are serious as they sing along with the children. When the song ends, Miss Louisa goes to the window and gazes out with a worried frown. Gerri and Dan jump up and draw their guns.

Gerri. Stay away from that window, ma'am. We're not giving you the chance to signal for help.

Dan. You may be a schoolmarm, but you can't outsmart us. Nobody has ever outsmarted Gerri the Kid and Dead-Eye Dan.

Miss Louisa (*speaking matter-of-factly*). It looks a bit like rain. William, will you and Theodora please go out and bring in the flag?

Gerri. Do you think we're stupid? Why, the minute those kids leave this room they'll run for the sheriff.

William (*nervously*). Don't insist that we go, Miss Louisa! It really doesn't look like rain.

Miss Louisa. There are cumulus clouds forming in the west. It is October; showers begin suddenly in the fall. It is a rule of our school that we never allow the flag of the United States to become wet. One of you may go with them, also, if you wish. But our flag must not be rained upon! Do you hear?

Gerri. Oh, all right then.

Miss Louisa (*sternly*). What did you say?

Gerri (*meekly*). Yes, Miss Louisa.

Narrator. Gerri heads toward the door, motioning to William and Theodora to go ahead of her. They go out the door while Dan keeps his gun drawn. After a moment, Gerri, William, and Theodora return. They wipe their feet carefully, and William hands the flag to Miss Louisa, who folds it and lays it on her desk.

Miss Louisa. Now, boys and girls, we will have a spelling bee. Reginald and Clara may be captains. You may start choosing teams, captains.

Reginald. I choose Theodora for my team.

Clara. I choose William.

Reginald. I choose Daniel.

Clara. I choose Geraldine.

Gerri. Say, what is this? What's going on here?

Dan (*with enthusiasm*). A spelling bee, pal. Ain't you never been in a spelling bee before?

Miss Louisa. "Haven't you ever," Daniel. Watch that grammar!

Dan. Haven't you ever been in a spelling bee before?

Gerri. No, and I'm not going to now. Besides, it'll be train time soon. We have to stay on the alert.

Miss Louisa (*pauses, then sympathetically*). Very well, Geraldine. I will excuse you from participating in the spelling bee. Naturally, it would be most embarrassing for you to be spelled down by a group of young children.

Gerri (*blustering*). Who's scared of being spelled down? Look, maybe I haven't had much schooling, but I'm not so dumb that a bunch of little kids can lick me at spelling.

Miss Louisa. I admire your spirit, Geraldine. You won't mind joining Clara's team then.

Gerri (*sighing*). Oh, all right.

Miss Louisa (*severely*). What did you say, Geraldine?

Gerri. Yes, Miss Louisa.

Miss Louisa. Clara, would you please spell "doctor."

Clara. D-o-c-t-o-r.

Miss Louisa. Correct. Now Reginald, can you spell "lawyer."

Reginald. L-a-w-y-e-r.

Miss Louisa. Good. Now, Geraldine, I would like you to spell the word "thief."

Gerri. Uh—uh. Lemme see. It's t—h. It's t-h-e-i-f.

Miss Louisa. That is wrong, Geraldine. The correct spelling is t-h-i-e-f. You may take your seat.

William (*aside*). Gee whiz! She is a thief, and she can't even spell it!

Gerri (*sulkily*). Aw, so what if I'm not a good speller. I still make a good living. (*A faraway train whistles.*)

Dan (*suddenly*). What's that sound? Yeow! There goes the two-thirty freight train!

Gerri *(angrily).* I told you it was time to get out of here! But you had to let that crazy schoolteacher talk us into a spelling bee!

Narrator. Suddenly, the Sheriff and Ed, his deputy, enter, their guns drawn. They catch the outlaws off guard.

Sheriff. Hands up.

Ed. You're covered.

Narrator. Gerri and Dan raise their hands, as Ed takes their guns. The children cheer as the Sheriff steers the outlaws toward the door.

Theodora. Sheriff, how did you know the outlaws were here?

Sheriff. I didn't know, miss. But I gathered that something was wrong when I happened to look out of my office window and saw that the school flagpole was bare.

Ed. Why, you know as well as I do that, unless it's raining, Miss Louisa never lowers the flag until sundown. It's a rule of the school. Remember, Miss Louisa was our teacher, too.

Miss Louisa. Sheriff, I was hoping you or Ed would notice that the flag was down, and would remember that rule. Apparently my pupils remember some things that I teach them.

Annabelle (*laughing*). Miss Louisa was just like Paul Revere's friend. She used a signal to tell about the enemy!

Miss Louisa. That's right, Annabelle. And if Geraldine and Daniel were the slightest bit educated as to the ways of the weather, they would have known that cumulus clouds in the west rarely mean immediate rain.

Gerri. I had a hunch that we should have tied that teacher up in the closet the minute we came in!

Dan. Could you have tied her up?

Gerri. No, I guess I couldn't have at that. There's something about Miss Louisa. Well, you just can't imagine tying her up in a closet. (*pauses*) She doesn't scare easy, and before you know it, you're half-scared of her.

Miss Louisa. The proper grammar, Geraldine, is—"She doesn't scare easily."

Gerri. Yes, Miss Louisa.

Sheriff. Well, we'll take these scoundrels down to jail where they belong. You'll receive the hundred dollars' reward in a few days, Miss Louisa.

Miss Louisa. Thank you. I believe it will be just enough money to take the children on an outing to the Dodge City music festival. (*Children cheer.*)

Ed. Come on, you two. It's jail for you.

Miss Louisa. And now, children, I believe that I will dismiss you for the rest of the afternoon.

Class. Hooray! Hooray for Miss Louisa!

Narrator. The children run noisily out the door—all except William and Theodora. Miss Louisa sits limply at her desk. She holds her head in her hands. After a moment she looks up and sees them.

Miss Louisa. Well, children, why are you still here?

Theodora. You asked us to stay and learn the first three stanzas of "Paul Revere's Ride," Miss Louisa.

Miss Louisa. Oh, so I did. Well, I will excuse you just this once. You see, I'm feeling a bit shaky.

William (*thoughtfully*). Miss Louisa, you were afraid when the outlaws were here, weren't you?

Miss Louisa. Oh, yes. Very much afraid. I did everything in my power to delay them, so that they might miss the train and be captured. Yet, I longed for them to leave before they decided to use those wicked guns on some of us.

Theodora. Well, you didn't act scared. Not one bit!

William (*stoutly*). Naturally, she didn't! She behaved bravely when she was most afraid. That's courage. Remember?

Miss Louisa. Perhaps I taught something today after all. Before you leave, would you please take the flag and hoist it again. There are several hours until sundown. We must abide by the rules of the school, you know.

William (*with admiration*). Yes, Miss Louisa.

Theodora. Yes, indeed. Goodbye, Miss Louisa.

Flag, 1971,
WAYNE THIEBAUD.
Collection of the artist.
Courtesy of Allan Stone
Gallery, New York.

Developing Comprehension Skills

1. Make a plot diagram for *Miss Louisa and the Outlaws*. Show which parts of the play are in the introduction, rising action, climax, falling action, and resolution.

2. Which of the words below describes Miss Louisa? Find sentences in the play to support each of your choices.

stern	bewildered	shirking	efficient
merry	courageous	brisk	dignified

3. In a play, a writer tries to let the audience know quickly what each character is like. Usually, the first time the character speaks, he or she shows some important character trait. Find the first speech made by each character listed below. Does the character show any particular trait in that first speech? If so, what is the trait?

   a. Miss Louisa   b. Annabelle   c. Gerri   d. Dan

4. Both of the plays you have read had something to say about fear and courage. In your own words, state the theme of *Miss Louisa and the Outlaws*.

5. The story of *The Tinker of Toledo* obviously could not be real. The story of *Miss Louisa*, however, seems possible. Do you think that the action of this play was realistic? Do these characters seem like real people? Could these events actually happen? Give your opinion and reasons for it.

Reading Literature: Drama

1. **Recognizing a Radio Play.** How could you tell that this play, like *The Tinker of Toledo*, was written to be performed on the radio?

2. **Appreciating Levels of Language in Dialog.** The dialog in this play uses both standard and nonstandard English. The different levels of language help to show differences among the characters. Which character usually uses formal standard English? Which characters use informal standard English? Which characters use nonstandard English? What does the level of language tell about each character?

3. **Understanding Conflict.** Was the conflict in *Miss Louisa* internal? Was it external? Or did the play have both kinds of conflict? Explain your answer.

4. **Identifying Major Characters.** In *The Tinker*, there were only two major, or important, characters: Pedro and the ghost. Without each of them, there would be no play. All the townspeople were minor characters.

Who are the major characters in *Miss Louisa*? Why did you name the characters you named?

Developing Vocabulary Skills

Translating Nonstandard English. These speeches from *Miss Louisa and the Outlaws* contain nonstandard English, or English that is not acceptable everywhere. Rewrite each sentence in standard English. Also identify the slang word used in one of the speeches.

1. **Dan.** Nobody's going to get hurt, kiddies, as long as you set there quiet.

2. **Gerri.** Say, what is this? Dan and me got guns.

3. **Dan.** A spelling bee, pal. Ain't you never been in a spelling bee before?

4. **Gerri.** She doesn't scare easy, and before you know it, you're half scared of her.

Developing Writing Skills

1. **Comparing Characters.** In one or more paragraphs, compare Pedro and Miss Louisa. Tell how they are similar and how they are different. If you like, tell which one you like better or think is more interesting. If you give opinions, also give reasons for your opinions.

2. **Changing the Literary Form.** Imagine that you are one of the students in Miss Louisa's class. Write a letter to a friend describing the events of the day.

3. **Writing a Scene.** A scene in a play may sound like a normal, everyday conversation, but it is not. It must be more interesting than the usual conversation. If it is not exciting itself, it must lead into an exciting event. Otherwise, no one would read it.

Think back through your years in school. Try to remember one day or one class that was particularly interesting. Perhaps something funny happened in class. Perhaps something exciting or scary or sad happened. Write a scene in play form telling about that event. Follow the form used in the plays you just read. Include stage directions. Also use sound effects, if you like.

If you can't remember exactly what people said at the time, write new dialog that tells the same ideas. You may even add details to make the events easier to understand or more interesting. If you like, change the names of the people. You are starting with an event that was interesting to you; make it into a scene that is interesting to your reader.

Developing Skills in Study and Research

Practicing Good Study Habits. Imagine that you have been chosen to play one of the outlaws in *Miss Louisa and the Outlaws*. Decide which outlaw you want to play. Prepare for your role by studying the character. Carefully read over every speech the character makes. Notice how other characters speak to or about your character. How is your character different from the other outlaw? Take notes on what you think your character is like.

Then describe how you would speak when delivering that character's lines. If you were to play the role on stage, describe how you would dress and move and stand. Your description will show how thoroughly you understand your character.

Developing Skills in Speaking and Listening

Presenting a Reading of a Play. Work with a group to prepare a reading of *Miss Louisa and the Outlaws*, either the whole play or several pages of it. Each member of the group should choose a role, study the character, and practice reading the character's lines. The group should then read through the play, or portion of it, together at least once. Finally, present your reading to an audience.

Using Your Skills in Reading Drama

Read the following part of a play. Then answer these questions:

1. Who are the characters in this scene? Describe each one.
2. What conflict appears to be taking shape? Is it internal or external, or might it be both? Explain your answer.
3. Identify two sets of stage directions.

THE GOOSE THAT LAID THE GOLDEN EGGS

(As the curtain opens, a farmer and his wife are seated at their kitchen table, looking at a large notebook.)

Ed *(anxiously).* Jane, just look at these bills! I don't see how we're going to keep the farm! There's no way we can pay all these bills and pay the mortgage too.

Jane. I don't understand. I thought that when we bought the goose, our troubles were over.

Ed. The goose! The goose started our troubles! First, we took out that humongous loan to buy the bird. Then, since we thought we were on easy street, we started spending like there was no tomorrow. Now all the bills are in, and what do we have? One fat goose!

Jane. But that sweet goose has been worth every penny. She's been laying eggs every day, just like the salesman promised.

Ed. Sure. But only one a day. Jane, look at these bills! We need more than one-a-day gold deliveries! *(From offstage comes the honking of a goose. Ed listens for a moment.)* Jane, listen. I think I just got me an idea.

Using Your Comprehension Skills

In the scene above, find at least three sentence fragments. Restate each as a complete sentence.

Using Your Vocabulary Skills

Which character in the scene uses nonstandard English? Identify one slang word in that character's speeches. Also define the phrase "on easy street." Explain each in your own words, using standard English.

Using Your Writing Skills

Choose one of these writing assignments. Follow the directions.

1. You have learned that characters, setting, and plot or sequence are necessary in short stories, some types of nonfiction, and drama. Write three or more paragraphs comparing and contrasting these three selections: "The Dinner Party," "First to the South Pole," and *The Tinker of Toledo*. Discuss characters, setting, and plot or sequence. If you like, discuss other elements, also.

2. Complete the modern version of *The Goose That Laid the Golden Eggs*. You may follow the plot of the Aesop fable, or you may create a new ending. Invent new characters if you need them. Be sure to keep the characters consistent, or the same, from the beginning to the end of the play.

Using Your Skills in Study and Research

Imagine that you were given the entire script of *The Goose That Laid the Golden Eggs*, on page 440, and were told to study the part of Ed or Jane. Describe how you would study the play. What steps would you follow?

Using Your Skills in Critical Thinking

You have read two complete plays in this text. From what you knew before, and from what you learned in this chapter, answer this question: What are the requirements of a good play? List your requirements in order, from most important to least important. Your answer will be a personal one. Parts of it will be different from everyone else's. Be prepared to give reasons for your requirements and for the order in which you listed them.

Handbook for Reading and Writing

Literary Terms

Alliteration. The repetition of consonant sounds at the beginnings of words is called alliteration.

> Cattle, cockroaches, and kings,
> Beggars, millionaires, and mice
> Men and maggots all as one
> ("Earth," page 286)

For more about alliteration, see pages 120 and 121.

Allusion. A reference to another work of literature, or to a person, place, or event outside of literature is called allusion. In "The Fox and the Crow," Thurber refers to works by two other writers:

> 'Twas true in Aesop's time, and La Fontaine's (page 46)

For more about allusion, see page 47.

Biography. A true account of a real person's life is a biography. It is based on fact. A biography includes important events in the person's life, as well as interesting but less important facts. An example is "George Washington Carver" (pages 314 to 321).

For more about biography, see pages 296 and 302.

See also *Nonfiction*.

Cast of Characters. A list of all the characters who will take part in a play or drama is called the cast of characters. The list is provided at the beginning of most printed plays. For an example of a cast of characters, see the first page of "The Tinker of Toledo" (page 414).

For more about the cast of characters, see page 409.

Character. Each person or animal who takes part in the action of a story, play, or poem is called a character. Usually a story has one or two important characters. Each of these is a *major character*. Everyone else in the story is a *minor character*. In "The Dinner Party" (pages 184 to 185), the American naturalist is a major character. The native boy is a minor character.

For more about characters, see pages 141 and 297.

See also *Character Trait*.

Character Trait. A quality that a character shows by actions, statements, or thoughts is called a character trait. For example, in "The Necklace" (pages 147 to 153), Mathilde exhibits the character trait of vanity.

For more about character traits, see page 154.

Chronological Order. See *Time Order.*

Climax. The turning point of the story is the climax. It usually involves an important discovery, decision, or event. The climax is often the most exciting part of the story. In "The Jar of Tassai" (pages 210 to 214), for example, the climax comes when Tassai throws her jar at the snake.

For more about climax, see page 141. See also *Plot.*

Comparison. When a writer shows how two different things have something in common, he or she is using a comparison. A griddle is compared to a penny and a cover, below.

> The griddle started to spin as a penny does when it's ready to fall. It spun around and around and dug a deep hole in the ground before it flopped down like a cover over the hole. ("Paul Bunyan and Babe, the Blue Ox," page 61)

For more on comparison, see page 81. See also *Contrast, Metaphor, Simile.*

Conflict. The struggle that a character faces creates the conflict in a story. That struggle may be within one character, between two characters, or between a character and other forces. Conflict is necessary in any story or play.

For more about conflict, see page 182. See also *External Conflict, Internal Conflict,* and *Plot.*

Contrast. Writers sometimes use contrast to show how different two things are. In "The Fun They Had" contrast is used to tell of old and new ways of reading:

> When you're through with the book, you just throw it away, I guess. Our television screen must have had a million books on it, and it's good for plenty more. (page 217)

See also *Comparison.*

Description. In a description, a writer gives details that help the reader imagine a character, setting, or action. Often the details suggest a visual image, as below:

> The Royal Wizard was a little, thin man with a long face. He wore a high red peaked hat covered with silver stars and a long blue robe covered with golden owls. ("Many Moons," page 190)

A description may also provide details of sound, smell, touch, or other senses. Sometimes a description lists actions or attitudes of a character.

See also *Direct Description* and *Indirect Description.*

Dialect. A variety of language that is spoken in a certain place or among a certain group of people is called a dialect.

> Look-a yonder what I see—
> Your drill's done broke and your hole's done choke! ("John Henry," page 70)

For more about dialect, see page 87.

Dialog. Conversation between characters in a story or play is called dialog. In writing, the exact words are set off by quotation marks.

"There!" said the man triumphantly, "Look at that! Doesn't that prove to you that we are stronger than you?"

"Not so fast, my friend," said the lion, "That is only your view of the case." ("The Man and the Lion," page 14)

For more about dialog, see pages 82 and 409.

Direct Description. When a writer states how a character looks or acts, he or she is using direct description.

In the fourth row marched a tall powerful-looking American Indian. He had a shock of black hair. His big square jaw was set firmly. ("Jim Thorpe," page 336)

For more about direct description, see page 297.

See also *Description* and *Indirect Description*.

Drama. A story that is meant to be performed before an audience is a drama, or play. A drama is told through the words and actions of its characters. The word *drama* also refers in general to this type of writing. Like other forms of fiction, drama uses characters, setting, plot, dialog, and sometimes a narrator. In addition, a written drama makes use of stage directions and a cast of characters.

A long play is divided into parts called acts. Each act is divided into smaller scenes. In Chapter 7, there are two examples of drama: "The Tinker of Toledo" and "Miss Louisa and the Outlaws." Each of these is a one-act play.

For more about drama, see pages 408 and 409.

See also *Stage Directions* and *Cast of Characters*.

Essay. A type of nonfiction in which the writer expresses his or her own opinion is called an essay. An example of an essay is "A Changing Landscape" (page 402).

For more about the essay, see pages 392 and 393.

See also *Nonfiction*.

External Conflict. A struggle between two characters, or between a character and a force such as nature, is called external conflict. There are two external conflicts in "First to the South Pole!" (pages 351 to 360): the contest between the two exploring parties and the struggle between Scott's party and the severe weather.

For more about external conflict, see page 182.

See also *Conflict, Internal Conflict, Plot*.

Fable. A short story that teaches a lesson about human nature is called a fable. The lesson it teaches is called a moral. The characters in fables are often animals who speak and act like humans. An example of a fable is "The Wolf in Sheep's Clothing" (page 19).

For more on fables, see pages 2 and 3.
See also *Moral*.

Falling Action. That part of the plot in which the story draws to a conclusion is called the falling action. It follows the climax. For example, in "Two Ways To Count to Ten," the climax occurs when the antelope wins the contest. Then the falling action occurs:

The other animals stared stupidly at the winner. They did not understand yet what had happened.   (page 34)

For more about falling action, see page 141.
See also *Plot* and *Climax*.

Fiction. A work of fiction is one that comes from the writer's imagination. Some types of fiction are short stories, fables, folklore, and drama. An example of fiction is "The Great Detective" (page 223).

Figurative Language. A way of speaking or writing that looks at familiar things in a fresh, new way is called figurative language. Some particular kinds of figurative language are called figures of speech. Metaphor, simile, personification, and hyperbole are four figures of speech. They are all examples of figurative language.

Metaphor	The rocket was a bird in the sky.
Simile	The rocket soared like an eagle.
Personification	The rocket pushed the clouds out of its way.
Hyperbole	A year went by as we stood there, waiting for lift-off.

For more about Figurative Language, see pages 127 to 135 and 266 to 267.
See also *Hyperbole*, *Metaphor*, *Personification*, and *Simile*.

Folklore. Information passed on orally from generation to generation is called folklore. Folklore includes stories, riddles, rhymes, and other forms of spoken literature. It is based on the customs and beliefs of a whole group of people. "Davy Crockett" (pages 84 to 86) is an example of American folklore.

For more about folklore, see pages 52 and 53.

Humor. Writing that is funny has the quality of humor. A particular action in a story can suggest humor. For example, in "The Thief and the Bell" (page 36) the thief puts cotton in his ears to avoid having others hear him. A certain setting or character can also suggest humor. "Many Moons" (pages 189 to 197) has examples of both of these kinds of humor.

The language a writer uses can suggest humor, as in hyperboles of folklore.

The man so tall he must climb a ladder to shave himself ("They Tell Yarns," page 90).

For more about humor, see page 44. See also *Hyperbole* and *Irony*.

Hyperbole. An obvious exaggeration is called hyperbole. It often gives a reader a humorous image of what the writer is describing.

When the wind was with him, his whiskers arrived a day before he did.
("They Tell Yarns," page 89)

For more about hyperbole, see pages 53 and 134.

Imagery. Words and phrases that make an object or experience so real that we can imagine it with our senses is called imagery. Writers use sensory details to help us see, feel, smell, hear, or taste the things they describe. The following example appeals to sight.

In the morning the ground all around the farm house and the barn was covered with white popcorn so it looked like a heavy fall of snow.
("The Huckabuck Family," page 175)

For more about imagery, see pages 179 and 266.
See also *Figurative Language*.

Indirect Description. A writer who states directly how a character looks or acts is using direct description. Any other way in which the writer leads you to understand the character is called indirect description. For example, a character's comments may tell about himself or herself. This speech from "The Necklace" shows the character's concern for appearances.

"It annoys me," she said, "not to have a jewel. Not a single stone, even. Nothing to put on. I shall look out of place. I'd almost rather not go at all." (page 149)

A reader can also learn about a character through seeing how other characters react to him or her. The following example shows the popularity of Florence Nightingale with the British soldiers.

One day the troops in the front lines looked up to see Miss Nightingale riding out to visit them. She was a good horsewoman, and as she passed the Three Mortar Battery, the men broke into cheers. Many were soldiers returned to duty from her hospital. (page 308)

For more about indirect description, see pages 322 to 323.
See also *Description, Direct Description*.

Internal Conflict. The struggle within a character's own self is called internal conflict. This struggle usually involves a decision the character must make. In "Florence Nightingale," (pages 303 to 309), Florence must decide between living the life of a wealthy landowner's daughter or one of service to the sick and wounded.

For more about internal conflict, see page 182.

See also *Conflict, External Conflict, Plot.*

Introduction. The first part of the plot is the introduction. It introduces the reader to the characters and the setting.

The country is India. A colonial official and his wife are giving a large dinner party. They are seated with their guests—army officers, and government attachés with their wives, and a visiting American naturalist—in their spacious dining room. ("The Dinner Party," page 184)

For more about the introduction, see page 141.

See also *Plot.*

Irony. The contrast between what is expected or thought to be true and what actually happens is irony. For example, in "The King and the Shirt" (page 38) the King sent his messengers out to find a happy man and to bring back his shirt. The messengers went in to take off the man's shirt, but the happy man was so poor that he had no shirt.

For more about irony, see pages 154 and 273.

Metaphor. A figure of speech that compares two unlike things having something in common is called a metaphor. The comparison is made without the use of *like* or *as,* as in a simile.

You are better than all the ballads
    That ever were sung or said,
For you are living poems
    And all the rest are dead.
    ("To Young People," page 276)

For more about metaphor, see pages 130 and 131.

See also *Simile.*

Mood. The feeling you get as you are reading a selection is called the mood of that selection. *Cheerful, sad,* and *anxious* are three possible moods. The mood of "To Satch" (page 260), for example, is admiring.

For more about mood, see pages 183, 232, and 233.

Moral. The lesson that a fable teaches is called a moral. Sometimes the moral is stated at the end of a fable. For example, "The Goose That Laid the Golden Eggs" (page 8) ends with this moral: "Those who want too much lose everything." When a moral is not stated, the reader has to figure out what it is.

For more about moral, see page 3.

See also *Fable.*

Narrator. A narrator is the person who tells the story. There are different types of narrators. The first-person narrator is usually a character in the story, as the farmer in "The Snakebit Hoe Handle" (pages 95 and 96). The third-person narrator tells the story from outside the story, as in "The Emperor's New Clothes" (pages 166 to 170).

There are two types of third-person narrator. A narrator who knows all about the characters and how all of them think and feel is *omniscient*, as in "Pecos Bill" (pages 73 to 80). The third-person narrator may also be *limited*, telling only what one character thinks and feels, as in "Keplik, the Match Man" (pages 202 to 207).

For more about narrator, see pages 53 and 409.

See also *Point of View*.

Nonfiction. Writing that tells about real people, actual places, and true events is called nonfiction. It is based on fact. An example of nonfiction is "Neil Armstrong: First on the Moon" (pages 376 to 386).

For more about nonfiction, see page 296.

See also *Biography* and *Essay*.

Onomatopoeia. The use of words that sound like what they describe is called onomatopoeia. A writer can use words from the dictionary, such as *zoom* and *clang*. He or she can also invent words:

And just then, a train sped by: raketa, rake-ta, raketa, raketa, raketa.
("Keplik, the Match Man," page 206)

For more about onomatopoeia, see page 126.

Personification. A figure of speech that gives human qualities to animals, objects, or ideas is personification. The animals in Aesop's stories often remind us of humans.

The crow was hugely flattered by this, and, just to show the fox that she could sing beautifully, she gave a loud caw.
("The Fox and the Crow," page 23)

For more about personification, see pages 132 and 133.

Play. See *Drama*.

Plot. The sequence of events in a story is the plot. In most stories, one event follows the next. Usually, each thing that happens is caused by what comes before it. The parts of the plot include the introduction, the rising action, the climax, the falling action, and the resolution.

For more about plot, see pages 141, 154, and 155.

See also *Introduction*, *Rising Action*, *Climax*, *Falling Action*, and *Resolution*.

Poetry. Poetry is a form of writing with words arranged in lines and stanzas rather than sentences. The sounds of the words and the way they are arranged are important. "Faults" (page 268) is an example of a poem.

For more about poetry, see pages 230 and 231.

See also *Rhyme*, *Rhyme Scheme*, *Rhythm*, and *Stanza*.

Point of View. A story may be told from several points of view. This term refers to how the narrator tells the story. It may be a first-person point of view, as in "The Snakebit Hoe Handle" (pages 95 to 96). "The Learned Son" (page 39) is told from a third-person point of view.

For more on point of view, see page 183.
See also *Narrator*.

Repetition. When a word or a group of words is repeated in a selection, the writer is using repetition. Poets often repeat a word or phrase to give special emphasis to a thought or action.

> While I slept, while I slept and the night
>   grew colder
> She would come to my bedroom stepping
>   softly
> And draw a blanket about my shoulder
> While I slept.
> ("While I Slept," page 274)

For more about repetition, see pages 179, 199, and 267.
See also *Alliteration*.

Resolution. The loose ends in a story are tied up in the resolution. It is the last part of the plot.

> And from that day to this the Camel always wears a humph; but he has never yet caught up with the three days that he missed at the beginning of the world, and he has never yet learned how to behave. ("How the Camel Got His Hump," 163)

For more about resolution, see pages 141 and 155.
See also *Plot*.

Rhyme. The repetition of sounds at the ends of words is called rhyme. In poetry, rhyming words usually come at the ends of lines. The rhyming words in this example are *brother* and *another*, and *about* and *out*:

> I quarreled with my brother,
> I don't know what about,
> On thing led to another,
> And somehow we fell out.
> ("The Quarrel," page 271).

For more about rhyme, see pages 122, 123, and 231.
See also *Rhyme Scheme*.

Rhyme Scheme. The different patterns in which rhyme can be used are called rhyme schemes. When a rhyme scheme is written, different letters of the alphabet are used to stand for different rhyming endings. Here is an example of a rhyme scheme. It uses the letters *a*, *b*, and *c* to stand for the three endings.

> They came to tell your faults to me,   *a*
> They named them over one by one;   *b*
> I laughed aloud when they were done,   *b*
> I knew them all so well before—   *c*
> Oh, they were blind, too blind to see   *a*
> Your faults had made me love you
>   more.   *c*
> ("Faults," page 268)

For more about rhyme scheme, see pages 123 and 241.

See also *Rhyme*.

Rhythm. The pattern of accented syllables in poetry is called rhythm. The accented or stressed syllables may be marked with /, while the unaccented or light syllables may be marked ⌣. The following is an example of rhythm:

⌣ / ⌣ ⌣ / ⌣ ⌣ / ⌣
Your world is as big as you make it.
/ / ⌣ ⌣ / ⌣ /
I know, for I used to abide
⌣ ⌣ / ⌣ ⌣ / ⌣ ⌣ / ⌣
In the narrowest nest in a corner,
⌣ / ⌣ ⌣ / ⌣ ⌣ /
My wings pressing close to my side.
("Your World," page 248)

For more about rhythm, see pages 124, 125, and 231.

Rising Action. The second part of the plot, following the introduction, is the rising action. In this part it becomes clear that the characters face a problem, or conflict. One event follows the other. For example, in "The Great Detective" (page 223), the rising action occurs when the detective finds a hair on the dead man's coat and sets out to look for the person who lost the hair. The rising action is immediately followed by the climax.

For more about rising action, see page 141.

See also *Plot*.

Sequence. A series of events or ideas may be put in an order, called sequence. Often the writer tells about chronological sequence, or time order. Sometimes a selection, such as an essay, has ideas arranged in a logical sequence. For example, the writer might begin with an opinion and follow it with reasons to back it up.

For more about sequence, see pages 393 and 399.

See also *Time Order*.

Setting. The time and place in which the events in a story occur are referred to as the setting. All stories have a setting, but some are described in more detail than others.

Tassai lived on the top of a mesa that looked far out over the Painted Desert. ("The Jar of Tassai," page 210)

For more about setting, see page 53.

Short Story. A work of fiction short enough to be read at one sitting is called a short story. It usually tells about one major character and one set of events. "The Emperor's New Clothes," (pages 166 to 170) is an example of a short story.

For more about the short story, see page 140.

See also *Fiction*.

Simile. A figure of speech that compares two things that are not alike, but have something in common, is called a simile.

The comparison uses the word *like* or *as*. Below, earth and honey are compared:

> She was making a jar from clay that she found in a secret place, where the earth was smooth as honey to the touch. ("The Jar of Tassai," page 210)

For more about simile, see page 128. See also *Metaphor*.

Stage Directions. In drama, stage directions guide the actors in performing the play. These directions may tell the actors how to speak the words or what background sounds or actions are needed. In "The Tinker of Toledo," the following stage directions may be found: *whistles, puzzled, a great whirring sound as the ghost disappears.* (page 422)

For more about stage directions, see page 409.

Stanza. A group of lines in poetry is called a stanza. There is usually a space between two stanzas of a poem. An example of a poem with three stanzas is "One for Novella Nelson" (page 238).

For more about stanza, see page 231.

Tall Tales. Humorous, exaggerated stories about real or imaginary characters are called tall tales. American folklore includes many of these stories. "Paul Bunyan and Babe, the Blue Ox" (pages 58 to 64) is an example of a tall tale.

For more about tall tales, see page 52.

Theme. The main idea that the writer wants the reader to understand is the theme of the selection. In "Appointment in Baghdad" (pages 157 to 158), the theme is that one cannot escape death.

For more about theme, see pages 182 to 183.

Time Order. Events in a story follow a certain order. It is important to understand which event comes first and how it causes the next event. The progression of events is called time order. In "The Emperor's New Clothes," from the time the rogues agree to weave the cloth to the time of the procession, the events follow one another in time order.

For more about time order, see page 4.

Tone. The author's attitude toward what is being said is the tone. For example, in "The Huckabuck Family" (pages 174 to 178) the tone is humorous.

For more about tone, see page 178.

Understatement. Sometimes a writer tells about an object or event casually, as if it were small or unexciting, when it is actually great or exciting. That way of telling about something is understatement. In "How To Tell Bad News" (page 98) the foreman uses understatement to tell about terrible events that happened.

For more about understatement, see page 100.

Summary of Comprehension Skills

Cause and Effect. Events are often related by cause and effect. The first event causes the second event. The second event, then, is the effect of the first event.

Some clue words tell the reader to look for cause-and-effect relationships. Among these clue words are the following: *because, since, so that, in order that*, and *if—then*.

Here is an example of a cause and an effect. The clue word is *because*.

Because the rain showed no signs of stopping, the baseball game was postponed.

For more about understanding cause and effect, see pages 54 and 55.

Chronological Order. See *Sequence*.

Fact and Opinion. Writers often combine fact and opinion. Facts are statements that can be proved. Opinions, on the other hand, are statements that cannot be proved. They only express the writer's beliefs.

Sometimes writers list facts that lead you to believe their opinions, as in the example below. The opinion is underlined. Following the opinion are four sentences that state facts.

The anglerfish is the most unusual fish in the world. It "fishes" for its food. The anglerfish rests on the sea bottom and raises a long spine. To other fish, the spine looks like food. When curious fish come to investigate, the anglerfish devours them, sucking them into its huge mouth.

For more about separating fact and opinion, see page 299.

Figurative Language. Figurative language is a way of speaking or writing that forces the listener or reader to look at familiar things in a new way. While the words say one thing, their meaning can be very different.

For example, when people tell you to save your money for a rainy day, they don't mean to save coins and bills until it rains. The "rainy day" in the expression refers to any time of need. To understand this example of figurative language, you had to think about the words and look for a logical meaning.

For more about understanding figurative language, see page 232.

Fragments. See *Sentences and Sentence Fragments*.

Inferences. An inference is a logical guess based on evidence. You are often expected to make inferences as you read. You must infer what the writer hasn't said from what he or she has said. For example, a writer could describe a boy who is constantly looking out a window. He checks his watch every few seconds. He has a worried expression on his face. From this description, you can infer that the boy is waiting for someone who is late.

For more about making inferences, see pages 142 and 143.

Logical Sequence. See *Sequence.*

Main Idea. A paragraph is a group of sentences that work together to tell about one idea. This idea is the main idea. The main idea is often stated in one sentence called the topic sentence. The topic sentence may be at the beginning, middle, or end of a paragraph. Some paragraphs have no topic sentence at all. However, these paragraphs still have main ideas. All the sentences in a paragraph should be related to the main idea.

Read the following paragraph. The topic sentence has been underlined.

Sherry's trip to the mall was a success. Right away, she found the album she wanted. It was even on sale. Then, after trying on only three pairs of jeans, she found a pair that fit perfectly. Last, she treated herself to her favorite snack, a chocolate-marshmallow ice cream cone.

The main idea was stated in the topic sentence. The rest of the sentences gave details about the main idea.

For more about identifying the main idea of a paragraph, see pages 298 and 299.

Mood. Mood is the feeling you get when you read a piece of writing. Writers choose their words carefully to create the mood. For an example, read the following line from a poem.

I'm gonna reach up and grab me a hand-fulla stars.

The casual mood of this line was created by using words such as *gonna* and *grab me* and *handfulla*. As you read poems and other writing, pay attention to the words the writer has chosen. They will help you understand the mood the writer wants you to feel.

For more about understanding mood, see pages 232 and 233.

Opinions. See *Fact and Opinion.*

Outcomes. When you make a reasonable guess about what will happen next in a story, you are predicting an outcome.

Some outcomes are easy to predict. For example, if you hear thunder and see lightning, you can predict that it will rain soon. Predicting other outcomes is not so simple. Imagine that two friends have an argument. They might never speak to each other again. Perhaps one friend could apologize, and the quarrel would be forgotten. A third possible outcome might be that the next time the friends met, they would pretend that the disagreement never happened.

When you predict outcomes, base your guess on clues the writer gives you. To make a logical prediction, you should use what you know about the character, the plot, the setting, and your personal knowledge of what people usually do in certain situations.

For more about predicting outcomes, see pages 142 and 143.

Paragraphs. See *Main Idea.*

Punctuation. Periods, commas, and all the other marks used in writing to separate sentences or parts of sentences are called punctuation. Punctuation helps to make the meaning of the words and sentences clearer.

End punctuation, that is, punctuation at the end of a sentence, gives clues about how the sentence should be read.

1. **Period**. If a sentence ends in a period (.), the speaker is making a statement or giving a command. The voice probably goes down.

   The room is stuffy.
   Please open a window.

2. **Question Mark**. If a sentence ends in a question mark (?), the speaker is asking a question. The voice goes up.

   Would you like an orange?

3. **Exclamation Point**. If a sentence ends in an exclamation point (!), the speaker is excited or upset. The voice may be loud or high.

   Ready or not, here I come!

For more about understanding end punctuation, see pages 410 and 411.

Other **punctuation clues** give additional help in understanding a sentence.

1. **Dash**. Frequently a dash (—) is used to set off an explanation. At other times, it is used between two phrases or sentences to show excitement.

   Brad stepped on the running board—a narrow footboard under and beside the car door.
   That car—the red one—is a real classic, for sure!

2. **Series of Periods**. A series of three periods suggests that an idea is not complete. When the series of dots is used at the end of a sentence, a fourth period showing the end of a sentence is added to the series.

   Well . . . it's hard to say . . . .

For more about understanding dashes and a series of periods, see page 287.

3. **Quotation marks**. (" ") set off the words a character says. The quotation marks are placed before and after the character's words.

"Let me try to throw your spear, O King," the antelope cried.

For more about understanding quotation marks, see page 34.

Sentences and Sentence Fragments. Writers usually express themselves in sentences. A sentence is a group of words that tells a complete idea. Here is an example of a sentence:

My teacher helped me with my project.

A sentence has both a subject and a predicate. The subject tells who or what did something, or what the sentence is about. The predicate tells what the subject did or was.

Subject	Predicate
My teacher	helped me with my project.

Sentence fragments are groups of words that do not have both a subject and a predicate. We use fragments frequently in conversations. When they write dialog, authors often use fragments to make conversations sound realistic. For instance, what Terry says, below, is an example of a fragment:

Ray: Will you help me with this?
Terry: Right away!

The context in which you find the sentence fragment tells what it means. In this example, "Right away!" means that Terry will help Ray as soon as she can.

For more about identifying sentences and understanding sentence fragments, see pages 410 and 411.

See also *Punctuation*.

Sequence. To understand a selection, it is important to recognize the sequence, or order, in which the information is presented. Three kinds of sequence a writer can use are natural order, time order, and logical order.

Natural order is often used in descriptions. In natural order, a writer talks about things in the order in which you would notice them. Here, for example, is Mr. Keplik's plan for his model bridge:

It would run across the living room from the kitchen to the bedroom, and the two towers would stand as high as his head. (page 204)

Time order, or **chronological order**, is the order in which events happen. This order is usually used in stories.

Sometimes events are connected only by time order, as in this example:

Tom took a bite of hamburger and then drank some milk.

Usually, however, the first event must take place before the second event may occur. Here is an example:

Tom bought his lunch and then he sat down and ate it.

For more about recognizing time order, see pages 4 and 5, and Drawing a Time Line on page 16.

Logical order is usually used to relate ideas or reasons. It may be used in stories to explain why a character does something. For example, read the last paragraph on page 202 to find Mr. Keplik's reasons for taking up a hobby. Logical order is also used frequently in essays and similar nonfiction writing. It helps the reader understand why the writer believes or feels as he or she does.

For more about recognizing logical order, see page 297.

Time Order. See *Sequence*.

Summary of Vocabulary Skills

1. Word Parts

To unlock some unfamiliar words, you can separate each word into two or more parts. If you know the meaning of each word part, you can figure out the meaning of the unfamiliar word. The two kinds of word parts are base words and affixes. There are two kinds of affixes: prefixes and suffixes.

Base Word. A word to which other word parts are added is called a base word. For example, the base word in *cheerful* is *cheer*. The base word in *unhappy* is *happy*. Sometimes the spelling of a base word is changed when other word parts are added to it. For example, the *e* is dropped from *anger* when it is changed to *angry*. For further information about spelling changes caused by combining suffixes and base words, see *Making Spelling Changes* below.

Prefix. A word part added at the beginning of a base word is called a prefix. Each prefix has a certain meaning. Adding a prefix to the beginning of a word changes the meaning of the word.

Prefix	+	**Base Word**	=	**New Word**
re-	+	play	=	replay

In the example, adding *re-* changed the meaning from "play" to "play again." For a list of several frequently used prefixes, see page 6.

Suffix. A word part added at the end of a base word is called a suffix. Adding a suffix to a word changes the meaning of the word.

Base Word	+	**Suffix**	=	**New Word**
soft	+	-ly	=	softly

In the example, adding *-ly* changed the meaning from "soft" to "in a soft way." For a list of frequently used suffixes, see page 7.

Making Spelling Changes. Before endings can be added to some words, one of the following spelling changes may be necessary.

1. When a suffix beginning with a vowel is added to a word ending in silent *e*, the *e* is usually dropped.

   fame + -ous = famous

   Note that the *e* is not dropped when a suffix beginning with a consonant is added.

   hope + -ful = hopeful

2. When a suffix is added to a word ending in *y* preceded by a consonant, the *y* is usually changed to an *i*.

study + -ous = studious

Note that when the *y* is preceded by a vowel, it is not changed.

play + -er = player

3. Words of one syllable, ending in one consonant preceded by one vowel, double the final consonant before adding *-ing*, *-ed*, or *-er*.

run + -er = runner

Note that when two vowels appear in the one-syllable word, the final consonant is not doubled.

train + -er = trainer

For more about making spelling changes, see pages 12 and 13.

2. Context Clues

Context refers to the sentence or paragraph in which you find a word. Clues about the meaning of a new word are often given in context. Look for the following kinds of context clues.

Antonyms. An antonym, or opposite, may be given in the same sentence as the new word, or in a nearby sentence. Often the antonym appears in the same position in its sentence as the new word. An antonym leads you to understand a new word by explaining what it is not.

His condition was not improving. Instead, he was regressing.

The antonyms both appear after the verb *was*. *Regressing* means "the opposite of improving."

For more on antonyms, see page 200.

Comparison and Contrast Clues. Writers often compare one idea with another. They sometimes use an unfamiliar word in one part of the comparison. In that case, the other part of the comparison may give you a clue to the meaning of the word. Key words to look for in comparison clues are *like*, *as*, *similar to*, and *than*.

Here is an example of a comparison clue:

Our frigid weather lately has been similar to the cold climate of the North Pole.

The comparison tells you that *frigid* means "very cold."

Writers also use contrast clues to give you hints about the meaning of a new word. Writers show that certain things or ideas are opposites. A contrast clue tells you what the new word is not. Look for these key words in contrast clues; *although*, *but*, *however*, *yet*, *on the other hand*, *different from*, and *in contrast*.

Although the helmet looks <u>archaic</u>, it is actually new.

The contrast clue tells you that *archaic* is the opposite of *new*.

For more about comparison and contrast clues, see pages 300 and 301.

Definitions. In a definition clue, the writer tells the meaning of the new word. Certain words signal that a definition will follow. Look for these key words: *is*, *who is*, *which is*, *that is*, and *in other words*.

The foreign words were printed in <u>italics</u>, which is a slanted type of printing.

For more about definitions in context, see pages 144 and 145.

Example Clues. In an example clue, a new word is related to a group of familiar words. The new word may be an example of a familiar term. Other times, the familiar terms are examples of the new word.

Key words and phrases tell you to look for examples in a sentence. Some key words are *an example*, *for example*, *one kind*, *for instance*, *some types*, and *such as*.

The Olympic Games include tests of strength and endurance such as the <u>decathlon</u>.

For more about example clues, see page 323.

Inference: Using Clues from Different Parts of the Sentence. Clues to the meaning of an unfamiliar word can be found in different parts of the same sentence. For example, clues to a new word in the subject can sometimes be found in the predicate.

The huge <u>Cyclops</u> glared with its one terrifying eye.

From this sentence, you can guess that a *Cyclops* is a huge and frightening creature with one eye.

Inference: Using Clues from Different Parts of the Paragraph. Sometimes the sentence in which a new word appears has no clues to its meaning. However, it is often possible to find clues to the meaning somewhere else in the same paragraph. Here is an example.

Kim has taken up <u>spelunking</u>. Before she enters any cave, she checks her equipment carefully. She knows how dangerous it would be to depend on unsafe equipment when she's exploring an unknown cave passage.

You can figure out the meaning of the word *spelunking* by taking a guess based on clues. The paragraph gives us the following information: To spelunk, Kim must go into caves; she needs reliable equipment; exploring cave passages can be dangerous. Spelunking, therefore, must be an exciting pastime which involves exploring caves.

For more about inferring meanings from the context, see page 301.

Main Idea Clues. Sometimes you can figure out the meaning of a new word by understanding the main idea of the paragraph or selection in which it appears. Look for clues throughout the paragraph. In the following example, several clues will make the meaning of the underlined word clear.

> Craig is ambidextrous. He uses his right hand for throwing and batting. He uses his left hand for writing. When he plays tennis, he uses the hand that works best against his opponent.

The main idea of the paragraph shows that *ambidextrous* means "able to use either hand."

For more about main idea clues to meanings, see page 347.

Prefixes and Suffixes. Your knowledge of affixes, that is, prefixes and suffixes, can lead you to context clues.

> The simulator produced conditions like the ones the astronauts would encounter in space.

In this example, you know that the suffix *-or* means someone or something that does something. You can guess that a *simulator* is something that produces conditions similar to actual conditions.

For more about prefixes and suffixes as context clues, see pages 221 and 388.

Restatement. To help you understand an unfamiliar word, a writer will often restate it. In other words, he or she says the idea again in a different way. Key words and key punctuation tell you to look for the meaning. Some keys for restatements are the word *or*, dashes, commas, and parentheses.

> The pie had an exotic, or foreign, flavor.

For more about restatements in context, see pages 144 and 145.

3. Denotation, Connotation, and Multiple Meanings

Denotation refers to the dictionary meaning of a word. **Connotation** refers to the feelings, ideas, and thoughts the word brings to the reader's mind. In order to understand most directions, explanations, and statements of fact, you need only recognize the denotation of a word. However, in order to understand most literature, and especially poetry, you need to be aware of the connotations of words.

For example, the denotation of the words *chains* is "a series of metal links." However, its connotations may include loss of freedom, injustice, and suffering. These are the meanings suggested in the following sentence.

Some people are forced to live their lives in <u>chains</u>.

For more about the difference between connotation and denotation, see page 235.

Multiple Meanings. Many words have more than one meaning. To choose the denotation that the writer intended, read the words in context. Read the words and sentences before and after the word. Try out possible meanings in the context of the sentence. In most cases, it will be easy to choose the best meaning.

Use the context of this sentence to figure out which meaning of *duck* the writer intended.

"Duck!" shouted the careless golfer, as the golf ball sliced to the left.

There are at least three dictionary meanings for *duck*:

1. an aquatic bird with webbed feet
2. to dodge in order to avoid something
3. a heavy cotton or linen fabric

Try each of the meanings in the sentence. It is clear that the second meaning must be the one the writer meant.

For more about choosing among multiple meanings, see page 234.

4. Levels of Language

Standard English is English that is acceptable anywhere, either in speaking or writing. It follows traditional rules of grammar and uses words that can be found in the dictionary. Most writing is done in standard English.

Standard English may be formal, as in speeches and in most written literature. It may also be informal. Most conversations are in informal standard English. Some writing is in informal standard English, such as letters, diaries, and literature that is trying to sound like natural speech.

Nonstandard English is English used by particular groups of people in particular circumstances. It may not follow the traditional rules of grammar. It may use slang, words not found in the dictionary or with meanings not listed in the dictionary. Writers use nonstandard English only for special effects. For example, characters who are close friends might speak to each other in nonstandard English.

For more about recognizing the levels of language, see pages 412 and 413.

5. Reference Books: The Dictionary and the Thesaurus

A **dictionary** is an alphabetical listing of words and their meanings. Often context clues and word parts do not give enough information to understand unfamiliar words. Then you should use a dictionary to find the meaning.

If a word has multiple definitions, or meanings, they will all be listed. These denotations will probably be grouped by part of speech. To choose the right meaning for your selection, test each definition in the sentence in which you found the word.

Some dictionaries also give some information about connotations of a word. Another reference book that gives information about connotations is the **thesaurus**. In a thesaurus, a word is listed with other words of similar meanings, usually with some explanation of the differences.

For more about the dictionary, see pages 56 and 57. For more about the thesaurus, see page 278.

See also *The Dictionary* and *The Thesaurus* under Guidelines for Study and Research.

Guidelines for the Process of Writing

Every time you write, there are certain steps you should follow. Each of the steps is essential for good writing. All of these steps, taken together, are called the process of writing.

The process of writing includes the stages of **prewriting, drafting, revising**, and **sharing**.

Stage 1: Prewriting

Prewriting includes all the preparations you make before you begin to write. During the prewriting stage, writers think, plan, do research, and organize. Below are the five steps of prewriting.

1. Choose and limit a topic. Make a list of ideas that interest you. Go over the list carefully. Choose the topic that interests you most. Then make a second list. This time, write down the things you could say about the topic. Limit your list to the ideas you can handle in your story, poem, or other writing.

For example, one student was asked to write a paragraph comparing any two fables in Chapter 1. He read over the table of contents for Chapter 1 and chose the two versions of "The Fox and the Crow."

Then he listed all the ideas he might discuss in his paragraph.

moral	events	characters
setting	details	personification
language	tone	conversation

Finally, he circled the ideas he thought would be most interesting.

moral	events	(characters)
setting	details	personification
(language)	(tone)	conversation

2. Decide on your purpose. Decide why you are writing. What do you want to say about your topic? Do you want to explain it, describe it, or criticize it? Are you trying to teach your readers or persuade them to do something?

The student writing about fables decided he would give his opinion of two of his choices. He knew he would need to give good reasons for his opinion.

3. Decide on your audience. Decide who will read your writing. When you know who you are writing for, you will be better able to choose your level of language and to decide which details to include.

In a class assignment, for example, your language will be more precise and formal than in a postcard to a close friend.

4. Gather supporting information. List everything you know about the topic. It is possible that you will need more information. You may need to use reference sources such as encyclopedias. Take notes on all the information you find.

The student who was writing about fables reread both his selections. He wrote notes about what seemed important.

AESOP

"set his wits to work" — sounds nice
The fox makes fun of the crow.
The crow is stupid!
sort of preachy

THURBER

"attracted the eye and the nose" — funny
The crow makes fun of the fox.
"lion's share of the cheese" — sounds like other fable
The crow thinks he's so smart.
Writer says funny things, like "Bars may come and bars may go."
different moral
whole story sounds different

5. Organize your ideas. Read over your list of details and information. Some details will be useful. Others will not really belong there. Cross out the ones that don't belong. Then choose a logical order for the details.

For example, you may choose time order if you are writing a story. For a description, you may list details in the order you would notice them. Make a plan, or outline, showing the order in which you will present your ideas. Your outline should make sense to you.

Here is the student's outline for his paragraph. He has written out and underlined his main idea. This will help him keep his sentences on the subject.

COMPARISON OF FABLES
My opinion — I like Thurber's fable best.
My reasons —
    Thurber's fable is funnier
    characters are funnier
    his version sounds different, new

Stage 2: Writing Your First Draft

Now you are ready to get your ideas down on paper. At this point, don't concentrate on getting your words perfect. That careful work will come later. For now, keep your purpose and audience in mind. Follow your outline as much as possible. But remember that you can change your outline if you get better ideas as you write. Leave space between the lines of your draft for later corrections and changes.

This is the first draft of the comparison of two fables.

First Draft

> When I read the Fox and the Crow by Aesop and by James
>
> Thurber, I liked Thurbers best. Thurbers Version of the
>
> story was funnier. It kind of made me laugh when I read the
>
> words of the stupid crow. He thought he was so smart but
>
> the fox fooled him. Aesop fable was more serious, but
>
> thurbers fable was more good natured and it was just for
>
> fun. I liked thurber's fable because it sounded more
>
> modern. Also i heard this Aesop's falbe before but the way
>
> thurber wrote it made it seem new and different.

Stage 3: Revising and Sharing

When you revise, you make changes in your writing to improve it.

Read over your writing and make sure it is clear. Often you are not sure what you want to say until you have finished your first draft. Ask yourself these questions.

1. Is the writing interesting? Will others want to read it?
2. Is the organization clear and easy to follow? Do the ideas flow together smoothly?
3. Did I stick to my topic? Are there any unnecessary details? Should any other details be added?
4. Is every group of words a sentence? Does it express a complete thought? Is every word the best word to express my idea?

Mark any corrections and notes on your first draft. Don't be surprised if you make corrections to your corrections. If your paper becomes messy, rewrite it. You may need to write several drafts before you are satisfied with your work.

Proofreading. Your writing should be correct as well as clear and interesting. Read it over again. This time, check for any errors in capitalization, punctuation, grammar, and spelling. Correct your errors. Use the symbols in the box at the top of page 469.

Here is a draft that is being revised. Notice how the writer has improved the piece by crossing out unnecessary words, by adding precise words, and by moving ideas around. The writer has also corrected errors in capitalization, punctuation, grammar, and spelling. The writer has used proofreading symbols shown in the box on page 469. First study this draft, then compare it with the final draft on page 469. See how changes that were marked here have been carried out in the final copy.

Revised Draft

Both Aesop and James Thurber wrote versions
MY COMPARISON
of the fable "The Fox and the Crow."
After reading both versions, I decided that
When I read the Fox and the crow by Aesop and by James
, fable better.
Thurber, I liked Thurbers best. Thurbers Version of the
For one thing,
story was funnier. It kind of made me laugh when I read the
I enjoyed the clever way the fox fooled the proud
but words of the stupid crow. He thought he was so smart but
the fox fooled him. Aesop's fable was more serious, but
funny.
thurbers fable was more good-natured and it was just for
Another reason better was that
fun. I liked thurber's fable because it sounded more
had many times
modern. Also i heard this Aesop's falbe before but the way
thurber wrote it made it seem new and different.
modern.

Proofreading Symbols

Symbol	Meaning	Example
∧	insert	Thurber's
≡	capitalize	ḭ
/	make lowercase	Ⅴersion
∿	transpose (switch positions)	faḽbe
ℯ	omit letters, words	of the story
¶	make new paragraph	¶ Both Aesop and
⊙	insert a period	before○but the way

Writing the Final Copy. When you are sure that your writing is as clear and correct as you can make it, write your final copy. Use your best handwriting or type carefully. Indent paragraphs correctly. Then proofread your work again. Read it out loud. Look for any errors you might have missed.

Notice that in making this final copy, the student found and corrected a spelling error and a poorly worded phrase that had not been marked before.

Final Copy

```
          A COMPARISON OF TWO FABLES


     Both Aesop and James Thurber wrote versions of the fable
"The Fox and the Crow." After I read both versions, I
decided that I liked Thurber's fable better. For one thing,
Thurber's version was funnier. I enjoyed the clever way the
fox fooled the proud but stupid crow. Aesop's fable was
serious, but Thurber's fable was good-natured and funny.
Another reason I liked Thurber's fable better was that I had
heard Aesop's version many times before. The different way
Thurber wrote the story made it seem new and modern.
```

Checklist for the Process of Writing

Prewriting

1. Choose and limit a topic.
2. Decide on your purpose.
3. Decide on your audience.
4. Gather supporting information.
5. Organize your ideas.

Drafting

1. Begin writing. Keep your topic, purpose, and audience in mind at all times.
2. As you write, you may add new details.
3. Concentrate on ideas. Do not be concerned with grammar and punctuation at this time.

Revising and Sharing

1. Read your draft. Ask yourself these questions:
   a. Do you like what you have written? Is it interesting? Will others want to read it?
   b. Does your writing make sense?
   c. Is your writing organized well? Do the ideas flow smoothly from one paragraph to the next? Are the ideas arranged in a logical order?
   d. Is each group of words a complete sentence? Does it have a topic sentence? Does every sentence stick to the topic? Should any sentence be moved?
   e. Should any details be left out? Should any be added?
   f. Does every sentence express a complete thought? Are your sentences easy to understand?
   g. Is every word the best possible word?
2. Mark any changes on your paper.

Proofreading

Consider these questions as you check your writing for errors in grammar and usage, capitalization, punctuation, and spelling.

Grammar and Usage

a. Is every word group a complete sentence?
b. Does every verb agree with its subject?
c. Have you used the correct form of each pronoun?
d. Is the form of each adjective correct?
e. Is the form of each adverb correct?

Capitalization

a. Is the first word in every sentence capitalized?
b. Are all proper nouns and adjectives capitalized?
c. Are titles capitalized correctly?

Punctuation

a. Does each sentence have the correct end mark?
b. Have you used punctuation marks such as commas, apostrophes, hyphens, colons, semicolons, question marks, quotation marks, and underlining correctly?

Spelling

a. Did you check unfamiliar words in a dictionary?
b. Did you spell plural and possessive forms correctly?

Preparing the Final Copy

1. Make a clean copy of your writing. Make all changes and correct all errors. Then ask yourself these questions:

   a. Is your handwriting neat and easy to read?
   b. Are your margins wide enough?
   c. Is every paragraph indented?

2. Proofread your writing again. Read it aloud. Correct any mistakes neatly.

Guidelines for Study and Research

Entire libraries are filled with materials that can help you in your studies. Books, magazines, and other resources can also add to your enjoyment of hobbies and other activities. It is important to take advantage of what is available. A good reader finds the information he or she wants and applies it to his or her own situation.

In this section of the Handbook, you will be given some guidelines for finding and using printed materials. Here are the topics that will be discussed:

1. Using Reference Materials
   The Dictionary
   The Thesaurus

The Encyclopedia
The Nonfiction Book

2. Finding the Right Book
   The Library
   The Card Catalog

3. Preparing To Study
   Preparations in Class
   Your Study Area
   Your Schedule for Study Time

4. Studying
   Three Types of Reading:
      Scanning
      Skimming
      Study-Type Reading
   The SQ3R Study Method
   Note-taking

---

1. Using Reference Materials

The Dictionary

A **dictionary** is an alphabetical listing of words, called entry words, and their meanings. You can use the dictionary for many purposes, including the following:

1. to check the spelling of a word
2. to discover its pronunciation
3. to learn its part of speech
4. to find out its meaning or meanings

respelling

entry word

part of speech

cy·clone (sī′klōn) *n.* **1.** loosely, a windstorm with a violent, whirling movement; tornado or hurricane. **2.** a storm with strong winds rotating about a moving center of low atmospheric pressure.

meanings

How To Find a Word. In order to find a word in the dictionary, look first at the **guide words** on the pages. Two guide words are usually printed at the top of every page. They show the first and last words on the page. Keep looking until you find the guide words between which your word falls.

For example, imagine you needed the word *cyclone*. Here are the guide words for three pages of a dictionary. On which page will *cyclone* appear?

cut—cutout
cutover—cycle
cyclic—cynic

You needed to compare the guide words to the fifth letter in order to find the answer. *Cyclone* will appear on the third page, between *cyclic* and *cynic*.

What the Entry Word Tells You. Use the **entry word** itself, printed in boldface (dark) type, to see how the word is spelled. Use the entry word, also, to find out where to break the word into syllables if you need to break it at the end of a line of writing.

cy·clone

How To Find the Pronunciation. Use the **respelling** that follows the entry word to determine the pronunciation of the word. The respelling usually appears within parentheses. It uses letters and symbols to stand for the sounds of the spoken word. To find out what each letter and symbol stands for, you must refer to the **pronunciation key** on that page or the page across from it. (For the meaning of the symbols in the sample respelling, see the pronunciation key in the Glossary.)

Accent marks in the respelling indicate which syllable to stress when you say the word. If the word has more than two syllables, it may have more than one accent. The heavy accent is called the **primary accent**. The lighter one is called the **secondary accent**. In this example, the primary accent is on the first syllable and the secondary accent is on the third syllable.

ag·ri·cul·ture (ag′ri kul′ chər)

How To Find the Part of Speech and the Meaning. Immediately following the respelling is an abbreviation that tells the **part of speech** of the word. Then you will find the **definition**, or meaning, of the word. If the word may be used as more than one part of speech, all the definitions for one part of speech are grouped together. After that you will find a second abbreviation and the definitions that fit that second part of speech, and so on.

After some entries, you will find sub-entries listed in dark, or bold, type. **Sub-entries** are familiar phrases in which the entry word appears. The special meaning of the phase is then listed.

For more about the use of the dictionary, see pages 56 and 57.

The Thesaurus

A **thesaurus** is a list of words followed by related words. You use a thesaurus when you need to find a word to express your exact meaning. The related words may be synonyms for the listed word. Some of the related words may be different parts of speech from the entry word. Other related words are antonyms, words with meanings opposite from the entry word.

Imagine, for example, that you needed another word for the word *strange.* You would first find the listing for *strange* in the thesaurus. There you would read words such as *unusual, odd, fantastic,* and *mysterious.* See how each word fits into your sentence. Then choose one of those words to use.

Each thesaurus is organized in a different way. Look in the front of the thesaurus for directions. The index at the back of the book will also help you find a particular entry word.

For more about using a thesaurus, see page 278.

The Encyclopedia

The **encyclopedia** is a collection of articles on a wide variety of topics. The articles are arranged in alphabetical order, according to their titles. Usually, if an encyclopedia is several volumes long, an index appears in the last volume.

When you are looking for information in an encyclopedia, begin with the index. The index will tell you which articles have information on your topic. It will also tell the volume and page where each article appears.

For more information about using the encyclopedia, see pages 173, 227, and 334.

The Nonfiction Book

When you are looking for detailed information on a topic, your best source may be a nonfiction book concerning the topic. In order to decide whether the book you have found will be useful to you, examine these parts of the book:

The title page. Does the title mention your topic? Is the author or editor someone with knowledge about the topic?

The copyright page. If you need up-to-date information, is the copyright date a recent one?

The table of contents. Is the organization of the book clear? Do the part titles or chapter titles suggest what you can find in each section of the book, so that you can find your topic easily?

The index. Is there an adequate index? Does it list terms or names that you need information about? Does it use italic or boldface type to indicate the pages with maps, graphs, or illustrations?

2. Finding the Right Book

The Library

Books in a library are divided into two groups: fiction and nonfiction.

Fiction books are stories about imaginary happenings. They are arranged alphabetically according to the last name of the author. The author's last name is usually shown on the spine of the book.

Nonfiction books contain factual information. Most libraries arrange these books according to the **Dewey Decimal System**. Every book is assigned a number in one of ten categories. The number is printed on the spine of the book. The books are then arranged in numerical order.

THE DEWEY DECIMAL SYSTEM

000–099	General Works	encyclopedias, almanacs, handbooks
100–199	Philosophy	conduct, ethics, psychology
200–299	Religion	the Bible, mythology, theology
300–399	Social Science	economics, law, education, commerce, government, folklore, legend
400–499	Language	languages, grammar, dictionaries
500–599	Science	mathematics, chemistry, physics
600–699	Useful Arts	farming, cooking, sewing, radio, nursing, engineering, television, business, gardening, cars
700–799	Fine Arts	music, painting, drawing, acting, photography, games, sports
800–899	Literature	poetry, plays, essays
900–999	History	biography, travel, geography

The number assigned to each nonfiction book is called its **call number**. The call number tells you where the book is shelved and other important information.

The Card Catalog

The best way to locate a book in the library is to use the **card catalog**. The card catalog is a cabinet of small drawers filled with cards for each book in the library. These cards are arranged alphabetically according to the words in the top line of each card. On the top left corner of the card, you will find the call number for the book listed on the card. Using the call number, you can then locate the book on the shelves.

There are usually three cards for every book in the library: an author card, a title card, and a subject card. Each of the three cards contains the same information, but in a different order. The **author card** lists the author's name on the top line. The **title card** lists the title on the top line. The **subject card** lists the subject or topic of the book on the top line. Examine the sample cards on this page to see what other information is given on the cards.

If you know the author of the book you are looking for, use the author card to locate the book. If you know the title, use the title card. If you are looking for a book on a particular subject, use the subject cards to find possible books.

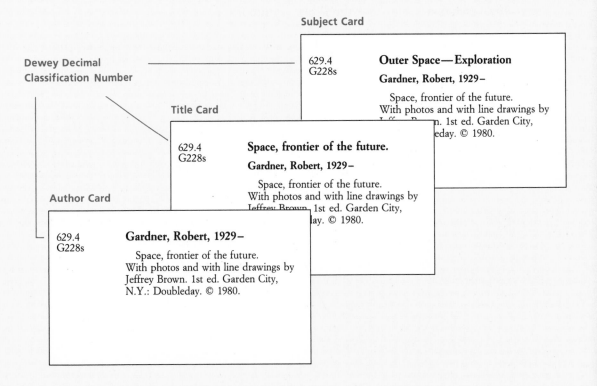

Subject Card

| 629.4
G228s | **Outer Space—Exploration** |
| | Gardner, Robert, 1929– |

Space, frontier of the future.
With photos and with line drawings by Jeffrey Brown. 1st ed. Garden City, N.Y.: Doubleday. © 1980.

Dewey Decimal Classification Number

Title Card

| 629.4
G228s | **Space, frontier of the future.** |
| | Gardner, Robert, 1929– |

Space, frontier of the future.
With photos and with line drawings by Jeffrey Brown. 1st ed. Garden City, N.Y.: Doubleday. © 1980.

Author Card

| 629.4
G228s | **Gardner, Robert, 1929–** |

Space, frontier of the future.
With photos and with line drawings by Jeffrey Brown. 1st ed. Garden City, N.Y.: Doubleday. © 1980.

3. Preparing To Study

Preparations in Class

Before you can begin an assignment, you must know what it is you are being asked for. Therefore, the first step to studying is listening carefully in class. Pay particular attention to **directions**.

1. Focus your attention on only the directions about to be given.
2. Notice how many steps are involved.
3. Relate a key word to each step, such as *Read, Answer,* or *Write.*
4. Ask questions about any step you do not understand.
5. Repeat the completed directions to yourself and then write them down.

Don't rely only on your memory. Keep an **assignment notebook** ready for making a record of what you must do. For each assignment, write the following:

1. The subject
2. The assignment itself and any special details
3. The date the assignment is given
4. The date the assignment is due

It's a good idea to write the four categories in separate columns in your notebook, as below:

Subject	Assignment	Date given	Date due

Your Study Area

The area where you read and study should meet these requirements:

1. It should be quiet.
2. It should be well lit.
3. It should be clean and neat.
4. It should be equipped with the tools you may need, such as pencils, paper, and a dictionary.

Your Schedule for Study Time

It is important to set aside time to study and complete assignments.

Some reading and writing assignments require a small amount of time. Some require more time. Assignments that can be completed in one day are called **short-term goals**. You should set aside a block of time each day to work on them.

Assignments that cannot be completed overnight are called **long-term goals**. These can sometimes seem impossible. If you break them down into smaller tasks, however, the job becomes manageable. Look at each task and decide how long it will take. Then develop a study plan for completing all of the tasks, one by one.

To make a **study plan**, write down what you will accomplish each day. On your plan, show the times each day when you will work on the project. If you stick to your study plan, you are sure to complete your assignment on time.

4. Studying

Three Types of Reading

There are three types of reading you can use when you are studying. Each is best for a particular purpose.

Scanning is a type of fast reading. It allows you to locate quickly a specific piece of information. To scan, move your eyes quickly over the page. Look for key words that will lead you to the facts and ideas you need to answer your question. Scanning is useful in answering true-false, fill-in, and multiple-choice questions.

Skimming is another type of fast reading. It helps you get a quick overview of the material you are about to read. It also allows you to become familiar with the most important facts. To skim, move your eyes quickly over the material. Look for titles, subtitles, and illustrations that will give you clues about the content of the material. You are skimming when you are doing the survey step in the SQ3R study method, described below.

The third type of reading is **study-type reading**. This is slower than scanning and skimming. When you do study-type reading, you are trying to get as much meaning as you can from the words. You are trying to find the order in which the information is arranged, and to make connections between statements. The SQ3R study method is a good description of effective study-type reading.

The SQ3R Study Method

You usually need to read and study to complete assignments and prepare for tests. The **SQ3R study method** is one sure way to improve your reading and study skills. SQ3R stands for these five steps: Survey, Question, Read, Recite, and Review.

Survey. Look over the material to get a general idea of what it is about. Read the titles and subtitles. Look at the illustrations, such as pictures, maps, graphs, or tables. Read the introduction or first few paragraphs.

Question. Read any study questions provided in the book or by your teacher. They will help you identify important points to look for when you read.

Read. Read the material. Identify the main ideas. Keep the study questions in mind.

Record. After reading, write the answers to the study questions. Write down brief notes to help you remember any other important ideas.

Review. Look back at the study questions and try to answer them without using your notes. You may need to review the material to find the answers. Last, study your notes so that you will be able to remember the information later.

Note-Taking

As you read, you will probably recognize some main ideas and important facts. Write them down in a notebook set aside for that textbook or subject. If you do not have separate notebooks for each subject use dividers between notes in a larger book.

Notes do not have to be written in sentences. They should be in your own words. Write them clearly so that, when you read these notes at a later date, they will still make sense to you.

You will find that taking notes will help you in many ways. Taking notes forces you to concentrate on the material. It also helps you understand the material, since you are always looking for the important facts and ideas. Last, notes are very useful as a study guide for later review.

Incidents that influenced Neil Armstrong to become an airline pilot:

1. Saw air races with his father (at the age of two)

2. Became interested in building models after his first airplane ride (age of six)

3. Enjoyed looking at the sky through his neighbor's telescope

Summary of Skills in Critical Thinking

Analysis. The skill of analysis, or analyzing, is the ability to study something carefully, piece by piece. Many elements go together to make up a story or a poem. When you analyze, you focus on each part individually.

For example, when you analyze a poem, you may want to look at its rhyme scheme, its rhythm, its mood, or another element.

As you study each part separately, you begin to understand the whole selection better. Analyzing also helps you identify the ways in which a particular selection is similar to or different from other writing.

Throughout this text, study questions in Developing Comprehension Skills, Reading Literature, and Developing Writing Skills focus the reader's attention on individual elements in the selections. In addition, study questions under Developing Skills in Critical Thinking develop specific skills of analysis on pages 17, 101, and 390.

Evaluation. When you evaluate a piece of writing, you study it carefully and decide on its value. You use certain standards to judge the worth of a selection. Does the writing meet the standards or does it fall short?

Writing can be evaluated in two ways. First, the skill of the writers can be judged. For this type of evaluation you might ask yourself questions such as these: How well has the writer achieved his or her purpose? Has the writer chosen effective ways of presenting ideas? Is the organization logical? Does it help explain the ideas?

You can also evaluate *what* the writers are saying. Is their writing truthful and accurate? How do you know the writers are qualified to write about this subject? Are the writers telling the whole truth or is their view incomplete? Are they biased in any way? What are the qualities of this piece that make it worth reading?

As you evaluate *what* writers write, stay alert for examples of faulty thinking such as the following:

1. unsupported generalizations
2. hidden confusion of fact and opinion
3. slanted writing

When you write, try to be as skillful and accurate as possible. When you read, demand that other writers do the same.

For more about establishing standards for evaluation, see page 428. Some of the study questions involving evaluation are on pages 289, 313, and 428.

Fact and Opinion. Facts can be proved to be true. Opinions are only one person's beliefs. They may or may not be based on facts.

Fact: Water boils at 100 degrees Celsius.
Opinion: This soup is too hot.

As you read, watch out for statements that sound like facts but cannot be proved. The writer's opinions will also influence his or her choice of details, and may result in slanted writing.

Some of the many study questions on identifying fact and opinion in the selections are on pages 299, 361, 372, and 401.

See also *Personal Opinions.*

Generalizations. Writers sometimes notice that some things occur in a pattern, that is, over and over again. They may make a general statement about what they notice happening. For example, a generalization about spring could be "Many trees grow new leaves in the spring."

Writers can make mistakes in generalizations. Sometimes they don't look at the facts in enough cases. They apply the generalization to more instances than the facts will support. Then the generalizations are too broad. They are not completely true.

For example, this generalization is too broad: *All trees lose their leaves in the fall.* In reality, some trees do not lose their leaves in the fall. In fact, if you can think

of one tree that doesn't lose its leaves in fall, the generalization is faulty.

For more about identifying generalizations, see page 216.

Personal Opinions. You are often asked to give your opinion about an issue or question. Your opinion should be based on evidence. You should be able to point out and explain the reasons why you feel as you do.

Say, for example, you believe a certain story is realistic. If you want your opinion to be considered valid, you must be ready to back it up with evidence from the story. To explain your opinion, you might find examples of true-to-life situations and conversations in the story. You might point out the ways in which the story is like your own life or the lives of people you know.

Throughout this text, study questions in Developing Comprehension Skills, Reading Literature, and Developing Writing Skills ask the reader to form and present opinions, with supporting reasons. Some of these are on pages 25, 94, 253, and 362.

Slanted Writing. Writers are careful to choose words with the meanings they want. Denotations, or dictionary meanings, are important, of course. However, connotations, or the feelings or ideas the words give you, are equally important. In slanted writing, a writer uses many words with strong connotations. The connotations may lead readers to feel strongly in favor of a point of view. Other words with strong connotations may make a reader feel strongly against a subject.

Be aware of the power of slanted writing as you read. Don't permit the writer to trick you into agreeing with him or her without a good reason.

Read the following three sentences. Although they all deal with the same happening, they are very different. The first sentence is not slanted. The next two sentences are slanted. They use words with strong connotations.

1. Bill sold his red bike to Todd for fifty dollars.
2. Bill cheated Todd when he sold him his old bike for fifty dollars.
3. Bill practically gave his classic bike to Todd for only fifty dollars.

For more about slanted writing, see the study question on pages 348 and 349.

Glossary

The **glossary** is an alphabetical listing of words from the selections, along with their meanings. The glossary gives the following information:

1. **The entry word broken into syllables.**

2. **The pronunciation of each word.** The **respelling** is shown in parentheses. The most common way to pronounce a word is listed first. The Pronunciation Key below shows the symbols for the sounds of letters and key words that contain those sounds. A key is repeated on every second page.

   A **primary accent** ′ is placed after the syllable that is stressed the most when the word is spoken. A **secondary accent** ′ is placed after a syllable that has a lighter stress.

3. **The part of speech of the word.** The following abbreviations are used:

   n. noun   *v.* verb   *adj.* adjective   *adv.* adverb

4. **The meaning of the word.** The definitions listed in the glossary apply to selected ways a word is used in these selections.

5. **Related forms.** Words with suffixes such as *-ing, -ed, -ness,* and *-ly* are listed under the base word.

ra·tions (rash′ənz *or* rā′ shənz) *n. plural* food, or a supply of food.

Pronunciation Key

a	fat	**i**	hit	**o͞o**	look	ə {	a *in* ago	**ch**	chin
ā	ape	**ir**	here	**o͞o**	tool		e *in* agent	**sh**	she
ä	car, lot	**ī**	bite, fire	**ou**	out		i *in* unity	**th**	thin
							o *in* collect	**th**	then
e	ten	**ō**	go	**u**	up		u *in* focus	**zh**	leisure
er	care	**ô**	law, horn	**ur**	fur			**ng**	ring
ē	even	**oi**	oil			**′l**	able		

A

a·bide (ə bīd′) *v.* dwell. —*abide by* to give in to and carry out.

a·broad (ə brôd′) *adv.* outside one's own country.

ac·com·plish·ment (ə käm′plish mənt) *n.* an art or skill that has been learned.

ac·cu·rate (ak′yer it) *adj.* careful and exact; correct; without mistakes or errors.

ac·quaint (ə kwānt′) *v.* to cause to know personally; to make familiar.

ad lib (ad′ lib′) *v.* to make up words not in the script, as one is performing.

ad·mi·ra·tion (ad mə rā′shən) *n.* a feeling of delight and pleased approval at something.

a·do (ə do͞o′) *n.* fuss; trouble.

aer·o·nau·tics (er ə nô′tiks) *n. plural* the science of making and flying aircraft.

ag·o·ny (ag′ə nē) *n.* very great pain in the body or mind.

ag·ri·cul·ture (ag′ri kul′chər) *n.* the science and work of growing crops; farming. —**agriculturist** *n.*

al·ti·tude (al′tə to͞od *or* al′tə tyo͞od) *n.* height above the earth's surface.

am·a·teur (am′ə chər *or* am′ə to͝or) *n.* a person who does something for the pleasure of it rather than for money.

an·tic (an′tik) *n.* a playful or silly act, trick, or prank.

anx·ious (aṇgk′shəs) *adj.* worried.

ap·pa·ra·tus (ap′ə rat′əs *or* ap′ə rāt′əs) *n.* the tools, instruments, or equipment needed to do a certain job or experiment.

ap·pease (ə pēz′) *v.* to satisfy or relieve.

ap·pro·ba·tion (ap′rə bā′shən) *n.* official approval; satisfaction.

ar·ma·dil·lo (är mə dil′ō) *n.* a burrowing animal with bony plates around its back and head, living in the Southwest.

ar·ro·gant (ar′ə gənt) *adj.* overly proud and self-important. —**arrogantly** *adv.*

as·cent (ə sent′) *n.* a climbing or rising.

as·sume (ə so͞om′) *v.* **1.** to decide without evidence; **2.** to take on a certain look or form. —**assuming**.

as·tron·o·my (ə strän′ə mē) *n.* the science that studies the sun, moon, stars, planets, and comets.

at·ta·ché (at′ə shā′) *n.* a person with special duties on the staff of an ambassador or minister to another country.

au·di·ble (ô′də b'l) *adj.* loud enough to be heard. —**audibly** *adv.*

awe (ô) *n.* deep respect mixed with fear and wonder.

B

baf·fle (baf′'l) *v.* to confuse; puzzle.

ball (bôl) *n.* a large, formal dancing party.

bal·lad (bal′əd) *n.* **1.** a song or poem that tells a story in short verses; **2.** a popular love song.

bar·racks (bar′aks) *n. plural* a building or group of buildings where soldiers live.

ba·sin (bās′'n) *n.* all the land drained by a river and its branches.

bat·ter (bat′ər) *n.* a thin mixture of flour, milk, and eggs beaten together for making things like pancakes, cookies, or cakes.

be·lay (bi lā′) *v.* in mountain climbing, to secure a person or thing with a rope that is securely fastened at the other end.

be·wil·der (bi wil′dər) *v.* to make confused; puzzle very much.

bin·oc·u·lars (bi näk′yə lerz) *n. plural* a pair of small telescopes fastened together for use with both eyes.

bi·o·log·i·cal (bī ə läj′i k'l) *adj.* having to do with biology, the science of plants and animals.

bleak (blēk) *adj.* opened to wind and cold; not sheltered.

bleat (blēt) *v.* to make the sound of a sheep, goat, or calf.

bluff (bluf) *n.* a high, steep bank or cliff.

bot·a·ny (bät″n ē) *n.* the science that studies plants and how they grow.

bray (brā) *v.* to make a loud, harsh cry or noise.

bri·dle (brīd′l) *n.* the part of a horse's harness that controls the head.

brit·tle (brit″l) *adj.* easily broken because it is hard and not flexible.

bronze (bränz) *n.* a reddish-brown metal that is a compound of copper and tin.

brute (brōōt) *n.* **1.** a beast; **2.** a person who is brutal or stupid, coarse, and crude.

bur·ro (bur′o) *n.* donkey, especially one used as a pack animal in the Southwest.

C

ca·ble (kā′b'l) *n.* a thick, heavy rope, now usually made of wires twisted together.

cache (kash) *n.* anything hidden in a safe place.

cac·tus (kak′təs) *n.* a plant with spines or scales, growing in hot, dry places.

ca·det (kə det′) *n.* a student in training to become an officer in the army, navy, or air force.

cal·cu·lus (kal′kyə ləs) *n.* a kind of mathematics, used for difficult science or statistics problems.

can·o·py (kan′ə pē) *n.* a cloth or other covering fastened as a roof above a throne or bed, or held on poles over a person or sacred thing.

cap·sule (kap′s'l *or* kap′syōōl) *n.* the enclosed part of a spacecraft that holds the people and instruments. It can separate from the rocket for the return to earth.

cas·cade (kas kād′) *n.* **1.** a small, steep waterfall. **2.** something like a waterfall, as sparks falling in a shower.

cast (kast) *n.* a form or impression of something, such as an object or animal.

cat·a·mount (kat′ə mount) *n.* a wild cat, such as a cougar or lynx.

caw (kô) *n.* the loud, harsh cry of a crow or raven.

cham·ber·lain (chām′bər lin) *n.* a high official in a royal court.

chem·ist (kem′ist) *n.* a druggist: a British meaning.

chlo·ro·form (klôr′ə form) *n.* a colorless liquid that changes into a vapor quickly. In earlier times, it was used by doctors to make a patient unconscious, as during an operation.

chrys·an·the·mum (kri san′thə məm) *n.* a plant with round, many-petalled flowers grown in a variety of sizes and colors.

cin·der (sin′dər) *n.* a tiny particle of partly burned wood or coal.

ci·vil·ian (sə vil′yan) *n.* a person who is not a member of the military.

clad (klad) *adj.* clothed; covered.

cli·max (klī′maks) *n.* the final and strongest idea or event in a series; highest point of interest or excitement; the turning point in a story.

clum·si·ly (klum′zə lē) *adv.* in an ungraceful, awkward way.

co·bra (kō′brə) *n.* a very poisonous snake of Asia and Africa.

colo·nel (kur′n'l) *n.* an army or air force officer.

---

at, āte, fär; pen, ēqual; sit, mīne; sō, côrn, join, took, fōōl, our; us, turn; chill, shop, thick, they, sing; **zh** *in* measure; 'l *in* idle; ə *in* alive, cover, family, robot, circus.

co·lo·ni·al (kə lō′nē əl) **1.** *adj.* concerning the thirteen British colonies that were to become the United States. **2.** *n.* a person who lives in a colony.

col·o·ny (käl′ə nē) *n.* a land that is ruled by a country some distance away.

co·ma (kō′mə) *n.* a deep, long sleep, often caused by injury or disease.

com·et (käm′ət) *n.* a bright heavenly body with a fiery tail.

com·mis·sion (kə mish′ən) *n.* a group of people chosen to do a certain thing.

com·mo·tion (kə mō′shən) *n.* confusion or noisy rushing about.

com·pli·cat·ed (käm′plə kāt′id) *adj.* not simple; hard to solve or understand.

com·pu·ter (kəm pyōōt′ər) *n.* an electronic device used as a calculator or to store and select information.

con·ceiv·a·ble (kən sēv′ə b'l) *adj.* that can be imagined or thought of.

con·jur·er (kän′jər ər *or* kun′jər ər) *n.* a magician.

con·quest (käng′kwest) *n.* the act of getting or reaching a thing or goal, by trying hard.

con·test·ant (kən tes′tənt) *n.* a person who takes part in a contest.

con·ti·nent (känt′'n ənt) *n.* any of the main large land areas of the earth.

con·tract (kän′trakt *or* kən trakt′) *n.* an agreement, often a written agreement that one can be held to by law. *v.* to make or become smaller; to shrink.

con·va·les·cent (kän və les′'nt) *adj.* getting back health and strength after illness.

cor·don (kôr′d'n) *n.* a line or circle around a person or place.

cor·nice (kôr′nis) *n.* an overhanging mass of snow, ice, or rock usually on a mountain ridge.

cor·po·ral (kôr′pər əl) *n.* an officer in the armed forces.

corpse (kôrps) *n.* a person's dead body.

course (kôrs) *n.* a part of a meal served at one time.

cour·ti·er (kôr′tē ər) *n.* an attendant at a royal court.

coy·o·te (kī ōt′ē *or* kī′ōt) *n.* a small wolf of the western prairies of North America.

cram·pon (kram′pan) *n.* an iron plate fastened on a shoe to prevent slipping.

cra·ter (krāt′ər) *n.* a bowl-shaped hollow, as on the surface of the moon.

cre·o·sote (krē′ə sōt) *n.* an oily liquid made from wood or coal tar and used to keep wood from rotting.

cre·vasse (kri vas′) *n.* a deep crack or crevice, especially in a glacier.

crib (krib) *n.* a bin for storage of grain.

crock (kräk) *n.* a pot or jar made of baked clay.

crow[1] (krō) *n.* a large black bird known for its harsh cry or caw. —*as the crow flies*, in a straight line between two places.

crow[2] (krō) *v.* **1.** to make the shrill cry of a rooster. **2.** to make loud sounds like this, as in happiness, delight, or boasting (to *crow* over a victory).

crow·bar (krō′bär) *n.* a long metal bar used as a lever for prying things.

crow's-foot (krōz′foot′) *n. usually* **crow's feet**, *plural* any of the wrinkles that often develop at the outer corners of the eyes.

crow's nest (krōz′nest′) *n.* a small box or platform near the top of a ship's mast, where the lookout stands.

crys·tal·line (kris′tə lin) *adj.* like a crystal; transparent; clear; sparkling.

cu·mu·lus (kyōōm′yə ləs) *n.* a kind of cloud in which round masses are piled up on each other.

cun·ning (kun′iṅg) **1.** *adj.* crafty; sly. **2.** *n.* skill in cheating or tricking.

cur·a·ble (kyōōr′ə b′l) *adj.* able to be cured, or made well.

curt (kʉrt) *adj.* in an unfriendly or abrupt manner.

D

daunt·less (dônt′lis) *adj.* that cannot be frightened or discouraged.

debt (det) *n.* something that one owes to another.

de·ceit·ful (di sēt′fəl) *adj.* lying; misleading.

de·ceive (di sēv′) *v.* to make someone believe what is not true; to fool or trick.

de·feat (di fēt′) *v.* to win victory over.

de·ny (di nī′) *v.* to say that something is not true or right.

de·pot (dē′po) *n.* a place for storing supplies.

de·scend (di send′) *v.* to move down to a lower place.

des·ert (dez′ərt) *n.* a hot, dry region with little or no plant life.

des·o·late (des′ə lit) *adj.* not lived in; deserted.

de·tach·ment (di tach′mənt) *n.* the state of being aloof; separation.

de·tect (di tekt′) *v.* to discover something hidden or not easily noticed.

de·vour (di vour′) *v.* to eat up in a hungry or greedy way.

di·a·ry (dī′ə rē) *n.* a record written day by day of the things done, seen, or thought.

dig·ni·ty (dig′nə tē) *n.* a noble or stately appearance or manner.

di·min·ish (də min′ish) *v.* to make or become smaller in size or less in force.

di·min·u·tive (də min′ yōō tiv) *adj.* very small; tiny.

din (din) *n.* a loud, steady noise.

dis·ci·pline (dis′ə plin) *v.* to train; control.

dis·cus (dis′kəs) *n.* a heavy disk of metal and wood that is thrown in an athletic contest.

dis·gust (dis gust′) *n.* a strong dislike.

dis·po·si·tion (dis′pə zish′ən) *n.* one's general nature or mood.

dis·tin·guish (dis tiṅg′gwish) *v.* to see the difference in.

dis·tin·guished (dis tiṅg′gwisht) *adj.* outstanding; important.

dis·tress (dis tres′) *n.* pain, sorrow, or worry; suffering.

dock (däk) *v.* to join together in outer space.

dom·i·nant (däm′ə nənt) *adj.* most important.

don (dän) *v.* to put on, as one's hat or coat.

down (doun) *n.* soft, fluffy feathers used for stuffing pillows or lining clothing.

downs (dounz) *n. plural* treeless hills or dunes.

drought (drout) *n.* a long period of dry weather, with little or no rain.

drove (drōv) *n.* a group of cattle or sheep driven along together; herd; flock.

dune (dōōn *or* dyōōn) *n.* a rounded hill or ridge of sand heaped up by the wind.

E

ear·nest·ly (ʉr′nist lē) *adv.* seriously or sincerely.

earth·ling (ʉrth′liṅg) *n.* one who lives on earth.

---

at, āte, fär; pen, ēqual; sit, mīne; sō, côrn, join, took, fōōl, our; us, tʉrn; chill, shop, thick, *th*ey, siṅg; **zh** *in* measure; ′l *in* idle; ə *in* alive, cover, family, robot, circus.

e·gret (ē′gret) *n.* a kind of bird that lives along the shore.

em·broi·der (im brɔi′dər) *v.* to make fancy designs on cloth with needlework.

em·per·or (em′pər ər) *n.* a man who rules over an empire (a country or group of countries).

en·dure (in dʊr′ *or* in dyʊr′) *v.* to hold up under pain or weariness.

en·trails (en′trālz) *n. plural* the parts inside an animal's body.

en·vel·op (in vel′əp) *v.* to cover on all sides; wrap up or wrap in.

en·vi·ron·ment (in vī′rən mənt) *n.* all the conditions of a place; surroundings.

er·a (ir′ə *or* er′ə) *n.* a period of history having some special characteristic.

es·sence (es′′ns) *n.* that which makes something what it is; most important or basic quality of a thing.

es·tate (ə stāt′) *n.* a large piece of land with a large home on it.

e·ter·ni·ty (i tʉr′nə tē) *n.* all time, without beginning or end; endless time.

e·ther (ē′thər) *n.* a colorless liquid used to make a person unconscious, as during an operation in a hospital.

ev·i·dent (ev′ə dənt) *adj.* easy to see or understand; clear; plain.

ex·cru·ci·at·ing (iks krʊ′shē āt′iŋ) *adj.* causing great pain.

ex·hib·it (ig zib′it) *v.* to show or reveal.

ex·pe·di·tion (ek′spə dish′ən) *n.* a long journey or voyage by a group of people, as to explore a region.

ex·press (ik spres′) *n.* a way of sending goods or packages.

ex·qui·site (eks′kwi zit *or* ik skwiz′ it) *adj.* very beautiful.

ex·traor·di·nar·i·ly (ik strôr′d′n er′ə lē) *adv.* very much different from the ordinary.

F

face (fās) *n.* a surface or side; especially the main, top, or front side.

fair (fer) *n.* a gathering of people with amusements, displays, buying and selling of goods.

fetch (fech) *v.* to go after and bring back.

flare (fler) *v.* to blaze up with a bright flame.

flar·ing (fler′iŋ) *n.* **1.** a short burst of bright light. **2.** a sudden outburst.

flat·ter (flat′ər) *v.* to praise too much or without meaning it.

flu·id (flʊ′id) *adj.* like something that moves or changes; not fixed.

fore·fa·ther (fôr′fä′thər) *n.* a person who comes before one in a family; ancestor.

fore·man (fôr′mən) *n.* a person in charge of something.

for·feit (fôr′fit) *v.* to give up or lose something because of what one has done or has failed to do.

forge (fôrj) *v.* to move with sudden speed and energy.

for·mi·da·ble (fôr′mə də b′l) *adj.* admirable; awesome; causing fear or dread.

franc (fraŋk) *n.* the basic unit of money in France.

Frau (frou) *n.* a title meaning Mrs.: a German word.

frost·bit·ten (frôst′bit′′n) *adj.* damaged by having been exposed to great cold.

fum·ble (fum′b′l) *v.* to handle or grope about in a clumsy way.

fur·row (fʉr′ō) *n.* a long, narrow groove made in the ground by a plow.

G

gale (gāl) *n.* a strong wind.

gal·leon (gal′ē ən) *n.* a large Spanish sailing ship of olden times.

gal·oot (gə lo͞ot′) *n.* a disreputable-looking person.

gauge (gāj) *n.* any device for measuring something.

gear (gir) *n.* tools and equipment needed for doing something.

ges·ture (jes′chər) *n.* a motion made with some part of the body, especially the hands or arms, to show some idea or feeling.

Gi·la mon·ster (hē′lə män′stər) *n.* a large lizard of the Southwest.

gla·cier (glā′shər) *n.* a large mass of ice and snow that moves very slowly down a mountain or across land until it melts.

grav·i·ty (grav′ə tē) *n.* the force that tends to draw objects toward the center of the earth.

grease·wood (grēs′wo͝od) *n.* a low stiff shrub common in the Western part of the United States.

greed·y (grēd′ē) *adj.* wanting or taking all that one can get with no thought of what others need.

grid·dle (grid′′l) *n.* a heavy, flat metal pan for cooking pancakes.

grin (grin) *v.* to draw back the lips and show teeth, as in a big or foolish smile.

grudg·ing·ly (gruj′iɳ lē) *adv.* giving or doing something without wanting to.

gru·el (gro͞o′əl) *n.* a watery food made by cooking meal in milk or water.

H

har·di·hood (här′dē ho͞od) *n.* boldness or daring.

haunch (hônch) *n.* the hip, buttock, and upper part of the thigh.

head·long (hed′ lôɳ) *adj.* with wild speed or force.

heed (hēd) *v.* to pay attention to; to listen and consider.

her·it·age (her′ət ij) *n.* something handed down from one's ancestors or the past, as certain skills or rights, or a way of life.

hes·i·ta·tion (hez′ə tā′shən) *n.* pausing for a moment.

hoist (hoist) *v.* to lift or pull up; raise, especially with a crane, pulley, or rope.

hol·low (häl′ō) *adj.* sunken in.

hol·o·caust (häl′ə kəst *or* hô′lə kôst) *n.* a complete destruction by fire.

home·stead (hōm′sted) *v.* to become a settler on a piece of public land given by the U.S. government.

ho·ri·zon (hə rī′z'n) *n.* the place where the land and sky appear to meet.

hos·pi·ta·ble (häs′pi tə b'l *or* häs pit′ə b'l) *adj.* liking to have guests and treating them well.

host (hōst) *n.* a man who has guests in his home or at another place.

hos·tile (häs′t'l) *n.* unfriendly; against.

hu·mil·i·ty (hyo͞o mil′ə tē) *n.* the quality of being humble or feeling insignificant.

hu·mun·gous (yo͞o muɳ′gəs) *adj.* a slang word for huge.

hur·dle (hʉr′d'l) *n.* a small fence or frame that runners or horses must jump over in a race.

I

i·dle (ī′d'l) *adj.* not busy.

ig·ni·tion (ig nish′ən) *n.* the switch that starts an engine.

ig·no·ra·mus (ig′nə rā′məs *or* ig′nə ram′əs) *n.* an ignorant person.

---

at, āte, fär; pen, ēqual; sit, mīne; sō, côrn, join, to͝ok, fo͞ol, our; us, tʉrn; chill, shop, thick, *th*ey, siɳg; **zh** *in* measure; '**l** *in* idle; ə *in* alive, cover, family, robot, circus.

il·lu·mine (i lōō′min) *v.* to light up.

i·mag·i·nar·y (i maj′ə nər′ē) *adj.* not real.

im·men·si·ty (i men′sə tē) *n.* the fact of being immense; great size; vastness.

im·pass·a·ble (im pas′ə b'l) *adj.* that cannot be traveled on or across.

im·pe·ri·al (im pir′ē əl) *adj.* of an emperor, empress or empire.

im·pres·sion (im presh′ən) *n.* a mark or imprint made by pressing, as in marks found on fossils.

in·dis·sol·u·ble (in′di säl′yōō b'l) *adj.* that cannot be broken up; lasting; durable.

in·es·ti·ma·ble (in es′tə mə b'l) *adj.* cannot be estimated or measured.

in·fec·tious (in fek′shəs) *adj.* tending to spread to others.

in·hab·it (in hab′it) *v.* live in or on; to occupy.

in·her·i·tance (in her′it əns) *n.* the property that passes at the owner's death to his or her heirs.

in·let (in′let) *n.* a narrow strip of water running in to land, as from a river, lake, or ocean.

in·su·per·a·ble (in sōō′pər ə b'l *or* in syōō′ pər ə b'l) *adj.* that cannot be passed over or overcome.

in·ter·cept (in tər sept′) *v.* to stop or seize on the way.

in·ter·fer·ence (in′tər fir′əns) *n.* the act of blocking players in football to clear the way for the ball carrier.

in·va·lid (in′və lid) *n.* a person who is sick or injured, especially one who is likely to be so for some time.

in·vis·i·bil·i·ty (in viz ə b'l′ə tē) *n.* state of not being seen.

i·so·la·tion (i′sə lā′shən) *n.* the action of being kept apart from others.

J

jav·e·lin (jav′lin *or* jav′ə lin) *n.* a light spear used in an athletic contest.

jes·ter (jes′tər) *n.* a clown hired by a ruler to do tricks and tell jokes.

jolt (jōlt) *n.* a sudden bump or jerk.

K

kaf·ir (kaf′ər) *n.* a grain with juicy stalks, used to feed cattle.

ki·mo·no (kə mō′nə) *n.* a loose robe with wide sleeves and a sash.

kink (kiŋk) *n.* a short twist or curl, as in a hair or thread.

knob·by (näb′ē) *adj.* like a knob; having a round part that sticks out.

knot (nät) *n.* **1.** a small group (a *knot* of people). **2.** a hard lump on a tree where a branch grows out.

L

lab·o·ra·to·ry (lab′rə tôr′ē *or* lab′ər ə tôr′ē) *n.* a room or building where scientific work or tests are carried on.

la·bor·er (lā′bər ər) *n.* a worker.

la·con·ic (lə kän′ik) *adj.* using few words; brief.

la·goon (lə gōōn′) *n.* a shallow lake; pond.

la·ma (lä′mə) *n.* a Buddhist priest or monk.

land·lord (land′lôrd) *n.* a person who owns land or houses that are rented to others.

land·scape (land′skāp) *n.* a stretch of scenery that can be seen in one view.

la·pel (lə pel′) *n.* either of the front parts of a coat that are folded back.

leav·en (lev′'n) *v.* to spread through, slowly causing a change.

leg·end (lej′ənd) *n.* **1.** a story handed down through the years. **2.** a remarkable person who is much talked about while still alive.

leg·is·la·ture (lej′is lā′cher) *n.* a group of people who make laws.

lei·sure (lē′zhər *or* lezh′ər) *n.* free time, when one isn't busy with something else.

lens (lenz) *n.* a piece of clear glass or plastic used in a telescope.

lo·co·mo·tive (lō′kə mō′tiv) *n.* a steam, electric, or Diesel engine on wheels, that pulls or pushes railroad trains.

loom (lo͞om) *n.* a machine for weaving thread or yarn into cloth.

lop (läp) *v.* to trim by cutting off branches.

lum·ber·jack (lum′bər jak) *n.* a person whose work is cutting down trees and taking the logs to a sawmill.

lu·nar (lo͞o′nər) *adj.* of or like the moon.

lute (lo͞ot) *n.* an early musical instrument played like a guitar.

lux·u·ry (luk′shə rē *or* lug′zhə rē) *n.* the use and enjoyment of costly things. —**luxurious** *adj.*

M

mag·got (mag′ət) *n.* an insect in an early stage when it looks like a worm.

mag·nif·i·cent (mag nif′ə s′nt) *adj.* beautiful in a grand way.

man·sion (man′shən) *n.* a large, stately house.

mar·bled (mar′b′ld) *v.* made to look like marble (stone) that is streaked.

mar·tyred (mär′tərd) *v.* killed for not giving up one's beliefs.

meek·ly (mēk′lē) *adv.* mildly; humbly.

me·sa (mā′sə) *n.* a large, high rock having steep walls and a flat top.

mes·mer·ize (mez′mər īz) *v.* **1.** to hypnotize; **2.** to fascinate.

mim·ic·ry (mim′ik rē) *n.* the art of imitating speech or action.

min·is·ter (min′is tər) *n.* **1.** a person in charge of a department in government; **2.** one who leads people in worship.

mis·sion (mish′ən) *n.* **1.** a special duty or errand that a group is sent out to do. **2.** a group of persons who live and work together for a church or government. **3.** the special task that a person seems to be meant for in life.

mis·sion·ar·y (mish′ən er′ē) *adj.* having to do with religious missions.

moc·ca·sin (mäk′ə s′n) *n.* a soft leather shoe.

mod·est (mäd′ist) *adj.* not boastful about one's worth, skills, or deeds.

mod·ule (mäj′o͞ol) *n.* a section of a machine or device that can be detached for some special use.

mole (mōl) *n.* a small, dark-colored spot on the skin.

mol·ten (mōl′t'n) *adj.* melted by heat.

mon·arch (män′ark) *n.* one who rules, as a king, queen, or emperor.

mon·as·ter·y (män′ə ster′ē) *n.* a place where men in a religious order live together according to certain rules.

mon·i·tor (män′ə tər) *v.* to listen to or watch in order to check up on.

mon·o·tone (män′ə tōn) *n.* a keeping of the same tone or pitch without change, as in talking or singing.

moor (mo͞or) *n.* an area of open land, often swampy.

mot·ley (mät′lē) *n.* a wrap of many colors.

mount (mount) *n.* a horse for riding.

---

at, āte, fär; pen, ēqual; sit, mīne; sō, côrn, join, to͝ok, fo͞ol, our; us, turn; chill, shop, thick, they, sing; zh *in* measure; 'l *in* idle; ə *in* alive, cover, family, robot, circus.

mourn·ful (môrn′fəl) *adj.* feeling sorrow; being sad. —**mournfully** *adv.*

muck (muk) *n.* earth with rotting leaves, used as fertilizer.

mur·mur (mʉr′mər) *n.* a low, steady sound of voices.

mus·tang (mus′taṅg) *n.* a small wild or half-wild horse of the Southwest plains.

mu·ti·neer (myo͞ot ′n ir′) *n.* a person who resists or fights the leaders of a group, especially a sailor against an officer.

mut·ton (mut′′n) *n.* the flesh of a sheep, used for food.

muz·zle (muz′′l) *n.* the mouth, nose, and jaws of a horse.

N

nat·u·ral·ist (nach′ər əl ist) *n.* a person who makes a study of plants and animals.

near·sight·ed (nir′sīt′id) *adj.* able to see things that are near more clearly than things far away.

nut·hatch (nut′hach) *n.* a small bird that has a sharp beak and feeds on nuts.

O

or·bit (ôr′bit) *n.* the curved path of one heavenly body, planet, or satellite around another body in space.

or·bi·ter (ôr′bit ər) *n.* one who moves in an orbit.

out·law (ɷut′lô) *n.* a criminal, especially one who is being hunted by the police.

out·wit (ɷut wit′) *v.* to win out over by being clever or cunning. —**outwitted**.

o·ver·whelm (ō vər hwelm′) *v.* to overcome completely; make helpless.

ox·y·gen (äk′si jən) *n.* a gas that has no color or taste, and is a chemical element. All living things need oxygen.

oys·ter (ɷi′stər) *n.* a shellfish with a soft body enclosed in two rough shells hinged together.

P

pam·per (pam′pər) *v.* to be too gentle with.

pas·ture (pas′chər) *n.* land where grass and other plants grow and where cattle and sheep can graze.

pat·tern (pat′ərn) *n.* design.

peal (pēl) *n.* any loud sound that echoes, as of thunder.

peas·ant (pez′ənt) *n.* any person of the class of farm workers and farmers with small farms, as in Europe and Asia.

pell-mell (pel′mel′) *adv.* in a jumbled mass; in a confused way.

pen (pen) *v.* to shut up in a small yard with a fence.

pen·in·su·la (pə nin′sə lə *or* pə nin′syo͞o lə) *n.* a long piece of land almost completely surrounded by water.

per·cep·tion (pər sep′shən) *n.* knowledge or understanding got by perceiving (becoming aware of through the senses; seeing).

per·pet·u·al (pər pech′o͞o wəl) *adj.* lasting forever or for a long time.

phi·los·o·pher (fi läs′ə fər) *n.* a person who studies human thought about the meaning of life and the problems of right and wrong.

pit·tance (pit′əns) *n.* a small amount of pay, or money.

plough (plɷu) *v.* to turn the soil or make rows, as in farming: British spelling of *plow*.

plumb (plum) *n.* a metal weight hung at the end of a line called a **plumb line**. It is used to find out how deep water is or whether a wall is straight up and down.

pot·ter·y (pät′ər ē) *n.* pots and dishes made of clay and hardened by baking.

pov·er·ty (päv′ər tē) *n.* the condition of being poor, not having enough to live on.

prai·rie (prer′ē) *n.* a large area of grassy land without many trees.

pre·cious (presh′əs) *adj.* having a high price or value.

prec·i·pice (pres′ə pis) *n.* a steep cliff that goes almost straight.

pre·oc·cu·pa·tion (prē äk′yə pā′shən) *n.* the act of taking up one's time so that other things are not noticed.

prey (prā) *v.* to hunt other animals for food.

priv·i·lege (priv′′l ij) *n.* a special right, favor, or advantage given to some person or group.

pro·fes·sion·al (prə fesh′ən ′l) *n.* a person earning his or her living from a sport or other activity.

pro·file (prō′fīl) *n.* a side view or outline.

pro·vi·sions (prə vizh′ənz) *n. plural* a supply or stock of food.

pueb·lo (pweb′lō) *n.* an Indian town of homes built close together.

pulse (puls) *n.* the regular beating in the arteries, caused by the movements of the heart in pumping the blood.

pu·ny (pyōō′nē) *adj.* small or weak.

py·thon (pī′thän *or* pī′thən) *n.* a very large snake that crushes its prey.

Q

quail (kwāl) *n.* a small, wild bird hunted for sport or for food.

Quak·er (kwāk′ər) *n.* a member of a religious group that believes in a plain way of life and worship and is against violence of any kind.

R

raft·er (raf′tər) *n.* any of the sloping beams used to hold up a roof.

rap·ture (rap′chər) *n.* a deep feeling of joy and love.

ra·tions (rash′ənz *or* rā′shənz) *n. plural* food, or a supply of food.

re·ac·tion (rē ak′shən) *n.* an action in response to some other happening.

re·cite (ri sīt′) *v.* to say aloud before an audience. —**reciting**.

ref·uge (ref′yōōj) *n.* shelter or protection, as from danger.

ref·u·gee (ref′yōō jə′) one who flees his or her country to escape danger.

re·fuse[1] (ri fyōōz′) *v.* to say that one will not accept something.

ref·use[2] (ref′yōōs *or* ref′yōōz) *n.* rubbish.

rel·ish (rel′ish) *n.* enjoyment; zest.

re·plen·ish (ri plen′ish) *v.* to furnish a new supply for.

re·serves (ri zʉrvs′) *n. plural* extra players on an athletic team, used as replacements.

rev·er·ence (rev′ər əns *or* rev′rəns) *n.* great love and respect.

rick·ets (rik′its) *n.* a disease which causes bones to get soft.

ridge (rij) *n.* a top or high part that is long and narrow; crest.

rift (rift) *n.* an opening made, as by splitting; crack.

rogue (rōg) *n.* a dishonest or tricky person.

rus·set (rus′it) *adj.* a reddish-brown color.

ru·ta·ba·ga (rōōt′ə bā′gə *or* rōōt′ ə bā′gə) *n.* a turnip with a large, yellow root.

---

at, āte, fär; pen, ēqual; sit, mīne; sō, côrn, join, took, fōōl, our; us, tʉrn; chill, shop, thick, *th*ey, sing; **zh** *in* measure; ′l *in* idle; ə *in* alive, cover, family, robot, circus.

S

sage·brush (sāj′brush) *n.* a shrub that grows on the Western plains.

san·i·tar·y (san′ə ter′ē) *adj.* **1.** having to do with bringing about health or healthful conditions. **2.** free from dirt that could bring disease.

san·i·ta·tion (san′ə tā′shən) *n.* the science and work of bringing about healthful conditions.

sap (sap) *n.* the juice that flows through a plant or tree, carrying food, water, and other necessary things to all its parts.

sat·el·lite (sat′′l īt) *n.* an artificial object put into orbit around the earth, the moon, or some other heavenly body.

sav·age (sav′ij) *adj.* fierce; wild.

saw·mill (sô′mil) *n.* a place where logs are sawed into boards.

Scan·di·na·vi·an (skan′də nā′vē ən) *adj.* a person who comes from the part of Europe in which Norway, Sweden, Denmark, and Iceland are located.

scent (sent) *n.* a smell; odor.

schol·ar (skäl′ər) *n.* **1.** a person who has learned much through study. **2.** a student or pupil.

sci·en·tist (sī′ən tist) *n.* an expert in science, such as a biologist.

scorn·ful·ly (skôrn′fəl ē) *adv.* angrily; showing contempt.

scoun·drel (skoun′drəl) *n.* a bad or dishonest person; villain.

scur·ry (skur e′) *v.* to run quickly; scamper.

se·quoi·a (si kwoi′ə) *n.* a giant evergreen tree of California, as the redwood.

set·tle·ment house (set′′l mənt hous) *n.* a place in a poor, crowded neighborhood where people go to get advice or take classes.

shaft (shaft) *n.* a long, slender thing or part, as a column or a long handle.

shil·ling (shil′ing) *n.* a silver coin of Great Britain.

shirk·er (shurk′ər) *n.* one who wants to get out of doing something or who leaves something undone.

shriv·el (shriv′′l) *v.* to curl up and shrink or wither. —**shrivelling**.

shud·der (shud′ər) *v.* to shake or tremble in a sudden and violent way.

shut·tle (shut′′l) *n.* a device in weaving that carries a thread back and forth.

siege (sēj) *n.* the surrounding of a city, fort, or castle by an enemy army trying to capture it.

skil·let (skil′it) *n.* a frying pan.

skim (skim) *v.* to glide lightly, as over a surface.

slab (slab) *n.* a piece that is flat, broad, and fairly thick.

sledge (slej) *n.* a large, heavy sled for carrying loads over ice and snow.

sly (slī) *adj.* able to fool or trick others; cunning; crafty.

so·ci·e·ty (sə sī′ə tē) *n.* the wealthy upper class.

sol·emn (säl′əm) *adj.* serious.

spear (spir) *n.* a weapon made up of a long shaft (stem) with a sharp head. It is thrust or thrown by hand.

spec·i·men (spes′ə mən) *n.* one chosen from a group to show what the others are like; sample.

spec·ta·tor (spek′tāt′ər) *n.* one who attends and watches a show, sport, or event.

spike (spīk) *n.* a pointed piece of metal.

spin·dly (spin′dlē) *adj.* having very long and thin legs.

spring (spring) *n.* water flowing up from the ground.

spur (spur) *n.* **1.** a metal piece with sharp points, worn on the heel by horsemen to urge the horse forward. **2.** something that sticks out, as a ridge on a mountain.

spy (spī) *v.* to find out by watching carefully.

squad (skwäd) *n.* a group of people on a team.

squash (skwäsh) *n.* a fleshy fruit that grows on a vine and is cooked as a vegetable.

squire (skwīr) *n.* In England, a country gentleman who owns much land.

stance (stans) *n.* the way a person stands; position of one's feet.

stock–still (stäk'stil') *adj.* not moving at all; motionless.

store (stôr) *n.* a supply or stock for use as needed.

stout (stout) *adj.* **1.** fat. **2.** sturdy.

strad·dle (strad''l) *v.* **1.** to stand or sit with a leg on either side of. **2.** to sit, stand, or walk with the legs wide apart. —**astraddle,** *adv.*

strand (strand) *v.* to leave or be put in a difficult, helpless position.

stren·u·ous (stren'yoo wəs) *adj.* needing much energy or effort.

stress (stres) *n.* strain or pressure, such as in time of crisis.

suit·a·ble (soot'ə b'l) *adj.* proper for the purpose.

suite (swēt) *n.* a group of attendants or servants.

sul·tan (sul't'n) *n.* a ruler of a Muslim country, especially in earlier times.

sum·mit (sum'it) *n.* the highest point; top.

sum·mon (sum'ən) *v.* call or send for.

su·perb (soo purb') *adj.* excellent; splendid.

sur·feit (sur'fit) *n.* too much, especially food or drink.

sur·viv·or (sər vīv'ər) *n.* one who lives or lasts longer than others.

sus·te·nance (sus'ti nəns) *n.* that which sustains life; food or nourishment.

swathe (swäth) *v.* to surround or cover completely.

sym·pa·thet·ic (sim'pə thet'ik) *adj.* showing agreement; sharing somebody else's feelings. —**sympathetically** *adv.*

syn·thet·ic (sin thet'ik) *adj.* made by putting together chemicals rather than by using natural materials.

T

tam·a·risk (tam'ə risk) *n.* a tree or shrub with thin branches and clusters of flowers.

tan·gi·ble (tan'jə b'l) *adj.* that can be touched or felt; real or solid.

tan·ta·lize (tan'tə līz) *v.* to tease; tempt.

tar·ry (tar'ē) *v.* to stay for a time.

tart·ly (tärt'lē) *adv.* sharply spoken.

ten·don (ten'dən) *n.* the cord of tough fiber that fastens a muscle to a bone.

ten·e·ment (ten'ə mənt) *n.* an old, crowded apartment house.

thatch (thach) *n.* straw or leaves, usually for a roof.

thrash (thrash) *v.* to move about in a violent or jerky way.

thun·der (thun'dər) *v.* to cause a loud noise; shout in a forceful way.

tin·ker (tiŋ'kər) *n.* a person who mends pots and pans, often one who travels about doing this.

---

at, āte, fär; pen, ēqual; sit, mīne; sō, côrn, join, took, fool, our; us, turn; chill, shop, thick, they, sing; zh *in* measure; 'l *in* idle; ə *in* alive, cover, family, robot, circus.

ti·tan·ic (tī tan′ik) *adj.* very large, strong, or powerful.

tor·rent (tôr′ənt) *n.* a wild, rushing flow.

trag·ic (traj′ik) *adj.* bringing great harm and suffering; dreadful.

trans·par·ent (trans per′ənt) *adj.* so clear that it can be seen through.

trans·port (trans′pôrt) *n.* the act of carrying from one place to another.

tra·verse (tra vurs′ *or* trav′ərs) *v.* to pass over; cross.

treach·er·ous (trech′ər əs) *adj.* not safe; having hidden dangers.

tree (trē) *v.* to chase up a tree.

trek (trek) *n.* a long, slow journey.

trel·lis (trel′is) *n.* a frame of wood on which vines or other climbing plants are grown.

tribe (trīb) *n.* a group of people or animals.

tri·fling (trī′flin̄g) *adj.* **1.** of little value or importance. **2.** not at all serious.

tri·um·phant (trī um′fənt) *adj.* happy or joyful over a victory or success.

trum·pet (trum′pit) *v.* to announce in a loud voice.

tur·ret (tur′it) *n.* a small tower on a building, usually at a corner.

U

un·doubt·ed·ly (un dout′id lē) *adv.* certainly.

un·fit (un fit′) *adj.* not fit or suitable.

u·ni·corn (yōō′nə kôrn) *n.* an imaginary animal like a horse with one long horn in the center of its forehead.

u·nique (yōō nēk′) *adj.* remarkable; unusual.

un·ob·served (un əb zurvd′) *adj.* not seen.

un·sta·ble (un stā′b'l) *adj.* not stable; not firm or steady.

u·ten·sil (yōō ten′s'l) *n.* a container or tool used for a special purpose.

V

valve (valv) *n.* a device that controls the flow of a gas or liquid.

va·por (vā′pər) *n.* a thick mist or mass of tiny drops of water in the air, as steam or fog.

var·mint (vär′mənt) *n.* **1.** a wild animal or bird considered a pest. **2.** a contemptible person.

vast (vast) *adj.* very great or very large.

ven·ture (ven′chər) *v.* to do at some risk.

ve·ran·da (və ran′də) *n.* an open porch along the outside of a building.

ver·sa·tile (vur′sə t'l) *adj.* able to do many things well.

ves·sel (ves′'l) *n.* **1.** anything hollow for holding something; container. **2.** a large boat.

vi·brate (vī′brāt) *v.* to move rapidly back and forth; quiver.

vul·ner·a·ble (vul′nər ə b'l) *adj.* that can be hurt, destroyed, or attacked.

W

war·bler (wôr′blər) *n.* a bird that sings.

whet (hwet) *v.* to make stronger; stimulate.

whine (hwīn) *v.* to make a long, feeble sound or cry, as in complaining.

wit (wit) *n.* the ability to say clever things in an amusing way.

wits (wits) *n.* the power to think and reason.

wiz·ard (wiz′ərd) *n.* a magician; sorcerer.

wretch·ed (rech′id) *adj.* causing misery.

Y

yarn (yärn) *n.* a tale or story.

yoke (yōk) *n.* a wooden frame that fits on the necks of a pair of oxen to join them.

yon·der (yän′dər) *adv.* at or in that place; over there.

yuc·ca (yuk′ə) *n.* a tall plant with long, stiff, pointed leaves and large flowers.

Biographies of Authors

Aesop

Samuel Allen

Hans Christian Andersen

Aesop *(perhaps 620–564 B.C.)* was said to be a Greek slave who made up many fables. There is no proof that Aesop was a real person, but there are many legends about him. Most popular is the belief that he was a slave who was freed in appreciation of his wit and learning. The animals in Aesop's fables remind us of people. Their actions illustrate the virtues and failings of human nature. "The Tortoise and the Hare," "The Lion and the Mouse," and "The Ant and the Grasshopper" are three popular fables that have been translated into many languages. Even though Aesop's fables are over two thousand years old, the lessons they teach are still useful in today's world.

Samuel Allen *(born 1917)* grew up in Columbus, Ohio. He was an enthusiastic student and graduated from Fisk University in Tennessee. Allen went on to study at Harvard University Law School and the Sorbonne in Paris. At first, Allen decided on a law career. However, his love of writing steered him into becoming a successful poet and teacher of Afro-American literature. Samuel Allen's poems have appeared in magazines as well as books, sometimes under the pen name of Paul Vesey.

Hans Christian Andersen *(1805–1875)* was born in Denmark. His father died when he was eleven, and his mother wanted her son to learn a trade. Andersen's main interests, however, were his homemade puppets. At fourteen, he went to the city of Copenhagen to try for a life in the theater. He had no success, even after years of struggling. When he was twenty-four, he began to write poems, stories, and novels. Hans Christian Andersen's most successful efforts turned out to be his fairy tales, which have been translated into many languages and are still read throughout the world.

Isaac Asimov

Walker Chapman

Emily Dickinson

Isaac Asimov *(born 1920)* came with his family to the United States from Russia at the age of three. As a boy, he loved reading science-fiction magazines. This reading stimulated Asimov's interest in science. He studied at Columbia University and then became a professor at Boston University School of Medicine. Isaac Asimov has written hundreds of books and articles on scientific and other subjects, but is best known for his science fiction stories.

Frances Carpenter *(1890–1972)* was the daughter of a well-known geographer. Her father traveled all over the world on research trips and often took his family along. Frances Carpenter used information gained on those trips as background for much of her writing. Two of her popular books are *Tales of a Chinese Grandmother* and *African Wonder Tales.*

Walker Chapman *(born 1935)* also writes under the name of Robert Silverberg. Ever since he was a teen-ager, Chapman has been interested in the lives of famous people. He is especially fascinated by the experiments and discoveries of scientists and explorers, and enjoys putting this information into story form. Walker Chapman is also interested in science-fiction. He has not only written science-fiction stories, but has also edited a collection of other people's stories.

Emily Dickinson *(1830–1886)* lived in Massachusetts. She led a normal life until the age of twenty-six, when she suddenly began to spend most of her time alone. Dickinson stayed indoors and had few visitors. Secretly, she wrote more than a thousand poems—most reflected deep feelings about life, love, and nature. Only seven of Emily Dickinson's poems were published while she was alive. The rest were discovered after her death, written on scraps of paper and hidden away in her bedroom.

Eleanor Farjeon *(1881–1965)* grew up in England, part of a family of actors and writers. She began writing poems at the age of seven and continued writing throughout her childhood. At sixteen, Farjeon wrote the words for an opera. She and her three

Robert Francis

Walker Gibson

Michael Gorham

brothers all became successful writers. One brother wrote mystery stories, another was a music critic, and a third wrote mainly for young people, as Eleanor did. Farjeon's poetry, fiction, music, and plays expressed her zest for life and her understanding of human nature.

Robert Francis *(born 1901)* has devoted his life to writing and teaching. In his home on the outskirts of Amherst, Massachusetts, Francis lives a quiet life, gardening, reading, and writing. His award-winning works include fiction, essays, autobiography, and poetry. Robert Francis has published many collections of poems, including *Come Out into the Sun, The Orb Weaver,* and *The Sound I Listened For.*

Mona Gardner grew up in Seattle, Washington. Every summer her family left the United States to spend a few months in Japan. There she became acquainted with Oriental life. Gardner enjoyed meeting Japanese people and learning their customs. After graduating from Stanford University, she began her writing career. Gardner has written many stories and books about the Far East. She lived in Hong Kong for many years.

Walker Gibson *(born 1919)* has appeared on television, teaching a modern literature course to college students. Using a text he wrote called *The Limits of Language,* Gibson has also been a professor at the University of Massachusetts and at Amherst. His enthusiasm for writing has encouraged many of his students to follow in his footsteps.

Michael Gorham *(born 1907)* is a pen name for Franklin Folsom. His father was a football coach and his mother a Physical Education teacher. This helped spark Gorham's interest in sports and sports heroes. During his college years, he camped, hiked, skied, and led mountain climbing expeditions. After graduation, he became a teacher at Swarthmore College and also a writer. Michael Gorham especially enjoys writing about famous American leaders and cowboys.

Sir Edmund Hillary

Rudyard Kipling

Jean de La Fontaine

Oliver Herford *(1863–1935)* was born in England, but moved to the United States with his family at an early age. He attended Antioch College in Ohio, and he also spent time studying in London and Paris. Herford was a popular literary figure of the early 1900's. His poems and humorous stories were published in many magazines, including *Life* and *Harper's Weekly.* Herford was also an artist. Animals were his favorite subjects, and his drawings often accompanied his writings.

Sir Edmund Hillary *(born 1919),* a New Zealander, wrote a book called *High Adventure,* in which he described his climb to the top of Mount Everest in 1953. That mountain is located in the Himalayan Mountains near Nepal. Hillary was accompanied by a native resident of the area, Tensing Norgay. After the success of the Everest trip, Hillary embarked on another adventure—to the South Pole. He finally reached that destination in 1958 in a tractor. Because of the Everest expedition, the Queen of England gave him the honor of knighthood and named him Sir Edmund Hillary.

Georgia Douglas Johnson *(1886–1966)* opened her heart and her home to many young writers. Born in Georgia, Johnson studied music and literature at Atlanta University and Oberlin College. Eventually, she settled in Washington, D.C. There she worked as a writer, teacher, and government employee. Georgia Douglas Johnson inspired many young black people, encouraging them to have pride in their heritage and confidence in their writing abilities. Her published works include *Heart of a Woman, Bronze,* and *Share My World.*

Rudyard Kipling *(1865–1936)* was born in India. At the age of six, his British parents sent him back to England for his schooling. Kipling returned to India as a journalist, and remained there for seven years. He wrote stories and poems in his spare time, and he eventually brought them back to England for publication. In 1892 he married an American woman and moved to Vermont. Kipling continued to write, producing nonsense stories, poetry, and longer works of fiction. *Just-So Stories* and *The Jungle Book* are two of his well-known books. He won a Nobel Prize in 1907.

Jean de La Fontaine *(1621–1695)* was a French fable writer who lived in Paris. La Fontaine had read Aesop's fables and enjoyed telling them to his friends. He began to put them into writing and eventually was able to publish a book of fables. La Fontaine achieved worldwide recognition when the fables were translated into many languages.

Stephen Leacock *(1869–1944)* had a marvelous sense of humor. He shared it with the public by speaking and writing. Leacock received his college education at the University of Chicago and in Canada. He was interested in government, and taught Political Economics at McGill University. Stephen Leacock enjoyed making fun of crime-solvers in his series of short stories about detectives. His published works include *Nonsense Novels* and *Literary Lapses.*

Myron Levoy writes about events that take place in New York City, his home town. His stories tell about true-to-life people living and working in a big city. Often Levoy's stories are about the struggles of immigrants trying to make a new life in America. He describes the experiences of these people with humor and sympathy. Levoy also writes drama. One of his plays, *Eli and Emily*, was staged in 1969.

Anne Morrow Lindbergh *(born 1907)* was the wife of the famous aviator, Charles Lindbergh. She met her husband in Mexico, where her father was the United States ambassador. Charles and Anne Lindbergh shared a strong sense of adventure. She, too, learned how to fly and navigate an airplane. Her writings describe many of the experiences she and her husband had while flying all over the world. Anne Morrow Lindbergh has written numerous essays, an autobiography, and a collection of letters from her young adulthood, *Bring Me a Unicorn.*

Myra Cohn Livingston *(born 1926)* lives in California, but travels all over the United States. She visits schools and talks to students about poetry and story writing. Livingston encourages young people to develop self-awareness and to find beauty in ordi-

Stephen Leacock

Anne Morrow Lindbergh

Myra Cohn Livingston

Henry Wadsworth Longfellow

nary day-to-day things. She has had many of her own poems published and also has been the editor of collections of poetry written by others.

Henry Wadsworth Longfellow *(1807–1882)* was one of the most popular and respected poets of his time. One of his narrative poems, "The Song of Hiawatha," sold more than one million copies in his lifetime. Longfellow was born in Portland, Maine, and graduated from Bowdoin College. He traveled and studied in Europe, and then returned to the United States to teach college. Much of his life was spent at Harvard University, inspiring students in their creative writing. Other well-known poems by Longfellow are "Evangeline," "Paul Revere's Ride," and "The Village Blacksmith."

Alonzo Lopez writes poetry in his native Navajo language, as well as English. His poems reflect the culture of the Navajo people and their love of the land. Lopez was born in Arizona and attended Yale University, Wesleyan University, and the Institute of American Indian Arts.

Archibald MacLeish

Archibald MacLeish *(1892–1982)* was a man of many talents. During his long life, he was a soldier, lawyer, poet, playwright, essayist, and journalist. He also served as an Assistant Secretary of State to Franklin D. Roosevelt. Attending Yale University and Harvard Law School provided the foundation for all of these pursuits. MacLeish won two Pulitzer Prizes for his poetry and numerous other awards for his other writings.

Guy de Maupassant *(1850–1893)* was born in France, the son of a stockbroker. His mother's literary friends in Paris had a great influence on his writing career. Maupassant became interested in writing at an early age, but he had to serve in the army and work at a government job to earn money, before he met with literary success. A famous French author, Flaubert, spent years helping Maupassant, until he perfected his skill in story writing. Before illness cut short his promising career, Maupassant achieved fame for "The Umbrella," "The Piece of String," and "The Necklace."

Guy de Maupassant

Nellie McCaslin

May McNeer

Grace Moon

Nellie McCaslin *(born 1914)* has shared her appreciation of drama with people all over the United States. Born in Cleveland, Ohio, she attended Western Reserve University and New York University. After teaching drama at Tudor Hall in Indianapolis, McCaslin went on to lecture at Columbia University and the National College of Education in Evanston, Illinois. She has written numerous plays as well as books, including *Legends in Action* and *Act Now.*

Phyllis McGinley *(1905–1978)* grew up on a ranch in Colorado. She, and her brother rode to a rural school on horseback. Often they were the only students. After college, McGinley spent time teaching in Utah, then moved to New York City. Most of her poems, essays, and stories deal with the problems and events of everyday life. In 1961 she won the Pulitzer Prize for *Times Three: Selected Verse from Three Decades.*

May McNeer *(born 1926)* grew up in Florida. She attended college at the University of Georgia and the Journalism School at Columbia University. There she met an art student, Lynd Ward, who eventually became her husband. After traveling in Europe, they settled down to their life's work—writing and illustrating books for young people. McNeer has written about many famous Americans, including Abraham Lincoln and Mark Twain.

Grace Moon *(1877–1947)* had a deep interest in native American Indian culture. Together with her husband, Carl, she lived on reservations in the Southwest. The Moons spent many years among the Hopi and Navajo tribes, where they gathered much interesting information for her books. Grace Moon won a Newbery Medal in 1929 for *Runaway Papoose.*

Lilian Moore is an editor as well as an author. She lives in New York City, where she was born and raised. Moore has been a reading specialist, always having a deep interest in the welfare of her students. Her poetry and stories have been very popular. Among Moore's well-known stories are *Bear Trouble* and *Too Many Bozos,* which were also produced as films.

Edwin Morgan

Raymond Richard
Patterson

Carl Sandburg

Edwin Morgan *(born 1920)* was born in Scotland and educated at the University of Glasgow. He is a man of many talents, including writing poetry, essays, and words for operas, and editing, translating, and lecturing. Morgan has amazed his readers with the variety and imagination of his writing. The Scottish Arts Council presented him with an award for *Beowulf: A Verse Translation into Modern English.*

Raymond Richard Patterson *(born 1929)* grew up in New York City. He attended Lincoln University in Pennsylvania and then New York University. Patterson taught in a junior high school and supervised a boys' youth home. He has written a newspaper column, "From Our Past," which highlights events in black history. Patterson's well-known works include *Twenty-Six Ways of Looking at a Black Man* and *Get Caught: A Photographic Essay.*

Carl Sandburg *(1878–1967)* was the son of Swedish immigrants who settled in Illinois. As a young man, Sandburg held a variety of jobs, including truckdriver, dishwasher, farmhand, and floorsweeper. He also served in the army and traveled around the country. In his travels, he sang and played his guitar, collected folk music, and listened to folk tales. All of those experiences are reflected in his poetry, fiction, and nonfiction. Sandburg's language of writing—free verse, slang, dialect, and street talk—make his writing come alive with the sights, sounds, and feelings of America of the past. Sandburg's four-volume biography of Abraham Lincoln, which won a Pulitzer Prize, is still popular reading.

Adrien Stoutenburg *(born 1916)* attended the Minneapolis School of Arts, where she studied English, art and music. Stoutenburg worked as a librarian, reporter, and editor before turning to creative writing as a career. She has published more than thirty books, including poetry, short stories, biographies, and novels. One of Stoutenburg's most popular books, *American Tall Tales,* is a collection of folklore. These include stories about Paul Bunyan and Pecos Bill, retold with imagination and humor.

May Swenson

Sara Teasdale

James Thurber

May Swenson *(born 1919)* grew up and attended school in Utah. She became a teacher at Purdue University and then served as a Poet-in-Residence there. Swenson's poems often take on unusual shapes, such as typed pictures. Swenson wants her readers to enjoy the sight as well as the sound of poetry. Her verse has been published in many magazines as well as in books. Two of her well-known collections of poems are *A Cage of Spines* and *Half Sun Half Asleep.* She has won numerous prizes and awards, including a Guggenheim Fellowship.

Sara Teasdale *(1884–1933)* was born and educated in St. Louis, Missouri. She was a shy, sensitive young woman who withdrew from a normal life after an unhappy marriage. Teasdale's poems have an easy rhythm and usually tell her personal feelings about love. During her lifetime she had six volumes of poetry published. One of Teasdale's collections of poems, *Love Songs,* won the 1918 Poetry Society award, an honor that was later renamed the Pulitzer Prize.

James Thurber *(1894–1961)* was a humorist and cartoonist who focused on the problems of people trying to cope in modern society. He wrote numerous stories and essays, many of which appeared in the *New Yorker* magazine. They were accompanied by his drawings of animals and sad-looking people. James Thurber grew up and attended college in Ohio. A book based on his life, *My Life and Hard Times,* was very popular, along with *The Secret Life of Walter Mitty* and Thurber's modern retellings of Aesop's fables.

Leo Tolstoy *(1828–1910)* was a Russian author whose plays, novels, and stories were translated into many languages. He wrote about his early life, religious themes, and military experiences. Tolstoy's short stories often have humorous plots. One of his most famous novels, *War and Peace,* has been filmed both by

Leo Tolstoy

Americans and by Russians. Tolstoy was a man who believed strongly in education, peace, and love, and was against violence.

Guernsey Van Riper, Jr. *(born 1909)* has admired sports figures ever since he was a boy growing up in Indiana. After attending De Pauw and Harvard Universities, Van Riper found employment with an advertising agency. His work there involved some creative writing, and that led to writing stories about baseball and football players, Olympic heroes, and cowboys. Van Riper's stories combine the telling of facts and people's feelings in a style that makes good reading.

Lynd Ward

Lynd Ward *(born 1905),* a native of Illinois, is an artist as well as a writer. He has illustrated and co-authored biographies and stories, often with his wife, May McNeer. One of Ward's best known books, *The Biggest Bear,* won a Caldecott Medal in 1953. He got the inspiration for that story from his experiences living in the Canadian wilderness. Ward's parents took him as a child to live in a log cabin, as a way of improving his health. He and his family enjoy the outdoors and often revisit that area.

Paul Westman *(born 1956)* started writing when he was in sixth grade in Minneapolis, Minnesota. His interest in writing continued throughout high school and college. After he graduated from the University of Minnesota, Westman became a freelance writer. His favorite subjects are national figures, such as John Glenn, Neil Armstrong, Walter Mondale, and Jesse Jackson. He won a *Scholastic Magazine* award for *A Christmas Story.*

Edith Wharton

Edith Wharton *(1862–1937)* was born in New York City. After attending college, she married a banker and moved to Massachusetts. There she collected information for one of her most popular books, *Ethan Frome.* In 1907 Wharton moved to France. During World War I, she became active in war relief activities. For this work, the French government awarded her the Legion of Honor. In 1920 Edith Wharton received the Pulitzer Prize for *The Age of Innocence,* the story of a young woman growing up in New York.

Index of Titles and Authors

Index of Fine Art

Index of Skills

Skills in Comprehending Literature

Study and Research Skills

Speaking and Listening Skills

Skills in Critical Thinking

Conclusions
    Drawing Conclusions, 24, 35, 154, 199,
        207, 214, 240, 255, 261, 326, 350, 387
    See also *Outcomes.*
Connotations See *Slanted Writing.*
Context Clues See *Inference.*
Definition of Terms
    Establishing Definitions, 12, 87, 92, 93,
        105, 240
    Recognizing Multiple Meanings, 46, 92,
        156, 239
Evaluation
    Defined, 480
    Establishing Standards for, 387, 424, 427
    Of Accuracy of Content, 214
    Of Author's Credibility, 277, 401
    Of Author's Slant, 178, 224, 310
    Of Author's Style, 44, 92, 100, 179, 198,
        261, 270
    Of Believability of Characters, Setting,
        Plot, 20, 81, 178, 214, 224, 424, 437
    Of Elements of a Work 46–47, 66, 87,
        92, 96, 105, 154, 186, 249, 285, 425
    Of Reasons for Conclusions, Opinions, or
        Generalizations, 25, 154, 163, 198,
        207, 361, 366, 389, 437, 441
    Of Soundness of Opinions, 72, 240, 253,
        261, 333
    Of Soundness of Reasoning, 9, 30, 81,
        224, 269, 310, 371, 389
    Of Success of Literary Techniques, 46,
        65, 67, 179
    See also *Fact and Opinion,*
        Generalizations.
Fact and Fiction 20, 220
    See also *Evaluation, Of Accuracy;*
        Evaluation, Of Believability.

Fact and Opinion
    Defined, 481
    Separating Fact and Opinion, 16, 94, 188,
        361, 376, 398, 401, 405
    Relating Fact and Opinion, 310, 376, 387
Figurative Language
    Interpretation of Meaning 12, 248, 251,
        263, 292, 333
Generalizations
    Defined, 481
    Identifying Generalizations, 215, 216
    Making Valid Generalizations, 214, 239,
        255, 333
    Qualifying Generalizations, 9, 216, 220,
        240
    Using Generalizations, 259
Inference
    About Author's Purpose, 171, 179, 198,
        221, 224, 277, 289
    About Characters, 9, 12, 16, 20, 30, 34,
        43, 72, 143, 171, 215, 310, 425
    About Plot, 20, 34, 96, 99, 178, 208, 214,
        216, 371–372
    About Setting, 65, 71, 87, 100, 186, 208,
        361, 371, 402
Interpretation 20, 24, 28, 35, 40, 65, 86,
    163, 207, 263, 274, 289, 387, 402
Main Idea
    Distinguishing Between Main Idea and
        Details, 214, 310
    Identifying the Main Idea of a Paragraph,
        159, 249, 289, 299
    Relating Main Ideas of Several Paragraphs,
        264
Outcomes
    Outcomes and Conclusions, 154, 158,
        208, 215, 287

Art Credits

Cover

Plum, 1959, Kenneth Noland.
The Art Institute of Chicago, Wilson L. Mead Fund.

Illustrations

Kinuko Y. Craft, 22, 23, 76, 160–161, 162, 168–169, 191, 194, 197, 248, 249, 415, 418–419, 422; Robert Masheris, 8, 14, 15, 18, 19, 26, 27, 91, 284; James Watling, 43, 95–96, 256; Glenn Wolff, 45, 59, 62, 64; Jean Helmer, 67, 114–115; John Sandford, 86; Gary Kelley, 149, 150, 151; Christa Kieffer, 185; David Cunningham, 207; Yoshi Miyake, 210, 212, 213, 316–317; Roberta Polfus, 244; Judith Friedman, 431, 434; Ben Coblentz of Precision Graphics, 356.

Photographs of Authors

Atheneum Publishers: Myra Cohn Livingston. The Bettmann Archive: Aesop, Emily Dickinson, Rudyard Kipling, Stephen Leacock, Archibald MacLeish, Carl Sandburg, Sara Teasdale, Edith Wharton. Carcanet Press: Edwin Morgan. Culver Picture Service: Henry Wadsworth Longfellow, Guy de Maupassant, James Thurber. Bauer Englewood: Lynd Ward. Historical Picture Service: Hans Christian Anderson, Jean de La Fontaine, Leo Tolstoy. Suzanne Lee Houfek: Walker Chapman. Jill Krementz: Isaac Asimov, Anne Morrow Lindbergh. Jerome Liebling: Robert Francis. Layle Silbert: Raymond Richard Patterson, May Swenson. University of Massachusetts: Walker Gibson. Wide World Photos: Sir Edmund Hillary.

Acknowledgments

(continued from copyright page)

from *The Bashful Earthquake*; copyright under the Berne Convention, reprinted with the permission of Charles Scribner's Sons. For "The First" by Lilian Moore, from *Think of Shadows*; copyright © 1980 by Lilian Moore. For "74th Street," "Little Dead," and "One for Novella Nelson," from *The Malibu and Other Poems*; copyright © 1972 by Myra Cohn Livingston, a Margaret K. McElderry Book. Baker's Plays: For *The Tinker of Toledo* by Nellie McCaslin; copyright 1950, 1963 by Harper and Row Publishers. Bill Berger Associates, Inc.: For "The Dinner Party" by Mona Gardner; reprinted by permission of *Saturday Review*, January 31, 1942. The Bobbs-Merrill Company, Inc.: For "Greatest Athlete in the World" by G. Van Riper, Jr., from *Jim Thorpe: Indian Athlete*; copyright © 1956, by Guernsey Van Riper, Jr. Marchette Chute: For "Weather," from *Around and About* by Marchette Chute; copyright 1957, reprinted by permission of the author. Dodd, Mead & Company: For "The Great Detective" by Stephen Leacock, from *Laugh with Leacock*; copyright 1930 by Dodd, Mead & Company, renewed 1958 by George Leacock. Doubleday & Company, Inc.: For "Two Ways To Count to Ten" by Frances Carpenter, from *African Wonder Tales*; copyright © 1963 by Frances Carpenter Huntington. For "Endless Search" by Alonzo Lopez, from *The Whispering Wind* by Terry Allen; copyright © 1972 by The Institute of American Indian Arts. For "The Fun They Had" by Isaac Asimov, from *Earth is Room Enough*, reprinted by permission of Doubleday & Company, Inc. and NEA Service, Inc. Harcourt Brace Jovanovich, Inc.: For "The Huckabuck Family and How They Raised Popcorn in Nebraska and Quit and Came Back" by Carl Sandburg, from *Rootabaga Stories*; copyright 1922, 1923 by Harcourt Brace Jovanovich, Inc.; renewed 1950, 1951 by Carl Sandburg, reprinted by permission of the publisher. For "Morning—The Bird Perched for Flight" by Anne Morrow Lindbergh, abridged and reprinted from *Earth Shine*; copyright © 1969 by Anne Morrow Lindbergh. For "Yarns" by Carl Sandburg, abridged from selection #45 in *The People, Yes*; copyright 1936 by Harcourt Brace Jovanovich, Inc.; renewed 1964 by Carl Sandburg. For six lines from "Primer Lesson," from *Slabs of the Sunburnt West* by Carl Sandburg; copyright 1922 by Harcourt Brace Jovanovich, Inc.; copyright 1950 by Carl Sandburg. Harper & Row, Publishers: For "The Quarrel," from *Eleanor Farjeon's Poems for Children* (J. B. Lippincott); copyright 1933, 1961 by Eleanor Farjeon. For "Keplik, the Match Man" (text only), from *The Witch of Fourth Street and Other Stories* by Myron Levoy; text copyright © 1972 by Myron Levoy. Hastings House, Publishers, Inc.: For "Before Starting," from *Come As You Are* by Walker Gibson; copyright © 1958 by Walker Gibson. Hodder & Stoughton Limited: For an excerpt from "The Summit," from *The Ascent of Everest* by Sir Edmund Hillary, edited by Lord Hunt. Lerner Publications Company: For "Neil Armstrong: First on the Moon" by Paul Westman, from *Neil Armstrong, Space Pioneer*; copyright 1980. Little, Brown and Company in association with the Atlantic Monthly Press: For "Orbiter 5 Shows How Earth Looks from the Moon," from *New & Selected Things Taking Place* by May Swenson; copyright © 1969 by May Swenson. For "The Camel," from *Verses from 1929 On* by Ogden Nash; copyright 1933 by The Curtis Publishing Company, first appeared in *The Saturday Evening Post*. Macmillan Publishing Co., Inc.: For "Faults," from *Collected Poems* by Sara Teasdale; copyright 1917 by Macmillan Publishing Co., Inc., renewed 1945 by Mamie T. Wheless. Mrs. Frank M. Moon: For "The Jar of Tassai" by Grace P. Moon, from *All Kinds of Courage*. Edwin Morgan and Carcanet Press Ltd., Manchester: For "The Computer's First Christmas Card," from *Poems of Thirty Years* by Edwin Morgan. The New American Library, Inc.: For "The King and the Shirt," "The Learned Son," "Equal Inheritance," and "Three Rolls and a Pretzel," from *Fables and Fairy Tales* by Leo Tolstoy and translated by Ann Dunnigan; copyright © 1962 by Ann Dunnigan. The New York Times Company: For "A Changing Landscape" by Archibald MacLeish, December 25, 1968; copyright © 1968 by The New York Times Company. Hugh Noyes: For "Daddy Fell into the Pond" by Alfred Noyes. Raymond R. Patterson: For "A Love Song" by Raymond Richard Patterson. Plays, Inc., Publishers: For an edited version of *Miss Louisa and the Outlaws* by Frances B. Watts, from *Popular Plays for Classroom Reading* by A. S. Burack and B. Alice Crossley; copyright © 1963, 1974, by Plays, Inc. This play is for reading purposes only; for permission to perform the play, write to Plays, Inc., 8 Arlington St., Boston, MA 02116. Random House, Inc.: For "The Diamond Necklace," from *The Best Stories of Guy de Maupassant*, selected by Saxe Commins; published by Random House, 1945. Willie Reader: For "When Paul Bunyan Was Ill," from *Back Packing* by Willie Reader, New Collage Press, 1975. Scott, Foresman & Company: For an excerpt from "Rodeo" by Edward Lueders, from *Reflections on a Gift of Watermelon Pickle . . .* by Stephen Dunning, Edward Lueders, Hugh Smith; copyright © 1966 by Scott, Foresman & Co. Robert Silverberg: For "First to the South Pole," adapted from *The Loneliest Continent* by Walker Chapman; reprinted by permission of Agberg, Ltd. Simon & Schuster, Inc.: For pronunciation key from *Webster's New World Dictionary*, Basic School Edition; copyright © 1979 by Simon & Schuster, Inc. For "Stealing the Bell," from *Tales the People Tell in China* by Robert Wyndham; copyright © 1971 by Robert Wyndham, reprinted by permission of Julian Messner, a division of Simon & Schuster, Inc. Franklin Folsom and Evelyn Singer Literary Agency: For "Davy Crockett" by Michael Gorham, from *The Real Book of American Tall Tales*, Doubleday & Company, Inc. Evelyn Singer Literary Agency: For "Squares and Angles" by Alfonsina Storni, from *Spanish-American Poetry—A Bilingual Selection*; copyright © 1962 by Seymour Resnick, published by Harvey House. William Jay Smith: For an excerpt from "Lion" by William Jay Smith, from *Poems* 1947–1957. Sally Stolte: For "Fall" by Sally Andresen. Mrs. James Thurber: For "The Fox and the Crow," from *Further Fables For Our Time* by James Thurber; copyright © 1956 James Thurber, published by Simon & Schuster, Inc. For